Contents

Heinle Exam Essentials is a new series of materials for students preparing for the major EFL/ESL examinations, such as First Certificate in English (FCE), Certificate in Advanced English (CAE), Certificate of Proficiency in English (CPE), International English Language Testing System (IELTS), Test of English as a Foreign Language (TOEFL®), Test of English for International Communication (TOEIC®), and others. The series is characterised by the close attention each component pays to developing a detailed knowledge of the skills and strategies needed for success in each paper or part of the exams.

CAE Practice Tests helps learners become aware of CAE exam requirements, offers details about the format and language in the exam, and helps learners develop exam skills necessary for success. The book also provides extensive practice in all parts of the exam, using the actual test format.

Taking the CAE Exam

The CAE is at Level 4 of the series of Cambridge ESOL Examinations: Level 1 is the Key English Test, Level 2 the Preliminary English Test, Level 3 the First Certificate in English, and Level 5 the Certificate of Proficiency in English. CAE is also at Level 4 of the ALTE framework (ALTE, the Association of Language Testers in Europe, promotes transactional recognition of levels of language proficiency and certification). It is also classified as being at C1 level of the Common European Framework. The CAE is widely recognised in commerce and industry, and by universities and similar educational institutions, as proof that the holder of this qualification can do office work or take a course of study in English.

The exam, which is usually held twice a year, consists of five Papers:

Paper 1 Reading (1 hour 15 minutes)

- Part 1 consists of three short texts from a variety of sources. They all have a common theme. There are two four-option multiple-choice comprehension questions for each text. Part 1 tests your ability to read for detail, opinion, tone, purpose, main idea, implication, attitude, and to understand text organisation features (exemplification, comparison, reference).

- Part 2 consists of a long text from which six paragraphs have been removed and placed in jumbled order after the text. You have to decide from where in the text the paragraphs have been removed. Part 2 tests your understanding of how a text is structured.

- Part 3 consists of a long text with seven four-option multiple-choice questions. Part 3 tests your ability to read for detail, gist, opinion and attitude.

- Part 4 consists of a long text with several sections or several short texts. There are 15 questions which require you to decide which section of the text/short text each one refers to. Part 4 tests your ability to read for specific information, detail, opinion and attitude.

Paper 2 Writing (1 hour 30 minutes)

- Part 1 is compulsory. You are required to write an article, a formal or informal letter, a proposal or a report in 180–220 words. Before you write your answer, you must read the instructions as well as an input text or texts. There may also be input in the form of a diagram, graph, etc. Part 1 focuses on your ability to evaluate, express opinions, hypothesise, etc. Persuasion is always an important element in your writing in Part 1.

- There are four questions to choose from in Part 2. For questions 2–4, you are required to write an article, an essay, a letter, a proposal, a report, a review, a competition entry or a contribution to a longer piece in 220–260 words. Part 2 focuses on your ability to give opinions, persuade, justify, give advice, compare, etc. For question 5, you choose from one of two tasks on the set texts. You are required to write an article, an essay, a report or a review.

Both parts of the Writing Paper test your ability to write a text according to instructions in an appropriate style and register for a given purpose and target reader. Effective text organisation, accuracy and a good range of vocabulary are also important.

Paper 3, Use of English (1 hour)

- Part 1 is a multiple-choice cloze task. You read a text with 12 gaps. This is followed by 12 four-option multiple-choice questions. You need to complete each gap with the correct option. Part 1 tests your knowledge of vocabulary, including idioms, fixed phrases, phrasal verbs and semantic precision.

- Part 2 is an open cloze task. You read a text with 15 gaps. You need to complete each gap with an appropriate word. Part 2 tests your knowledge of the structure of the language.

- Part 3 is a word formation task. You read a short text with 10 gaps. You need to complete each gap with an appropriate word formed from a prompt word in capitals that appears to the right of the text on the same line as the gap. Part 3 tests your knowledge of how words are formed from other words.

- Part 4 consists of five sets of three gapped sentences. You need to complete the gaps in each set with an appropriate word which will be the same for all the sentences in a set. Part 4 tests your knowledge of vocabulary and lexical patterns such as collocations and phrasal verbs.

- Part 5 consists of eight sentences, each of which is followed by a word and a gapped sentence. You need to complete the gapped sentence so that its meaning is the same as the first sentence using three to six words, including the word given. Part 5 tests your knowledge of vocabulary and grammar.

Paper 4 Listening (approximately 40 minutes)

- Part 1 consists of three short monologues or texts involving interacting speakers. You are required to

CAE
Practice Tests
with key

**Charles Osborne with
Carol Nuttall**

HEINLE
CENGAGE Learning™

Australia • Brazil • Japan • Korea • Mexico • Singapore • Spain • United Kingdom • United States

**Heinle Exam Essentials CAE Practice Tests,
Second Edition**
Charles Osborne with Carol Nuttall

Publisher: Jason Mann

Development Editor: Process ELT (www.process-elt.com)

Production Editor: Natalie Griffith

International Marketing Manager: Marcin Wojtynski

Manufacturing Manager: Helen Mason

Project Manager: Howard Middle/HM ELT Services

Production Management: Process ELT

Copy Editor: Process ELT

Compositor: Process ELT

Illustrator: Nick Dimitriadis

Cover/Text Designer: Studio Image & Photographic Art
(www. studio-image.com)

ISBN: 978-1-4240-2827-6

Heinle
Cheriton House, North Way, Andover,
Hampshire, SP10 5BE

Cengage Learning is a leading provider of customized learning solutions with office locations around the globe, including Singapore, the United Kingdom, Australia, Mexico, Brazil and Japan. Locate our local office at: **international.cengage.com/region**

Cengage Learning products are represented in Canada by Nelson Education, Ltd.

Visit Heinle online at **http://elt.heinle.com**
Visit our corporate website at **www.cengage.com**

Text Credits
Page 10: From "Peach of an Idea", by Richard Wray. Copyright © THE GUARDIAN 2004. **Page 34:** From "Mind your languages", by Matthew Brace. Copyright © GEOGRAPHICAL 1999. **Page 58:** Adapted from "Explorers Still Seek El Dorado in the Mountains of Peru", by Juan Forero. Copyright © 2004 by the New York Times Co. Reprinted with permission. Text has been modified to facilitate reading comprehension. **Page 60:** From "On yer bike", by Tim Dowling, THE GUARDIAN. Copyright © Tim Dowling 2003. **Page 102:** From "Countdown to extinction for world's great apes", by Tim Radford. Copyright © THE GUARDIAN 2003. **Page 124:** From "Hybrid Homes", by William Underhill and Malcolm Beith. From Newsweek, September 20 © 2004 Newsweek, Inc. All rights reserved. Reprinted by permission. **Page 148:** From "Bred to soar", by Jeffrey P.Cohn. Copyright © ORGANIZATION OF AMERICAN STATES 2004. **Page 168:** "Close encounters of the wild kind", by Christian Amodeo. Copyright © GEOGRAPHICAL 2004. **Page 170:** From "Back to basics", by Ashley Seager. Copyright © THE GUARDIAN 2004.

Photo Credits
The publishers would like to thank the following for permission to use copyright images:
Page 192 top © AP Photo/Marco Ugarte, middle © AP Photo/Kathy Willens; page 193 bottom © Brand X Pictures/PictureQuest; page 194 middle left © Brand X Pictures/PictureQuest; page 195 left © Corbis; page 196 bottom left © Bob Evans (pp 50%)/Painet, bottom right © 2007 Rubberball/Jupiterimages; page 198 top © Bill Bachmann/Painet, bottom right © AP Photo/Chria O'Meara; page 200 top © Comstock Images/Picture Quest, middle right © AP Photo/Richard Drew, bottom © AP Photo/Marcio Jose Sanchez; page 201 top © AP Photo/Mariana Eliano, middle © AP Photo/Kevin Frayer, bottom © Jack Iddon/Painet; page 203 bottom centre © Words & pictures LLC/Painet; page 204 middle © Andre Jenny/Painet, bottom © 2007 PhotoAlto Agency/Jupiterimages; page 205 top © Corbis/PictureQuest, bottom left © Steve Skjold/Painet, bottom right © 2005 Thinkstock/Jupiterimages; page 207 top © Brand X Pictures/PictureQuest, bottom left © Blend Images/PictureQuest, bottom right © IT Stock Free/PictureQuest; page 209 top left © Rubber Ball/PictureQuest, top right © Corbis/PictureQuest, middle right © AP Photo/Michel Euler; page 210 bottom left © Bill Bachmann/Painet, bottom right © AP Photo/David Brauchli; page 211 top © Comstock Images/PictureQuest; page 212 bottom right © Corbis/PictureQuest; page 213 top © AP Photo/Peter Morgan, middle © AP Photo/Damian Dovarganes, bottom © AP Photo/Lennox; page 214 middle © AP Photo/Gaurav Tiwari, bottom © Painet Inc.
© Photos.com: Page 193 middle; page 194 top upper, middle right, bottom right; page 195 bottom right; page 198 bottom left; page 199 middle, bottom; page 200 middle left; page 202 top, bottom left, bottom right; page 203 top, middle left; page 204 top; page 209 middle left, bottom left; page 210 top; page 212 top left, top right, middle right, bottom left; page 214 top.
© Index Open: Page 192 bottom; page 193 top; page 194 top lower, bottom left; page 195 top right; page 196 top; page 199 top; page 203 middle right, bottom left, bottom right; page 208 top, bottom left, bottom right; page 209 bottom right; page 211 bottom left, bottom right; page 212 middle left.

Printed by C&C Offset, China
2 3 4 5 6 7 8 9 10 - 11 10 09

answer two three-option multiple-choice questions for each extract. Part 1 tests your ability to understand feeling, attitude, opinion, purpose, function, agreement, course of action, general gist, detail, etc.

- Part 2 consists of a long monologue or prompted monologue. You are required to complete eight gapped sentences with information you hear on the recording. Each gap is completed by one, two or three words, or a number. Part 2 tests your ability to understand specific information and stated opinion.

- Part 3 consists of a long monologue or text involving interacting speakers. You are required to answer six four-option multiple-choice questions. Part 3 tests your ability to understand attitude and opinion.

- Part 4 consists of five short monologues on a related theme. There are two tasks in this part. Both tasks require you choose from a list of options the opinion that each speaker expresses. Part 4 tests your ability to understand gist, attitude and main point and to interpret context.

Paper 5, Speaking (15 minutes)
The Speaking Paper generally involves two candidates and two examiners.

- In Part 1 you have a brief conversation with the examiner. Part 1 tests your ability to give personal information and use social and interactional language.

- In Part 2 the examiner gives you and the other candidate visual and written prompts. Each candidate is required to use the prompts he/she is given to talk for a minute. He/She is also required to answer a question based on the other candidate's prompts in 30 seconds. Part 2 tests your ability to organise a larger unit of discourse to compare, describe, express opinions and speculate.

- In Part 3 the examiner gives you and the other candidate visual and written prompts. You are required to use the prompts to have a conversation with the other candidate. Part 3 tests your ability to sustain an interaction, exchange ideas, express and justify opinions, agree and/or disagree, suggest, evaluate, reach a decision through negotiation, etc.

- In Part 4 the examiner asks you questions based on the topics you talked about in Part 3. You are required to have a three-way discussion with the examiner and the other candidate. Part 4 tests your ability to exchange information, express and justify opinions, agree and/or disagree.

Preparing for the CAE Exam

In preparing for the five Papers, the following points should be taken into account:

Reading: To prepare for this Paper, you should read from a range of material: newspapers, magazines, journals, novels, leaflets, brochures, etc. When you read, pay attention to text organisation features, train yourself to recognise the author's purpose in writing and his or her tone, and learn to read between the lines for what is implied rather than stated explicitly. It is important to practise different reading strategies that can be used for different parts of the Reading Paper, for example skimming for the main idea and gist, scanning to locate specific information or reading closely to determine the writer's precise meaning.

Writing: You need to be familiar with all the text types you may be required to write in the exam. You should also be aware of the criteria that will be used in marking your texts:

- Has the candidate achieved the purpose stated in the instructions?
- Does the text have a positive general effect on the target reader?
- Does the text cover all the content points?
- Is the text organised effectively and are ideas linked appropriately?
- Has language been used accurately?
- Does the text have a good range of vocabulary and grammatical features?
- Is the register appropriate for the task?
- Is the layout appropriate?

Use of English: You need to develop grammatical awareness and become familiar with grammatical patterns and collocations. You also need a good knowledge of vocabulary, so learn whole phrases rather than single words in isolation. Build up your knowledge of vocabulary and how words and phrases are used. When you come across a new word, don't just learn its meaning in context. Does it have any other meanings or uses?

Listening: You should practise listening to a wide variety of spoken English: announcements, speeches, lectures, talks, radio broadcasts, anecdotes, radio interviews, discussions, etc. You should also practise listening for different purposes: to understand gist, identify context or attitude or find specific information.

Speaking: You should practise speaking English as much as possible. It is important to master conversational skills such as turn taking and the appropriate way to participate in a discussion, giving full but natural answers to questions and requesting clarification.

Further information can be obtained from the Cambridge ESOL website: www.cambridgeESOL.org.

CAE Practice Tests: contents

CAE Practice Tests in the **Thomson Exam Essentials** series prepares candidates for the CAE examination by providing **8 full practice tests**, which accurately reflect the latest exam specifications.

There are **3 guided tests** at the beginning, which feature **essential tips** to practise exam strategy. These tips offer guidance and general strategies for approaching each task. Other tips offer advice relevant to specific questions in the guided tests. These 3 guided tests will help students prepare for each paper, while the following **5 tests (without guidance)** will offer students thorough practice at a realistic exam level.

The CDs or cassettes accompanying the book include the audio materials for all the Listening Papers. These accurately reflect the exam in both style and content. Moreover, the audio materials for Tests 1 and 2 have been recorded with the repetitions and full pauses, exactly as in the exam itself.

A **writing bank** includes sample answers for the kinds of tasks that occur in Paper 2 (Writing), writing tips in the form of notes and **useful phrases** for the particular task types. Varied **visual materials** for Paper 5 (Speaking) have also been included, while a **language bank** supplies useful phrases and expressions for use in the Speaking Paper.

There is also a **glossary** for each test, explaining vocabulary that is likely to be unfamiliar to students.

Clear and straightforward design simplifies use of the book. **Exam overview** tables ensure that key information is readily accessible, while a specially designed menu makes it easy to navigate through the different parts and papers of each practice test.

CAE Practice Tests: principles

In writing this book, three guiding principles have been observed:

Firstly, that it should be useful for teachers, students sitting the CAE exam for the first time and students re-sitting the exam, whether they are working alone or in a class. Students approaching CAE for the first time would be best advised to work through the book linearly, developing their skills and confidence; those re-sitting the exam can consult the Exam overview tables to concentrate on particular areas for targeted revision. The **"without key"** edition can be used by students working in a class, while the **"with key"** edition includes a detailed **Answer key**, ensuring that students working alone can benefit from support while attempting these tests.

The second principle is that the questions should accurately reflect the range of questions found in the CAE exam. Thus students obtain guidance concerning the general content and the best way of approaching the tasks from the questions themselves. Seeing the questions in this light – as instructions to the candidate from the examiner rather than intimidating challenges – also helps students feel less daunted by the whole experience of sitting a major exam like this.

The third principle is that the texts used in the practice tests should be varied, representative of those used in the exam, and interesting. Everyone finds it easier to learn if the subject matter is relevant to his or her lifestyle and interests. In choosing, editing and creating the texts here, we have done our utmost to ensure that the experience of working with this book is as stimulating and rewarding as possible.

Charles Osborne, April, 2009

PAPER 1 Reading	▶	Part 1
PAPER 2 Writing		Part 2
		Part 3
PAPER 3 Use of English		Part 4
PAPER 4 Listening		
PAPER 5 Speaking		

You are going to read three extracts which are all concerned in some way with extraterrestrial life. For questions **1–6**, choose the answer (**A, B, C** or **D**) which you think fits best according to the text.

Mark your answers **on the separate answer sheet**.

Essential tips

▶ This part of the exam tests your general understanding of a whole short text or text organisation, and some questions may also focus on details. Read each text through in order to get the general meaning before attempting the questions.

▶ Look at key words in each question and see how they relate to the relevant part of the text. The text may use different words from those that appear in the questions and answer options. Look for phrases in the text which convey the same meaning as one of the options. The option you choose must express the same idea as that which appears in the text.

Question 1: The answer to this question may not be immediately obvious. What is the magazine trying to do, according to the advertisement? You may find it useful to eliminate the incorrect options first.

Question 2: Notice the word 'must' in the question stem. It is important that the completed question stem conveys the same meaning as that expressed in the text.

Wanted: **Assistant Editor for new science publication**

Are you a science enthusiast with a journalistic flair? Or perhaps you are a journalist with a passion for science? If so, then you could be the person we are looking for!

In September we will be launching *Is There Anybody Out There?*, a monthly science magazine specialising in astrobiology and astrophysics. It will report on the latest research and findings regarding the study of life in the universe. We are looking for a creative and innovative Assistant Editor to help develop a magazine that will be accessible to the layman.

Job description
The Assistant Editor will be expected to propose ideas for stories and feature articles and be involved in some of the initial research. He or she will be responsible for editing the news stories and help to set up the magazine's web site. This will include online articles and information services.

Qualifications required
The suitable candidate will have a Bachelor's degree in journalism or science, and preferably some knowledge of astrobiology and/or astrophysics. He or she will be familiar with standard office computer software and will demonstrate creative writing skills. The ability to handle stress and meet tight deadlines is of the utmost importance.

If you think you fulfil these requirements and are interested, send us your resumé with a covering letter explaining why you think you would be suitable for the job.

1 The new magazine aims to
   A attract a readership of non-specialists.
   B publish articles about life on Earth.
   C conduct research into astrobiology.
   D develop an interest in general science.

2 To be considered for the job, a candidate must
   A have experience as a journalist.
   B know about specialist software.
   C be able to work under pressure.
   D have studied astrobiology or astrophysics.

Life in the Universe

Until recently, we have confined ourselves to our own solar system in the search for life, partly because we have not had evidence for the existence of other solar systems. Furthermore, our telescopes have not been powerful enough to detect planets. But not long ago, a technique was developed that could ascertain reliably whether stars have planets orbiting them. Basically, this technique relies upon our ability to detect with some degree of precision how much light a star is giving off. If this changes for a brief period, it is probably because a large object – a planet – is passing in front of it. At first, the technique could only establish the existence of a very large planet with an elliptical orbit that brought it into close proximity to the star. This was one of the limitations of the technique: life could not exist on such large planets. Furthermore, the orbit of the planet would preclude the possibility of other, smaller planets orbiting the same star. Therefore, that particular planetary system could be effectively ruled out in terms of the search for life.

However, astronomers using an Anglo-American telescope in New South Wales now believe they have pinpointed a planetary system which resembles our own. For the first time, they have identified a large planet, twice the size of Jupiter, orbiting a star like the sun, at much the same distance from its parent star as Jupiter is from the sun. And this is the vital point about their discovery: there is at least a theoretical possibility that smaller planets could be orbiting inside the orbit of this planet.

3   According to the article, the initial flaw in the technique for detecting new planets lay in
    A   its inability to determine how much light a star was emitting.
    B   the fact that it could detect large objects passing in front of a star.
    C   its dependence on the amount of light that was emitted by a star.
    D   its inability to detect a planet where life could exist.

4   What is important about the recent discovery in New South Wales?
    A   Astronomers have discovered a planet which resembles Jupiter.
    B   Smaller planets may exist within the new planetary system.
    C   The new planet lies as far from its star as Jupiter does from the sun.
    D   There is a possibility that life exists on this new planet.

Essential tips

Question 5: The writer has many positive things to say about the film, but the question focuses on what makes it so convincing.

Question 6: Be careful about the use of words in the options! What does the writer actually say about the use of special effects in the film?

EXTRACT FROM A FILM REVIEW

The Sci-Fi Film Festival retrospective begins this week, and science buffs and UFO enthusiasts might do a lot worse than go and see Zemeckis's 1997 classic, *Contact*, starring Jodie Foster. Foster plays a research scientist called Ellie Arroway who intercepts a message from outer space. This message indicates the existence of intelligent life and it triggers a whole chain of extraordinary events.

The film is based on the novel by the celebrated astronomer Carl Sagan. Its strength lies in the fact that it manages to retain much of the power and compelling nature of the book, while at the same time maintaining a relatively high level of technical accuracy. This is largely thanks to Sagan's involvement in the making of the film. As many of you may know, Sagan died before the film was completed.

The main plot, concerning the discovery of the message, the struggle to interpret it, and the eventual contact between humans and aliens, is interwoven with the intrigues that arise from the ambitions of scientists, politicians and industrialists for fame and power.

As is usually the case with Zemeckis, special effects are used both creatively and effectively, serving to enhance the plot rather than swamp it, and there are fine performances, particularly by Ms Foster, Matthew McConaughey, James Woods and Tom Skerritt. While the method with which Arroway receives the alien communication is a far cry from the advanced technology actually in operation, the story is nevertheless convincing, and contributed to a renewed interest in UFOs and the search for extraterrestrial life.

5 The review suggests that one reason the film is so convincing is because
    A Jodie Foster is a very fine actress.
    B an astronomer was involved in its creation.
    C it used accurate techniques.
    D it was directed by Zemeckis.

6 In the reviewer's opinion, the special effects
    A are the most important aspect of the film.
    B effectively suffocate the plot.
    C are used to the film's advantage.
    D enhance the actors' performances.

PAPER 1 Reading ▶
PAPER 2 Writing
PAPER 3 Use of English
PAPER 4 Listening
PAPER 5 Speaking

Part 1
Part 2
Part 3
Part 4

You are going to read a newspaper article. Six paragraphs have been removed from the article. Choose from the paragraphs **A–G** the one which fits each gap (**7–12**). There is one extra paragraph which you do not need to use.

Mark your answers **on the separate answer sheet**.

Peach of an Idea

Regent's Park in central London was recently the site of a festival of music and fruit, marking the fifth birthday of Innocent, the drinks company set up by three college friends who wanted to bring a bit of nature to the table. It all began five years ago, when Adam Balon, Richard Reed and Jon Wright were contemplating starting their own business. They took 500 pounds worth of fruit to a music festival in west London, made a huge batch of smoothies – fruit drinks blended with milk and yoghurt – and asked their customers for a verdict.

7

Looking back, they now admit that they were amazingly naive about starting a business, thinking it would just take off once they had the recipes and packaging figured out. In fact, the three budding businessmen had nine months living on credit cards and overdrafts before they sold their first smoothie.

8

The appeal of Innocent's products lies in their pure, unadulterated ingredients, plus a dash of quirky advertising. As one campaign put it, their drinks are not made *from* fruit, they *are* fruit. Innocent's refusal to compromise on this point presented them with some problems when they first started talking to potential suppliers, Adam says. This was when they discovered the truth about the majority of so-called 'natural fruit drinks'.

9

'Naivety', adds Richard, who is always ready with a soundbite, 'can be a great asset in business because you challenge the status quo.' Although Innocent's drinks are fiendishly healthy, the company has always been very careful not to preach. 'Everyone knows what they're supposed to do,' says Richard. 'But we just

don't, especially when you live in a city and it's pints of lager and a kebab at the end of the night. We just thought, "Wouldn't it be great to make it easy for people to get hold of this natural fresh goodness?" Then at least you've got one healthy habit in a world of bad ones.'

10

In essence, explains Jon, Innocent plans to simply freeze some of its smoothies, possibly with a bit of egg thrown in to make it all stick together. To help testers make up their minds about which combinations work, the yes and no bins will be dusted off and put out again.

11

'You've just got to put that in the category of "never say never",' says Richard. 'But the three of us go away once every three months to talk about what we want out of the business and we are all in the same place. So as long as we are excited and challenged and proud of the business, we are going to want to be a part of it.'

12

'We have got annoyed with each other,' admits Adam. 'But the areas we have had fallings-out over are things where we each think we have reasons to be right. So it's been about really important stuff like the colour of the floor, the colour of the entrance, or what to paint the pillar.' 'We really did nearly jump on each other about that,' adds Jon. 'Was it going to be blue or green?'

A Despite the temptation to do so, they have so far refused all offers. This might not last, of course, but while it does, it will have positive consequences for the fruit drinks market.

B At the Regent's Park event the team tried out one of their new ideas – extending their range of products into desserts. 'We always try and develop something that we actually want, and for us there is this problem of Sunday evenings when you sit down with a DVD and a big tub of ice cream and it's nice to munch through it, but my God, is it bad for you,' Richard adds.

C Most are made from concentrated juice with water – and perhaps sweeteners, colours and preservatives – added. 'We didn't even know about that when we started,' Adam explains. 'It was when we started talking to people and they said, "OK, we'll use orange concentrate," and we said, "What's concentrate?" and they explained it and we said, "No, we want orange juice." '

D 'We originally wrote this massive long questionnaire,' says Richard. 'But then we thought, if you're at this festival and it's sunny, the last thing you want is to fill out a survey. So we decided to keep it simple and ask literally, "Should we stop working and make these things?" We had a bin that said yes and a bin that said no, and at the end of the weekend the yes bin was full of empty bottles. We all went in to work the next day and quit.'

E They also seem to have managed to stay friends. They still take communal holidays, and the fact that each member of the team brings a different and complementary set of skills to Innocent seems to have helped them avoid any big bust-ups over strategy.

F Innocent now employs 46 people and Fruit Towers – as they call their base – has slowly expanded along the line of industrial units. The company has managed to establish a dominant position in the face of fierce competition. This year Innocent became Britain's leading brand of smoothie, selling about 40% of the 50 million downed annually by British drinkers.

G Having created a successful business from this base, is there a temptation to sell up and go and live on a desert island? With consumers becoming increasingly concerned about what they put in their stomachs, premium brands such as Innocent are worth a lot of money to a potential buyer.

Essential tips

▸ This part of the exam tests your understanding of how a text is organised and, in particular, how paragraphs relate to each other. For example, a paragraph might give details about an idea mentioned or discussed in a previous paragraph, or it may present another side of an argument discussed in a previous paragraph.

▸ Read through the main text quickly to get a general idea of what it is about. Don't worry if there are words or phrases you don't understand. Find the main idea in each paragraph.

▸ Look for links between the main text and the gapped paragraphs. The gapped paragraph may have links either to the paragraph before it or to the paragraph after it, or even to both.

▸ Look for theme and language links. For example:
  • references to people, places and times.
  • words or phrases that refer back or forward to another word, phrase or idea in the text. For example, if the first line of a paragraph says something like 'This becomes clear when we look at ...', 'This' refers back to something expressed in the previous paragraph.
  • linking devices such as 'firstly', 'secondly', 'furthermore', 'on the other hand', 'however'. These will help you to find connections between paragraphs.

▸ When you have found a paragraph that may fill a gap, read the paragraph that comes before it and the one that comes after it to see that they fit together.

▸ Re-read the completed text and make sure it makes sense.

Question 7: The last sentence in the previous paragraph describes how Balon, Reed and Wright 'asked their customers for a verdict'. Which gapped paragraph describes how customers gave their opinion?

Question 9: The previous paragraph ends with 'This was when they discovered the truth about the majority of so-called "natural fruit drinks" '. Look for a gapped paragraph which describes this 'truth'.

Question 11: In the paragraph following the gap, one of the owners of Innocent implies that something seems unlikely because he and his colleagues are still a good team. Which gapped paragraph poses a question which this paragraph answers?

PAPER 1 Reading
PAPER 2 Writing
PAPER 3 Use of English
PAPER 4 Listening
PAPER 5 Speaking

Part 1
Part 2
Part 3
Part 4

You are going to read a magazine article. For questions **13–19**, choose the answer (**A, B, C or D**) which you think fits best according to the text.

Mark your answers **on the separate answer sheet**.

The Beauties of the Stone Age

Jane Howard views some works of ancient art

I have just come home after viewing some astonishing works of art that were recently discovered in Church Hole cave in Nottinghamshire. They are not drawings, as one would expect, but etchings, and they depict a huge range of wild animals. The artists who created them lived around 13,000 years ago, and the images are remarkable on a variety of counts. First of all, their sheer number is staggering: there are ninety all told. Moreover, fifty-eight of them are on the ceiling. This is extremely rare in cave art, according to a leading expert, Dr Wilbur Samson of Central Midlands University. 'Wall pictures are the norm,' he says. 'But more importantly, the Church Hole etchings are an incredible artistic achievement. They can hold their own in comparison with the best found in continental Europe.' I am not a student of the subject, so I have to take his word for it. However, you do not have to be an expert to appreciate their beauty.

In fact, it is the wider significance of the etchings that is likely to attract most attention in academic circles, since they radically alter our view of life in Britain during this epoch. It had previously been thought that ice-age hunters in this country were isolated from people in more central areas of Europe, but the Church Hole images prove that ancient Britons were part of a culture that had spread right across the continent. And they were at least as sophisticated culturally as their counterparts on the mainland.

News of such exciting discoveries spreads rapidly, and thanks to the Internet and mobile phones, a great many people probably knew about this discovery within hours of the initial expedition returning. As a result, some etchings may already have been damaged, albeit inadvertently, by eager visitors. In a regrettably late response, the site has been cordoned off with a high, rather intimidating fence, and warning notices have been posted.

An initial survey of the site last year failed to reveal the presence of the etchings. The reason lies in the expectations of the researchers. They had been looking for the usual type of cave drawing or painting, which shows up best under direct light. Consequently, they used powerful torches, shining them straight onto the rock face. However, the Church Hole images are modifications of the rock itself, and show up best when seen from a certain angle in the natural light of early morning. Having been fortunate to see them at this hour, I can only say that I was deeply – and unexpectedly – moved. While most cave art often seems to have been created in a shadowy past very remote from us, these somehow convey the impression that they were made yesterday.

Dr Samson feels that the lighting factor provides important information about the likely function of these works of art. 'I think the artists knew very well that the etchings would hardly be visible except early in the morning. We can therefore deduce that the chamber was used for rituals involving animal worship, and that they were conducted just after dawn, as a preliminary to the day's hunting.'

However, such ideas are controversial in the world of archaeology and human origins. Dr Olivia Caruthers of the Reardon Institute remains unconvinced that the function of the etchings at Church Hole can be determined with any certainty. 'When we know so little about the social life of early humans, it would be foolish to insist on any rigid interpretation. We should, in my view, begin by tentatively assuming that their creators were motivated in part by aesthetic considerations – while of course being prepared to modify this verdict at a later date, if and when new evidence emerges.'

To which I can only add that I felt deeply privileged to have been able to view Church Hole. It is a site of tremendous importance culturally and is part of the heritage, not only of this country, but the world as a whole.

▸ This part of the exam tests your detailed understanding of a text, including the views and attitudes expressed.

▸ Read through the text quickly to get a general idea of what it is about. Don't worry if there are words or phrases you don't understand.

▸ The questions follow the order of the text. Read each question or question stem carefully and underline the key words.

▸ Look in the text for the answer to the question. One of the options will express the same idea, but don't expect that it will do so in the words of the text.

▸ The final question may ask about the intention or opinion of the writer. You may need to consider the text as a whole to answer this question, not just the last section.

Question 13: An option can only be correct if all the information contained in it is accurate. Look at option A: are the images in Church Hole 'unique examples of ceiling art'? The text says they are 'extremely rare in cave art' – is this the same? Look at option B: are the images in Church Hole 'particularly beautiful'? And are they 'paintings'?

Question 15: Look at option A. What does the writer say about the discovery of the images being made public? Look at option B. If something is 'vulnerable to damage', what might happen to it? Look at option C. The text says 'many people probably knew about the discovery within hours of the initial expedition returning'. Is this the same as saying many people visited the cave within hours? Look at option D. Have the images definitely been damaged? When may the damage have taken place: before or after the measures were taken?

Question 17: Sometimes you will find words from the options in the

text. Be careful: the meaning in the text is not necessarily the same as that in the answer options. Here, option D says the hunters 'worshipped animals in the cave', but the text says the cave was used for 'rituals involving animal worship', which is not the same thing.

13 According to the text, the images in Church Hole cave are
A unique examples of ceiling art.
B particularly beautiful cave paintings.
C superior in quality to other cave art in Britain.
D aesthetically exceptional.

14 What is the cultural significance of these images?
A They indicate that people from central Europe had settled in Britain.
B They prove that ancient Britons hunted over large areas.
C They reveal the existence of a single ice-age culture in Europe.
D They suggest that people in Europe were more sophisticated than Britons.

15 According to the text,
A the discovery of the images should not have been made public.
B the images in the cave are vulnerable to damage.
C many people visited the cave within hours of its discovery.
D the measures taken to protect the images have proved ineffective.

16 Why were the images not discovered during the initial survey?
A They were not viewed from the right angle.
B People were not expecting to find any images.
C Artificial light was used to explore the cave.
D The torches used were too powerful.

17 What conclusions does Dr Samson draw from the lighting factor?
A Rituals are common in animal worship.
B The artists never intended to make the images visible.
C The images were intended to be visible at a certain time of day.
D Ice-age hunters worshipped animals in the cave.

18 According to Dr Caruthers,
A we cannot make inferences from cave art.
B the images in Church Hole do not serve any particular function.
C experts know nothing about life 13,000 years ago.
D the function of such images is open to question.

19 It seems that the writer
A can now envisage the life of ice-age hunters more vividly.
B was profoundly impressed by the images in the cave.
C has now realised the true significance of cave art.
D thinks the images should receive more publicity.

PAPER 1 Reading ▶	Part 1
PAPER 2 Writing	Part 2
PAPER 3 Use of English	Part 3
PAPER 4 Listening	**Part 4**
PAPER 5 Speaking	

You are going to read a newspaper article containing reviews of performances. For questions **20–34**, choose from the reviews (**A–D**).

Mark your answers **on the separate answer sheet**.

Essential tips

▶ In this part of the exam, you are required to read one or more texts to find specific information, which may include an opinion or the expression of an attitude.

▶ Read the instructions, the title and the questions.

▶ Skim through the text quickly to get a general idea of what it is about. Don't worry if there are words or phrases you don't understand, especially since this text is long.

▶ Read each question again and make sure you understand what it is asking. Underline the key words in the question (the words that show you what you should look for in the text).

▶ Scan the text for ideas or words that relate to the question. Read the relevant part of the text carefully.

▶ Remember that the part of the text that gives the answer for each question will almost certainly not use the same words; instead, it will express the idea in a different way.

Question 22: The word 'reminded' is used in the statement. Think of other words or phrases that convey this idea and scan the text for them. Then check that the part of the text you find also expresses the idea of an experience that was both unusual and enjoyable.

Question 26: If the statement is expressed in difficult language, you need to examine it carefully. What is meant by 'the conventions' of an art form? This must refer to the conventional or usual way of doing something. Find a performance that was unusual in relation to a conventional or ordinary performance of that art form (opera, puppet show, jazz or theatre).

Question 28: A 'prejudice' is a negative opinion someone has about a person or thing. Find a section of a review that describes how someone reconsidered an opinion or changed their mind about the art form.

In which review are the following stated?

Performers worked seasonally at one time.	**20** ....
The venue did not allow for a performance of a particular art form.	**21** ....
The performance reminded the writer of an unusual performance he had once enjoyed.	**22** ....
The performers were free to devise their own programme.	**23** ....
The performers had been recommended to the writer.	**24** ....
The behaviour of the performers was contrary to the writer's expectations.	**25** ....
The performance challenged the conventions of an art form.	**26** ....
Performances of this sort used to be very popular.	**27** ....
The performance prompted someone to reconsider a prejudice about an art form.	**28** ....
The performance had unexpectedly sophisticated requirements.	**29** ....
An element of the performance was distressingly realistic.	**30** ....
One of the artists performed despite a handicap.	**31** ....
The performance comprised a number of extracts from various works.	**32** ....
The performers derived pleasure from audience participation.	**33** ....
One participant revealed an unexpected talent.	**34** ....

That's Entertainment!

Felix Masterson decided to engage artists to put on performances in his own home for his family's private enjoyment. Here is his report.

A Opera Recital

For the first of our 'home performances' we decided on opera, a form of art that especially moves me. The other art form that I adore – ballet – could hardly be performed in the confined space of a normal house, no matter how much ingenuity was employed! My wife and I were particularly looking forward to the performance by Footstool Opera, a touring company that specialises in mounting productions in confined spaces, often coming up with a programme to order as suits the occasion. When I was planning the event, I imagined the opera company would bring with them a high-quality sound system of some sort to provide musical accompaniment, but the manager informed me that all they required was 'a piano in good working order'. I hastily arranged for our ancient upright to be tuned, and to my relief, pianist Antonia Holmes pronounced it entirely satisfactory when she tested the instrument before the performance. We had made it clear that no particular requirements would be imposed upon the performers, so they gave us a medley of familiar pieces from popular operas, and my daughter – who had previously been of the view that opera was unspeakably idiotic – was entranced. If I were to be brutally honest, I would have to say that the performers, apart from one tenor, were not in the top class. But I don't imagine many people would notice this, and it certainly didn't detract from our enjoyment of the evening.

B Puppet Show

Having grown up with that curiously British phenomenon of puppet theatre, the Punch and Judy show, I was determined to find one of the traditional practitioners of the art and secure his services. Alas, times have changed. There was once a time when no seaside resort in the country was complete without a Punch and Judy show on the pier, but today puppet theatre of this sort can hardly compete with video games at holiday resorts. Besides, who can afford to work only during the summer months? Consequently, there are, according to the theatrical agencies I contacted, none of the old-fashioned puppeteers left. However, I did manage to find a puppet theatre company called Little Man Theatre that included traditional Punch and Judy shows in its repertoire, so I went ahead and booked them. They arrived with a surprising number of boxes and cases. Naively, I had expected a miniature theatre to require a minimal amount of equipment. In this case, the size of the venue did indeed present a problem, though the nature of the difficulty was the reverse of what I had feared. We actually had some trouble making out the words of the crocodile character, largely – I suspect – because William Daniels, one of the two puppeteers, was suffering from a terrible cold, complete with high fever and a voice virtually reduced to a croak. Like a true pro, though, he struggled through the performance bravely. And once the first act was under way, I began to appreciate why so many props were needed. This wasn't Punch and Judy as I remembered it but a twenty-first century version of the story, requiring a staggering number of scene changes. A breathtaking performance, and though I felt sad at the demise of the old-time favourites, our children enjoyed it immensely.

C Jazz Concert

I had initially set myself the task of finding performers of whom I knew absolutely nothing, simply by sitting down with the Yellow Pages, when a colleague of my wife's started raving about a particular jazz ensemble. It seemed churlish to do otherwise than engage them and The Hot Jazz Quintet turned out to be a group of highly professional musicians who appeared to make a point of being scrupulously polite and tidy. It was as though the stereotype image of the egocentric musician were being overturned in front of my very eyes: a surprising experience for anyone old enough to have seen The Who smash their instruments live onstage several decades ago.

Despite being in such close proximity to the musicians, it had not occurred to me that we would be required to adopt a more active role until the saxophone player handed my son a set of bongo drums and invited him to join in. As luck would have it, Mike is a percussionist with his school orchestra, and he was able to acquit himself creditably, to the delight of the professionals performing for us. Not being a connoisseur of this type of music myself, I had frankly not been prepared to enjoy this evening as much as the other members of my family. This perhaps makes it more of a tribute to the Quintet that I found myself getting quite carried away by the intricate rhythms and spectacular solos.

D Murder Mystery Theatre

We invited Murder Incorporated, a theatre company that specialises in murder mysteries, to perform *Death Calls* for us, and to those of you who have not been initiated in the workings of 'murder mystery theatre', a word of explanation is needed. This is no ordinary production. In fact, one could claim that it doesn't really come under the category of theatre at all, and it is not normally presented on a stage, either. The basic idea is that a murder is 'committed' just out of sight of the audience. After the 'body' is found, the task of the audience is to work out who the murderer is by following up on certain clues.

A few moments after the actors had arrived, when we were still under the impression that preparations were being made for the performance, a piercing scream caused us all to rush out into the hall. There we stumbled – literally – over a body oozing fake blood that was so convincing it almost caused my wife to faint. Yes, it had started. As we followed the actors around the house for scenes in various locations, we tried to work out who the murderer could be. It was a fascinating experience, and I have to report that my wife proved to be a brilliant sleuth, solving the mystery in record time. *Death Calls* was a masterpiece of condensed theatre that had me fondly recalling a production of *2001, A Space Odyssey* at the Edinburgh Fringe Festival, which featured a cast of two, an audience of two and an old car as the venue. Highly recommended.

Essential tips

▶ In Paper 2 you must answer two questions. The question in Part 1 is compulsory. In Part 2 there are four questions, and you have to answer one of them.

▶ In Part 1 you may be asked to write an article, a report, a proposal, or a formal or informal letter. All of these will be written for a particular purpose and target reader.

▶ Part 1 tests your ability to respond to the input material in an appropriate style, evaluating information, expressing opinions, etc. All tasks require you to be persuasive. Read the instructions carefully and underline the key words that tell you what you are being asked to do.

▶ The input information in Part 1 may be from a variety of different texts: notes, letters, reports, advertisements, diagrams, etc. Make sure you read it carefully and understand what information it conveys before you start writing.

▶ Think about the appropriate register for your writing: formal, semi-formal, neutral or informal. If you are writing a report or proposal, consider whether to use headings and bullet points or numbered lists.

▶ Don't try to write out your answer in a rough draft before you produce a final draft; you will not have enough time. Instead, plan carefully what you will say in each section/paragraph of your writing.

▶ Divide your writing into three sections: introduction, main body and conclusion. Think about what you will say in each part. Plan approximately how many words should be in each section of your writing.

▶ Write your article, letter, report, etc. Use your own words as far as possible; don't copy the information from the input texts.

▶ When you have finished, check your spelling and punctuation. Make sure the examiner can read your writing.

▶ See the **Writing bank** on page 214 for examples of different types of writing.

PAPER 1 Reading

PAPER 2 Writing ▶ Part 1
Part 2

PAPER 3 Use of English

PAPER 4 Listening

PAPER 5 Speaking

You **must** answer this question. Write your answer in **180–220** words in an appropriate style.

---

1 The Northgate Town Planning Department has announced that it intends to build houses on a piece of open land called Northgate Common.

You have been asked by the local residents' committee to write an article for the local newspaper in response to the announcement, explaining why you are opposed to the plan. Read the announcement below, on which you have made notes, and write the article.

NORTHGATE COMMON

Consultation? When?

After consultation with local residents, the Northgate Town Planning Department hereby announces that planning permission has been granted for a housing project on the area of unused land known as Northgate Common. Work is scheduled to begin in September of this year.

Not unused: parkland for sports, children playing, walks, etc.

Only 3 months away: should have been told earlier!

Cheap housing for local people?

12 semi-detached private residences will cover 62% of the common, and the remaining 38% will be developed into private gardens for the use of the residents.

Why not public gardens?

Now write your **article**.

Essential tips

▶ When you write an article, think carefully about the appropriate register and tone for the question you are answering. What publication is the article for? Who is going to read your article?

▶ In your article, you must describe 'the situation'. What information should you give? Is it necessary to mention who 'you' are in this article?

▶ Think carefully about why you are writing the article. What effect do you want it to have on readers? What do you hope to achieve by writing it? Do you want to convince readers about anything? Think about the language you will need to achieve this goal.

▶ The handwritten comments next to the announcement provide you with information, but you need to expand them into sentences. For example, the first comment is 'Consultation? When?' How could you express the idea conveyed by these words in a full sentence?

PAPER 1 Reading

PAPER 2 Writing ▶
Part 1

PAPER 3 Use of English
Part 2

PAPER 4 Listening

PAPER 5 Speaking

Essential tips

▶ In Part 2 you must choose one task. However, you should be familiar with all the possible types of text you might need to write.

▶ Read each question carefully. Before you choose a question, ask yourself if you know enough vocabulary on the subject and can employ it in the required register and text type.

▶ In Part 2 questions you have more freedom to use your imagination and come up with information that is not in the input material.

Question 2

▶ Although the word is not mentioned in the question, you are being asked to write an article expressing your opinions.

▶ Think about the style that would be appropriate: formal, semi-formal or informal?

▶ The question makes it clear that you should concentrate on two aspects of travel: (a) why it is important and (b) how you would benefit. This suggests that the two main sections of your article should be about these aspects.

▶ Plan carefully what to say in each part of your answer to avoid repeating yourself, and to ensure you include as many relevant points as possible.

▶ You also need an introduction and a conclusion. What could you say here?

▶ Remember that you should use your imagination – when you explain what you would like to do on a journey, for instance.

▶ Make sure you have enough time to check your answer.

Write an answer to **one** of the questions 2–5 in this part. Write your answer in **220–260** words in an appropriate style.

2 You see the following announcement in a travel magazine and decide to enter the competition:

FREE TRAVEL IN EUROPE!

Are you under the age of 25?
Are you interested in travelling around Europe?

Write to us explaining why travelling is good for young people, and indicate how you yourself would expect to benefit from a trip around Europe.

The writer of the best entry will win a free EuropeRail monthly travel pass.

Send your entry to:
EuropeRail, P.O. Box 242, London

Write your **competition entry**.

3 You have seen the following announcement in an international magazine:

Modern technology:
saving our time or wasting our money?

Does modern technology really make our lives easier, or are the machines and devices we buy a waste of money? We want to know what you think.

Write an article, giving at least two examples of useful machines or devices and two examples of machines or devices that we could easily do without.

Write your **article**.

4 Read the following extract from a letter that you received from an international youth organisation:

> We are conducting a survey on the importance of regional culture to young people around the world. Please write us a report for this survey, describing how young people in your region feel about the history and culture of that region, and how you think this may change in the future.

Write your **report**.

5 Answer **one** of the following two questions based on your reading of **one** of the set books.

Either

5(a) A well-known literary magazine has invited readers to send in reviews of a book they have read recently. You have decided to write a review of the set book, outlining the plot and saying whether or not you would recommend the book to other readers and why.

Write your **review**.

Or

5(b) Your teacher has asked you to write an essay on the main characters in your set book, examining their personality and saying whether or not their actions are justified in the story.

Write your **essay**.

Essential tips

Question 4

▶ In order to answer this question, you must be familiar with the format of a report. You need to write clear paragraphs and use headings. You may also want to use other features such as bullet points or numbered lists.

▶ Remember that a report must have a clear introduction and conclusion as well. In your introduction, state what the report is about and who it is for. In your conclusion, summarise the information contained in your report. See the Writing bank on page 216.

▶ You need to include information about the culture and history of your region. At the same time, your task is to produce a good piece of writing, so as long as the points you make sound reasonable, they do not all have to be factually correct. For instance, if you want to say that young people in your region are interested in the history of this part of the country, you could invent a survey that shows 65% of young people say they are 'very interested' in history. It doesn't matter if this survey was never actually carried out.

▶ The question asks you to give your opinion about how the situation may change in the future. Therefore, you can use the first person to say what you think (e.g. 'I think', 'I believe'), but keep the formal style that is appropriate for a report.

Question 5

▶ In this question, you may be asked to write an essay, a review, an article or a report. It is therefore important to practise writing these text types in relation to your chosen set book.

▶ The tasks will focus on character study, the development of the plot and the main themes within the story. As you read the set book, make notes on characters' personalities. Practise making comparisons between different characters and also think about why you like or dislike them. You must be able to outline the plot and talk about themes such as greed, ambition, love, hate, etc.

▶ You may be asked to compare the set book with a film that is based on it, especially if the latter is well known, so check whether or not there is a film based on the book you are reading, and try to ensure that you see it before the exam.

▶ For question 5(a), your review should outline the plot. Think carefully about what you like and dislike about the book. Even if you like it very much, it might be useful to mention one weak point; this will make your review sound more convincing and realistic. If you recommend it to other readers, you might like to mention what kind of reader you think would enjoy it, e.g. a particular age group, lovers of thrillers, romantic novels, etc.

▶ For question 5(b), you need to have a good understanding of the main characters. Think about the decisions they make in the story and whether they are the right ones, in your opinion. Remember to support what you say with examples from the book.

For questions **1–12**, read the text below and decide which answer (**A, B, C** or **D**) best fits each gap. There is an example at the beginning (**0**).

Mark your answers **on the separate answer sheet**.

Example:

0　　**A** event　　**B** aspect　　**C** field　　**D** division

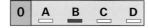

Essential tips

▶ Read through the whole text to get a general idea of what it is about.

▶ The correct option must have the correct meaning. It can also be part of a phrase, collocation, idiom, phrasal verb or expression.

▶ The correct option must fit in the sentence structurally. All the four options will be the right part of speech (noun, adjective, verb, adverb etc.), but only one will be correct in the context of the sentence. For instance, the correct option may be the only word that is followed by a preposition which comes after the gap. So check the words on either side of the gap carefully to see what collocates with them.

Question 2: One of the options does not collocate with 'time'. Of the other three options, only one has the correct meaning of 'best'.

Question 4: Only one of the options forms a fixed expression with 'what is' which has the required meaning here: 'in addition' or 'moreover'.

Question 7: Only one option collocates with 'convinced'.

Question 12: Is 'people' countable or uncountable? Think about what you would use each option to describe.

Nature's Clocks

Our biological clocks govern almost every (**0**) ...... of our lives. Our sensitivity to stimuli (**1**) ...... over the course of the day, and our ability to perform certain functions is subject to fluctuations. Consequently, there is a(n) (**2**) ...... time for tasks such as making decisions: around the middle of the day. Anything that (**3**) ...... physical co-ordination, on the other hand, is best attempted in the early evening. What is (**4**) ...... , there is a dramatic drop in performance if these activities are (**5**) ...... out at other times. The risk of accident in a factory, for example, is 20% higher during the night (**6**) ....

Primitive humans lived their lives in tune with the daily cycle of light and dark. Today we are (**7**) ...... convinced that we can impose schedules on our lives at will . Sooner or later, however, we pay a (**8**) ...... for ignoring our natural rhythms. A good example is jet lag, caused when we confuse our body's biological clocks by (**9**) ...... several time zones. People suffering from jet lag can take several days to adjust to new time zones, and have a reduced ability to make decisions, which is a worrying thought, as serious (**10**) ...... of judgement can be made. And this may be just the (**11**) ...... of the iceberg. An increasing (**12**) ...... of people suffer from seasonal affective disorder (SAD), a form of depression that can be triggered by living in artificial conditions. SAD can be serious, and sufferers may even need to take antidepressant drugs.

1	**A** modifies	**B** ranges	**C** varies	**D** wavers
2	**A** peak	**B** summit	**C** maximum	**D** optimum
3	**A** requests	**B** demands	**C** dictates	**D** stipulates
4	**A** more	**B** else	**C** different	**D** up
5	**A** made	**B** done	**C** carried	**D** performed
6	**A** labour	**B** work	**C** duty	**D** shift
7	**A** powerfully	**B** firmly	**C** steadily	**D** highly
8	**A** price	**B** fine	**C** fee	**D** cost
9	**A** landing	**B** penetrating	**C** crossing	**D** travelling
10	**A** errors	**B** mistakes	**C** inaccuracies	**D** fallacies
11	**A** peak	**B** pinnacle	**C** top	**D** tip
12	**A** amount	**B** quantity	**C** number	**D** proportion

For questions **13–27**, read the text below and think of the word which best fits each gap. Use only **one** word in each gap. There is an example at the beginning (**0**).

Write your answers **IN CAPITAL LETTERS on the separate answer sheet**.

Example:

0	*THERE*	0

Essential tips

▶ Read through the whole text to get a general idea of what it is about.

▶ Decide what word or words in the sentence are grammatically related to the gapped word; this will help you decide what part of speech is needed (auxiliary verb, pronoun, article, preposition etc.).

▶ Read the whole sentence to see if the word you need is part of a longer or parallel structure such as 'not only ... but also ...'.

▶ It may be that two or even three words could fit in the gap, so do not assume the word you are thinking of is wrong if you can also think of one or two alternatives.

Question 13: Read the whole sentence carefully. You will notice that each half talks about a certain type of tourist. The second group is referred to as 'others', so what word could be used together with 'tourists' to refer to the first group?

Question 15: The gapped word is part of a phrase: 'follow ... somebody's footsteps'. If you can't immediately think of the gapped word, try to find a word that sounds right: you may well have heard the phrase before.

Question 21: Think of the meaning of the sentence and the text as a whole. If oil dispersed effectively, would there be a problem?

Question 24: It should be clear that you need a preposition here. The previous sentence mentions cruise ships, and now the possibility of a collision involving an iceberg is raised. Which preposition is used with 'collision' in this context?

Question 26: The word you need may be part of a simple expression. You may be able to find the correct word by reading the sentence aloud.

Danger Facing Antarctica

Antarctica is becoming a popular tourist destination and in the last decade (**0**) .... has been a dramatic increase in visitors to the area. (**13**) .... tourists simply want to see the last unspoiled continent, (**14**) .... others have more active pursuits such as adventure sports in mind. And of course, there are also those adventurous souls who want to follow (**15**) .... the footsteps of the great polar explorers. (**16**) .... , environmentalists are concerned that the booming tourist industry may (**17**) .... endangering the Antarctic environment and sowing (**18**) .... seeds of its own destruction.

One of the problems facing the area is pollution resulting from tourism. Careless visitors throw rubbish into the sea, not realising (**19**) .... harmful this can be to wildlife. (**20**) .... danger is oil spills. In the freezing waters, oil does (**21**) .... disperse effectively. Consequently, oil from even a small spill (**22**) .... remain a hazard to wildlife for many years. And this is a very real danger: some of the cruise ships visiting Antarctica have not been reinforced to (**23**) .... into account the dangers. A collision (**24**) .... an iceberg could cause a disaster of major proportions. This is (**25**) .... no means a far-fetched notion. From (**26**) .... to time icebergs do appear in these waters, and global warming means that massive chunks of ice are breaking (**27**) .... the continental ice sheet more and more frequently. If a ship collided with one of these, it could spell disaster for tourism.

Essential tips

Question 28: Think carefully about the part of speech you need here. You may need both a prefix and a suffix.

Question 30: The gapped word forms part of an expression: 'in ... with', which means 'matching something'.

Question 31: The gapped word is a compound adjective which means 'lasting for the whole of one's life'.

Question 32: The gapped word must be a noun. Do you need the singular or plural form?

For questions **28–37**, read the text below. Use the word given in capitals at the end of some of the lines to form a word that fits in the gap **in the same line.** There is an example at the beginning (**0**).

Write your answers **IN CAPITAL LETTERS on the separate answer sheet.**

Example:

0	*PARTICIPATE*	0 __ __

Elephant Training

If you are travelling in Thailand and have a taste for adventure, you can now (**0**) .... in an unusual kind of activity. For an (**28**) .... modest sum, you can spend a few days at an elephant conservation centre training to be a mahout or elephant driver. Be prepared to get wet, however, because you spend most of the day atop an elephant, during which time this (**29**) .... beast can take up to three baths!   **PART**
CREDIBLE

MAJESTY

Primarily set up in an endeavour to preserve the Thai elephant, the centre offers such activities to tourists as a means of funding itself. Nevertheless, its training programme remains strictly in (**30**) .... with the traditions of Kachasart, the ancient method of studying elephants, and the mahouts that work with the elephants build up a close, (**31**) .... relationship with them, founded on mutual respect and love.   **KEEP**

LIFE

The type of training depends on the (**32**) .... that different animals display, and care is taken not to overtire them. Training is believed to be (**33**) .... to the elephants, providing them with physical and mental (**34**) .... Their well-being is of utmost importance, and the success of the centre's breeding programme bears witness to this.   **ABLE**

BENEFIT
STIMULATE

While it may not be ideal to keep such magnificent beasts in (**35**) .... – and the centre has come in for plenty of criticism – (**36**) .... deforestation has left wild elephants struggling to survive in habitats that are shrinking almost on a (**37**) .... basis. The centre offers them a sanctuary – for the time being at least.   **CAPTURE**
EXTEND

DAY

PAPER 1 Reading

PAPER 2 Writing

PAPER 3 Use of English   Part 1
PAPER 4 Listening   Part 2
PAPER 5 Speaking   Part 3
                            Part 4
                            Part 5

Essential tips

▸ Make sure you read all three sentences in a set before deciding on a word. The correct word must fit all three sentences!

▸ Decide what kind of word you are looking for. The missing word will have the same form in all three sentences.

▸ The missing word will usually be a common word, although it may be used as part of a phrasal verb, collocation, expression or idiom in at least one of the sentences.

Question 38: The third sentence should help you find the word that fits all three sentences.

Question 39: In the third sentence, the missing word is part of an idiomatic phrase. The first and second sentences contain clues to help you find the word.

Question 42: Read the second sentence. What can you look at to find the answers to an exercise in a textbook?

For questions **38–42**, think of **one** word only which can be used appropriately in all three sentences. Here is an example (**0**).

Example:

0 ● We will do all the work, but they will .... all the credit, as usual!

   ● She will .... offence if you tell her that hairstyle doesn't suit her.

   ● They threatened to .... David to court unless he stopped playing his drums at night.

0	*TAKE*	0

Write **only** the missing word **IN CAPITAL LETTERS on the separate answer sheet**.

---

38 ● When Frank was entertaining the children, I saw a .... of him I hadn't seen before.

   ● Ken works as a teacher, but he also sells insurance on the ....

   ● Ellen fell off her bike and got scratches all down her left ....

39 ● That kind of music leaves me .... , I'm afraid.

   ● Jenny has been so .... towards me lately that I think I may have done something to upset her.

   ● Tom and Bianca were supposed to get married last month, but she got .... feet and now the wedding's off!

40 ● It is only possible to dive safely from the .... end of the pool.

   ● Sally was nervous as she walked onto the stage, but she took a .... breath and began to sing.

   ● You'll get into .... trouble if you get caught.

41 ● The house .... south, with a beautiful view of the sea.

   ● Sanchez .... Martinez in the final of the tournament, and won.

   ● Wendy finally .... up to the fact that Fred wouldn't be coming back.

42 ● Our football coach always said that teamwork was the .... to success in life.

   ● If you aren't sure of the answer to a question, there's a .... on page 274.

   ● I pressed the wrong .... and I deleted the file from the computer!

PAPER 1 Reading

PAPER 2 Writing

PAPER 3 Use of English | Part 1

PAPER 4 Listening | Part 2

PAPER 5 Speaking | Part 3

| Part 4

| **Part 5**

Essential tips

▶ For each question, read both sentences carefully. The second sentence must convey the same information as the first sentence, but in different words.

▶ The key word must be used without changing its form in any way.

▶ You may need to change the order in which you give the information, and the form of some words from the first sentence.

▶ Some questions may require you to change from a negative sentence to a positive one, or from a passive structure to an active one. Be prepared for this!

▶ You must use between three and six words in your answer. If you write too few words or too many, you will lose marks.

Question 43: The key word is a reporting verb. There is more than one possible structure which follows it. It does not matter which one you use in your answer.

Question 45: You need an inversion here.

Question 46: You need an emphatic structure here.

Question 49: How can you express the idea of possibility? You need a structure with a modal verb. You will also need a suitable linking word.

For questions **43–50**, complete the second sentence so that it has a similar meaning to the first sentence, using the word given. **Do not change the word given.** You must use between **three** and **six** words, including the word given. Here is an example (**0**).

Example:

0 Jane regretted speaking so rudely to the old lady.
 MORE
 Jane .... politely to the old lady.

0	*WISHED SHE HAD SPOKEN MORE*	**0**

Write the missing words **IN CAPITAL LETTERS on the separate answer sheet.**

---

43 'Honestly, I didn't cheat in the test!' said John.
 DENIED
 John .... in the test.

44 Pop in for a chat whenever you are in town.
 HAPPEN
 If .... in town, pop in for a chat.

45 Paula had just reached the gate when it began to rain.
 THAN
 No sooner .... it began to rain.

46 'Mark wrote that poem, not Ian,' said Helen.
 IT
 According to Helen, ... that poem, not Ian.

47 Even if it is expensive, they want to go on the London Eye.
 MAY
 Expensive .... , they want to go on the London Eye.

48 Unless you tell the truth, the school trip will be cancelled.
 MEAN
 Your failure .... the cancellation of the school trip.

49 Jill has never been here before, so it is possible that she has got lost.
 HAVE
 Jill .... it is the first time she has ever been here.

50 Instead of spending money on clothes, I prefer to spend it on books.
 SPEND
 I would .... on books than on clothes.

You will hear three different extracts. For questions **1–6**, choose the answer (**A, B** or **C**) which fits best according to what you hear. There are two questions for each extract.

Extract One

You hear two friends talking about an experience one of them had as a volunteer.

1   Nigel joined the Blue Ventures project because

    A a friend of his encouraged him to do volunteer work.

    B he had always dreamed of going to Madagascar.

    C he thought the experience would be useful to him.   **1**

2   Which word best describes Jenny's reaction to Nigel's account?

    A enthusiasm

    B disinterest

    C envy   **2**

Extract Two

You hear two people talking on a radio programme about how to deal with a compulsive disorder.

3   When did Alice realise she had a problem?

    A when she had a strong urge to go shopping all the time

    B after she had got into serious financial difficulty

    C once she had talked to a professional about how she felt   **3**

4   Alice now goes to a gym in order to

    A stop herself spending money.

    B get fit and lose a bit of weight.

    C get to know new people.   **4**

Extract Three

You hear two friends talking about a football match they have just watched.

5 The woman thinks that England

    A deserved to lose.

    B were not confident enough.

    C were unfortunate.   **5**

6 According to the man,

    A Gerrard was unfairly treated.

    B England played badly.

    C Russia didn't play well.   **6**

Essential tips

▶ Before you listen to each extract, you will be given time (fifteen seconds) to read the questions. Make good use of this time, and try to predict what you are going to hear.

▶ Listen carefully before choosing the answer. The options may contain words you hear on the recording, but the meaning of the sentence may be different!

▶ Some questions ask you about the speaker's feelings or attitude to something. Listen to the speaker's tone of voice and the way he/she speaks. It may be necessary to listen to the whole extract before making your choice.

Question 1: More than one option may seem possible here. Why did Nigel join the project?

Question 2: Listen carefully to Jenny's tone of voice.

Question 4: Alice spends time at the gym that she would otherwise spend somewhere else. Where?

Essential tips

▶ Read the instructions and find out the subject of the recording.

▶ Read the questions carefully and think about the sort of information you might need to complete the gaps.

▶ Each gap is completed by one, two or three words, or a number.

▶ Decide what grammatical form the gapped word or words should have.

▶ You will hear the words you need on the recording, but not in the same sentences as the questions. You need to listen for the ideas expressed on the recording.

▶ You will hear the recording twice, so you will have a chance to fill in any gaps you miss the first time.

Question 7: What sort of word could come after 'in': a time, a place, or an expression with the preposition 'in'? Listen for any of these.

Question 10: The recording is about a medicine, and this sentence mentions an acid that can affect something or somebody quite badly. Who or what could this be?

Question 12: The sentence is about something that happened or lasted for nearly seventy years, so you should listen for information about this period. Also consider what could fit with the phrase 'into the way aspirin works'.

Question 14: The gapped word must describe something like a plant, which can be grown without artificial chemicals, so listen for a word with this meaning.

You will hear a writer talking about a book she has written on the subject of aspirin. For questions **7–14**, complete the sentences.

The story of aspirin

Doctors in [____ 7 ____] treated their patients with a medicine derived from the bark of the willow.

Edward Stone believed that [____ 8 ____] was similar to quinine.

The active ingredient of aspirin was isolated in [____ 9 ____]

Unfortunately, salicylic acid can affect the [____ 10 ____] quite badly.

The first commercially available aspirins were made by Bayer, a [____ 11 ____]

However, there was little [____ 12 ____] into the way aspirin works for nearly seventy years.

Some scientists think that people over [____ 13 ____] should take aspirin to prevent certain diseases.

It appears that [____ 14 ____] grown without artificial chemicals also contain the active ingredients of aspirin.

Essential tips

This part of the exam is usually a multiple-choice task, but it could also be a sentence-completion task. If it is a sentence-completion task, look back at the tips for Parts 1 and 2. If it is a multiple-choice task, read the following tips:

▶ Read the instructions and find out the subject of the recording.

▶ Read the questions or question stems carefully and underline the key words.

▶ The questions follow the order of the recording, but the final question may be about the recording as a whole.

Question 15: Option A suggests most people, especially the critics, liked the ballet; option B implies some people liked it and some didn't; option C implies most people didn't like it; and option D implies that people who love animals liked the ballet. Which of these ideas does the recording convey?

Question 18: Think about different ways to express that something 'is of greatest interest to audiences'. You should also be prepared for the information to be given in a different order. For example, the speaker may describe something that happened and then say afterwards that it interested audiences.

Question 19: The question tells you that Stan will talk about something that went wrong when he saw the ballet. Which option best describes what happened?

You will hear part of an interview with Stan Levin, a dance critic, about a modern ballet production involving animals. For questions **15–20**, choose the answer (**A, B, C** or **D**) which fits best according to what you hear.

15 We gather that the ballet being discussed here
  A has received general critical acclaim.
  B has caused considerable controversy.
  C has not been well received on the whole.
  D has become popular with animals-lovers.

16 It appears that the function of the dogs in the ballet is to
  A reflect what happens to the human characters.
  B act as a contrast to the human characters.
  C show how wild animals behave in a civilised society.
  D symbolise homeless people.

17 How does Stan feel about the increasing use of technology in dance?
  A He thinks this trend has gone too far.
  B He prefers more traditional approaches to dance.
  C He does not approve of it in principle.
  D He believes it is creating a new art form.

18 What aspect of the ballet is of greatest interest to audiences?
  A the way the dogs behave during dance sequences
  B the way the dogs perform their tricks
  C the sight of the dogs in a pack
  D the way the dogs copy the actions of one character

19 What caused the lapse in mood during the performance Stan saw?
  A the inability of the dogs to concentrate
  B the audience's unwillingness to accept the dogs
  C the behaviour of a member of the audience
  D the inability of dogs and humans to work as a team

20 What aspect of the performance made the most powerful impression on Stan?
  A the implicit potential for violence
  B the aggression shown by the dogs
  C the bond between the dogs and the tramp
  D the primitive appearance of the dogs

Essential tips

▶ Read the instructions and find out who will be talking and what they will be talking about.

▶ You have two tasks to think about at the same time, each relating to one type of statement made by the speakers. So the first time you hear each speaker be prepared for a piece of information that corresponds to an option in the first task; the second time listen for a piece of information that corresponds to an option in the second task.

▶ The answer options do not repeat what the speakers say; they express the ideas in different words. Read each option carefully, and be prepared to hear the information expressed in a different form.

▶ Each task has three options you do not need.

Questions 21–25
Option A: If something has a 'social function', what does it have? How might you express the idea that learning English has a social function?

Option H: If this option is correct for one of the speakers, it must mean that the person had 'an injury'. What words could be used to express that you were injured?

Questions 26–30
Option G: What ways are there to express that something is a commitment? If you commit yourself to do something, what do you do or say to yourself or to other people?

Option H: How else could a speaker talk about 'genetic make-up'? Can you think of any expressions, perhaps more informal ones, that convey the idea that some characteristics are genetically controlled?

You will hear five short extracts in which people talk about fitness and health.

While you listen you must complete both tasks.

Task One
For questions **21–25**, choose from the list **A–H** what each speaker says about his or her reasons for attending a gym regularly.

A   The gym has a social function for me.

B   I want to be fit for a specific event.

C   My company pays for me to attend a gym.

D   I must keep fit because of my medical condition.

E   Being fit gives me a sense of achievement.

F   Attending a gym is an absolute necessity for me.

G   I come here with the members of my cycling club.

H   I started exercising regularly after an injury.

Speaker 1	21
Speaker 2	22
Speaker 3	23
Speaker 4	24
Speaker 5	25

Task Two
For questions **26–30**, choose from the list **A–H** what opinion each speaker expresses about fitness and health generally.

A   My lifestyle is unhealthy in the long run.

B   Keeping fit is a habit.

C   I find it hard to commit myself to exercising.

D   City life doesn't encourage walking for exercise.

E   Exercise machines are extremely boring.

F   You can't separate health and lifestyle.

G   It's easier to get fit if you think of it as a commitment.

H   I'm sure your genetic make-up has a lot to do with fitness.

Speaker 1	26
Speaker 2	27
Speaker 3	28
Speaker 4	29
Speaker 5	30

Essential tips

Part 1

▶ In this part of the exam, you must show that you can use English appropriately to interact with another person in a social context. You will be expected to answer questions about yourself your family, home, interests, education and future plans.

▶ Make sure you answer the question you have been asked and don't go off at a tangent to talk about something different.

▶ Don't try to prepare for this part of the exam by learning a speech off by heart – it will sound unnatural.

Part 2

▶ In this part of the exam, you have to talk on a subject for one minute. This is a long time when you have to talk in an exam. Make sure you practise talking for this length of time.

▶ The examiner could ask you to compare things, contrast them, identify them or speculate about them. He/She will give you three photographs and ask you to talk about two of them.

▶ Here you are asked to compare and contrast the photographs, and to speculate why someone is doing something or what advantages something might have. Make sure you answer both parts of the question.

▶ While the other candidate is talking, listen carefully. The examiner will ask you a question related to what he/she has been talking about. You should answer this question in about thirty seconds.

Part 1 (3 minutes)

The examiner will ask you a few questions about yourself and then ask you to talk to your partner. For example, the examiner may ask you:

- Where do you both live?
- What do you like and dislike about this area?
- If you moved to another area, where would you like to live?

Part 2 (4 minutes)

You will each be asked to talk on your own for a minute without interruption. You will each be given a set of three photographs in turn to talk about. After your partner has finished speaking, you will be asked a brief question connected with your partner's photographs. You will have thirty seconds to answer.

Costumes (compare, contrast and speculate)

Turn to pictures 1–3 on page **190**, which show people in costumes.

Candidate A, compare and contrast two of these pictures and imagine what could have prompted these people to dress in this way. How do you think they are feeling?

Candidate B, which of these costumes would you feel most comfortable in, and why?

Working environments (compare, contrast and speculate)

Turn to pictures 1–3 on page **191**, which show different working environments.

Candidate B, compare and contrast two of these workplaces, saying what advantages and disadvantages you could imagine for them.

Candidate A, which of these environments would you prefer to work in, and why?

Part 3 (4 minutes)

Modern times (discuss, evaluate and select)

Turn to the pictures on page **192**, which show aspects of modern life.

Talk to each other about which two of these pictures you would choose to illustrate that modern life has both advantages and disadvantages.

Part 4 (4 minutes)

The examiner will encourage you to develop the topic of your discussion in Part 3 by asking questions such as:

- Which aspects of life in the past, which no longer exist, do you think were positive? Could they be revived? Why (not)?
- Should developments in technology be restricted in any way? Why (not)?
- What sort of difficulties do young people face today, but that previous generations did not have to confront, or not to the same extent?
- Why do older people sometimes become nostalgic about the past?

Essential tips

Question 2: Read the question stem carefully. Remember that 'implies' means 'says indirectly', and think about the writer's attitude towards the Ethical Fashion Forum. What does she believe the Ethical Fashion Forum is trying to do? Does she think they genuinely want to improve the situation?

You are going to read three extracts which are all concerned in some way with ethical fashion. For questions **1–6**, choose the answer (**A, B, C** or **D**) which you think fits best according to the text.

Mark your answers **on the separate answer sheet**.

Ethical Fashion

It is hip to be eco-friendly in the business world nowadays, and even the fashion industry has jumped on the bandwagon. A network of designers and businesses connected with the industry have collaborated to form the Ethical Fashion Forum. Its aims are, ostensibly, to bring together all the components in the global garment supply chain and to promote sustainable practices in the manufacture of clothing, particularly in developing countries. The Ethical Fashion Forum encourages manufacturers to improve working conditions by reducing the use of dangerous chemicals and dyes in the treatment of fabrics. This is one of the ways, it is hoped, that the clothing industry can alleviate the negative impact it has on the environment.

All noble intentions, and admirable indeed. However, the cynics among us cannot help but question the sincerity of entrepreneurs in an industry as notoriously exploitative as this one. Is the fashion industry honestly becoming more socially aware? Or is it simply capitalising on the eco-friendly fad of the moment in an attempt to combat the growing number of anti-consumerism campaigns by marketing the idea that the fashion industry is also now socially and environmentally aware? The industry appears to be saying that it is still acceptable, in fact necessary, to buy lots of clothes and accessories. In other words, 'buy ethically, but don't stop buying'!

The truth of the matter is that it will be extremely difficult to persuade all the links in the supply chain to act responsibly, especially when profits are at stake. Furthermore, we cannot ignore the fickle nature of fashion itself, which is constantly subject to changing tastes.

1 The Ethical Fashion Forum
   A   is an environmentally-friendly fashion company.
   B   promotes the clothing industry in developing countries.
   C   is an organisation made up of fashion designers.
   D   seems to be encouraging the clothing industry to change.

2 The writer implies that the Ethical Fashion Forum's real motives are to
   A   improve working conditions within the fashion industry.
   B   coordinate the different stages in the manufacture of clothing.
   C   take advantage of current trends in favour of ecologically sound practices.
   D   reduce the use of dangerous chemicals and dyes in the treatment of textiles.

Essential tips

Question 4: You need to read the whole of the third paragraph. All of the options may appear possible, but what does the advertisement actually say?

STOMPING GREEN!

✔ You think ethically
✔ You eat ethically
✔ You buy ethically
✔ You dress ethically

Now you can also walk ethically with our new range of ethical footwear! Made from a special material that breathes, and looks and feels like supple leather, our shoes are not only ethical, they're STOMPING GREEN!

Our footwear is genuinely animal- and environment-friendly. It is made in European factories in worker-friendly environments. We use high-tech synthetics that are bio-degradable where possible to provide you with shoes that suit your requirements aesthetically, ethically and economically.

Most of our shoes are made to order, so check out our web site to see the full range of the colours and styles we offer in boots, shoes and sandals, as well as details about the materials we use in their manufacture. And of course, if you live in Portsmouth or are passing through, do visit our shop. We guarantee that you will walk out wearing one of our models! You will be amazed at the quality and the variety available!

STOMPING GREEN – Footwear for the Environment.

3   According to the advertisement, Stomping Green footwear
  A   does not harm the environment in any way.
  B   is handmade on the premises of the shop.
  C   is designed to suit people with different tastes.
  D   is made specifically for vegetarians.

4   The advertisement implies that Stomping Green
  A   care for the people who work in the manufacture of their footwear.
  B   would prefer customers to order their footwear online.
  C   pride themselves on their unique designs.
  D   sell most of their footwear in Portsmouth.

Recycle that suit!

Have you taken a good long look in your wardrobe recently? How full is it, and how many of the clothes do you actually wear? Did you know that in Britain alone, people throw away an estimated one million tonnes of clothing material every year? And yet we regularly seem to need to buy new clothes.

Discarded textiles present a health hazard because of the chemicals used to treat them, such as dyes and bleaches. As these decompose, they release toxic gases into the atmosphere. There is a wealth of sites on the Internet devoted to recycling old clothes, and several offer useful practical advice on how to revamp items like old suits, aprons, curtains, etc.

Recycling old clothes can help reduce the amount of waste generated, and with a little imagination, you can customise an outfit and create your own individual style. At the same time, you save money. Some very innovative people have set up sewing groups dedicated to recycling old clothes, and exchange ideas and tips on how to do it. If you aren't interested in sewing, then at least you can take your old clothes to charity shops, pass on children's clothes to friends and neighbours, and support fashion businesses which use recycled products. You will be making a difference, no matter how small.

5　The purpose of the first paragraph is to
- **A**　persuade readers to be more adventurous when choosing new clothes.
- **B**　make people aware of how wasteful they are with their clothing.
- **C**　discuss the problems involved in achieving an individual style.
- **D**　warn people against spending money on fashionable clothes.

6　The article suggests that people should
- **A**　save money by making their own clothes.
- **B**　stop buying clothes in order to reduce waste.
- **C**　make new outfits using old clothes.
- **D**　only buy clothes from charity shops.

PAPER 1 Reading ▶
PAPER 2 Writing
PAPER 3 Use of English
PAPER 4 Listening
PAPER 5 Speaking

Part 1
Part 2
Part 3
Part 4

You are going to read a magazine article. Six paragraphs have been removed from the article. Choose from the paragraphs **A–G** the one which fits each gap (**7–12**). There is one extra paragraph which you do not need to use.

Mark your answers **on the separate answer sheet**.

Mind your languages

Thousands of the world's languages are dying, taking to the grave not just words but records of civilisations and cultures that we may never come to fully know or understand. It is a loss of which few people are aware, yet it will affect us all. Linguists have calculated that of the 6,000 languages currently spoken worldwide most will disappear over the next hundred years. As many as 1,000 languages have died in the past 400 years. Conversely, the handful of major international languages are forging ahead.

| 7 | |

But the vast majority of the world never had need of phrases in Heiltsuk (a Native Indian language from the Canadian Pacific coast of British Columbia which is now dead). Nor will most people be interested in learning any of the 800 languages spoken on the island of New Guinea or the 2,400 spoken by Native American Indians (many of which are threatened), but their deaths are robbing us of the knowledge needed to write many chapters of history.

| 8 | |

Documenting a threatened language can be difficult and dangerous, requiring consummate diplomacy with tribes, some of which may be meeting outsiders for the first time and may well be wary about why these strangers need so much information about their language. 'Some peoples are extremely proud of their language while others are sceptical of the "white man", believing he now wants to rob them of their language as well,' says Kortlandt.

| 9 | |

'There are about 200 Tibeto-Burman languages, only about ten of which have been properly described,' says Kortlandt. 'We now have fourteen PhD students describing different, unknown languages.' The problem is it can take years to document a language. 'We are generally happy when we have a corpus of texts which we can read and understand with the help of a reliable grammar and dictionary provided by a competent linguist, preferably including texts of some particular interest,' says Kortlandt.

| 10 | |

To non-linguists it must seem an odd issue to get worked up about. Why waste so much time saving languages spoken by so few and not concentrate on the languages of the future that most of us speak? Why look back instead of forward? 'Would you ask a biologist looking for disappearing species the same question?' Kortlandt asks. 'Or an astronomer looking for distant galaxies? Why should languages, the mouthpiece of threatened cultures, be less interesting than unknown species or galaxies? Language is the defining characteristic of the human species. These people say things to each other which are very different from the things we say, and think very different thoughts, which are often incomprehensible to us.'

| 11 | |

Take, for example, the vast potential for modern medicine that lies within tropical rainforests. For centuries forest tribes have known about the healing properties of certain plants, but it is only recently that the outside world has discovered that the rainforests and coral reefs hold potential cures for some of the world's major diseases. All this knowledge could be lost if the tribes and their languages die out without being documented.

| 12 | |

Kortlandt is blunt about why some languages have suffered. 'If we look back to the history of the Empire,' he says, 'for social, economic and political reasons, a majority never has an interest in preserving the culture of a minority.'

A Frederik Kortlandt, Professor of Comparative Linguistics at Leiden University in Holland, has a mission to document as many of the remaining endangered languages as he can. He leads a band of language experts trekking to some of the most inaccessible parts of the earth to save such threatened languages.

B This is one of the factors worrying Paul Qereti, a linguist in Fiji in the South Pacific. There are hundreds of known remedies in Fiji's forests. The guava leaf relieves diarrhoea, the udi tree eases sore throats, and hibiscus leaf tea is used by expectant mothers. There are possibly scores more yet to be discovered. We will only be able to find them and benefit from their properties through one or more of the 300 languages and dialects spoken on the Fijian islands. If the languages die, so too will the medicinal knowledge of naturally occurring tonics, rubs and potions. Science could be left wondering what we might have found. English is now spoken by almost everyone in Fiji and Qereti is teaching Fijians how to speak their own disappearing native languages and dialects.

C In September this year, like-minds met in Kathmandu for a conference on how to save some Himalayan languages spoken by just a handful of people. A great number of languages in the greater Himalayan region are endangered or have already reached the point of no return.

D As Kortlandt stresses, 'If you want to understand the human species, you have to take the full range of human thought into consideration. Language is the binding force of culture, and the disappearance of a language means the disappearance of culture. It is not only the words that disappear, but also knowledge about many things.'

E Kortlandt knows a language is disappearing when the younger generation does not use it any more. When a language is spoken by fewer than forty people, he calculates that it will die out. Every now and then language researchers get lucky. Kamassian, a southern Samoyed language spoken in the Upper Yenisey region of Russia, was supposed to have died out, until two old women who still spoke it turned up at a conference in Tallinn, Estonia in the early 1970s.

F According to the *Atlas of Languages*, Chinese is now spoken by 1,000 million people and English by 350 million. Spanish, spoken by 250 million people, is fast overtaking French as the first foreign language choice of British schoolchildren.

G Kortlandt is one of several linguists who have sounded the alarm that humankind is on the brink of losing over fifty percent of its languages within the next generation or two. 'This loss may be unavoidable in most cases,' says one authority, 'but at the very least, we can record as much as we can of these endangered languages before they die out altogether. Such an undertaking would naturally require support from international organisations, not to mention funding.'

Essential tips

- Remember: in this part of the exam you need to understand the structure and organisation of a text: how its paragraphs work together.

- First look at the instructions and the title of the text. Then skim the gapped text for the general meaning and notice how it develops ideas, opinions or events.

- You may need to consider more than one gap at a time in order to work out which paragraph goes where. Do not rely simply on recognising repeated names, dates etc.

Question 7: In the paragraph after the gap, the word 'But' shows that a contrast is being described. It is likely that the contrast is between the extinct or threatened languages referred to and the 'major international languages' mentioned in the paragraph before the gap.

Question 8: In the paragraph following the gap, the name of a person – Kortlandt – is mentioned, but there is no indication who this person is. It is likely that the gapped paragraph gives some details about him.

Question 11: The paragraph after the gap describes the kind of knowledge that could be lost if certain languages become extinct. Which gapped paragraph introduces this theme?

PAPER 1 Reading ▶
- Part 1
- Part 2
- **Part 3**
- Part 4

PAPER 2 Writing

PAPER 3 Use of English

PAPER 4 Listening

PAPER 5 Speaking

You are going to read a magazine article. For questions **13–19**, choose the answer (**A, B, C** or **D**) which you think fits best according to the text.

Mark your answers **on the separate answer sheet**.

The Cinderella Story

The basic story is very old indeed and familiar to most of us. The heroine, Cinderella, is treated cruelly by her stepmother and mocked by her two ugly stepsisters. And even though her father loves her, she can't tell him how unhappy she is because her stepmother has bewitched him. One day Cinderella's stepmother and stepsisters are invited to a ball at the royal palace. Cinderella is told she cannot go and is understandably very unhappy. However, her fairy godmother comes to the rescue and, waving her magic wand, produces some beautiful clothes for Cinderella as well as a carriage to convey her to the ball. There, she dances with the handsome prince, who falls in love with her, not only because she is beautiful but also because she is good and gracious. Cinderella has been warned that the magic will wear off at midnight, so when the clock strikes twelve, she hurries away, leaving behind her a glass slipper. Next day, the prince, smitten by her charms, comes looking for the girl whose foot fits the glass slipper. He finds Cinderella and they marry amid general rejoicing.

Just a sweet, pretty tale? Not in the view of Ellen MacIntosh, who has written extensively about fairy tales. 'This story features the stock, two-dimensional characters of most fairy tales, and little character development is attempted,' she says. Indeed, although her comment does make one wonder why simplicity of this sort should be out of place in a story for children. Be that as it may, Ellen's main problem is with what the story implies. 'Instead of standing up to her cruel stepmother and absurd stepsisters, Cinderella just waits for a fairy godmother to appear and solve her problems. But wouldn't you want a daughter of yours to show more spirit?'

The story is enduring, whatever its shortcomings, and it doesn't take much in the way of analytical skills to see its influence on a number of recent Hollywood productions, all aimed at girls aged five to fifteen. In these versions for the silver screen, the Cinderella character no longer has to clean the house and has no siblings to make her life a misery, though she persists in not showing much backbone. The character of the rich and handsome stranger, however, is retained, and in some cases really is a prince. The role of the fairy godmother is often played by coincidence or sheer luck; we live in an enlightened age when even very young children might reject the notion of fairies. The wicked stepmother may be transformed into a villain of some sort. In the majority of film versions, the heroine has a profession and is even permitted to continue working after marrying her prince – this is the twenty-first century, after all.

Doesn't the success of these films indicate that the story has relevance to children even today? 'Yes,' admits Ellen, who sees its message as being rooted in a fundamental childhood desire for love and attention. 'Most children experience a sense of inner loneliness as they are growing up and empathise with the protagonist who faces some sort of test or challenge. This can be seen in the original story of Cinderella, where the fairy godmother tells the heroine that she must learn to be gracious and confident if she is to go to the ball. She has to grow spiritually, and by maturing, she becomes attractive to the prince, thus ensuring that the ending of the story will be happy. 'In the later versions, this element is missing,' says Ellen, 'and the theme of the story is simply that a girl's role in life is to be more beautiful than other little girls so that she can carry off the prize: the handsome prince. Is this really what we want girls to grow up believing?'

- Remember: in this part of the exam you need to understand the details of a text, as well as the writer's opinion, attitude and purpose.

- You can approach this part in two slightly different ways. However, you should begin by reading the instructions and the title of the text. Then you can either skim the text first before you read the questions, or read the questions first before you skim the text.

- There will be seven questions or question stems. Read each question carefully and, without looking at the options, scan the text for the answer or for a suitable and accurate way to complete the question stem.

- Think about the meaning of what you read, and only then see if you can match the relevant section of the text with one of the options.

- The correct option is unlikely to use the same words as the text to express an idea.

Question 13: You are being asked about the writer's view, not Ellen MacIntosh's. Look for a section of the text where the writer describes Ellen's ideas and then gives her opinion of these ideas.

Question 15: This question is about films based on the Cinderella story. Look in the text for the word 'film' or any other word which means the same thing, for example, 'movie'. When you find the relevant section of the text, read it carefully. Then see which option corresponds precisely to what the text says.

Question 19: Even though you may be nervous and in a hurry, you must think carefully about the meaning of the questions. Which word in the question stem shows you are being asked to find a *difference* between the original story and the modern version?

13 What does the writer imply about fairy tales?
- **A** Fully developed characters would improve them.
- **B** The stories are very basic.
- **C** It is unrealistic to expect character development.
- **D** It is a mistake to consider them sweet and pretty.

14 What is Ellen's main objection to the Cinderella story?
- **A** The heroine is treated cruelly.
- **B** The heroine is not assertive enough.
- **C** The ugly stepsisters are figures of ridicule.
- **D** The stepmother is a stereotypical character.

15 In film versions of the Cinderella story
- **A** the prince is invariably replaced by a rich stranger.
- **B** two characters from the original story are omitted.
- **C** there is no longer a wicked stepmother.
- **D** the Cinderella character no longer has to work.

16 Modern film adaptations of the story tend to present a Cinderella
- **A** whose character remains basically unchanged.
- **B** who is luckier than she is in the original story.
- **C** whose circumstances are unusual.
- **D** that many children might find unconvincing.

17 Modern variants on the story generally
- **A** portray Cinderella as a successful professional.
- **B** imply that Cinderella will become a real princess.
- **C** reflect children's beliefs.
- **D** make concessions to modern women's lives.

18 In Ellen's view, what makes the Cinderella story so appealing?
- **A** Children can identify with the heroine.
- **B** Little girls enjoy being challenged.
- **C** It has an element of magic.
- **D** Cinderella is more beautiful than other girls.

19 Unlike the original tale, modern versions of the Cinderella story
- **A** suggest that girls do not need strength of character.
- **B** do not require the heroine to develop.
- **C** underestimate the power of love.
- **D** are aimed solely at young children.

PAPER 1 Reading ▶ | Part 1
PAPER 2 Writing | Part 2
PAPER 3 Use of English | Part 3
PAPER 4 Listening | **Part 4**
PAPER 5 Speaking

Essential tips

▶ You can approach this part of the Reading paper in two ways. However, you should begin by reading the instructions and the title of the text. Then you can either skim the text first before you read the questions, or read the questions first before you skim the text. Experiment and see which way works better for you.

▶ Don't waste time reading the text in detail. You only need to match specific information in the text with the questions.

▶ The text is on two pages, so be careful. In the exam, you will be able to fold out the second page so that you can access any part of the text at a glance.

Question 25: Some questions use language which you will need to think about carefully. Here, for example, the question is about the need to do other jobs to make money, but this simple idea is expressed formally. The reverse may also occur: the question may express an idea in simple language but the text will use more formal language.

Question 28: A 'leisure pursuit' is a hobby; an 'alternative' leisure pursuit is one different to the hobby already mentioned. You know from the title that this text is about people who have made their hobbies into their careers, so find a section of the text where someone talks about taking up another hobby.

Question 32: Here, a key word is 'unexpected'. All the people in this text were able to turn their hobby into their career, so they all probably had a talent or, at least, a certain ability. But which person had an unexpected talent?

You are going to read an article in which people talk about turning their hobbies into careers. For questions **20–34**, choose from the sections of the article (**A–F**).

Mark your answers **on the separate answer sheet.**

In which section of the article are the following mentioned?

the pleasure of teaching young people	**20** ....
valuable experience gained from voluntary work	**21** ....
an enhanced appreciation of other people's work	**22** ....
neglecting a job	**23** ....
thoughts about the future	**24** ....
the financial necessity for engaging in other ventures as well	**25** ....
encouragement from a family member	**26** ....
advice from a specialist	**27** ....
finding an alternative leisure pursuit	**28** ....
the value of assessing one's abilities objectively	**29** ....
identifying potential customers	**30** ....
an impulsive decision	**31** ....
un unexpected talent for a particular job	**32** ....
a feeling of apprehension before making a major change	**33** ....
academic qualifications which were never used	**34** ....

Turning a **Hobby** into a **Career**

*It may seem idealistic or risky to exchange one's regular job
for the uncertainty of earning your living from a hobby –
but more and more people are attempting to do just that.*

A   I had piano lessons when I was young, and I did have some talent. But it soon became obvious I'd never be good enough for a career on the concert stage. In a way, I was lucky. If I hadn't realised early on that I'd never make it as a performer, I probably would have carried on dreaming that my big break would come. As it is, I became a music teacher instead, and in my free time I started to dabble in the technical side of music production. Then an aunt died, leaving me some cash, and I suddenly realised I could finally set up my own recording studio! Of course, there is a downside to turning a hobby into a career. I love my job so much that I used to work seven days a week, but after a while I realised I was getting burnt out – you need to switch off occasionally. My job has definitely added depth to the way I listen to music; now I can really understand why someone's using a certain technique or piece of equipment.

B   I studied medicine, but when I finished medical school I had a sort of crisis. I suddenly knew I couldn't go on with it! I'd have been an awful doctor. But I was keen on amateur dramatics and I enjoyed putting on plays at the local youth centre, especially coaching budding actors. So I started wondering if I could make a living from teaching drama. A friend suggested I should set up as a freelance teacher and offer acting lessons for children. It was tricky and at first, I couldn't work out how to find customers who would pay for their children to attend the kind of courses I wanted to run. Then someone at an organisation called Business Link, which helps people set up their own businesses, suggested advertising on the Internet! I was contacted by a surprising number of interested people, and five years down the line I'm doing all right. The classes themselves aren't terribly lucrative, but I supplement my income by giving talks to amateur dramatics societies, writing articles for magazines and organising trips to see shows in London. It's not a bad life.

C   When I left college I started working in a bank, but my heart was never really in it. The problem was partly the environment: I don't like working in an office. I'm more of an outdoor person – and I'd always been crazy about surfing. Well, one summer while I was in Cornwall on holiday, I got chatting to the owner of a surf shop. He said he wanted to sell up and I jumped at the chance to buy the business from him! Looking back, I can see how lucky I was. It's incredibly difficult to set up a shop like that from scratch. Besides, being such an avid surfer myself, I assumed a lot of other people must share that interest – which isn't the case! Obvious when you think about it, but it took me a while to realise what a naive attitude that was. Now that I've learnt the ropes, I'm thinking either of expanding – more shops, managers and so on – or diversifying, perhaps producing my own surf boards! I actually think the second option is more likely because it's a subject which interests me a lot.

D   I'd always been a serious amateur photographer, and when I left school I wanted a job that would allow me a lot of free time for my hobby. So I got a job as a waiter, working evenings only. Around that time I also offered to help my uncle out in his studio. He was a professional photographer, and I'd go along at the weekends and act as general unpaid dogsbody. I got an insight into the business, which made me wonder whether I too could earn a living from photography. So I saved, set myself up as a professional photographer and tried to survive solely on my earnings from selling pictures. However, after a while I realised it simply wasn't going to happen. So I swallowed my pride and got some work as a sales representative for one of the big camera manufacturers, which takes me round the country to trade fairs and so on, demonstrating the latest equipment. I'm doing quite well in that line of work, although I've noticed one odd thing: now that my hobby is my work, more or less, I've had to find another way to switch off. In fact, I've taken up fishing.

E My first job was with an insurance company, but I was hardly a model employee. I loathed my job, and instead of selling insurance, I used to wander around the city's numerous art galleries. I have no creative talent of my own, but I can recognise it in the work of others. I soon picked up quite a lot of knowledge about contemporary art. Then one day I got talking to the manager of an art gallery. She mentioned a new gallery that was going to be opened and suggested I apply for the job of manager. At first, I was doubtful, but I realised I had nothing to lose, so I applied and was asked to go for an interview. I think the fact that I was so obviously crazy about art impressed the owners. To my surprise, I've turned out to be quite a good saleswoman. Of course, most people come into the gallery just to look around, but when someone shows an interest in one of the works on show, I don't immediately start to persuade them to buy it. I just chat about the work and what makes it interesting to me. People feel reassured when they sense your enthusiasm.

F I wanted to study graphic design when I left school, but I didn't have good enough grades to go on to art school. Instead, I got a job in a garage, and for the next ten years I worked as a car mechanic. But while I was working, I did some evening courses in industrial design and got lots of books on the subject. I was interested in the practical side of construction, too: I even built a car of my own from spare parts. Then I got the idea of building a bike – a four-wheel delivery bike – and the next thing I knew, my wife was urging me to set up my own company! I had to take a very deep breath before I finally took the plunge. I'd done my best to prepare for it, taking a course in business management in my spare time, and I knew I'd be working longer hours for less money, at least at first. The big difficulty was the uncertainty of not knowing how much would be coming in each month. And things were pretty tough for the first few years, although I never regretted it. Looking back, I can see that I underestimated the amount of paperwork I'd have to do. I somehow thought I could just concentrate on the nice stuff – designing!

Essential tips

▸ In Paper 2 you must answer two questions, so it is essential to use your time effectively. This does not mean you should start writing at once and write as much as you can! You must take the time to prepare before you begin writing.

▸ Make sure you understand the instructions. Read the question several times, underlining the key words that describe your task.

▸ Think about the register of your writing: should it be formal or informal? What layout is appropriate?

▸ Part 2 tasks will include an article, a letter, a proposal, a report, a review, a competition entry, a contribution to a longer piece such as an entry for a travel book, or an essay. Question 5 will be a task based on set texts, and it will take the form of an essay, a review, an article or a report. Your answer for Part 2 must be between 220 and 260 words.

▸ The input for Part 2 questions is much shorter than that for Part 1. You must use the information given, but also use your imagination intelligently to come up with more information. You will need to spend time preparing your answer, as for Part 1.

▸ In Part 2 you must answer one question, so think carefully about the task that you feel most comfortable with. Are you confident you know which register to use and if a particular format or layout is necessary? Do you have a good range of vocabulary relevant to this task? Can you express clear views on the subject (if the question requires you to do so)?

▸ Don't write a rough draft – there isn't time for that. Make a plan instead.

• Your writing should normally have three sections: an introduction, the main body and a conclusion. Note down approximately how many words should be in each section.

• Note down a few words or phrases to remind yourself what you must say in each section.

• Take a few minutes to look at your plan and make sure the information flows well. If it doesn't, you can still change your mind and put something in the conclusion instead of the main body, for instance.

▸ See the **Writing bank** on page 214 for examples of different types of writing.

You **must** answer this question. Write your answer in **180–220** words in an appropriate style.

1 You are the student representative on the executive committee of Oldtree College, where you are studying. Recently, an article from a former student was published in the local newspaper, criticising the way the college has changed. The principal of the college has asked you to write to the newspaper, responding to the article.

Read the extract from the former student's article below, on which the principal has made some notes. Then write a letter to the editor as requested by the principal.

Essential tips

▶ You are asked to write a letter to a local newspaper, so what register is appropriate? Should you use headings? What about abbreviations or contractions?

▶ Underline the important information, which includes the handwritten comments next to the article. Then decide where to include this information when you plan your letter.

▶ Your letter is in reply to an article, so what would you put in the introduction to your letter? How would you explain who you are and why you are writing?

▶ It may be effective to end your letter with a simple and powerful statement. Could you say anything personal (in your character here as 'student representative')? Perhaps you could give your own personal, positive view of the college.

Oldtree Gone Downhill

A former student expresses disappointment

by *Hilda Cooper*

Twenty years after graduating from Oldtree College I thought I'd have a look at the old place again. Oh, how sad! The lovely sports pavilion has gone – don't students enjoy cricket and football these days? In its place is an ugly new accommodation block. There was litter everywhere and the students looked distinctly unfriendly with their sloppy clothes and surly faces. In an atmosphere like this, how can academic standards be maintained? What can explain this sad state of affairs?

New sports centre shared with City College. Wider range of sports available to students.

Accommodation needed: 70% more students over last 15 years. 20% from overseas.

College provides more cultural events, plays, etc.

We offer a wider range of courses, and a higher proportion of students get top grades than 20 years ago!

Now write your **letter** to the editor of the newspaper. You do not need to include postal addresses.

Essential tips

Question 2

▶ What style would be appropriate for this proposal? Bear in mind that the proposal is written by a college student to the principal of the college.

▶ Consider your three sections: introduction, main body and conclusion. The introduction could state simply what you want, and the conclusion could repeat this request, perhaps with some extra force or promise of success. The words 'Introduction' and 'Conclusion' could also be headings. What will the main body contain? What will the heading(s) be?

▶ Don't worry about precise figures, for example, how much money would be needed to start the radio station. You are not expected to know this.

Write an answer to **one** of the questions 2–5 in this part. Write your answer in **220–260** words in an appropriate style.

2 You would like to start a radio station at the college where you are a student. You have decided to send a proposal to the principal, asking for permission and practical assistance. Your proposal should include the following:
- why you think the radio station would be beneficial
- what sort of programmes you would begin with
- what sort of support, practical and financial, you would need

Write your **proposal**.

3 You have seen the following advertisement in an international magazine for young people:

Competition

All over the world, more and more people are migrating from the countryside to cities. What are the attractions of city life? What about the disadvantages? What will life in our cities be like in the future?

**Write and tell us your views.
We will publish the best entry.**

Write your **competition entry**.

Essential tips

Question 5(a): You could begin your article by defining what you understand to be a fictional hero/heroine, and then mention the one of your choice. You should give examples of his/her actions which you find particularly admirable. It may be useful to compare your hero/heroine with one from another book, and say why you think your choice is more exceptional.

Question 5(b): When writing a report, you need to give your paragraphs headings. Use the details of the question to help you organise your answer into paragraphs with suitable headings. This will help you focus on what information you need to include.

4 A British television channel is interested in making a documentary called *Transports of Delight*, which will feature public transport all over the world. You have been asked to write a report for the channel, addressing the following questions:
   • What means of public transport in your region are the most popular?
   • What is being done to improve these facilities and encourage the use of public transport?
   • What more could be done?

Write your **report**.

5 Answer **one** of the following two questions based on your reading of **one** of the set books.

Either

5(a) An online book shop is holding a competition to find the most popular fictional hero or heroine. It has invited its web site visitors to send articles about their favourite protagonists, explaining why they think the character of their choice is a 'hero/heroine', and what makes him/her exceptional, using examples. You have decided to enter the competition. Write about the protagonist of the novel you have been reading.

Write your **article**.

Or

5(b) Your teacher has asked you to write a report on the novel you have been reading, describing the most dramatic events and how they affect the main characters. In your report you should also say who you would recommend this book to, and why.

Write your **report**.

Essential tips

▸ Read the title and the whole text quickly for general meaning.

▸ Remember: the gapped word may be part of an idiom, expression or phrasal verb. It may collocate with another word, or be part of a fixed phrase.

▸ If you do not know which option to choose, read out the sentence with each of the options in turn. Choose the option that sounds best in context.

▸ Check the clauses and phrases on each side of the gap to see whether the presence of a word here dictates the choice of word for the gap.

Question 5: Two options have the correct meaning, but only one of them is followed by 'with'.

Question 6: Sometimes it helps to picture a scene. How would a horse walk along the side of a canal pulling a boat? Quickly or slowly? With effort or easily? In a straight line or wandering from side to side? One of the options suggests the appropriate way of walking.

Question 9: Two options seem possible here, but you must choose the one which expresses the idea of 'so full of something that things cannot move through it'.

Question 11: The word 'up' after the gap suggests that the correct option is part of a phrasal verb. The meaning is clear here – the boats can be renovated to make them attractive.

For questions **1–12**, read the text below and decide which answer (**A, B, C** or **D**) best fits each gap. There is an example at the beginning (**0**).

Mark your answers **on the separate answer sheet**.

Example:

0   **A** prime   **B** fundamental   **C** downright   **D** deep-rooted

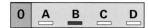

Modern barging

There has been a (**0**) ...... change in the way the canals of Britain are used. The (**1**) ...... network of canals that covers much of the country (**2**) ...... back to the industrial revolution, when goods were transported along these routes. The canals themselves, the (**3**) ...... waterways of the country, were dug by teams of men. This was no (**4**) ...... feat in the days before mechanised diggers. It was also necessary to construct a system of locks, which raise and lower boats so they can (**5**) ...... with the varying height of the canals themselves. Barges – simple boats without engines – were used to carry the freight, and horses would (**6**) ...... along the side of the canal pulling these vessels. Many of the people working on the boats would themselves live on the water, in a long boat with cramped living quarters: a narrowboat.

As the railways and roads (**7**) ...... in popularity as ways of transporting freight, the canals fell into (**8**) ...... ; many of them became (**9**) ...... with weeds and rubbish. But over the last few decades Britain appears to have rediscovered these (**10**) ...... of engineering. A growing number of people each year sample the delights of canal holidays. Narrowboats can be (**11**) ...... up to be very comfortable, and these days they are (**12**) ...... by an engine and not pulled by a horse.

1	**A** extensive	**B** far-flung	**C** ample	**D** widespread
2	**A** comes	**B** looks	**C** throws	**D** dates
3	**A** inbuilt	**B** inland	**C** internal	**D** interior
4	**A** modest	**B** mean	**C** minor	**D** tiny
5	**A** balance	**B** compensate	**C** cope	**D** handle
6	**A** trudge	**B** canter	**C** stroll	**D** meander
7	**A** increased	**B** obtained	**C** gained	**D** assumed
8	**A** disuse	**B** obsolescence	**C** redundancy	**D** negligence
9	**A** impeded	**B** choked	**C** hindered	**D** congested
10	**A** records	**B** testimonies	**C** constructions	**D** monuments
11	**A** done	**B** worked	**C** customised	**D** converted
12	**A** equipped	**B** supplied	**C** drawn	**D** powered

For questions **13–27**, read the text below and think of the word which best fits each gap. Use only **one** word in each gap. There is an example at the beginning (**0**).

Write your answers **IN CAPITAL LETTERS on the separate answer sheet**.

Example:

0	*ORDER*	0

Finding the Right Word

A recent study has suggested an answer to a question that has occupied philosophers for centuries: Do people need words in (**0**) .... to think? A tribe living in the Amazon basin could provide the answer. The Piraha tribe (**13**) .... be small – there are only about 200 members all told – (**14**) .... they exhibit a fascinating cultural peculiarity. These people have no words for numbers, (**15**) .... from 'one', 'two' and 'many'. What is more, (**16**) .... words for 'one' and 'two' are very similar. As (**17**) .... as anyone can tell, this tribe has never had (**18**) .... sort of vocabulary for numbers, but (**19**) .... appear to survive quite well without it.

It was soon realised that these people might supply an insight (**20**) .... the way our minds work. Studies have shown that adult members of the tribe are no (**21**) .... at counting than a baby is at speaking. (**22**) .... they were shown a row of objects and asked (**23**) .... duplicate the number they saw, they could not get beyond two or three before starting to make mistakes. This applies even to adults who appear reasonably intelligent in (**24**) .... other way.

So it looks (**25**) .... though the Piraha are not very good at counting simply because they (**26**) .... not have a vocabulary for numbers. This would suggest that human beings in general cannot think if they have no words to do (**27**) ....

Essential tips

▶ Read through the whole text to get a general idea of what it is about.

▶ Remember: the gapped words will probably not be complex or specialised words. Most of them will be structural items like articles, pronouns or prepositions. A few may form part of common expressions etc.

▶ Look at the whole sentence, or even bigger sections of the text, to see if the word you need is part of a longer or parallel structure. For example, you might need the word 'other' in the expression 'on the other hand', which will be clear if you find 'on one hand' in the previous sentence.

Question 17: The structure 'as ... as' is often used with adjectives to compare two things which are the same. Can you think of an expression with 'as ... as' that has the more abstract meaning of 'to the extent that'?

Question 19: This gap is in a long sentence, so read the whole sentence carefully. There is a verb after the gap: 'appear'. What is its subject? Can it be 'the tribe', which occurs earlier in the sentence?

Question 21: The word 'than' later in the sentence indicates that the gapped word must be part of a comparative structure. The context tells us that these people are not good at counting. What adjective could be used with 'no' to express the idea that they are as good at counting as a baby is at speaking?

Question 25: Read the whole sentence. The first part of the sentence must mean something like 'it seems that the Piraha ...'.

Essential tips

Question 30: What part of speech do you need? You need to read the whole paragraph in order to be sure of the meaning of this sentence. Does the missing word have a positive or negative meaning?

Question 33: 'Vary' means 'change'. However, the word you need here means 'always'. What part of speech do you need, and what changes do you need to make to 'vary' in order to form the missing word?

Question 35: What word could we use here to mean 'add new information to something'?

For questions **28–37**, read the text below. Use the word given in capitals at the end of some of the lines to form a word that fits in the gap **in the same line.** There is an example at the beginning (**0**).

Write your answers **IN CAPITAL LETTERS on the separate answer sheet.**

Example:

0	*INTRIGUING*	0 __ __

The Jigsaw History Puzzle

Of all the games in the world, the jigsaw puzzle has got to be among the most ubiquitous. Yet the history of its origins presents an (**0**) .... puzzle of its own.   **INTRIGUE**

Officially, the jigsaw puzzle (**28**) .... in England,   **ORIGIN**
and its (**29**) .... was John Spilsbury, a London   **INVENT**
engraver and map maker. It is also an apparently
(**30**) .... fact that in 1767 Spilsbury created a puzzle,   **DISPUTE**
(**31**) .... known as a 'dissected map', by mounting   **INITIAL**
one of his maps on a piece of hardwood and cutting around
the borders of the countries. His puzzles came to be used as
(**32**) .... tools in schools to help children learn   **EDUCATION**
Geography.

However, as is almost (**33**) .... the case with   **VARY**
inventions, some doubts have been raised about whether
Spilsbury's puzzle was the first, and there is evidence that
two Dutch map makers, Covens and Mortier, may have
produced the first puzzle ten years earlier. The controversy
arises from the fact that their puzzles were first made using
maps that had been printed in the 1720s. However, this was
an age of exploration, and new (**34**) .... demanded   **DISCOVER**
that maps be constantly (**35**) .... Consequently,   **DATE**
the maps used in the puzzles would have been out of date by
1760, suggesting that Covens and Mortier produced their first
puzzles before then. The evidence is (**36**) .... ,   **CONCLUDE**
however, and advertising for their dissected maps only appears
in 1779. So it is (**37**) .... that they simply thought   **CONCEIVE**
this was a good way of making use of old maps.

PAPER 1 Reading
PAPER 2 Writing
PAPER 3 Use of English ▶
PAPER 4 Listening
PAPER 5 Speaking

Part 1
Part 2
Part 3
Part 4
Part 5

Essential tips

Question 38: The first sentence can help a lot here. The speaker wants to sit down, so what has she been doing all day?

Question 40: In the first sentence, the missing word is part of a compound noun. In the third sentence, the missing word is part of a phrase which means 'the number of crimes committed during a certain period'.

Question 42: In the second sentence, the missing word is part of an expression which means 'determined to do something (bad)'. Read the third sentence; if something is not straight, what is it?

For questions **38–42**, think of **one** word only which can be used appropriately in all three sentences. Here is an example (**0**).

Example:

0
- We will do all the work, but they will .... all the credit, as usual!
- She will .... offence if you tell her that hairstyle doesn't suit her.
- They threatened to .... David to court unless he stopped playing his drums all night.

0	*TAKE*	0

Write **only** the missing word **IN CAPITAL LETTERS on the separate answer sheet.**

38
- I've been on my .... all day, and I'm looking forward to sitting down with a nice cup of tea!
- Martha thought she was going to be out of work for months, so she really landed on her .... with that new job!
- He's been living here for two years now, but he's getting itchy .... and wants to leave.

39
- Although it was a warm day, she was wearing a .... winter coat.
- I have a .... schedule next week, so I won't be able to go out with you.
- He wasn't used to doing such .... physical work and got blisters on his hands.

40
- What's today's exchange .... between the dollar and the euro?
- We're stuck in traffic, and at this .... , we're going to arrive late.
- The crime .... has risen alarmingly in the last five years.

41
- Selling their flat was a silly thing to do, in my ....
- As we entered the valley, the village came into ....
- A tall man with a big head is blocking my .... of the stage, and I can't see the actors.

42
- Stand with your knees .... and then slowly straighten them.
- Sally is angry and seems .... on quarrelling with everyone again.
- This key is .... out of shape and I can't use it.

Essential tips

Question 45: You need a phrasal verb here which means 'think of something'. Be careful! Do you need a two-part or three-part phrasal verb?

Question 46: You need to make two changes to the second sentence. First, you need a causative structure. Secondly, think about the word you have been given. It is part of an expression that means 'decorated'.

Question 50: This is a conditional, but not a simple structure!

For questions **43–50**, complete the second sentence so that it has a similar meaning to the first sentence, using the word given. **Do not change the word given.** You must use between **three** and **six** words, including the word given. Here is an example (**0**).

Example:

0   Jane regretted speaking so rudely to the old lady

MORE

Jane .... politely to the old lady.

| 0 | *WISHED SHE HAD SPOKEN MORE* | 0 |

Write the missing words **IN CAPITAL LETTERS on the separate answer sheet.**

---

43   'Do your homework first, and then you can go to the cinema,' said Jim's mother.

LONG

Jim's mother agreed to let him go to the cinema .... his homework first.

44   'Yes, I took the money, but Ned told me to do it!' said George.

WHO

George claimed that it .... to take the money.

45   Harry thought of throwing a surprise party for Katie's birthday.

CAME

Harry .... of throwing a surprise party for Katie's birthday.

46   They are decorating our living room, so the house is a mess.

DONE

We are .... , so the house is a mess!

47   I really hate it when people speak to me like that!

BEING

I really object .... like that!

48   I was just about to call him when he rang me instead.

POINT

I was .... when he rang me instead.

49   The manager gave her secretary strict instructions that no one should be allowed to disturb her.

CIRCUMSTANCES

'Under .... to be disturbed!' the manager told her secretary.

50   I learnt a lot about gardening, thanks to Kevin.

FOR

If .... , I wouldn't have learnt so much about gardening.

Essential tips

Question 2: Read the options carefully during the pause before you hear the recording. Then listen to the speaker talking about doing Tai Chi. What does she say takes years of practice?

Question 3: Read the question stem carefully. What information do you have to focus on?

Question 6: All the options may appear possible, but listen carefully to what the speaker actually realised.

You will hear three different extracts. For questions **1–6**, choose the answer (**A, B** or **C**) which fits best according to what you hear. There are two questions for each extract.

Extract One

You hear part of an interview with a Tai Chi instructor.

1 According to Ruth, Tai Chi
  A needs to be performed indoors.
  B is a series of exercises.
  C represents a way of life.

2 One of the most difficult things about learning Tai Chi is
  A that you have to do it out of doors.
  B achieving harmony between your movements.
  C remembering the complex dance sequences.

Extract Two

You hear two people discussing taking a year off before going to university.

3 Before going to work in China, the man had not expected the job to be
  A rewarding.
  B easy.
  C boring.

4 The woman's experience made her realise that
  A marketing was a difficult career for women.
  B working in a hotel was very challenging.
  C she had made the wrong choice of career.

Extract Three

You hear part of an interview with an illusionist.

5 Daniel's interest in magic arose from
  A his ambition to become an entertainer.
  B his desire to impress someone.
  C his trips to the cinema as a boy.

6 According to Daniel, one similarity between magic and film making is
  A the debt they owe to technology.
  B the disbelief they arouse in the audience.
  C the power they have over the audience.

You will hear part of a talk by a writer who has written a biography. For questions **7–14**, complete the sentences.

An interesting character

The speaker has written a book about [____ 7 ____] called Robert Tewbridge.

Tewbridge's father was a [____ 8 ____] in Scotland.

Tewbridge's parents wanted him to become [____ 9 ____]

Tewbridge earned his living by writing [____ 10 ____] for various publications.

The speaker learnt a great deal about Tewbridge's character from studying his [____ 11 ____]

It appears that Tewbridge and his [____ 12 ____] were close friends.

Tewbridge spent many years studying [____ 13 ____]

He lived in [____ 14 ____] for the last thirty years of his life.

Essential tips

▶ As with all listening tasks, make the best use of the time you are given before you hear the recording. Read the instructions carefully, look at the title and the questions, and imagine what the recording might say.

▶ Remember: you will hear the words you need but not in the same context as the question. Note, however, that you can answer a question with a synonym, or paraphrase an idea, as long as the synonym or paraphrase completes the question appropriately.

▶ Bear in mind the question after the one you are trying to answer, so if you miss the information you need, you can move on to the next question.

Question 7: The word or words you need must describe the person's occupation or role. This sort of information might be given at the beginning of the talk, so make sure you are listening carefully from the very start of the recording!

Question 10: From the context you can guess that the speaker will mention a profession. You might try to imagine which professions a farmer and his wife might aspire to for their son.

Question 11: The speaker will say that he studied something, but remember that another way to say that you did something is to imagine what would have happened if you had not done it.

Question 14: There are many phrases with 'in' which might fit here, such as 'in luxury', but that is unlikely. Probably the word you need will be the name of a place. The text may use a different structure, so you might not hear the preposition 'in'.

Essential tips

▶ Prepare for what you will hear on the recording: read the instructions and think about the subject. Consider who the speakers will be.

▶ Remember: you will not hear the exact words of the question in the recording, so concentrate on the ideas expressed.

▶ The questions follow the order of the recording, but the final question may be about the recording as a whole.

Question 16: The question refers to Betsy's feelings about expensive shops. If you hear one of the words in the options, check that Betsy is using it to talk about expensive clothes shops.

Question 17: To prepare for this question, think how you would explain the feelings in the options. In the recording you will hear one of these feelings expressed in different words.

Question 19: How might Betsy express 'most rewarding' in other words? Now think about the meaning of the options. What does 'overcome their inhibitions' in option A mean, for example?

You will hear part of an interview with Betsy Boom, owner of a chain of fashion shops. For questions **15–20**, choose the answer (**A**, **B**, **C** or **D**) which fits best according to what you hear.

15 What aspect of shopping does Betsy enjoy most?
   A experimenting with different styles
   B finding a bargain
   C comparing items in different shops
   D being given advice

16 What does she dislike about expensive clothes shops?
   A There isn't a wide selection of goods.
   B The assistants are unfriendly.
   C Customers are ignored.
   D Customers are expected to spend a lot of money.

17 When people first went into one of Betsy's shops, they often felt
   A flattered.
   B amused.
   C awkward.
   D dizzy.

18 The members of staff in Betsy's shop
   A were offended at the demands Betsy made.
   B found it hard to adjust to the new surroundings.
   C disliked dealing with shy and difficult customers.
   D came to enjoy the atmosphere after a while.

19 What is the most rewarding aspect of the business for Betsy?
   A seeing customers overcome their inhibitions
   B proving to others that her idea was a good one
   C watching the staff relax in their new roles
   D being able to provide fashionable clothes at low prices

20 What does Betsy feel is the danger she faces now?
   A becoming complacent
   B growing arrogant
   C being afraid to try something new
   D suffering financially if fashions change

Essential tips

▸ Read the instructions carefully. Look at the options for Task One, and consider what each person's job entails before you attempt this task.

▸ Aim to complete Task One the first time you listen, and Task Two the second time. Then check that you feel happy with your choices for Task One. On listening the second time, you may notice something you missed the first time.

Question 22: Listen carefully to what the speaker says. She mentions helping 'university students'. Who might she be?

Question 24: The speaker says that 'Here at Head Office, we show our employees exactly how much energy can be saved by adopting particular practices.' Who would be likely to talk about the company and its staff in this way?

Question 26: Listen to everything the speaker says before making your choice. What point does he make about workers' awareness?

Question 29: The speaker talks about how the company goes further than simply imposing new regulations at work. What do they do?

You will hear five short extracts in which people talk about environmental initiatives in the workplace.

While you listen you must complete both tasks.

TASK ONE

For questions **21–25**, choose from the list **A–H** the person who is speaking.

A a public health officer

B a sales representative

C the company manager

D a company's customer

E a careers advice officer

F a marketing executive

G an environmental activist

H an office cleaner

Speaker 1	21
Speaker 2	22
Speaker 3	23
Speaker 4	24
Speaker 5	25

TASK TWO

For questions **26–30**, choose from the list **A–H** what view each speaker is expressing.

A Consumers should put more pressure on companies to adopt environmental schemes.

B Few companies consider conservation a priority.

C We should be more optimistic about what companies are doing about the environment.

D Few office workers realise how much they could do to conserve energy.

E Companies need to explain environmental initiatives to their employees.

F Young people no longer buy products from companies that don't have sound environmental policies.

G The provision of incentives will encourage staff to adopt company schemes.

H Young job seekers demand a work environment that reflects their values.

Speaker 1	26
Speaker 2	27
Speaker 3	28
Speaker 4	29
Speaker 5	30

Essential tips

Part 3

▶ In this part of the exam you and the other candidate have to work together to perform a task such as finding a solution to a problem.

▶ Listen carefully to the examiner's instructions.

▶ You have three minutes for the task, so it is important that you really discuss the issue. You must ask your partner about his/her views and not only give your own.

▶ There is no right or wrong answer. The only important thing is to come to a conclusion. However, don't try too hard to persuade your partner; it is perfectly acceptable if you each come to different conclusions.

Part 4

▶ In this part of the exam you will be asked to talk about the subject discussed in Part 3. Usually, the discussion will be more abstract and general.

▶ You should listen carefully to your partner and then commenting on what they have said, perhaps agreeing or disagreeing, or adding a new idea.

▶ Make sure you don't just give one-word responses to your partner's questions. Practise the conversational devices used in discussions, including expressions like 'In my opinion', 'It seems to me', 'I don't entirely agree'.

Part 1 (3 minutes)

The examiner will ask you a few questions about yourself and then ask you to talk to your partner. For example, the examiner may ask you:

- What kind of outdoor activities do you enjoy?
- Which sports are popular in your region?
- Which sports do you enjoy watching and playing, and which do you find boring?

Part 2 (4 minutes)

You will each be asked to talk on your own for a minute without interruption. You will each be given a set of three photographs in turn to talk about. After your partner has finished speaking, you will be asked a brief question connected with your partner's photographs. You will have thirty seconds to answer.

> **Anticipation** (compare, contrast and speculate)

Turn to pictures 1–3 on page **193**, which show people anticipating something.

Candidate A, compare and contrast two of these pictures and imagine what these people could be anticipating that makes them look this way. How do you think they are feeling?

Candidate B, what sort of things do you anticipate with pleasure?

> **Being Alone** (compare, contrast and speculate)

Turn to pictures 1–3 on page **194**, which show people alone.

Candidate B, compare and contrast two of these situations. Why do you think the people are alone, and how do you think they feel?

Candidate A, when do you enjoy being alone, and when does it disturb you?

Part 3 (4 minutes)

> **Motivation** (discuss, evaluate and select)

Turn to the pictures on page **195**, which show how motivation is part of modern life.

Talk to each other about the importance of motivation in each of these situations and then decide in which one a powerful sense of motivation can have a positive and in which a negative effect.

Part 4 (4 minutes)

The examiner will encourage you to develop the topic of your discussion in Part 3 by asking questions such as:

- When do you think it is important for people to be motivated? Are there any times when being motivated is undesirable?
- It is often said that motivation is important in education. Do you agree? Why (not)?
- What factors motivate people to achieve something? Are these factors external or internal?
- How can people motivate themselves?

You are going to read three extracts which are all concerned in some way with environmental issues. For questions **1–6**, choose the answer (**A, B, C** or **D**) which you think fits best according to the text.

Mark your answers **on the separate answer sheet**.

Essential tips

Question 1: What was the writer's initial reaction when laws were passed restricting the use of pesticides? Was her reaction justified? What does 'With hindsight' mean?

How much does the environment matter?

I've always been keen on environmental matters, but in the seventies, when I was growing up, the subject wasn't discussed as much as it is today. Perhaps the problem was just as bad then, but fewer people understood the implications of what was going on or realised something ought to be done about it. I remember being pleased when laws restricting the use of certain pesticides came in. They appeared to signal the start of a vast movement to improve the environment, an acknowledgement that all human beings had a right to clean air and water.

With hindsight, I think we were naive. There is much greater awareness of environmental issues these days, but I still don't think enough is being done about the problem. And since it's a global issue, individual countries can't tackle it by themselves. Reducing damage to the environment really must be an international effort. In a paradoxical way, the more we discover about the extent of the problem, the less we do about it. This is because problems like global warming are so huge that ordinary individuals don't feel they could possibly make any difference. I think that's the real danger facing us today – that we'll succumb to a feeling of helplessness instead of making a concerted effort to make our planet a safer and cleaner place for future generations.

1   Why does the writer mention the law restricting pesticides?
   A   to show that her initial optimism about the environment was misplaced
   B   to illustrate the steps that have been taken to protect the environment
   C   to make people aware of the dangers of using pesticides indiscriminately
   D   to demonstrate her early involvement in environmental movements

2   What fear does she express in the second paragraph?
   A   People are still not aware of the extent of the problem.
   B   Individuals' actions won't make any difference to the problem.
   C   Nothing can be done to stop the effects of global warming.
   D   The scale of the problem may prevent action being taken.

Essential tips

Question 4: Read the options carefully. Then read the text to find out what the overall long-term effects of overfishing will be.

Overfishing Alert!

The problem and its causes

Illegal fishing is a thriving business, aided by the fact that international efforts to reduce it are achieving very little. The main problem is that the high seas do not fall under the jurisdiction of any one country, making restrictions difficult to impose. Advances in fishing technology mean that large factory ships can stay out for weeks on end, using huge nets which indiscriminately scoop up everything in their path, including many small fish which are unsuitable for the market. These get thrown away or crushed for animal food and fertiliser.

Long-term impact

Each year 20,000 porpoises and an even higher number of dolphins die in fishing nets. The overfishing of krill in the Antarctic threatens wildlife further up the food chain such as whales, seals and penguins, which rely on the krill for food. In some Canadian coastal areas, cod fish populations have been fished to commercial extinction, thereby destroying the livelihood of whole communities.

What needs to be done

- Marine protected areas need to be established on the high seas.
- International laws restricting fishing need to be passed to safeguard fish stocks.
- The public needs to put pressure on governments so that the aforementioned measures are implemented.

You can help by joining the World Wildlife Fund and becoming involved in the fight.

Don't delay! Take action TODAY!

3   According to the text, illegal fishing is able to continue unchecked due to
   A   technological developments in the fishing industry.
   B   the fact that it is difficult to enforce laws in international waters.
   C   both technological developments and difficulties to do with enforcing the law.
   D   disputes between countries over fishing rights in Antarctic waters.

4   Ultimately, overfishing will affect
   A   the nature of the fishing industry.
   B   both societies and the environment.
   C   community lifestyles in Canada.
   D   the eating habits of whales and seals.

How Green Is My House!

We've got new neighbours. Now I won't try to influence your impression of them in any way; I'll allow them to do that. Suffice it to say, they do *not* care. In fact, they don't approve of those who do, and do little to disguise their feelings. I've tried. I mean, at first I made a real effort to be friendly – I believe in freedom of choice, after all – but was met with a brick wall from the husband and derisive sarcasm from the wife.

The wife. Shirley, with her permed hair and red fingernails that look like a hawk's talons, mini-skirt and fag hanging permanently from the corner of her scarlet lips. Shirley, whose reaction to my home-knitted jacket lovingly made from recycled yarn was to ask if I'd made it from an old bedspread! She only wears designer labels, of course. Does she realise what sweat-shop they've probably come from, or what toxic chemicals have been used to dye the fabric? Claiming to be house-proud, she totters to the rubbish bin three times a day, throwing away everything from plastic bottles and pizza boxes to unwanted clothes and toys into the one bin. No recycling for that family! Bruce (the husband) scoffs at our neat row of separate recycling bins for plastic, paper and metal, dismissing them as a waste of time: 'Why bother? It won't make any difference, anyway.' When I patiently explained how important each individual's contribution could be, his eyes took on a bored, glazed expression, and he quickly made his excuses and disappeared into his twenty-year-old, fume-belching Mercedes.

5 Which word best describes the writer's feelings towards her new neighbours?
  A indifference
  B hatred
  C indignation
  D resentment

6 We can infer that the writer is
  A open-minded.
  B environmentally aware.
  C house-proud.
  D fashion-conscious.

PAPER 1 Reading ▶

PAPER 2 Writing

PAPER 3 Use of English

PAPER 4 Listening

PAPER 5 Speaking

Part 1
Part 2
Part 3
Part 4

You are going to read a newspaper article. Six paragraphs have been removed from the article. Choose from the paragraphs **A–G** the one which fits each gap (**7–12**). There is one extra paragraph which you do not need to use.

Mark your answers **on the separate answer sheet**.

Seeking El Dorado in the Mountains of Peru

It was just a sparkle on the horizon, where the sun hit what appeared to be a flat plain on an otherwise steep mountain in the Peruvian Andes. But Peter Frost, a British-born explorer and mountain guide, surmised that the perch would have made a perfect ceremonial platform for Inca rulers. So Frost and the adventure hikers he was leading slogged through heavy jungle growth and uncovered remnants of the Inca civilisation that flourished here. They found looted tombs, a circular building foundation and the stonework of an aqueduct.

7

Recent carbon dating at Caral, north of Lima, has shown that an advanced civilisation existed here nearly 5,000 years ago. The Lord of Sipian tomb, considered one of the richest pre-Columbian sites ever found, was discovered in 1987, firing the ambitions of those hoping to make similar spectacular finds.

8

It is the mountains of the Vilcabamba range that perhaps hold the most tantalising, spectacular ruins. Vilcabamba was the centre of a great empire that 500 years ago stretched from modern-day Colombia to Chile. The Spaniards wiped out the last Inca holdouts in 1572 and then promptly abandoned much of the region. That left it to men like Mr Bingham, who in one remarkable year discovered Machu Picchu and several other important settlements.

9

The finds are significant because while modern Peru is synonymous with the Inca, archaeologists actually know very little about their civilisation. 'About ninety percent has not been investigated,' said a Peruvian archaeologist. 'There are maybe 1,000 books on Machu Picchu, but only five or six are really scientific.'

10

To many, like Frost and Reinhard, the powerful hold of discovering ruins swallowed by jungle is as strong today as it was early last century. 'It's the Indiana Jones fantasy,' said Scott Gorsuch, whose sharp eye led to the discovery of Qoriwayrachina with Frost. 'It's really not more complicated than that – the search for El Dorado, this idea that there are lost cities out there waiting to be found.'

11

Frost is not an archaeologist, but through his work as a tour guide, photographer and author of the popular travel book, *Exploring Cuzco*, he has dedicated much of the last thirty years to learning everything he can about the ancient highlanders. 'Some people like the thrill of finding something and moving on to something else,' he said. 'But you want to do something useful with it.'

12

Frost is now trying to raise money for future expeditions to Qoriwayrachina, but he is already dreaming of other finds. 'I know of two sites that are sort of undiscovered, that I'd like to discover,' he said, explaining with a wry smile that he cannot reveal their locations. 'It's not a big thing, but I feel it's wise not to broadcast intentions.'

A But he did not find them all, leaving much of Vilcabamba open to modern-day explorers. 'I've run across foundations of buildings, foundations of roads, water channels, probably dozens of them,' Frost said.

B In two lengthy expeditions to Qoriwayrachina in 2001 and 2002, a team led by Frost found a sort of blue-collar settlement spread across more than sixteen square miles. They found the ruins of 200 structures and storehouses, an intricately engineered aqueduct, colourful pottery and tombs. The people who once lived there toiled in mines or cultivated diverse crops at various altitudes. The explorers believe that Qoriwayrachina may have been used to supply a more important Inca centre, Choquequirau, but much remains unknown.

C But exploring is not all about adventure. Serious explorers carefully read the old Spanish chronicles, pore over topographical maps and charts and interview local residents, who often lead them to sites. The work also requires raising money to finance expeditions. 'Anyone can blunder around in a jungle,' writes Hugh Thompson in his recent book about exploring for Inca ruins, *The White Rock*. And indeed, the annals of Peruvian exploration are littered with failures.

D 'Peru has one of the oldest continuous civilisations in the history of the planet,' Frost explained. 'That amounts to an awful lot of culture buried under the ground or under vegetation.'

E Johan Reinhard, who holds the title of explorer in residence at *National Geographic*, is a proponent of vigorous exploration combined with serious scientific research. He says it is important to find and catalogue sites in Peru before they are looted or destroyed. 'If you don't do it now, some of these things will be gone, and they'll be gone forever,' he said.

F The previous year, 1989, saw a number of expeditions to the region in search of the mythical lost city, but the end result was similarly disappointing. Undeterred, the courageous explorer refuses to abandon his attempts to raise money for one last try.

G The discovery in 1999 of Qoriwayrachina was instantly hailed as a major find. It evoked the romantic image of the swashbuckling explorer unearthing a Lost City, an image embodied by Hiram Bingham, the American who in 1911 made the greatest Inca discovery of them all, Machu Picchu. In the twenty-first century it would seem that the remote, rugged mountains around Cuzco would have given up all of their secrets. But this region of southern Peru is still full of ruins.

Essential tips

Question 8: The last sentence of the previous paragraph mentions 'spectacular finds'. In which gapped paragraph is this theme continued?

Question 9: Look at the previous paragraph and underline the names mentioned. Are any of them mentioned in a gapped paragraph? The last sentence talks about the discoveries of Bingham. Which gapped paragraph has pronouns that could refer to them?

Question 10: Remember that when a person's name is first mentioned, the writer will often give some basic information about that person. So if a name is mentioned in the main text without any such information, look for it in one of the gapped paragraphs.

PAPER 1 Reading ▸ | Part 1
PAPER 2 Writing | Part 2
PAPER 3 Use of English | **Part 3**
PAPER 4 Listening | Part 4
PAPER 5 Speaking

You are going to read a magazine article. For questions **13–19**, choose the answer (**A, B, C** or **D**) which you think fits best according to the text.

Mark your answers **on the separate answer sheet**.

On Your Bike *On Your Bike* On Your Bike

Every generation has its emblematic boy's toy. Once upon a time there was the golf cart: a little toy car specifically designed for middle-aged men too rich to care about looking ridiculous. Later came the beach buggy, a briefly fashionable, wildly impractical, single-terrain vehicle. One might include the motorcycle or the snowmobile on this list, were they not, in certain contexts, quite useful, but there is no doubt which pointless recreational vehicle has captured the imagination of the landed, middle-aged celebrity: it's the quad bike.

What is it about this squat, ungainly, easy-to-flip machine that celebrities love so much? As recreational vehicles go, the quad bike is hardly sophisticated. They are to the countryside what the jet-ski is to Lake Windermere. 'There's nothing cool about a quad,' says Simon Tiffin, editor of a well-known magazine. 'It's a strange thing to want to hare round beautiful bits of the country in a petrol-guzzling machine.'

But celebrities love quad bikes. Musicians, comedians, DJs, actors and sportsmen have all been photographed aboard quads. 'They're the latest rich person's toy,' says Tiffin. 'Spoilt children get them for Christmas.' Provided you've got a large estate to go with it, however, the quad bike can remain a secret indulgence. You can go out and tear up your own piece of countryside without anyone knowing you're doing it.

The quad bike's nonsensical name – 'quad' means four, but 'bike' is an abbreviation of 'bicycle', which means two – that comes to six – hints at its odd history. Originally the ATV, or all-terrain vehicle, as quads are sometimes known, was developed in Japan as a three-wheeled farm vehicle, an inexpensive mini-tractor that could go just about anywhere. In the seventies it was launched in America as an off-road recreational vehicle. In the 1980s the more stable four-wheeled quad was officially introduced – enthusiasts had been converting their trikes for some time – again primarily for farming, but its recreational appeal soon became apparent. At the same time a market for racing models was developing.

Paul Anderson, a former British quad racing champion, says the quad's recreational appeal lies in its potential to deliver a safe thrill. 'It's a mix between a motorbike and driving a car; when you turn a corner, you've got to lean into the corner, and then if the ground's greasy, the rear end slides out,' he says. 'Plus they're much easier to ride than a two-wheeled motorcycle.' The quad bike, in short, provides middle-aged excitement for men who think a Harley might be a bit dangerous. Anderson is keen to point out that quad bikes are, in his experience, much safer than motorcycles. 'With quad racing it's very rare that we see anybody having an accident and getting injured,' he says. 'In the right hands, personally, I think a quad bike is a very safe recreational vehicle,' he adds.

Outside of racing, quad bikes are growing in popularity and injuries have trebled in the last five years. Although retailers offer would-be purchasers basic safety instructions and recommend that riders wear gloves, helmets, goggles, boots and elbow pads, there is no licence required to drive a quad bike and few ways to encourage people to ride them wisely. Employers are required to provide training to workers who use quad bikes, but there is nothing to stop other buyers hurting themselves.

For the rest of the world, quad bikes are here to stay. They feature heavily in the programmes of holiday activity centres, they have all but replaced the tractor as the all-purpose agricultural workhorse and now police constables ride them while patrolling the Merseyside coastline. It has more or less usurped the beach buggy, the dirt bike and the snowmobile; anywhere they can go the quad bike can. They even race them on ice. You can't drive round Lake Windermere on one, or at least nobody's tried it yet. Just wait.

Question 13: Be careful that you don't assume an option is correct simply because you may find similar words in the text. Option C says the quad bike is 'pointless as a recreational vehicle'. Are any of the key words also in the text? Does the sentence where they occur express the same idea as the option?

Question 16: The question is about what Paul Anderson says, so it doesn't matter whether some of these ideas are expressed in the rest of the article. The correct option must describe, in other words, an idea that *this person* expresses.

Question 17: This question is about the legal requirements for riders of quad bikes. In the part of the text where this subject is mentioned, what *obligations* – not simply suggestions – are mentioned?

13 The writer claims that the quad bike
  A   now serves the same function as the beach buggy once did.
  B   is as useful as a snowmobile or motorcycle.
  C   is pointless as a recreational vehicle.
  D   will only be fashionable for a brief period.

14 What is Simon Tiffin's attitude to the people who ride quad bikes?
  A   He doesn't understand them.
  B   He thinks they are amusing.
  C   He is scornful of them.
  D   He believes they have too much money.

15 Originally, the quad bike
  A   was popular only in America.
  B   was a utilitarian vehicle.
  C   had four wheels.
  D   was used as a recreational vehicle.

16 What view is expressed by Paul Anderson?
  A   The only danger is when the rider is turning a corner.
  B   Anyone who can ride a quad bike can ride a motorcycle.
  C   Most accidents occur when people are racing quad bikes.
  D   A quad bike can be exciting without being dangerous.

17 Quad bike riders have to
  A   wear gloves, helmets, goggles, boots and elbow pads.
  B   follow basic safety instructions.
  C   take lessons if they use the bike as part of their job.
  D   have a motorbike licence.

18 According to the writer, why will quad bikes remain popular as working vehicles?
  A   They are used by the police.
  B   They are used a great deal on farms.
  C   They have virtually replaced horses.
  D   They can be used on ice.

19 What is the writer's opinion of the quad bike?
  A   It serves no useful purpose.
  B   It is a toy for sophisticated men.
  C   It is a safe way to have fun.
  D   It is unattractive and unsafe.

PAPER 1 Reading ▶ Part 1
PAPER 2 Writing   Part 2
PAPER 3 Use of English   Part 3
PAPER 4 Listening   **Part 4**
PAPER 5 Speaking

Essential tips

Question 23: Even if you are unfamiliar with the word 'fusion', you can work out that this question is about something successful involving 'words and graphics'. Which other words or phrases could be used to talk about these elements of a book?

Question 27: To find the answer to this question, think about what a person could conjure up in his or her mind as a result of having a strong imagination.

Question 32: The words in the question are very simple, which may mean that the words used in the text will not be. Can you find a different word for 'ending' in one of the texts, and an expression or idiom that means 'unexpected'?

You are going to read a newspaper article containing book reviews. For questions **20–34**, choose from the reviews (**A–H**).

Mark your answers **on the separate answer sheet**.

In which review are the following mentioned?

a subject whose fascination never fades	20 ....
particularly fine illustrations	21 ....
an accidental transgression	22 ....
a successful fusion of words and graphics	23 ....
an adult who helps a child	24 ....
travel between completely credible worlds	25 ....
a previous work by the same author	26 ....
the potential danger of having a powerful imagination	27 ....
children who are not interested in certain kinds of books	28 ....
children who lack self-confidence	29 ....
doubts about who the book is intended for	30 ....
a powerful evocation of a particular time and place	31 ....
an unexpected ending	32 ....
the ability to make adult themes accessible to children	33 ....
the tendency to patronise	34 ....

Books for Children

Reviews of the best children's books published this year

A Lost and Found by Peter Osgood
Ages 10+

Anje was abandoned by her mother as a baby and has grown up with foster parents, but now she resolves to track down the mother who deserted her. Osgood avoids all the traps inherent in a tale of family life, refusing to describe events in such a way as to justify the adults' actions. Instead, he portrays the situation as Anje herself experiences it, with stunning insight and accuracy, producing a moving and hard-hitting story. What is more, there is plenty of action to keep you turning the pages, and the breathtaking finale comes right out of the blue. Sensitive youngsters may find the subject emotionally haunting, but by this age children should be able to cope with the issues handled here. Highly recommended.

B Bird Fly Away by Helen Hunter-Smith
Ages 8–11

Children may well be natural conservationists, enchanted by floppy bunnies and cute doggies, but rather than simply exploit this yearning for anthropomorphic animals, Hunter-Smith has decided to tackle head-on the whole problem of how we treat animals in western society. The story revolves around a farm where Cal lives with his parents, who are desperately trying to get away from the countryside and move to the big city. The haunting pictures of the dilapidated farm buildings and scruffy animals are just one of the outstanding features in this first novel, but perhaps the major attraction of *Bird Fly Away* is that it refuses to compromise in its portrayal of poverty-stricken farmers and neglected animals. This enables young readers to understand fully the awkward issues facing the grown-ups in this world, though there is a tribute to the genre of fairy tales in the shape of a happy ending. A fine work with serious undertones.

C Cuddle by Seth Ashton
Ages 0–4

Everyone likes a cuddle; that's the premise of this charming, chunky book for the very young. Even toddlers who show no interest in the usual baby bathtime books will be entranced by the delightful narrative. In fact, this book could hardly be bettered as an introduction to the world of stories. As Eddy the Baby Elephant wanders sadly through the jungle in search of his parents, he encounters all sorts of adorable creatures, from Harold the Hippo to Tim the Toothy Tiger, and each of them sends him on his way with a nice cuddle. All Eddy has to learn to do is ask for a cuddle – and be prepared to return the favour and give someone else a cuddle when asked to do so. The sparse text is cleverly interwoven with the line drawings in such as way as to encourage reading without being too overtly didactic.

D Step Aside by Diana Courtland
Ages 8–11

Having grown up in an orphanage, Bob can only imagine what normal family life is like, and he indulges in these fantasies whenever his drab reality becomes too depressing. Problems begin to emerge when he discovers he is slipping in and out of his imaginary world without realising it – and then he finds he can't control which world he is living in. This powerful and original tale demonstrates with stunning clarity how strongly we can be drawn into our fantasies and what an uncomfortable (and ultimately terrifying) experience it can be. While Courtland clearly has talent as a writer, the younger members of the target market for this work may find the subject matter too unsettling. After all, she is really hinting at the psychological basis of a wide range of mental problems, not to mention abuse of alcohol and narcotics. If this marketing mismatch could be addressed, the book would deserve unreserved praise.

E Not in Time by Laura Rose
Ages 8–11

Child psychologists tell us that round about the age of six or seven most children are gripped by an interest in the phenomenon of time, though the extent to which they articulate this naturally varies. Books and films for older children (and adults) that deal with time travel indicate just how, well, timeless, that interest is. Laura Rose's third book once again features her popular protagonist, Heather Hornet, who discovers an old garden that is a portal to a world of the future. As Heather ventures backwards and forwards in time, she learns fascinating details about life in different epochs, each of which is entirely plausible and very real. The writer also dares to address the thorny but fascinating philosophical question of whether a visitor from the future who changes the past could thereby nullify his own existence. To discover what conclusion Rose comes to, you will have to buy the book!

F Colour My World by Ashton Lyle
Ages 2–5

My three-year-old niece loved this book, though I can't promise that every three-year-old will feel the same way. This is the story of Viji, the little boy who absolutely refuses to paint pictures in his nursery class. In a clever touch we see how the pictures themselves feel (neglected, since you ask) when Viji only paints them under extreme pressure. But a new teacher at nursery school brings out the artist in Viji by helping make his pictures come to life for him, showing him what they think and feel. So the moral here is that even though grown-ups want you to do something that you yourself have no desire to do, you might still enjoy it if you give it a go. A useful message for every child who is unwilling to try something new because of doubts about his or her ability.

G The Ghost at Number 54 by Fred Wilmot
Ages 8–11

This marvellous tale manages to make England in the 1950s seem like an interesting place – and as someone who was growing up there at the time, I can only say this is a huge tribute to the writer's skills! Wilmot captures brilliantly the drabness and grey uniformity, but also the quaint quality of life in that decade. Against this backdrop he tells the story of Alice and John as it slowly dawns on them that their house, number 54 Mafeking Place, is haunted. One striking quality in this work is Wilmot's ability to demonstrate what is going on in the minds of the adults in the story – without talking down to his young readers, as so many writers do. I won't reveal how the tale ends, except to remark that we were very fond of happy endings in the 1950s.

H The Enchanted Tree by Samantha Carson
Ages 11+

The tree in this story is not just enchanted in the figurative sense of the word: Haball the wizard has actually cast a spell over it, and this means that nobody must look at the old oak. Everyone in the village knows this, for such matters are common in this medieval world of witches, wizards and spells. Everyone except Arthur, that is, for Arthur is the son of a travelling musician who is passing through the village. We learn what happens to Arthur when he looks at the tree, and as in her first novel, Carson depicts brilliantly the isolation of childhood, the sensation that everyone except you knows the rules of the game. A gripping read that will be popular with boys and girls alike.

You **must** answer this question. Write your answer in **180–220** words in an appropriate style.

Essential tips

Question 1

▶ Make sure you know who you are writing for. Think about the format and register that would be appropriate for the task.

▶ Include all the essential points from the input in your writing. You will lose marks if you neglect to cover all of them.

▶ Organise your writing clearly into paragraphs and present your ideas in a logical order.

▶ Use a good range of structures and vocabulary.

1 You are studying at a college in Brighton, on the south coast of England. Recently the college social club organised a trip to Edinburgh, and you went on the trip. Now the president of the club has asked you to write a report about it.

Read the extract from the president's memo and the extract from the publicity leaflet about the trip, together with your comments. Then write your report.

> I have heard various reactions about the trip, including some criticisms. The Social Club would like to organise similar trips in future, so I would be grateful if you could write a report for me. We want to know what problems there were as well as what aspects of the trip were successful. Perhaps you could also suggest how we could do better in future?
>
> Sam Samson, President

**See a completely different part of Britain!
Enjoy the beautiful scenery!
Listen to <u>musical Scottish accents</u>!**

Better if we'd had practice before?

Faster by train?

Sun: <u>Coach to London</u>, arrive at hotel
Free time in evening

Save time by taking sleeper?

Mon: <u>Train</u> to Edinburgh

Tues: <u>Guided tour of city</u>

Great!

Wed: Day at MacTavish College:
• <u>lectures</u> on Scottish culture
• <u>language classes</u>

Some young students bored

Everyone loved it

Thur: Free day, Scottish <u>country dancing</u> in evening

A bit hard for most

Interesting, but too much for one day?

Fri: Edinburgh's <u>museums and art galleries</u>

Sat: Back to London, then Brighton

Now write your **report**.

PAPER 1 Reading

PAPER 2 Writing ▶ Part 1

PAPER 3 Use of English Part 2

PAPER 4 Listening

PAPER 5 Speaking

Essential tips

Question 2: Your main task is to produce a good piece of written English, so it is not very important if the factual details you include are not entirely accurate.

Question 3: When writing about an experience you have had, make sure you include a balanced mixture of information about the experience. Don't only describe the facts, but also your views or feelings relating to them. You should also consider the best way to organise your ideas.

Question 4: Note that there are four points you must include in this piece of writing. Make sure you cover them adequately, and use your imagination to come up with the details.

Question 5(a): You are asked for your opinion, but you must support your ideas with examples from the book. Choose the characters you want to write about carefully. Preferably, they will be the protagonist and one of his/her adversaries.

Question 5(b): You should only attempt this question if you have seen a film version of the book you have read. Read the instructions carefully, and make sure you address the relevant points.

Write an answer to **one** of the questions **2–5** in this part. Write your answer in **220–260** words in an appropriate style.

2 A college in your region would like to send a leaflet to foreign students, giving them helpful information about the local leisure facilities. You have been asked to write the text. You should provide information about:
- sports and recreational opportunities
- cinemas and theatres
- cafés and restaurants

Write the **text for the leaflet**.

3 You have seen the following announcement in an international magazine:

'Education today often concentrates on theory and intellectual processes, but young people also need the satisfaction that comes from doing manual work.'

Have you ever had any experience of physical work – anything from building a piece of furniture to cleaning windows – that gave you a sense of satisfaction?

Write an article about your experience for us!

Write your **article**.

4 You recently witnessed a car accident. Nobody was seriously hurt, but there was a disagreement about who caused the accident and you had to make a statement to the police, which was an interesting experience. Write a letter to a friend describing:
- the events leading up to the accident
- the accident itself
- the reaction of the drivers and passers-by
- your experience with the police

Write your **letter**.

5 Answer **one** of the following two questions based on your reading of **one** of these set books.

Either

5(a) Your teacher has asked you to write an essay on the question of guilt and responsibility in the book you have read. Are the main characters responsible for what happens to them? Compare two characters in the book, giving examples.

Write your **essay**.

Or

5(b) A web site that specialises in film reviews has asked you to write a review of a film version of the book you have read, comparing the film to the book. You should comment on the portrayal of characters, the development of the main themes, and say whether you think the film is as good as the book or not, and why.

Write your **review**.

PAPER 1 Reading

PAPER 2 Writing

PAPER 3 Use of English ▶ Part 1

PAPER 4 Listening   Part 2

PAPER 5 Speaking   Part 3

Part 4

Part 5

Essential tips

Question 2: The meaning of all four options could be appropriate here, but look at the structure of the sentence after the gap. Which verb can be followed by 'other people to read it'?

Question 6: Two options can be used with 'than', but only one forms a phrase with the meaning of 'except', which is the meaning required by the context.

Question 11: The correct option is clearly part of a phrasal verb, and the meaning should be apparent: 'become successful or popular'.

For questions **1–12**, read the text below and decide which answer (**A, B, C** or **D**) best fits each gap. There is an example at the beginning (**0**).

Mark your answers **on the separate answer sheet**.

Example:

0   **A** unlikely   **B** impossible   **C** unbelievable   **D** unique

0	A	B	C	D

The Video Loggers

One rather (**0**) ...... word that has recently entered the language is 'blog', a shortened form of 'web log'. A blog is a diary (**1**) ...... on the Internet by the person writing it – the 'blogger' – who presumably (**2**) ...... other people to read it. It is ironical that modern technology is being used to (**3**) ...... new life into such an old-fashioned form as the personal journal. And now, as the technology behind video cameras is making them easier to use, we have the video log, or 'vlog'. Vlogging does not require (**4**) ...... sophisticated equipment: a digital video camera, a high-speed Internet connection and a host are all that is needed. Vloggers can put anything that (**5**) ...... their fancy onto their personal web site. Some vloggers have no ambitions (**6**) ...... than to show films they have shot while on holiday in exotic places. However, vlogs can also (**7**) ...... more ambitious purposes. For instance, amateur film-makers who want to make a (**8**) ...... for themselves might publish their work on the Internet, eager to receive advice or criticism. And increasingly, vlogs are being used to (**9**) ...... political and social issues that are not newsworthy enough to (**10**) ...... coverage by the mass media. It is still too early to predict whether vlogging will ever (**11**) ...... off in a major way or if it is just a passing fad, but its (**12**) ...... is only now becoming apparent.

1	**A** released	**B** sent	**C** posted	**D** mounted
2	**A** believes	**B** expects	**C** assumes	**D** supposes
3	**A** add	**B** inhale	**C** insert	**D** breathe
4	**A** absolutely	**B** largely	**C** utterly	**D** highly
5	**A** grasps	**B** appeals	**C** takes	**D** gives
6	**A** except	**B** apart	**C** rather	**D** other
7	**A** serve	**B** employ	**C** function	**D** play
8	**A** publicity	**B** fame	**C** name	**D** promotion
9	**A** emphasise	**B** publicise	**C** distribute	**D** circulate
10	**A** earn	**B** warrant	**C** excuse	**D** cause
11	**A** fly	**B** show	**C** take	**D** make
12	**A** potential	**B** possibility	**C** ability	**D** feasibility

PAPER 1 Reading
PAPER 2 Writing
PAPER 3 Use of English ▶ Part 1
PAPER 4 Listening   **Part 2**
PAPER 5 Speaking   Part 3
   Part 4
   Part 5

Essential tips

Question 13: If you look at the whole sentence, you will see that a comparison is being made using the expression 'makes more sense'. How would you expect this comparison to continue?

Question 19: The punctuation here shows that this is a question. The sentences that follow provide reasons for using this reclamation material. Which question with 'bother' is answered by giving reasons?

Question 24: The sentence explains that the clients of reclamation centres want 'items that simply can't be found these days', and then goes on to give an example: 'stone fireplaces'. Which expression using 'as' can be used to give an example?

For questions **13–27**, read the text below and think of the word which best fits each gap. Use only **one** word in each gap. There is an example at the beginning (**0**).

Write your answers **IN CAPITAL LETTERS on the separate answer sheet.**

Example:

0	*WHO*	0

Second-hand
but better than new

Many people (**0**) .... are building their own homes or renovating existing buildings have discovered that it makes more sense to buy second-hand goods (**13**) .... to buy new doors, fireplaces or radiators. These days a large (**14**) .... of businesses offer second-hand material, though many of (**15**) .... cater exclusively for professional builders. However, there are outlets that sell to members of the public, so someone who wants to indulge (**16**) .... a spot of DIY will probably be able to find reclamation material, (**17**) .... second-hand building supplies are known, anywhere in the country.

Searching for (**18**) .... one wants can be time-consuming, so (**19**) .... bother? Is there, for example, any financial reason to make it (**20**) .... one's while? The answer, in many cases, is yes. An oak door in good condition will be considerably (**21**) .... expensive than a new one, even (**22**) .... it is only a few years old. However, the majority of clients of reclamation yards are on (**23**) .... lookout for items that simply can't be found these days, (**24**) .... as stone fireplaces several centuries old. Items like this (**25**) .... , of course, be expensive, but there are a lot of people who do not (**26**) .... paying a high price for a second-hand fireplace that is, (**27**) .... their view, better than new.

Essential tips

Question 29: The gapped word comes before an adjective. What part of speech do you need?

Question 31: The gapped word is an adjective. Does it have a positive or negative meaning?

Question 32: The gapped word follows an article, so it must be a noun. How do you make a noun from 'grow'?

For questions **28–37**, read the text below. Use the word given in capitals at the end of some of the lines to form a word that fits in the gap **in the same line**. There is an example at the beginning (**0**).

Write your answers **IN CAPITAL LETTERS on the separate answer sheet**.

Example:

0	*REGULATIONS*	0

Product Placement

Due to the enforcement of advertising (**0**) .... ,   **REGULATE**
an indirect form of advertising known as product placement
is growing in (**28**) .... It involves using branded   **POPULAR**
products in films and television programmes, and its success
at selling these products is making it (**29**) ....   **INCREASE**
desirable. For instance, commercials for alcohol are banned
in the UK, but a scene in a film showing the hero enjoying a
particular brand of whisky is not subject to (**30**) ....   **CENSOR**
Yet it is an effective way of advertising. Understandably,
this has raised concerns that young children may be tempted
by unsuitable products, and parents are (**31**) .... to   **POWER**
prevent it.

What other factors have contributed to the (**32**) ....   **GROW**
of product placement? One is the (**33**) .... of   **TEND**
consumers to become more (**34**) .... in their   **CRITIC**
response to an advertisement if they are exposed to it over
a period of time. They become tired of being urged to buy a
product by a disembodied voice in a conventional
commercial. Advertisers are being forced to recognise
a (**35**) .... in their customers which did not exist   **SOPHISTICATED**
in the past. People these days are more likely to be influenced
by watching role models using a product. And if this is true of
consumers in general, it is particularly (**36**) .... to   **APPLY**
the young, who are intensely aware of fashion and image but
(**37**) .... forceful in their rejection of authority.   **EQUAL**

Essential tips

Question 38: The gapped word is used very differently in each sentence. In the first sentence, when the police catch a suspected criminal, they arrest him. What might they do once they have questioned him at the police station? Read the third sentence, and think of a word which means 'run in order to attack'.

Question 39: What word do we use to describe both things and people that no longer 'work' or 'exist'?

Question 42: Think of extraterrestrial beings and a word that means 'foreign'!

For questions **38–42**, think of **one** word only which can be used appropriately in all three sentences. Here is an example (**0**).

Example:

0 ● We will do all the work, but they will .... all the credit, as usual!

   ● She will .... offence if you tell her that hairstyle doesn't suit her.

   ● They threatened to .... David to court unless he stopped playing his drums all night.

0	*TAKE*	0

Write **only** the missing word **IN CAPITAL LETTERS on the separate answer sheet.**

---

38 ● The police .... the man with attempted burglary.

   ● The taxi driver .... me ten euros for taking me to the station.

   ● Breaking the door down, the soldiers .... into the building.

39 ● She picked up the phone only to find that the line was ....

   ● Latin and Ancient Greek are .... languages, and are no longer spoken in daily life.

   ● The ambulance rushed the woman to hospital, but she was pronounced .... on arrival.

40 ● I work freelance because working in an office .... me down to a routine, which I hated.

   ● Eileen .... her hair back in a ponytail to keep it off her face.

   ● Jack's description of the driver .... in with that given by the other witness.

41 ● Could you give me an .... of how many people are coming to dinner tonight?

   ● Sitting in the freezing cold watching a football match is not my .... of a romantic night out!

   ● I have no .... why Bill left the party so suddenly.

42 ● Having been brought up in a city, Julie found the rural environment .... to her.

   ● The aim of the festival is to bring together people from .... cultures, and enhance understanding between them.

   ● 'The message seems to be coming from an .... spacecraft, Commander,' said the astronaut.

Essential tips

Question 44: The speaker is speculating based on things he knows. Which structure do you need? Which idiomatic phrase means 'escape'?

Question 46: You need a phrase with 'placed'. What word can be used with 'place' to mean that something is someone's fault?

Question 48: You need a phrasal verb which means 'regret saying something'.

For questions **43–50**, complete the second sentence so that it has a similar meaning to the first sentence, using the word given. **Do not change the word given.** You must use between **three** and **six** words, including the word given. Here is an example (**0**).

Example:

0 Jane regretted speaking so rudely to the old lady.

MORE

Jane .... politely to the old lady.

| 0 | WISHED SHE HAD SPOKEN MORE | 0 |

Write the missing words **IN CAPITAL LETTERS on the separate answer sheet.**

43 Although he studies hard, Derek never does well in his exams.

MATTER

Derek never does well in his exams, ... he studies.

44 It looks as though the thieves escaped in a white Mercedes van.

GETAWAY

The thieves may .... in a white Mercedes van.

45 The town council rarely seem to consider the wishes of the residents.

INTO

The wishes of the residents rarely .... by the town council.

46 Carrie's mum said it was her fault the party was ruined.

PLACED

Carrie's mum .... for the party being ruined.

47 When thieves broke into our home, they took our computer and all our CDs as well.

ONLY

As a result of the break-in, we lost .... all our CDs.

48 I'm sorry I said that your new hat looked like a lampshade.

BACK

I .... about your new hat looking like a lampshade.

49 There were a lot of people at the resort, but Mandy still had a great time.

FACT

Mandy had a great time at the resort .... crowded.

50 'You left my MP3 player on the bus, Joe!' shouted Oliver.

ACCUSED

Oliver .... MP3 player on the bus.

Essential tips

Question 2: Does the woman refute everything the man says, or does she counter some of his points?

Question 4: Read the wording of the options in this question carefully. What does Rusty say about the purpose of having a samba referee?

Question 5: Listen to the way the man talks, as well as what he says. What is his attitude towards the problem of depression in today's society?

You will hear three different extracts. For questions **1–6**, choose the answer (**A, B** or **C**) which fits best according to what you hear. There are two questions for each extract.

Extract One

You hear two people talking about the benefits of garlic.

1   According to the man, garlic
    A raises cholesterol levels in the body.
    B should be applied directly to the skin.
    C has an aroma which repels mosquitoes.

1

2   How does the woman feel about garlic?
    A She does not believe it is beneficial.
    B She is sceptical about its properties.
    C She thinks it can cure skin problems.

2

Extract Two

You hear part of an interview with Rusty Upshaw, a bossaball referee.

3   According to Rusty, bossaball is played
    A on trampolines and sand.
    B on inflatables.
    C on trampolines and inflatables.

3

4   Rasta believes the samba referee
    A enhances the attraction of the sport.
    B distracts the crowd from the game.
    C keeps the crowd under control.

4

Extract Three

You hear two people talking about research into depression.

5   How does the man feel about the subject of depression?
    A He is not convinced about the extent of the problem.
    B He believes scientists should be more concerned.
    C He is optimistic that treatment will soon be available.

5

6   According to the article,
    A research reveals that activity in two specific regions of the brain increases when a person is unhappy.

    B autopsies show that optimistic people have an abnormally small number of cells in certain regions of the brain.

    C it is not known whether reduced activity in certain regions of the brain is a cause of depression.

6

PAPER 1 Reading

PAPER 2 Writing

PAPER 3 Use of English

PAPER 4 Listening ▸
- Part 1
- **Part 2**
- Part 3
- Part 4

PAPER 5 Speaking

Essential tips

Question 7: What kinds of constructions are built these days? Do you need to include an article in your answer? Is an adjective necessary?

Question 9: From the structure of the sentence you can see that an adjective is needed here. If the wheels of a vehicle don't match so that it can't be used for practical purposes, what sort of function might the vehicle have?

Question 12: What kind of word might complete the phrase: 'The Parisii came to Britain from ...'? It could be the name of a place: a city, country etc. Remember that you will hear the word or words you want, but not in the same context as in the question.

You will hear an archaeologist talking about a recent find. For questions **7–14**, complete the sentences.

An Ancient Chariot

The chariot was found at a site where [**7**] is being built.

It was buried in a limestone chamber with a man's [**8**] inside it.

The chariot's wheels don't match, suggesting it had a [**9**] function.

The remains of a large number of [**10**] were also discovered near the chariot.

The chamber was probably the tomb of the [**11**] of a tribe.

The Parisii came to Britain from [**12**]

Until the discovery of the chariot, it was not known that the Parisii had lived so far [**13**]

It is hoped that the chariot can be moved to [**14**]

Essential tips

Question 15: The question is expressed in simple language. However, in the recording, you will hear the correct answer expressed in less straightforward language, perhaps using an idiom or informal expression. Even if you are not familiar with the idiom or expression, you may still be able to guess the correct answer from the context and tone of voice.

Question 19: Ellen says she thinks Tim is 'trying to dodge the responsibility for the problem'. Even if you don't know the word 'dodge', the context tells you Ellen is not pleased with what Tim has said. What could 'dodge' mean, in connection with 'responsibility'?

Question 20: Listen for an expression meaning 'make the protest effective'. It may well be that Ellen does not express this idea in a simple or direct way.

You will hear part of a radio discussion with Ellen Harrington of the Meadow Lane Residents Group, and Tim Barlow from Carton Town Planning Department. For questions **15–20**, choose the correct answer (**A**, **B**, **C** or **D**) which fits best according to what you hear.

---

15   What was Ellen's first reaction when the town centre was closed to traffic?
  A   She was terrified.
  B   She was miserable.
  C   She was delighted.
  D   She was suspicious.

16   The mood of the Meadow Lane residents can best be described as
  A   resigned.
  B   dissatisfied.
  C   furious.
  D   dejected.

17   How does Tim feel about the changes in the town centre?
  A   He regrets they were made so quickly.
  B   He believes they were inevitable.
  C   He thinks the town council should have foreseen the problem.
  D   He is proud the town council went forward with them.

18   What does Tim think about the protest Ellen's group is planning?
  A   He doesn't think it will accomplish anything.
  B   He thinks it is not aimed at the right people.
  C   He doesn't think drivers will be affected.
  D   He thinks it will be dangerous.

19   How does Ellen react to Tim's comments?
  A   She thinks he is being evasive.
  B   She accepts his main point.
  C   She thinks he doesn't understand human nature.
  D   She considers his comments unrealistic.

20   What does Ellen think will make the protest effective?
  A   the amount of publicity it will generate
  B   the inconvenience it will cause to drivers
  C   the number of demonstrators who will take part
  D   the forthcoming election

Essential tips

Questions 21–25: Since you will probably not hear most of the key words in the options, you need to be prepared for words and expressions with a similar meaning. For example, instead of saying 'at school' (option A), the speaker might refer to a type of school, a certain class at school, the name of a school etc. Similarly, a speaker may use a word for a certain relative (option B), such as 'aunt', or even a description of who that person is, such as 'my sister's husband'.

Questions 26–30: Think about how someone might describe an activity to convey the idea that it is 'very dangerous' (option A), perhaps by saying what sort of accident might happen. What kind of language could be used to express this? And consider different ways of expressing the idea of 'spirit of cooperation' (option F): what would we call a 'group' in a sport?

You will hear five short extracts in which people talk about children's free time activities.

While you listen you must complete both tasks.

Task One

For questions **21–25**, choose from the list **A–H** the explanation each speaker gives about how his or her child became interested in an activity.

A Our child began this activity at school.

B A relative was indirectly responsible for our child taking up this activity.

C A newspaper article sparked off interest in this activity.

D We encouraged our child to take up this activity.

E Our child began this activity as a result of a medical condition.

F A television programme inspired our child to take up this activity.

G Our child became interested in this activity while staying with friends.

H The idea for doing this activity came from reading about it.

Speaker 1		21
Speaker 2		22
Speaker 3		23
Speaker 4		24
Speaker 5		25

Task Two

For questions **26–30**, choose from the list **A–H** what each speaker expresses about these activities.

A This activity is very dangerous.

B Our child's physical condition has improved.

C We were opposed to this activity at first.

D Our child takes this activity too seriously.

E We didn't understand what the activity entailed at first.

F This activity develops a spirit of cooperation.

G This activity has become quite fashionable recently.

H Our child has benefited socially.

Speaker 1		26
Speaker 2		27
Speaker 3		28
Speaker 4		29
Speaker 5		30

Essential tips

Part 1: Think about the vocabulary you need to talk about the topic. You should also consider which tenses are appropriate. For instance, you might say your father 'comes from' a certain city, using the present tense – but if you want to say when he left that city, you could use a past tense. When you describe how long you have been living in your home, you will probably need to use the present perfect continuous.

Part 2: To describe how people might feel in a certain situation, or what might have happened, you need expressions that express possibility, such as 'he might have just arrived' or 'they must be feeling tired because it looks as though ...'. However, to describe something that has happened to you, you will need to use appropriate past tenses. For instance, you might say something like: 'I remember once I was walking home and I fell over. I had been to a party, and I was feeling very tired ...'.

Part 3: An emotion or an abstract concept can be interpreted in different ways. The concept of 'pride' can be positive or negative, for example, so you should be prepared to consider different aspects of the idea given to you. Remember that the point here is not to convince the examiner or the other candidate, but to show you can express your views, argue, negotiate and reach a conclusion.

Part 4: In this part, you are asked to talk about actual events or situations and to give your opinions. After answering the question, you may go on to talk more generally about the subject, but you should always first show that you have understood the question.

Part 1 (3 minutes)

The examiner will ask you a few questions about yourself and then ask you to talk to your partner. For example, the examiner may ask you:

- Would you tell me something about the members of your family?
- Where are the members of your family from?
- Which people from your extended family do you have most contact with?

Part 2 (4 minutes)

You will each be asked to talk on your own for a minute without interruption. You will each be given a set of three photographs in turn to talk about. After your partner has finished speaking, you will be asked a brief question connected with your partner's photographs. You will have thirty seconds to answer.

> **Departing** (compare, contrast and speculate)

Turn to pictures 1–3 on page **196**, which show people departing.

Candidate A, compare and contrast two of these pictures. Why do you think the people are leaving, and how might they be feeling?

Candidate B, can you describe a situation when you felt very excited about leaving a place?

> **Exhaustion** (compare, contrast and speculate)

Turn to pictures 1–3 on page **197**, which show tired people.

Candidate B, compare and contrast two of these situations. Why might these people be tired? What kind of exhaustion – mental or physical – do they feel, and why?

Candidate A, which kind of exhaustion do you find most difficult to get over, and why?

Part 3 (4 minutes)

> **Pride** (discuss, evaluate and select)

Turn to the pictures on page **198**, which show examples of pride.

Talk to each other about the different sorts of pride suggested by these pictures, and then decide which two pictures you would choose to illustrate that pride has different forms.

Part 4 (4 minutes)

The examiner will encourage you to develop the topic of your discussion in Part 3 by asking questions such as:

- When was the last time you felt proud of something you had achieved?
- Do you think there are forms of pride that can be harmful?
- Would someone who never felt proud of himself or herself be unhappy?
- Are there times when you feel proud of other people? Can you give an example?

You are going to read three extracts which are all concerned in some way with the performing arts. For questions **1–6**, choose the answer (**A, B, C** or **D**) which you think fits best according to the text.

Mark your answers **on the separate answer sheet**.

Reaching for the stars

My first single has reached number one in the charts. This success has come overnight, and I'm still taken aback when people recognise me in the street. I've even had some trouble with a couple of fans following me, which is a bit disconcerting! There is a plus side, though – I enjoy being invited to parties. Knowing that my single is selling well is hugely satisfying, of course, but it doesn't compare with the pleasure I get from performing for a live audience. To see so many people responding positively to your music is really gratifying, and being able to connect with them makes me feel like I'm participating in their pleasure. I've just completed a national concert tour, and the response of my fans was overwhelming.

I'm not from a musical family. I only became interested in singing when I was sixteen, when some friends asked me to join their group as a vocalist – I took to singing like a duck to water. Naturally, I had daydreams of being a star, but some aspects of performing came as a surprise. I never would have imagined I'd get back pain from standing on stage for so long, for instance. But on balance, I'm delighted with the way things have turned out, and I'm looking forward to recording my next album in June.

1   In general, the writer
   A   prefers recording to performing before a live audience.
   B   has become accustomed to being recognised.
   C   relishes the social aspects of her success.
   D   is annoyed by fans who pester her in the street.

2   An unexpected aspect of her career is that
   A   she has had no formal musical training.
   B   singing came quite naturally to her.
   C   audiences respond to her with enthusiasm.
   D   she suffers physically from performing.

CROWN BALLET SCHOOL APPEAL

Loftside Lodge has been home to the Crown Ballet School since its establishment in 1956. A magnificent, seventeenth century manor house set in four acres of rolling countryside, it is now in need of renovation so that it may continue to offer a valuable contribution to dance education in Britain. Plans include the restoration of the original flooring in the east wing, and an extension to the west wing, which will allow for more boarding facilities, thus enabling the school to open its doors to a larger number of talented children from further afield.

Support has already been obtained from English Heritage and the Arts Council, and many generous parents and friends of the school have helped to raise over 60% of the ten million pounds we need for the project. However, another three and a half million pounds must still be found if we are to complete this important development.

The Crown Ballet School promotes passion and creativity in all forms of dance. Each contribution will help us not only to continue but also to expand our activities. Opportunities are available for donors to receive naming rights.

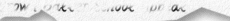

3 The Crown Ballet School
- **A** was built in the 1950s.
- **B** is under threat of demolition.
- **C** belongs to the Arts Council.
- **D** offers its students accommodation.

4 Why might some people wish to back the project?
- **A** because they would like to be recognised as benefactors
- **B** so that they will be allowed to watch performances
- **C** because they would like to benefit from dance education
- **D** so that they can become involved in the school's activities

Goodbye to Bip

Marcel Marceau, that master of illusion through mime, whose chalk-faced character Bip is known and loved in all corners of the globe, has died in his home in France, aged 84.

For over fifty years, he brought magic to the stage, captivating audiences with his extraordinary performances. Within seconds of walking onto an empty stage, he would create a whole scene with breathtaking precision. He was poetry in motion, his body movements speaking volumes to people the world over in a universal language which knew no racial or cultural boundaries. This made him accessible to a wider audience than almost any other theatrical artist. When interviewed once in the United States, Marceau said of himself: 'Mostly I think of human situations for my work, not local mannerisms. There is no French way of laughing and no American way of crying. My subjects try to reveal the fundamental essences of humanity.'

And they did just that. Touring the world many times, Marceau performed in over eighty countries, clocking an average of over two hundred and fifty performances a year. During the course of his long career, Marceau wrote and directed many mimodramas and acted in several films, but he is best remembered for his solo stage performances as the lovable character Bip, who was based on Pip, a character in Charles Dickens' novel *Great Expectations*. Marceau was inspired by both the great novelist and Charlie Chaplin, star of the silent movies, for both were champions of the downtrodden, the have-nots, the little people. Just as the moustache, enormous boots and walking stick of the tramp became Chaplin's trademark, so the white face, battered top hat and slightly bemused, childlike expression of Bip became Marceau's.

5 According to the writer, Marcel Marceau became internationally famous
   A due to the incredible accuracy with which he moved.
   B as a result of his talent for writing poetry.
   C because he needed no language to communicate.
   D because he made people both laugh and cry.

6 The writer implies that Marcel Marceau, Charles Chaplin and Charles Dickens
   A had similar physical characteristics.
   B shared an interest in the theatre.
   C performed successfully on the stage.
   D were concerned about the poor.

PAPER 1 Reading ▶
PAPER 2 Writing
PAPER 3 Use of English
PAPER 4 Listening
PAPER 5 Speaking

Part 1
Part 2
Part 3
Part 4

You are going to read a newspaper article. Six paragraphs have been removed from the article. Choose from the paragraphs **A–G** the one which fits each gap (**7–12**). There is one extra paragraph which you do not need to use.

Mark your answers **on the separate answer sheet**.

Wind of Change

The world's biggest wind farms are currently being constructed off the coast of Britain after a major policy decision by the government to invest time and money in renewable forms of energy. When the entire project is finished, it is estimated that almost eight percent of the electricity that the country needs will be generated in this way.

7

The wind farms themselves will consist of towers with fan-like blades at the top, arranged in groups of as many as 300. As these blades are turned by the wind, they generate electricity. The towers are tall enough to ensure that there will always be enough wind, even on the calmest days, to turn the rotor blades. The electricity generated from these turbines is fed by underground cable to the mainland, where it is incorporated into the national grid.

8

The reason for the delay is due to a conservative approach to new technology as well as economic considerations. Governments are notoriously reluctant to embrace new technology which has not yet proved itself, fearing that if it were to fail, the electorate would blame them. Moreover, until recently it was cheaper to generate electricity by traditional methods. However, now that fossil fuels are becoming more expensive – and the cost of mining them is also rising – the balance has shifted.

9

The way ahead is not without its problems, however. There have been a large number of complaints about wind farms on land, with critics maintaining that the tall towers and gigantic blades are an eyesore. Appearance is less likely to be a problem with offshore wind farms since they will be far enough from the coast to be virtually invisible unless the weather is exceptionally clear.

10

Environmental organisations hope that the government's commitment to wind power will encourage the use of other 'green' methods of producing electricity, though some technologies are less likely to be developed than others, at least in this country. The British Isles enjoy relatively few sunny days, so solar energy is hardly going to be a great success here.

11

It now appears likely that funds will be made available for the necessary research, especially since the British government has made it clear that it sees no future for nuclear power. Existing nuclear power stations are to be phased out gradually, though the government has been wary of providing precise dates for decommissioning.

12

In the meantime, it is encouraging to note that energy solutions which would have seemed unlikely, not to say laughable, just a few decades ago are finally starting to make an impact. It is to be hoped that this trend will continue.

A The most striking aspect of the project is the simplicity of the fundamental idea. Indeed, it seems odd that the principle, which has, after all, been applied to power windmills for thousands of years, has only very recently been used successfully to generate electricity on a large scale.

B There has been little attempt up to now to persuade the general public that wind power is the technology of the future. The government no doubt hopes that when the towers are in place and people realise they are neither a threat to the environment nor aesthetically ugly, attitudes will change.

C Some form of water power would seem a far more likely candidate for development, with tides off the coast of Britain being strong and, of course, regular. As has been the case with wind power, sizeable investment will be needed in order to produce the required technology, but the potential is certainly there.

D This is in line with the target the government set itself of producing ten percent of Britain's electricity from renewables – wind power being the most significant of these – by the year 2010. Environmental groups have hailed the government's commitment and are claiming that the future is definitely looking greener as far as energy is concerned.

E It has been pointed out by those who fear the terrible consequences of an accident that this is only a small step in the right direction. Even when the existing power stations are shut down, the huge problem of disposing of the radioactive materials from them will still have to be solved.

F Another cause for concern is voiced by wildlife organisations, fearful that migrating birds could crash into the rotating blades. Experience in other countries such as Denmark suggests this is unlikely, but the government has promised to monitor the progress of a pilot scheme at present in operation off the coast of Wales.

G Britain is not being particularly revolutionary in placing its trust in wind power. In fact, there is very little risk involved. The country is fortunate when it comes to this particular source of energy – it has a great deal of wind all year round. In a few years Britain may well become a world leader in offshore wind exploitation.

PAPER 1 Reading ▶
PAPER 2 Writing
PAPER 3 Use of English
PAPER 4 Listening
PAPER 5 Speaking

Part 1
Part 2
Part 3
Part 4

You are going to read a magazine article. For questions **13–19**, choose the answer (**A, B, C** or **D**) which you think fits best according to the text.

Mark your answers **on the separate answer sheet**.

Facing the Music

Declan Mayes, President of the Music Buyers Association, is furious at a recent announcement by the recording industry concerning people downloading MP3 music files from the Internet. Of course, there are files that can be downloaded legally for a small charge, but the uproar is not about these: it is about illegal downloads, which constitute an undoubted infringement of copyright. However, there is a great deal of controversy over whether the people who indulge in this activity should be regarded as actual criminals.

A few parallels may be instructive. If someone copies an audio music cassette for their own private use, they are, strictly speaking, breaking the law. But recording companies have usually turned a blind eye to this practice because prosecuting the few people involved would be difficult, and the financial loss to the company itself is not considered significant. At the other end of the scale, there are criminals who make illegal copies of CDs and sell them for a profit. This is far more serious, and the industry actively pursues and prosecutes pirates. Now the Music Recording Association has announced that it regards individuals downloading music from the Internet as pirates, claiming that they damage the industry in just the same way. 'The industry is completely over-reacting; it'll be a laughing stock,'

says Mayes. 'They're going to arrest some teenager downloading files in his bedroom – and sue him for thousands of dollars! This isn't going to frighten anyone into buying CDs.'

Mayes may have a point. There is a general consensus that CD pirates should be subjected to the full wrath of the law, but few would see an individual downloading music for his or her own pleasure in the same light. However, downloading music files illegally is not as innocuous as making private copies of audio cassettes. The scratchy, distorted cassette copy is a poor version of the original recording, whereas an MP3 file is of high quality and can be stored – on a CD, for example. It is this that makes the practice a powerful temptation for music fans, given the high cost of CDs.

What does Mayes think about claims that music companies could be forced out of business by people downloading music illegally? 'That's nonsense. Music companies are always whining about high costs, but that doesn't prevent them from recording hundreds of CDs by completely unknown artists, many of whom are "packaged" by marketing departments to appeal to young consumers. The companies are simply hoping that one of these new bands or singers will be a hit, and although it can be expensive to promote new artists, the cost of

manufacturing the CDs is actually very low.'

This last point would appear to be the focus of resentment against music companies: a CD is far cheaper to produce than its price in the shops would indicate, and profit margins for the music companies are huge. An adult with a reasonable income may not object to paying £15 for a CD of classical music, but a teenager buying a CD by the latest pop sensation may find that price rather steep – especially since the latest pop sensation is almost certain to be forgotten within a few months. And while the recording industry can't be held responsible for the evanescent nature of fame, given the teenage appetite for anything novel, it could lower the prices it charges – especially since technology is making CDs even cheaper to produce.

This is what Mayes hopes will happen. 'If the music industry stops exploiting the music-buying public, it can survive. Everyone would rather buy a CD, with an attractive jacket and booklet, than mess around downloading files, but the price has to be reasonable. The problem isn't going to vanish if the industry carries on trying to make a quick profit. Technology has caught up with the music companies, and trying to fight it by taking people to court will only earn money for the lawyers.' A frightening thought.

13 If someone downloads MP3 music files illegally, the Music Recording Association will now
    A turn a blind eye.
    B be indulgent towards them.
    C take them to court.
    D charge them a fee.

14 Mayes thinks that the recording industry's recent announcement
    A fails to take into account the difficulties of prosecuting offenders.
    B makes the industry appear ludicrous.
    C will deter consumers from buying CDs.
    D will encourage resentment of CD piracy.

15 According to the article, it is commonly accepted that
    A producing pirate CDs in order to make money is a serious offence.
    B downloading MP3 files is more serious than making audio cassettes.
    C the Music Recording Association should ignore infringements.
    D the laws regarding illegal music recordings should be amended.

16 Why does the writer feel that MP3s are unlike copies of audio cassettes?
    A Downloaded MP3 files are generally not for private use.
    B The financial losses to the music industry are greater.
    C The price of MP3s is greater than the price of audio cassettes.
    D There is a significant difference in quality.

17 Mayes implies that music companies
    A could cut costs by making cheaper CDs.
    B should not promote artists who are unknown.
    C are speculating when they promote new artists.
    D should use different manufacturing processes.

18 The writer points out that the music industry cannot be blamed for
    A the fact that fewer teenagers are buying classical music CDs.
    B the fact that fashions change quickly.
    C the poor quality of much modern music.
    D the prices that are charged for CDs in shops.

19 What does Mayes think is at the root of the dilemma facing the music industry?
    A the unprecedented speed of technological advances
    B unrealistic legal advice
    C its failure to adopt an appropriate long-term strategy
    D the rapidly changing nature of contemporary music

You are going to read a newspaper article in which women talk about their attitudes toward cars. For questions **20–34**, choose from the women (**A–D**). When more than one answer is required, these may be given in any order.

Mark your answers **on the separate answer sheet**.

Which woman ...

uses her car to get to work?	**20** ....
uses her car mainly to make short journeys?	**21** .... **22** ....
has only had a driving licence for a few years?	**23** ....
has a prejudice against a particular kind of car?	**24** ....
feels safety considerations are paramount when buying a car?	**25** ....
wanted a car that would have a minimal impact on the environment?	**26** ....
didn't want to be responsible for the car at first?	**27** ....
acknowledges that she knows little about cars?	**28** ....
uses other means of transport because of rising costs?	**29** ....
drives a kind of car which is becoming increasingly popular?	**30** ....
needs a large car?	**31** ....
is an enthusiastic driver?	**32** ....
wishes she didn't need to rely on a car?	**33** ....
dissuaded someone from buying a car?	**34** ....

Women Drivers

What do women think about the cars they drive? We talked to four women about their views.

A Megan Fields

Megan Fields lives in rural Hertfordshire, just outside a small village. In recent years the bus service in the village has improved, and there is also a good link now to the nearest town. Consequently, she uses a car mainly to commute to her office almost forty miles away. Megan works normal office hours, Mondays to Fridays, and this means she has to make a round trip of very nearly eighty miles a day in the enervating rush-hour traffic. However, since the latest increases in the price of fuel, she and her husband feel they have to think more carefully about car maintenance costs.

Megan was forced to purchase a new car only a short while ago: she was recently involved in a collision with a lorry. It was an unequal contest, and Megan's car was a write-off. Fortunately, nobody was badly hurt, but Megan was shaken by the experience. She promised herself that her next car would have more robust bodywork in case anything like that ever happens again. Since their old car had been on its last legs anyway, she and her husband had been looking at the options available on the market even before the crash, and they had narrowed the choice down to three or four models. Before they made their final decision, they took a number of other factors into consideration. They wanted a car that would be fuel-efficient and that would produce as few harmful emissions as possible. Megan left the choice of car to her husband; she claims she is ignorant of the technical issues involved and has no desire to learn. She stresses that she would rather be able to manage without a car at all. However, given their circumstances, doing without a car does not appear to be a viable option.

B Vera Aziz

Vera is one of the growing number of people who have purchased an SUV – a sports utility vehicle. In her view, there is something very reassuring about the height of the vehicle, which places the driver and passengers above the majority of other road users. Though she has no statistics to back up her opinion, she is convinced that this means she would be far better off in an accident. There is another practical factor at work in her choice of vehicle: her SUV seats eight people quite comfortably, and she needs this room since she regularly ferries her two daughters and their four friends to and from ballet classes.

Vera says that a car is an absolute necessity for her. Public transport in the part of Surrey where she lives is woefully inadequate and there is no school bus, so when the weather is bad she has to drive the children to their school nearby. About once a fortnight she and her husband go up to London for the day and they need the car to get them to the local train station. Otherwise, she admits, the car stays in the garage most of the time. When asked about what influenced her choice of vehicle, she is unequivocal: safety was the crucial point, and she imagines that this is the case for the vast majority of women.

C Sue Henderson

The new charges for drivers entering inner London, coupled with exhorbitant parking fees throughout the capital, means that the situation has changed for Sue. She says she would far rather take the train to the city instead of driving in from Faversham in Kent, so these days she mostly uses the car to stock up with groceries from the local supermarket on Friday evenings. But there has been another more radical change in her driving habits over the past few months. Some good neighbours of hers, who only used their car very occasionally, were thinking of buying a new one, and Sue suggested that instead of going to the expense and trouble this would involve, they should just use hers whenever they wanted to. Sue says that some careful planning is required to make this arrangement work smoothly, but it has resulted in considerable savings for everyone concerned. She also makes the point that a scheme like this works best if people are relaxed about the car they drive and don't insist on a spotlessly clean high-performance model. Sue's present car is fairly old, large and sturdy – one of the Scandinavian models that offer their owners a sense of security. She is rather dismissive of SUVs, which she doesn't consider particularly safe. This is because she read somewhere that they can roll over quite easily. Furthermore, they are a danger to cyclists because SUV drivers tend not to notice them. Sue also has strong opinions about the jokey stereotype of the bad woman driver, which she regards as absolute nonsense. She is similarly dismissive of the idea that men are natural born drivers, claiming that statistics prove the opposite, and that men cause far more accidents than women, especially serious ones.

D Heather Adams

Four years ago Heather Adams's husband injured his leg in an accident which left him unable to drive. Heather herself then reluctantly took charge of the car, not only driving it but also making sure it was serviced regularly and generally looking after it. The Adams's children are still very young, so Heather is the only one in the family who uses the car now. In fact, she only passed her driving test three and a half years ago, so she had little practical experience with vehicles of any kind until then. Their present car is the only one she has ever driven, apart from the car at the driving school when she was learning to drive. She says she never expected to get such enormous pleasure from sitting behind the wheel, and believes that learning to drive gave her a sense of independence and confidence that she lacked when she was younger. She regards a car as an essential part of her life now – public transport in the northern city where she lives is unreliable and not convenient for her needs.

Her husband has clearly influenced her views on road safety. He believes it is important to be able to put your foot down and accelerate away from trouble. Heather agrees and clearly relishes driving a car with a powerful engine. For her, this would be a prime consideration if she were to buy another car.

You **must** answer this question. Write your answer in **180–220** words in an appropriate style.

1   You are the social secretary at Blackstone College, where you are also a student. Recently you organised a party for children living in the area. In your view, it was a success. However, an article published in the local newspaper was rather critical about it.

Read the article, to which you have added some comments. Then write a letter to the newspaper responding to the article.

Not fair: most parents satisfied. Approx. 120 kids had good time!

OK, not enough rides – but other entertainment like clowns, jugglers, etc!

OK, bad layout

Complaints about College Children's Party

Blackstone College held its first Children's Party on Tuesday 15ᵗʰ, but parents say the event was not a success. 'They ran out of food early on – there was none left by half past two – and there weren't enough rides for all the kids,' said Helena Jackson, who brought her four-year-old son Steven. Fred Wormsley, who brought his twin eight-year-old girls, also felt that the party could have been better planned. 'We were given a map of the area but it didn't stop us getting lost!' Such criticisms are bound to make local residents wonder whether the college is spending tax payers' money wisely.

Refreshments scheduled from 12 to 2!

Party paid for by students, not college!

Now write your **letter** to the newspaper. You do not need to include postal addresses.

PAPER 1 Reading

PAPER 2 Writing ▶ Part 1
Part 2

PAPER 3 Use of English

PAPER 4 Listening

PAPER 5 Speaking

Write an answer to **one** of the questions **2–5** in this part. Write your answer in **220–260** words in an appropriate style.

2 You decide to enter a competition for writers run by an English language club in your area. The notice you see says:

> ## 'People can never hide their deepest emotions.'
>
> Write an account of an occasion when you were strongly affected emotionally, but attempted to hide your true feelings. Describe how the situation came about and indicate whether you succeeded in concealing your emotions or not.

Write your **competition entry**.

3 You have been asked to write a contribution for a tourist guidebook for your area, suggesting outings and day trips suitable for families. You should include information about:
- places of historical interest
- areas of natural beauty
- theme parks and amusement parks

Also include practical information about transport, opening and closing hours, etc.

Write your **contribution** for the guidebook.

4 You see the following announcement in an international magazine for language teachers:

> ## What makes an outstanding teacher?
>
> We want to hear your stories. Tell us about a teacher you had at school who really impressed you. Explain what it was about him or her that makes you remember this person as a great teacher.

Write your **article**.

5 Answer **one** of the following two questions based on your reading of **one** of the set books.

Either

5(a) A literary magazine is holding a competition, and has asked its readers to send in articles in response to the following question: 'In what sense is the main character in the novel a victim, and at what point does he/she cease to be one?' You have decided to enter. Write an article for the magazine, using examples from the book you have read to support your answer.

Write your **article**.

Or

5(b) You do market research for a publishing house. You have been asked to write a report on an enduringly popular novel, outlining its most successful features, its shortcomings and the reasons it has remained popular.

Write your **report**.

For questions **1–12**, read the text below and decide which answer (**A, B, C** or **D**) best fits each gap. There is an example at the beginning (**0**).

Mark your answers **on the separate answer sheet.**

Example:

0   **A** probable   **B** possible   **C** likely   **D** potential

All in the Stars

First-time visitors to India are (**0**) ...... to be impressed by how profoundly astrology influences almost every (**1**) ...... of life on the subcontinent. In fact, the belief that the motions of remote heavenly bodies can affect events on Earth is so (**2**) ...... that several Indian universities (**3**) ...... courses in the subject. It is not, therefore, surprising that many people will (**4**) ...... an astrologer before they take any important step. For example, Indian marriages are arranged with the aid of an astrologer, who will cast the horoscopes of the bride and groom, and also (**5**) ...... out the best date for the wedding to take place. A few years ago in Delhi, thousands of couples rushed to get married on a particularly auspicious day, with the (**6**) ...... that priests, brass bands and wedding photographers were in short supply.

The role of astrology is not (**7**) ...... only to the social aspects of Indian life. Few people (**8**) ...... business without resorting to their astrologer. Major films are only (**9**) ...... on auspicious dates. Even (**10**) ...... of state are not exempt from its influence: when India (**11**) ...... her independence from Britain in 1947, the (**12**) ...... of power was carefully timed to take place after a particularly inauspicious period had passed.

1	**A** division	**B** facet	**C** angle	**D** sector
2	**A** widespread	**B** overwhelming	**C** intensive	**D** capacious
3	**A** offer	**B** afford	**C** supply	**D** serve
4	**A** interrogate	**B** confer	**C** interview	**D** consult
5	**A** make	**B** work	**C** calculate	**D** determine
6	**A** effect	**B** outcome	**C** upshot	**D** result
7	**A** demarcated	**B** bound	**C** confined	**D** restrained
8	**A** engage	**B** perform	**C** carry	**D** conduct
9	**A** published	**B** released	**C** aired	**D** revealed
10	**A** affairs	**B** cases	**C** issues	**D** topics
11	**A** grabbed	**B** procured	**C** gained	**D** captured
12	**A** delivery	**B** inheritance	**C** succession	**D** transfer

For questions **13–27**, read the text below and think of the word which best fits each gap. Use only **one** word in each gap. There is an example at the beginning (**0**).

Write your answers **IN CAPITAL LETTERS on the separate answer sheet**.

Example:

0	ALL	0

Independent **Television**

Foreigners are often surprised that there are no advertisements at (**0**) .... on the BBC television channels. The absence of commercials, as television advertisements are known, is (**13**) .... to the fact that the constitution of the BBC forbids it to accept advertising. So (**14**) .... does the BBC get the money it needs to (**15**) .... it going? In fact, the BBC is financed from revenue (**16**) .... is raised by the sale of television licences. The fee for the licences is set by the government, but (**17**) .... this, the BBC is not state run, and it is proud of (**18**) .... independence. It (**19**) .... be said that the viewers themselves pay for the BBC, since (**20**) .... who owns a television has to purchase a licence. And of course, you have to have a valid licence whether you actually watch the BBC (**21**) .... not. This arrangement dates (**22**) .... to the 1920s, when the BBC was a radio broadcaster. Some people feel the system is unfair (**23**) .... those who watch other channels but not the BBC, and there are those who fail to buy a licence, which is (**24**) .... the law. (**25**) .... an effort to combat this, the BBC has a fleet of detector vans that tour the country, checking (**26**) .... a television is being used from an address when there is (**27**) .... record of a licence having been purchased.

TEST 4

PAPER 1 Reading

PAPER 2 Writing

PAPER 3 Use of English ▶

Part 1
Part 2
Part 3
Part 4
Part 5

PAPER 4 Listening

PAPER 5 Speaking

For questions **28–37**, read the text below. Use the word given in capitals at the end of some of the lines to form a word that fits in the gap **in the same line**. There is an example at the beginning (**0**).

Write your answers **IN CAPITAL LETTERS on the separate answer sheet**.

Example:

0	*HEIGHT*	0 __ __

From coin to paper

In ninth century China, at the (**0**) .... of the Tang dynasty, the government became concerned about the (**28**) .... of carrying around large amounts of coins in order to conduct business (**29**) .... Consequently, they devised a method of paying merchants with money certificates, which had a (**30**) .... to blow away. This quickly earned them the (**31**) .... 'flying cash'. These certificates could be exchanged for coin money on demand at the capital. They were (**32**) .... , so merchants began exchanging them with each other instead of using coins.

HIGH

CONVENIENT
ACTION

TEND
NAME

TRANSFER

It was not until the Song dynasty that actual paper money was created. (**33**) .... introduced by a group of merchants and financiers, each banknote had images of houses, trees and people printed on it. These were (**34**) .... by various intricate markings, the (**35**) .... of which could be made only by the issuing banks, thereby making counterfeiting difficult. For this reason, they became readily accepted for payment, and their circulation increased. Then, in 1023, the government decided to (**36**) .... the banknotes and issue government notes in their place, every one of them with a cash backing. These new banknotes could be exchanged for government-issued coins, and so could be used to buy simple groceries. As a result, the use of paper money soon became (**37**) ....

INITIAL

COMPANY
IDENTIFY

DRAW

SPREAD

For questions **38–42**, think of **one** word only which can be used appropriately in all three sentences. Here is an example (**0**).

Example:

0
- We will do all the work, but they will .... all the credit, as usual!
- She will .... offence if you tell her that hairstyle doesn't suit her.
- They threatened to .... David to court unless he stopped playing his drums all night.

| 0 | *TAKE* | 0 |

Write **only** the missing word **IN CAPITAL LETTERS on the separate answer sheet**.

38
- Sarah has that rare .... of being able to really listen to people.
- Joe's always had the .... of the gab, which is why he became a politician.
- There's a free .... in every pack of Busy Bee's Frosted Honey Flakes.

39
- Try .... some cornflour into that sauce to thicken it up.
- You can have some fun .... business with pleasure at these conferences.
- Sharon's twin daughters are so similar that I keep .... them up.

40
- Children who are .... to their own devices get up to all sorts of mischief.
- Charles felt .... out when the other children started playing a board game without him.
- After the party, Karen's mum was .... with all the tidying up to do.

41
- .... exercise will help you stay healthy.
- Walter used to be a long-distance lorry driver, but now he's got a .... job in an office.
- When the nurse checked the sleeping patient, his breathing was .... , with no sign of distress.

42
- You shouldn't drive a car .... the influence of alcohol.
- She wrote her first three books .... another name.
- 'You'll find his records filed .... the heading 'Non-resident,' said the clerk.

For questions **43–50**, complete the second sentence so that it has a similar meaning to the first sentence, using the word given. **Do not change the word given.** You must use between **three** and **six** words, including the word given. Here is an example (**0**).

Example:

0   Jane regretted speaking so rudely to the old lady.

   MORE

   Jane .... politely to the old lady.

| 0 | *WISHED SHE HAD SPOKEN MORE* | 0 |

Write the missing words **IN CAPITAL LETTERS on the separate answer sheet.**

---

43   The warmth of her welcome surprised me.

   ABACK

   I .... her warm welcome.

44   Tom hates parties, so don't try to persuade him to go.

   WORTH

   It .... Tom to go to parties because he hates them.

45   'You will have to travel a lot in this job,' the manager told her.

   INVOLVE

   The manager informed her that the job .... a lot.

46   We would have arrived here late if Neil's father hadn't taken us to the bus stop.

   FOR

   Had .... Neil's father taking us to the bus stop, we would have arrived here late.

47   It is possible that Teresa took your car keys this morning by mistake.

   ACCIDENTALLY

   Teresa .... your car keys this morning.

48   We had expected Alan to be late, but he came home early.

   EXPECTATIONS

   Contrary .... , Alan came home early.

49   I didn't recognise her until she took off her sunglasses.

   ONLY

   It .... her sunglasses that I recognised her.

50   'Why don't you go to the Loch Lomond Eco Lodge for the weekend?' Kevin said.

   SUGGESTED

   Kevin .... to the Loch Lomond Eco Lodge for the weekend.

You will hear three different extracts. For questions **1–6**, choose the answer (**A, B** or **C**) which fits best according to what you hear. There are two questions for each extract.

Extract One

You hear a mother talking to her teenage son about school.

1 Sam's mother is concerned that Sam

   A is having problems concentrating.

   B does not do his homework.

   C is putting his future at risk.

1

2 Which word best describes Sam's attitude towards his mother's concern?

   A dismissive

   B angry

   C disgusted

2

Extract Two

You hear part of a radio programme in which two people are discussing growing herbs.

3 According to Jerry, herbs are particularly useful

   A in a corner of the garden.

   B when they grow on windowsills.

   C if grown among vegetables.

3

4 Which of the following is not true about growing herbs?

   A Annual herbs are not used in cooking.

   B Herbs are easy to cultivate.

   C Perennial herbs add flavour to food.

4

Extract Three

You hear two friends talking about travelling alone.

5 What does Joy advise Tom to do?

   A choose his destination carefully

   B find groups to travel with

   C get used to travelling alone

5

6 Which of the following does Joy mention?

   A accommodation arrangements

   B having company in the evenings

   C guided tours

6

You will hear an anthropologist talking about a recent find. For questions **7–14**, complete the sentences.

A Significant Find

Several fossil skulls were dug up in Ethiopia

last ☐ **7**

There were at least ☐ **8** adult skulls
and one that belonged to a child.

It appears that the people these skulls belong to were

our ☐ **9** ancestors.

Anthropologists now believe that *Homo sapiens* is

☐ **10** from Neanderthals.

The reason why the Neanderthals ☐ **11**
is not known.

The people whose skulls have been found probably used

☐ **12**

They also lived in ☐ **13** ,
a factor which probably helped them to survive.

The early days of human evolution are still ☐ **14**
to modern scientists.

You will hear part of a radio discussion about iris recognition systems. For questions **15–20**, choose the answer (**A**, **B**, **C** or **D**) which fits best according to what you hear.

15 Jim says that the idea behind iris recognition systems (IRS)
   A   is based on state-of-the-art technology.
   B   was thought of many years ago.
   C   relies on a simple camera.
   D   requires sophisticated computer software.

16 He believes that iris recognition machines will be adopted on a large scale chiefly because
   A   they can be depended upon.
   B   they speed up the identification process.
   C   they can be connected to a wide range of secondary devices.
   D   the machines in use at present are proving very successful.

17 Iris recognition machines were used at a school
   A   to gauge the reaction of students.
   B   to stimulate interest in science lessons.
   C   to improve efficiency at a school canteen.
   D   to identify pupils entering a school.

18 Jim feels that people who object to iris recognition machines
   A   regard them as a threat to personal freedom.
   B   object to X-ray machines as well.
   C   are a very small minority.
   D   fail to appreciate how they work.

19 What does Jim say about the costs involved in registering the population?
   A   The government will not pay all the costs involved.
   B   They will depend on the scale of the project.
   C   They will be modest at the outset.
   D   They will be high initially.

20 According to Jim, what will convince governments to adopt iris recognition systems?
   A   reduced expenses
   B   public acceptance
   C   increased security
   D   ease of use

You will hear five short extracts in which people talk about holidays that went wrong.

While you listen you must complete both tasks.

Task One

For questions **21–25**, choose from the list **A–H** the person who is speaking.

A a teacher

B a pensioner

C a doctor

D a hotel manager

E a guide

F a racing driver

G a sales representative

H a tour operator

Speaker 1		21
Speaker 2		22
Speaker 3		23
Speaker 4		24
Speaker 5		25

Task Two

For questions **26–30**, choose from the list **A–H** what each speaker is expressing.

A acceptance of personal responsibility for events

B indignation because of inclement weather

C a determination to overcome setbacks

D frustration that the experience failed to satisfy expectations

E lack of respect for people's feelings

F relief that initial fears were unfounded

G irritation at other people's attitudes

H a reluctance to accept responsibility for a situation

Speaker 1		26
Speaker 2		27
Speaker 3		28
Speaker 4		29
Speaker 5		30

Part 1 (3 minutes)

The examiner will ask you a few questions about yourself and then ask you to talk to your partner. For example, the examiner may ask you:

- What do you enjoy doing when you go away for a holiday?
- How would you describe the best holiday you have had?
- What sorts of things can spoil a holiday for you?

Part 2 (4 minutes)

You will each be asked to talk on your own for a minute without interruption. You will each be given a set of three photographs in turn to talk about. After your partner has finished speaking, you will be asked a brief question connected with your partner's photographs. You will have thirty seconds to answer.

Sports (compare, contrast and speculate)

Turn to pictures 1–3 on page **199**, which show people taking part in different sports.

Candidate A, compare and contrast two of these pictures and say what kind of training each of these sports requires. What are the advantages and disadvantages of taking part in a team sport, as opposed to an individual sport?

Candidate B, which of these sports would you find most enjoyable?

Accommodation (compare, contrast and speculate)

Turn to pictures 1–3 on page **200**, which show different places where people live.

Candidate B, compare and contrast two of these homes, saying what you think would be the advantages of living in each one and what might be the impractical aspects of living there.

Candidate A, which of these homes do you think is most practical?

Part 3 (4 minutes)

Public Transport (discuss, evaluate and select)

Turn to the pictures on page **201**, which show different forms of transport in a certain city.

The tourist board in this city is publishing a brochure to attract visitors, and it has been decided to put three photographs on the cover, showing different forms of public transport. Which three photographs should be used in order to give the impression that this is an interesting city to visit?

Part 4 (4 minutes)

The examiner will encourage you to develop the topic of your discussion in Part 3 by asking questions such as:

- Should private cars be banned from city centres? Why (not)?
- What do you think could be done in your area to encourage people to use public transport?
- Some cities encourage people to take passengers in their cars to reduce congestion. Do you think this is a good idea, and would it work in your area? Why (not)?

You are going to read three extracts which are all concerned in some way with astrology. For questions **1–6**, choose the answer (**A, B, C** or **D**) which you think fits best according to the text.

Mark your answers **on the separate answer sheet**.

The roots of astrology are probably as old as humanity's first attempts to map the heavens. The oldest astrological records we know of come from Babylon, and astrology clearly played an important role in the life of Ancient Egypt, Greece and Rome. In fact, most cultures throughout history have believed that the stars influence our lives, and to judge by the avidity with which modern-day Britons scan the pages of newspapers for their daily horoscope, astrology is as popular today as ever it was. In fact, astrology is big business, and top astrologers with regular pages in newspapers and magazines earn huge annual incomes. Even the new technologies have been pressed into service; astrological web sites are visited by millions every day, and not just by the gullible or uneducated. There are students studying science at university who admit to believing that one's star sign determines personality. Hard-headed businessmen have been known to pay for astrological predictions about the rise and fall of the stock market, and a few years ago it emerged that one large bank was using astrology to help manage its five billion pound investment portfolio. Nor is it a secret that several politicians have relied on astrologers to provide insight into matters of state – believers include former American President Ronald Reagan. Even former British Prime Minister Margaret Thatcher once told MPs: 'I was born under the sign of Libra; it follows that I am well-balanced.'

But surely it is an irony that in our technological age so many people continue to put their faith in astrologers. After all, we are living in a period of history when science seems to have provided answers to many of the riddles and mysteries of nature. Paradoxically, however, the resultant mechanistic view of life has caused many to feel that their life has no purpose, a state of affairs also reflected by the decline in formal religious observance. Is this, perhaps, why growing numbers of people are turning to astrology with such fervour? Are they simply exhibiting a natural human longing for some meaning in their life?

---

1 Which observation does the writer make regarding astrology?
   A Its appeal is timeless.
   B It has gained credibility.
   C Its popularity is in decline.
   D Scientists have disproved its claims.

2 According to the writer, what is ironic about astrology today?
   A Science has provided answers to astrological questions.
   B Several high-ranking politicians believe in it.
   C It has gained adherents as a result of scientific progress.
   D Technological developments have led to a decline in religious beliefs.

Astrology Analysed

Books on astrology and its influence on our lives abound, so when *Astrology Analysed* landed on my desk, I can't say I was exactly fired with enthusiasm. Until, that is, I began to read it.

For here, at last, is a book that offers a genuine critical evaluation of the claims astrologers have been making for thousands of years. The author, Tom Maine, is an internationally acclaimed expert on the philosophy of science. In this book, he successfully brings together historical and scientific research in an account that is both informative and challenging to the reader.

Believers in astrology are often all too ready to blindly accept comments on their personality, suggestions about who is a suitable match for them, and predictions about their career, love life, etc. On the other hand, sceptics can be positively scathing in their determination to highlight astrology's flaws and inadequacies. Few people are willing to examine the subject empirically or objectively. Tom Maine is one of the few who has attempted to do so.

His approach is impartial yet probing, providing readers with a unique insight into this ancient art, and at the same time allowing them to draw their own conclusions regarding its value. Tracing its historical origins, he analyses how astrology works, and scrutinises various experiments that have been carried out to ascertain the accuracy of its claims. It makes for a fascinating read. As to my own conclusion regarding the validity of astrology, I am keeping that to myself!

3   According to the review, the author
   A   is a popular scientist and philosopher.
   B   has a balanced approach to the subject.
   C   encourages readers to regard astrology as a science.
   D   exposes the flaws in astrological predictions.

4   Regarding her own views on the subject of astrology, the writer is
   A   unequivocal.
   B   apathetic.
   C   noncommittal.
   D   explicit.

Nicholas Culpeper

Nicholas Culpeper is best remembered today as the author of the book commonly known as 'Culpeper's Herbal', which was published in 1653. What is not so well known about this accomplished healer is that he was also an astrologer.

In Culpeper's time, it was common practice for medicine to be linked with astrology, and had been for at least 2000 years. People saw astrology as directly affecting the efficacy of plants' healing properties. Thus, healers of the day were often also skilled astrologers. No doubt for this reason, after completing a long apprenticeship to an apothecary, where he learned about the healing properties of herbs, Culpeper went to work with the astrologer William Lilly in 1635. Lilly taught him a great deal about medical astrology, and greatly influenced his future work. Culpeper's philosophy was built on a combination of astrological and Greco-Arabic medical principles.

Believing that medical knowledge should be made available to whoever was interested, Culpeper made himself unpopular with the medical establishment of the day by writing and publishing guides in English rather than Latin, in which he outlined the principles of medical astrology and the use of medicinal herbs in healing. 'Culpeper's Herbal' was based on these principles, and was seen as a definitive work on herbal medicine for more than 250 years. Today, some astrologers still adhere to his philosophy. They argue that by studying an individual's natal chart in detail, it is possible to evaluate his or her tendency towards illness, and the body's ability to heal itself.

Although the development of Western conventional medicine has destroyed much of medical astrology's public credibility, the growing interest in alternative medicine such as acupuncture and homeopathy could stimulate a revival of interest in the subject.

5 In Culpeper's day, people believed that
   A plant growth was affected exclusively by astrology.
   B astrology determined a plant's ability to cure disease.
   C only astrologers could effectively cure illness.
   D medical knowledge was restricted to astrologers.

6 According to the writer,
   A people no longer question the validity of medical astrology.
   B Culpeper was admired in the medical circles of his day.
   C William Lilly was strongly influenced by Culpeper's writings.
   D Culpeper tried to make medical knowledge more accessible.

PAPER 1 Reading ▶
PAPER 2 Writing
PAPER 3 Use of English
PAPER 4 Listening
PAPER 5 Speaking

Part 1
Part 2
Part 3
Part 4

You are going to read a magazine article. Six paragraphs have been removed from the article. Choose from the paragraphs **A–G** the one which fits each gap (**7–12**). There is one extra paragraph which you do not need to use.

Mark your answers **on the separate answer sheet**.

Countdown to Extinction for World's Great Apes

Gorillas, chimpanzees, bonobos and orangutans – the closest living relatives of humanity – could vanish from the wild within fifty years, according to United Nations leaders who met recently in Paris. They have appealed for £15 million to save the world's great apes from extinction.

7

There is no doubt that dedicated researchers and writers have raised public awareness about the plight of the great apes, and commercially successful films like *Gorillas in the Mist* have also helped to shed light on the situation. Unfortunately, in spite of this, the decline in ape numbers has not only continued but accelerated.

8

Lowland and mountain gorillas range through nine African countries. Reliable figures on these animals are hard to come by, partly because the creatures are by nature reclusive and shy, and partly because the areas they inhabit are both remote and inhospitable. However, one estimate suggests that eighty to ninety percent of the population may have been lost in just five years, as new roads have opened up inaccessible forest to poachers, loggers and bush meat hunters. Only about 600 mountain gorillas survive in Uganda, Rwanda and the Democratic Republic of Congo.

9

The future looks equally bleak for the other African apes. Two chimpanzee species, *Pan troglodytes* and *Pan paniscus* (the bonobo or pigmy chimpanzee), are found in twenty-one African countries, but their populations are very small compared to the size of their potential range. There may be only 105,000 *Pan troglodytes*, and fewer than 20,000 bonobos left. The western chimpanzee has vanished from Benin, Gambia and Togo. Fewer than 400 remain in Senegal and 300 to 500 in Ghana. The population of chimps in Guinea-Bissau is below 200. And yet these animals are our closest relatives: chimpanzee DNA is so close to human DNA that one scientist has proposed that they should be reclassified as genus *Homo*.

10

By 2030 less than ten percent of Africa's remaining forest is likely to remain undisturbed. The picture from south-east Asia is also disturbing: by 2030 there will be almost no habitat that could be described as 'relatively undisturbed'. The total number of orangutans (*Pongo pygmaeus*) in the region is unknown, but the species is at 'extremely high risk' of extinction in Sumatra, where a population put at 6,000 three years ago has been falling by 1,000 a year. It is also endangered in Borneo.

11

'We cannot just put up fences to try and separate the apes from people,' says one official. 'Great apes play a key role in maintaining the health and diversity of tropical forests which people depend on. They disperse seeds throughout the forests, for example, and create light gaps in the forest canopy which allow seedlings to grow and replenish the forest ecosystem.'

12

It remains to be seen whether the great apes will fare any better than the dodo, or whether they will soon only survive in 2005 as sad reminders of our inhumanity. Time, which is fast running out, will tell.

A Another official has said: 'It's basic arithmetic: the multiplication of threats to the great apes, the division of their habitats, the subtraction of overall ape numbers.' To get the sums right, he added, would take the combined efforts of two UN agencies, four wildlife conventions and eighteen non-governmental organisations to raise awareness, funds and 'our conservation game to stop the great apes becoming history'.

B The UN first sounded an alarm about the rapidly dwindling numbers of great apes in 2001 and appealed for funds. But by last year, researchers on the ground had begun to reveal an even more ominous pattern of loss. They found that ape numbers in Africa had been slashed by logging, hunting and disease.

C 'The clock is standing at one minute to midnight for the great apes, animals that share more than 96% of their DNA with humans,' said Klaus Topfer, the head of the UN environment programme. 'If we lose any great ape species, we will be destroying a bridge to our own origins, and with it part of our own humanity.' He called the sum required 'the bare minimum we need, the equivalent of providing a dying man with bread and water'.

D To survive and breed, the great apes need undisturbed forest. But such earthly edens are becoming increasingly scarce. Logging, slash and burn agriculture and the ever-increasing pressure by human populations are taking their toll, and unfortunately, political instability and war have also had a devastating effect.

E UN agencies, conservation organisations, donor countries and officials from twenty-three African and south-east Asian nations have been meeting in Paris to work on survival strategies. Researchers have begun to use European satellite studies to measure forest destruction, and Unesco officials are working to improve law enforcement in African national parks.

F It is hoped that similar fund-raising activities will also prove effective in this case. Since the funds required have not been allocated by the UN as yet, it remains to be seen exactly how much will have to be supplied by private means. But it is likely to be a significant amount.

G In one population studied, researchers knew of 140 gorillas. After an outbreak of the Ebola virus, they could only find seven alive. 'The stark truth is that if we do not act decisively, our children may live in a world without wild apes,' they reported.

PAPER 1 Reading
PAPER 2 Writing
PAPER 3 Use of English
PAPER 4 Listening
PAPER 5 Speaking

Part 1
Part 2
Part 3
Part 4

You are going to read a newspaper article. For questions **13–19**, choose the answer (**A, B, C** or **D**) which you think fits best according to the text.

Mark your answers **on the separate answer sheet**.

The Land under the Sea

Underwater maps reveal hidden history

Ten thousand years ago, as the last ice age drew to a close, sea levels around the world were far lower than they are today. Much of the land under the North Sea and the English Channel was part of a huge region of forests and grassy plains, where herds of horses and reindeer roamed free and people lived in villages by the lakes and rivers. Then the climate gradually became warmer (a phenomenon certainly not confined to our own age!) and the water trapped in glaciers and ice caps was released. This ancient land was submerged in the resulting deluge and all that remains to tell us that it was once lush and verdant – and inhabited – is the occasional stone tool, harpoon or mammoth tusk brought up from the sea bed by fishing boats.

Now the development of advanced sonar technology, known as bathymetry, is making it possible to study this flooded landscape in extraordinary detail. A special echo sounder is fixed to the bottom of a survey vessel, and it makes wide sweeps across the sea bed. While previous devices have only been able to produce two-dimensional images, bathymetry makes use of computers, satellite positioning devices and special software to create accurate and remarkably detailed maps. For the first time an ancient river bed leaps out of the three-dimensional image, complete with rocky ledges rising up from the bottom of the valley. The sites of pre-historic settlements can now be pinpointed, and it is also possible to see in stunning detail the sunken shipwrecks that litter this part of the sea bed.

According to archaeologist Dr Linda Andrews, this technological development is of huge significance. 'We now have the ability to map the sea bed of the Channel and the North Sea as accurately as we can map dry land,' she says. She is, however, scathing about the scale of government funding for such projects. 'We have better images of Mars and Venus than of two-thirds of our own planet! In view of the fact that Britain is a maritime nation, and the sea has had such a massive influence on us, it's an absolute scandal that we know so little about the area just off our shores!'

Once bathymetric techniques have identified sites where people might have built their homes and villages, such as sheltered bays, cliffs with caves and the shores of freshwater lakes, divers could be sent down to investigate further. Robot submarines could also be used, and researchers hope they will find stone tools and wood from houses (which survives far longer in water than on dry land) as proof of human activity. The idea of Britain as a natural island kingdom will be challenged by these findings: Britain has been inhabited for about 500,000 years, and for much of this time it has been linked on and off to continental Europe. It remains to be seen how far this new awareness is taken on board among our 'island' people.

In fact, the use of bathymetry scanners will not be limited to the study of lost landscapes and ancient settlements. It will also be vital in finding shipwrecks. Records show that there are about 44,000 shipwrecks off the shores of Britain, but there is good reason to believe that the real figure is much higher. In addition, commercial applications are a real possibility. Aggregates for the construction industry are becoming increasingly expensive, and bathymetry scanners could be used to identify suitable sites for quarrying this material. However, mapping the sea bed will also identify places where rare plants and shellfish have their homes. Government legislation may prevent digging at such sites, either to extract material for a profit or to make the water deeper: there are plans to dredge parts of the English Channel to provide deeper waterways for massive container ships.

13 We are told that the area now under the sea

    A was not previously thought to have been populated.

    B was created by the last Ice Age.

    C has yielded some archaeological artefacts.

    D was flooded, drowning the inhabitants.

14 How does the new sonar technology work?

    A It has an echo sounder at the bottom of the sea.

    B It produces two-dimensional images of the sea floor.

    C It makes use of various devices.

    D It uses computers to locate pre-historic sites.

15 What is the most important aspect of the new scanning technique?

    A It can pinpoint the location of shipwrecks under the sea.

    B It is able to follow the course of ancient rivers.

    C It can measure the depth of the sea bed with accuracy.

    D It reveals important details of underwater topography.

16 How does Dr Andrews feel about the lack of accurate maps of the waters around Britain?

    A outraged

    B resigned

    C astonished

    D amused

17 The writer suggests that a better understanding of the settlements on the sea bed may

    A inspire more young people to take up archaeology.

    B modify the attitudes of the British to their country's history.

    C provide confirmation about the dangers of global warming.

    D alter the perception other countries have about Britain.

18 Quarrying is mentioned to show that

    A there will be little difficulty obtaining funds for research.

    B underwater research should be completed as soon as possible.

    C damage to the sea bed has not been recorded accurately so far.

    D the project may have practical benefits for industry.

19 The use of bathymetry scanners may help to

    A preserve the marine environment.

    B promote dredging in the English Channel.

    C identify new species of plants and animals.

    D obtain approval to look for shipwrecks.

You are going to read a newspaper article in which people talk about their experiences at job interviews. For questions **20–34**, choose from the people (**A–F**). When more than one answer is required, these may be given in any order.

Mark your answers **on the separate answer sheet**.

Which person mentions the following?

establishing how the interview will be conducted	**20** ....
the importance of keeping to the point	**21** ....
revealing what motivates you	**22** .... **23** ....
awareness of body language	**24** ....
sources of information about your prospective employer	**25** ....
dressing appropriately	**26** ....
taking responsibility for past errors	**27** ....
appearing to have rehearsed responses	**28** ....
preparing inquiries to put to a prospective employer	**29** ....
foreseeing the consequences of feeling apprehensive	**30** ....
an abrupt ending to an interview	**31** ....
indicating that you view the interview as a transaction	**32** ....
a relaxed atmosphere in the workplace	**33** ....
advantages in being honest about your failings	**34** ....

Tell us Something about Yourself

Being interviewed for a job can be a stressful experience. We asked six people what they learnt from being in that situation.

A My first interview for a job taught me a great deal. I was applying for the position of junior account executive in an advertising company, which involves dealing with clients on a face-to-face basis. It follows that you have to be good at interpersonal skills, and unfortunately, that's not the impression I gave. Like a lot of people, I tend to babble when I'm nervous. The interviewer began by asking me to say something about myself, and I started talking about my hobbies. But I got carried away and went off at a tangent, which made a bad impression. The other lesson I learnt was that if you are asked what your weaknesses are, you really shouldn't be evasive. You could mention a weakness that can also be a strength. For example, being pedantic is not always a bad thing in certain circumstances, and you should explain how you cope with that weakness, but you have to say something.

B In my present job I have to interview applicants, and I can offer a few general tips. Firstly, a candidate should not learn a speech off by heart; you will come across as insincere, as if you have practised everything in front of a mirror. Secondly, it is crucial to understand what the interviewer wants you to talk about. For instance, an interviewer might ask about a situation where your supervisor or manager had a problem with your work. Now, what the interviewer is really after is to see how you react to criticism, and the best thing is to say that you tried to learn from this. Finally, don't try to conceal your real character. When I was interviewed for a job many years ago, the interviewer asked me at the end of our talk if I had any questions. I was very keen to get the job, so I asked what opportunities there were for promotion if I were hired. I wondered if perhaps I had been too direct, but I later discovered that employers like you to seem eager, and I think they were impressed by my enthusiasm and ambition.

C One good way to prepare for an interview is to find out as much as you can about the company you have applied to from its website and promotional material. When you are asked if you have any questions, you can show that you have done this preparatory work, which will impress the interviewer. I also think a lot of candidates are too defensive in interviews. It's not enough just to avoid giving the 'wrong' answers; you should also actively try to make a good impression. Make it clear that the interview is a two-way process: after all, you want to be sure the company is the right place for you. It's acceptable to take the opportunity, when one is offered, to interview the interviewer! One way to do this is to ask him or her some penetrating questions such as why he or she has stayed with the company for so long. Some people might think such a question is arrogant, so size up the interviewer first and decide whether it would be an appropriate thing to ask.

D I remember one interview I attended with a company that makes ice cream and other dairy products. I didn't know much about the company, and it was brought home to me that I should have found out some basic facts. I turned up in a smart business suit and tie, only to find that my prospective employers were in jeans! They believed in being casual: no private offices, everyone ate in the same canteen, people all used first names with each other etc. I realised I should have done more research. Needless to say, I didn't get the job. On another occasion, at the end of an interview, I was asked if I had anything to say. I was so relieved that the interview was over that I just smiled and blurted out: 'No thanks!' I later realised this was a mistake. A candidate should decide in advance on at least ten things to ask the interviewer: it's not necessary to ask more than two or three questions, but you need to have some in reserve in case the question you wanted to ask is answered in the course of the interview.

E Preparation is of extreme importance; things like finding out what form the interview will have. Will there be any sort of written component, for instance, and will you be talking to one person or a panel? And of course, you need to prepare answers to those awkward questions designed to find out more about your character. For example, you might be asked about your most important achievement so far; don't answer this in a way that makes you seem swollen-headed or complacent as this will suggest that you don't learn easily. Actually, it's not so much what people say that makes them seem arrogant as the way they sit, how they hold their heads, whether they meet the interviewer's eye, so bear that in mind. Another question interviewers sometimes ask, to find out how well you work in a team, is about mistakes you have made. You should have an example ready and admit that you were at fault, otherwise it looks as though you are the kind of person who shifts the blame onto others. But you should also show that you learnt from the mistake and wouldn't make it again.

F Being nervous can make you forget things, so always take detailed notes with you to an interview, even about the simplest things – this will help you feel less nervous. I also think you have to strike the right balance between being too arrogant and too self-effacing. For example, if you are asked where you see yourself in five years' time, don't be diffident about showing that you are ambitious. You could even say you'd like to be doing the interviewer's job! Show that your ambition is the force that drives you – employers are happy to see this characteristic because it also suggests you will work hard. Take every opportunity to reinforce the impression that you are eager; one way is by asking questions about the job. This suggests that you will take it seriously. You could also ask what made the last person to fill the position you have applied for successful, or what you could accomplish in the job that would satisfy the interviewer. Naturally, the answers to questions like this are valuable in themselves, but frankly, the main reason for asking is to ensure you make the right impression.

You **must** answer this question. Write your answer in **180–220** words in an appropriate style.

1   You are the president of the student association at the college where you are studying. The principal of the college is planning an orientation weekend for new students at the beginning of the next academic year. She has asked you to come up with some ideas for the weekend, and you have invited students to send you their suggestions.

Read the principal's memo and the notes you have made on it. You should also read the suggestions you have received from other students, with your notes. Then, using all the information, write your proposal.

Memo

To: The President of the Student Association
From: The Principal
Re: Orientation Weekend

We have decided that the following events should be part of an orientation weekend for new students:

Saturday morning? →
* a talk on college regulations

Saturday early afternoon? →
* an introduction to using the library

Sunday morning? →
* an introduction to using the computer room

I'd welcome your suggestion for a timetable which would incorporate these and more informal events over the weekend.

Alison Watson, Principal

Show new students Sports Hall – late Saturday afternoon? Disco in evening? →

What about sports? Shouldn't new students be told about this side of college life?

Local volunteer groups and charities that students might want to become involved in?

Sunday afternoon, information stands of all college clubs in Main Hall? →

Introduction to student societies such as the Drama Club?

Now write your **proposal**.

Write an answer to **one** of the questions **2–5** in this part. Write your answer in **220–260** words in an appropriate style.

2 You read the following notice in a history magazine:

> History becomes fascinating when it is related to personal experience. Write an article about a situation when you found the past of your region or country suddenly became relevant to you because of a personal or direct experience.

Write your **article**.

3 A friend of yours has seen the advertisement below. Your friend would like to apply for the job and has asked you to write a character reference.

Hands Across the Sea – Regional Organiser

Hands Across the Sea is an organisation that arranges student exchange programmes between Britain and the rest of Europe. We need a regional organiser for our Northern England and Scotland office. The successful applicant will have relevant business skills, experience in marketing and sales and the ability to work in a team.

Write your **character reference**, explaining why your friend would be suitable for the position.

4 You have seen the following advertisement in a magazine on education:

Further Education

Every country needs well educated citizens, but a lot of youngsters still leave school as soon as they can. What are the benefits of further education? Why do many young people fail to appreciate these benefits? What could be done to motivate more youngsters to go on to college?

Send us your ideas: the writer of the best entry will win a laptop!

Write your **competition entry**.

5 Answer **one** of the following two questions based on your reading of **one** of the set books.

Either

5(a) Your teacher has asked you to write an essay on the importance of truth in the novel you have been reading. Using two characters, examine the role that truth, or the lack of it, plays in the story.

Write your **essay**.

Or

5(b) You are a student attending a college for the performing arts. Your tutor has asked you to create the opening scene for a film adaptation of a novel. He/She has asked you to examine the possibility of a film whose first scene is from the beginning or the middle of the book. You must write a report, discussing these possibilities in relation to the book you have read, and then say which first scene you would recommend and why.

Write your **report**.

For questions **1–12**, read the text below and decide which answer (**A, B, C** or **D**) best fits each gap. There is an example at the beginning (**0**).

Mark your answers **on the separate answer sheet**.

Example:

0	**A** apart	**B** even	**C** only	**D** alone

0	A	B	C	D
	—	—	—	▬

Mountain Rescue

Last year over 200 climbers were rescued from the mountains of Scotland (**0**) ...... by local rescue teams, who go out in all weathers to do whatever they can to help when disaster (**1**) .... These people are volunteers, giving their time and energy freely and, on (**2**) ...... , putting themselves in danger. They will risk life and (**3**) ...... in an emergency when they are (**4**) ...... on to rescue foolhardy or unlucky climbers.

A whole (**5**) ...... of things can go wrong up in the mountains. A storm can (**6**) ...... up without warning, reducing visibility to virtually zero. Then only the most experienced mountaineer could find their way back down to safety. And it is easy to come to grief, breaking a leg – or worse. Many climbers owe a huge (**7**) ...... of gratitude to the rescue teams!

While rescue teams work for no pay, there are considerable costs (**8**) ...... in maintaining an efficient service. Equipment such as ropes and stretchers is of (**9**) ...... importance, as are vehicles and radio communications devices. (**10**) ...... some of the costs are borne by the government, the rescue teams couldn't operate without donations from the public. Fortunately, fundraising for a good (**11**) ...... like this is not difficult; anyone who has ever been up in the mountains will gladly (**12**) ...... a contribution.

1	**A** hits	**B** rises	**C** strikes	**D** arrives
2	**A** situation	**B** event	**C** moment	**D** occasion
3	**A** limb	**B** blood	**C** bone	**D** flesh
4	**A** brought	**B** called	**C** summoned	**D** beckoned
5	**A** scope	**B** extent	**C** range	**D** scale
6	**A** brew	**B** arise	**C** whip	**D** lash
7	**A** recognition	**B** liability	**C** debt	**D** obligation
8	**A** implied	**B** involved	**C** featured	**D** connected
9	**A** lively	**B** vibrant	**C** essential	**D** vital
10	**A** Even	**B** Despite	**C** Though	**D** However
11	**A** effect	**B** cause	**C** reason	**D** exploit
12	**A** make	**B** take	**C** do	**D** hand

PAPER 1 Reading

PAPER 2 Writing

PAPER 3 Use of English ▸ Part 1

Part 2

Part 3

Part 4

Part 5

PAPER 4 Listening

PAPER 5 Speaking

For questions **13–27**, read the text below and think of the word which best fits each gap. Use only **one** word in each gap. There is an example at the beginning (**0**).

Write your answers **IN CAPITAL LETTERS on the separate answer sheet**.

Example:

0	*REST*	0

The Ubiquitous Shopping Mall

It is a trend which started in the United States and is rapidly spreading to the (**0**) .... of the developed world. Many towns and cities do not really have a centre (**13**) .... more. Instead, a shopping mall somewhere (**14**) .... the outskirts serves some of the functions of an urban centre. Here, shops and banks are all crowded together, (**15**) .... is very convenient, especially (**16**) .... those people who use a car. You can park in the basement car park, (**17**) .... all your shopping inside the mall, and then load up the car and drive home. You don't even (**18**) .... to go outside, so it doesn't matter what the weather's (**19**) ....

So (**20**) .... should anyone possibly object to the growing number of shopping malls springing up around our cities? (**21**) .... fact, many people do object, (**22**) .... only urban planners and politicians, but environmentalists as well. (**23**) .... most shops are concentrated in malls, it leaves city and town centres deserted and (**24**) .... any life of their own. Furthermore, malls do not take into (**25**) .... people without cars, who simply can't get to them easily. Ultimately, perhaps, the most damaging criticism is that malls are virtually identical. (**26**) .... a result, our towns and cities are losing (**27**) .... character, which has been created over centuries.

For questions **28–37**, read the text below. Use the word given in capitals at the end of some of the lines to form a word that fits in the gap **in the same line**. There is an example at the beginning (**0**).

Write your answers **IN CAPITAL LETTERS on the separate answer sheet.**

Example:

0	*AFFECTIONATELY*	0

Blogging and the media

The growing number of weblogs – or blogs, as they
are (**0**) .... known – on the Internet has   **AFFECTION**
become a cause for concern among mainstream media
organisations. Within a few years, blogs have developed
from personal musings on (**28**) .... events   **DAY**
to full-blown critical commentaries which are often
well-informed and (**29**) .... expressed.   **ELOQUENCE**
With an estimated fifty-two million bloggers writing
on almost every (**30**) .... subject each day,   **CONCEIVE**
corporate media can no longer ignore them or treat
them with (**31**) .... The ubiquity of blogs   **RESPECT**
means that they are increasingly (**32**) .... ,   **INFLUENCE**
as can be seen in the number of news stories that have
been (**33**) .... or called into question by   **CREDIT**
bloggers in recent years.

For bloggers have a freedom unavailable to mainstream
journalists. They bypass both editor and publisher, who
by their very presence (**34**) .... distort   **INEVITABLE**
stories by 'tailoring' them to suit their own ends. The
material on blogs is raw, (**35**) .... by editors,   **MODIFY**
and often harsh and direct in its criticism of the way
news is reported by the media. The advantages of this
for the reading public are obvious. Bloggers act as a
kind of media watchdog, able to check facts and verify
or (**36**) .... information in a way that   **PROOF**
journalists are often unable to, and this is shaking
mainstream media out of its (**37**) ....   **COMPLACENT**

For questions **38–42**, think of one word only which can be used appropriately in all three sentences. Here is an example (**0**).

Example:

0
- We will do all the work, but they will .... all the credit, as usual!
- She will .... offence if you tell her that hairstyle doesn't suit her.
- They threatened to .... David to court unless he stopped playing his drums all night.

0	*TAKE*	0

Write **only** the missing word **IN CAPITAL LETTERS on the separate answer sheet.**

38
- Let me give you a .... outline of our plan to develop the business.
- Lucy arrived at the party with a .... smile on her face, accompanied by her new boyfriend.
- The robbery took place in .... daylight, so it's amazing no one saw anything.

39
- Would you .... the baby for me while I go to the shops?
- I don't .... doing the washing up, but I object to drying the dishes as well!
- It's nothing to do with you, so why don't you .... your own business?

40
- The organisation has a strict .... of practice, and employees must make sure they adhere to it.
- I would like to make a phone call, but I don't know the international .... for Spain.
- I couldn't read the message because it was written in some kind of ....

41
- When she entered the competition, Amy never expected to .... off with the first prize.
- They returned home early only to .... in on thieves stealing their silver!
- If you don't tell me what's going on, I'll .... out the door and never come back!

42
- I think you need a different .... to deal with the problem.
- The .... to the city from the north affords the best views of the river.
- They decided that a direct .... was the best way to achieve results.

PAPER 1 Reading

PAPER 2 Writing

PAPER 3 Use of English ▶

PAPER 4 Listening

PAPER 5 Speaking

Part 1
Part 2
Part 3
Part 4
Part 5

For questions **43–50**, complete the second sentence so that it has a similar meaning to the first sentence, using the word given. **Do not change the word given.** You must use between **three** and **six** words, including the word given. Here is an example (**0**).

Example:

0   Jane regretted speaking so rudely to the old lady.
MORE
Jane .... politely to the old lady.

| 0 | *WISHED SHE HAD SPOKEN MORE* | 0 |

Write the missing words **IN CAPITAL LETTERS on the separate answer sheet.**

---

43   'Mr Brown, a holiday would do you good,' said Dr Mansley.
FROM
'Mr Brown, you .... a holiday,' said Dr Mansley.

44   It just isn't possible for me to take you to the party tonight.
QUESTION
It .... for me to take you to the party tonight.

45   They were never aware at any moment that something was wrong.
TIME
At .... that something was wrong.

46   'The gearbox of your car needs fixing,' Keith told Claire.
POINTED
Keith .... the gearbox of her car needed fixing.

47   If Gary hadn't had that accident, he would have become a professional football player.
FOR
If it .... , Gary would have become a professional football player.

48   We get on very well with Laura's parents.
TERMS
We .... Laura's parents.

49   I don't believe you've burned the dinner again!
HAVE
You .... again!

50   Someone snatched Sue's bag at the concert.
HAD
Sue .... at the concert.

You will hear three different extracts. For questions **1–6**, choose the answer (**A**, **B** or **C**) which fits best according to what you hear. There are two questions for each extract.

Extract One

You hear part of a radio programme in which a man is being interviewed about an unusual sport.

1 According to Chris, cheese rolling takes place
   A at only one venue in the world.
   B on muddy ground.
   C once a year.

        1

2 Which statement best sums up how Chris feels about cheese rolling?
   A It's too dangerous.
   B It's worth the risks.
   C It requires training.

        2

Extract Two

You hear a father and daughter discussing something that the daughter wants to buy.

3 Sophie's father doesn't want to buy her a mobile phone
   A on moral grounds.
   B because of the cost.
   C for health reasons.

        3

4 By the end of the conversation,
   A Sophie's father has agreed to consider the matter.
   B Sophie seems to have accepted her father's argument.
   C Sophie's father has given in to his daughter's wishes.

        4

Extract Three

You hear two people talking about yawning.

5 According to the woman, until recently, yawning was thought to
   A be simply a sign that we were tired.
   B help us breathe more deeply.
   C promote alertness.

        5

6 Research suggests that contagious yawning is a way of
   A maintaining alertness in the group.
   B expressing understanding in the group.
   C communicating with one another.

        6

You will hear an astrobiologist talking about her work. For questions **7–14**, complete the sentences.

What is Astrobiology?

It could be claimed that the science of astrobiology

has no | | **7** |

However, astrobiologists are also concerned with how life evolved

| | **8** |

There are some popular misconceptions about what

| | **9** | might look like.

For much of the Earth's history, single-celled | | **10** |

were the only life forms in existence.

Multi-cellular life evolved during the | | **11** |

known as the Cambrian.

Then, about | | **12** | years ago,

human-like creatures evolved.

Life on other planets will probably be | | **13** |

life on Earth.

Human beings might not have evolved if | | **14** |

had not become extinct.

You will hear part of a radio interview with Pete Birtwhistle, a playwright. For questions **15–20**, choose the answer (**A**, **B**, **C** or **D**) which fits best according to what you hear.

15 What was Pete's attitude to the theatre before he started writing?
  A He felt it had little relevance to his life.
  B He didn't feel qualified to judge it.
  C He thought it would be boring to watch a play.
  D He preferred comedies to tragedies.

16 How did he feel about leaving his previous job?
  A He felt very relieved.
  B He was anxious about his health.
  C He worried how others would see him.
  D He was very depressed.

17 What was the most difficult aspect of writing his first play?
  A disciplining himself to write every day
  B coming up with a suitable story
  C allowing the characters to develop
  D finding an appropriate ending

18 What is the biggest impact that writing has had on Pete's life?
  A It has made people respect him more.
  B It has enabled him to express himself.
  C It has opened up new professional opportunities.
  D It has allowed him to appreciate other plays.

19 How does Pete choose the theme of a new play?
  A He looks around for a challenging theme.
  B He looks for a subject that is in the news.
  C He looks for a theme that he understands.
  D He thinks about issues that affect society.

20 How does Pete feel about writing for films?
  A enthusiastic
  B worried
  C cautious
  D intimidated

PAPER 1 Reading

PAPER 2 Writing

PAPER 3 Use of English

PAPER 4 Listening
    Part 1
    Part 2
PAPER 5 Speaking
    Part 3
    Part 4

You will hear five short extracts in which people talk about tracing their ancestors.

While you listen you must complete both tasks.

Task One

For questions **21–25**, choose from the list **A–H** what each speaker says about the discoveries he or she made.

A One of my ancestors did a great deal of humanitarian work.

B A relative ran away from home when he was young.

C I am descended from immigrants.

D A family tradition turned out not to be true.

E At one time the family was wealthy.

F My great-grandmother came from a rich family.

G A relative emigrated to Australia.

H My great-great-grandfather changed his name.

Speaker 1		21
Speaker 2		22
Speaker 3		23
Speaker 4		24
Speaker 5		25

Task Two

For questions **26–30**, choose from the list **A–H** the emotion aroused in each speaker by these discoveries.

A I hate the thought of their suffering.

B Learning the truth caused considerable bitterness.

C I have become more curious about the story.

D The whole thing made us feel quite embarrassed.

E I was delighted to make contact with my relatives.

F The story saddened me.

G I am very proud of my ancestor.

H I was disappointed at first.

Speaker 1		26
Speaker 2		27
Speaker 3		28
Speaker 4		29
Speaker 5		30

Part 1 (3 minutes)

The examiner will ask you a few questions about yourself and then ask you to talk to your partner. For example, the examiner may ask you:

- When and how did you start learning English?
- In what ways is knowing a foreign language useful to you now?
- How do you expect language skills to be important to you in the future?

Part 2 (4 minutes)

You will each be asked to talk on your own for a minute without interruption. You will each be given a set of three photographs in turn to talk about. After your partner has finished speaking, you will be asked a brief question connected with your partner's photographs. You will have thirty seconds to answer.

Groups (compare, contrast and speculate)

Turn to pictures 1–3 on page **202**, which show people in groups.

Candidate A, compare and contrast two of these pictures. What are the advantages of doing these activities in a group? What might be the negative aspects of these activities?

Candidate B, in which situations do you cooperate with others as part of a group?

Experience (compare, contrast and speculate)

Turn to pictures 1–3 on page **203**, which show people who have gained experience.

Candidate B, compare and contrast two of these pictures, saying what sort of experience you imagine the people have gained and what might be the difficulties of gaining this experience.

Candidate A, can you think of a situation where you learnt something by going through a difficult experience?

Part 3 (4 minutes)

Time management (discuss, evaluate and select)

Turn to the pictures on page **204**, which show the need for time management.

Talk to each other about how these problems could be helped by better time management, and then decide which situation would benefit most and which would benefit least from better time management.

Part 4 (4 minutes)

The examiner will encourage you to develop the topic of your discussion in Part 3 by asking questions such as:

- Do you think it is a problem if someone is often late for appointments and meetings? Why (not)?
- Which aspects of modern life where time is managed badly do you find most annoying?
- Does modern life make us too anxious about punctuality? Why (not)?
- When was the last time you were late, and what caused you to be late?

PAPER 1	Reading	▶	Part 1
PAPER 2	Writing		Part 2
PAPER 3	Use of English		Part 3
PAPER 4	Listening		Part 4
PAPER 5	Speaking		

You are going to read three extracts which are all concerned in some way with the law. For questions **1–6**, choose the answer (**A, B, C** or **D**) which you think fits best according to the text.

Mark your answers **on the separate answer sheet**.

Acting and the Law

Barrister Michaela Duncan has returned to the stage after an absence of twenty-five years. No longer young enough to play ingénue roles, as she herself admits, what induced her to give up the law in order to play the relatively unglamorous parts available to older women? 'All my life I've been stage struck,' she laughs. 'When I was at school, I used to sneak off to matinées instead of doing my homework, and I enrolled in a drama school when I was eighteen.'

Duncan made her first professional stage appearance shortly afterwards. She went on to enjoy a considerable measure of success, yet, rather unusually, she also felt she was not being stretched intellectually. 'My father was a lawyer, and I thought the law would probably suit me, too,' she says. She put herself through university, and her acting career seemed to be over. In the years that followed, she proved herself as a barrister, eventually becoming a partner in a prestigious law firm. 'But I always maintained my stage contacts,' she remembers.

Then one day, she was asked for advice in a case involving Equity, the actors' union. 'Naturally, I was happy to help. I had worked as an actor, and I knew what it was like to struggle, to be unemployed. It was while I was working on the case that it suddenly struck me: I wanted to return to the stage! It's where I belong. It wasn't an easy decision to make, but at that point of my life, it was the right thing to do.'

1   Michaela initially abandoned her acting career as a result of
   A   pressure from her father to study law.
   B   her desire to do something more challenging.
   C   her frustration at having to play unglamorous parts.
   D   the lack of variety in the roles she was offered.

2   Concerning her decision to return to the stage, she says
   A   overall, she has no regrets.
   B   it was an easy one to make.
   C   she feels uncertain about it.
   D   she wishes she'd never left.

Magna Carta

Magna Carta, signed by King John of England in 1215, laid the foundation upon which Common Law was built, influenced the drawing up of the American Constitution, the creation of the Bill of Rights, and many other legal and political documents throughout the western world. It is often cited or quoted in political addresses and human rights campaigns, and is seen as a symbol of the principles of modern western civilisation.

In fact, in its original form Magna Carta, or Great Charter, represented little more than a bargaining tool in King John's struggle with his rebellious barons. They wanted to wrest some of his power from him, and forced him to sign the paper in order to retain his crown. Their intentions were in reality no nobler than the king's, neither side paying much attention to its content, so it is amazing that this paper has subsequently had such far-reaching effects on the judicial systems of the civilised world.

Magna Carta owes its fame and reputation to a relatively small number of its 63 chapters. In chapter 39, it confirmed the rights of the common man, and rendered the king, for the first time in British history, subject to the law of the land, in the following statement: 'No free man shall be arrested or imprisoned ... or outlawed or exiled or any way victimized, neither will we attack him or send anyone to attack him, except by the lawful judgement of his peers or by the law of the land.' This section formed the basis of the Habeas Corpus Act of 1679, which forbade the imprisonment of citizens without just cause, and perhaps explains why Magna Carta is still revered as a fundamental influence on many judicial systems today.

Critics of Magna Carta's contribution to democracy abound, and not without reason, when you consider the motives behind its creation. Yet, however unwittingly, those rebellious barons of the thirteenth century set the ball rolling in the battle for human rights, a battle which is being fought to this day.

3   According to the writer, Magna Carta
   A   was regarded as an important document in the thirteenth century.
   B   bestowed power on the common people.
   C   was originally used to manipulate the King of England.
   D   is known today as a symbol of righteousness throughout the world.

4   The writer suggests that Magna Carta
   A   effectively led to the destruction of the monarchy.
   B   is the object of more respect than it deserves in political circles.
   C   is responsible for causing a lot of the wars in the world.
   D   gained a significance that was unintended by its creators.

Wanted: Commercial Litigation Secretary

- Are you a trained legal secretary looking for a change of scene?
- Are you bored with the routine of your present position, and searching for something more challenging – and with a more rewarding salary?
- Do you want to develop your skills and broaden your experience?

Then you could be the person for us!

We are looking to employ a legal secretary, preferably with a background in either commercial law or litigation, who is interested in expanding his/her activities. Apart from carrying out general secretarial duties, the successful applicant will be assigned to one of the partners in the Litigation Arbitration Team as his/her personal assistant, and will be responsible for compiling detailed information from a variety of sources. He/She will also be required to liaise with other members of the team, as well as clients.

The ideal candidate will be self-motivated and proactive, and show initiative in solving problems. He/She will be organised and meticulous in his/her work, and have excellent communication skills. The job is challenging and varied, so we are looking for someone who is versatile and confident. The successful candidate will occasionally be required to handle sensitive documents, so he/she must be trustworthy, as confidentiality is vital.

The successful candidate will benefit from a generous salary, an excellent benefits package and a stimulating working environment, with colleagues who are dedicated to what they do.

Apply online to: Greaves, Barker, Coles and Associates

---

5 According to the advertisement, which applicant is least likely to get the job?
- **A** a dynamic and efficient young person with secretarial skills, but no experience in litigation
- **B** an experienced legal secretary who has worked in litigation for a number of years
- **C** a shy young person who has worked as a secretary in a law firm for three months
- **D** an ambitious person who has worked for a firm specialising in company law, and would like more challenge

6 Above all, the successful applicant must be
- **A** ambitious.
- **B** trustworthy.
- **C** experienced.
- **D** confident.

PAPER 1 Reading ▸
PAPER 2 Writing
PAPER 3 Use of English
PAPER 4 Listening
PAPER 5 Speaking

Part 1
Part 2
Part 3
Part 4

You are going to read a newspaper article. Six paragraphs have been removed from the article. Choose from the paragraphs **A–G** the one which fits each gap (**7–12**). There is one extra paragraph which you do not need to use.

Mark your answers **on the separate answer sheet**.

Hybrid Homes

New building technologies are making nearly zero-energy houses a real possibility

Imagine a community for the deeply green. Walls nineteen inches thick keep temperatures comfortable year-round. Windows are triple-glazed. A wind-driven ventilation system feeds fresh air into each house – and grabs the heat from stale outgoing air. Outsize conservatories face south to trap the light and warmth of the sun. Solar panels provide enough power to run electric cars. The architecture is modish, and even the most modest apartment has its own garden.

7

In Europe and the United States buildings guzzle about forty percent of all energy – about ten percent more than transport – and create the same proportion of carbon dioxide emissions. BedZED and other initiatives show that trimming excess energy consumption needn't be difficult or even high tech – just a matter of intelligent design.

8

It's no wonder such ideas are gaining admirers. Over the past two years, BedZED has attracted thousands of visitors from as far away as India and China, and more zero-energy communities are under construction elsewhere in Britain as well as in the United States.

9

Major momentum for these changes has come from Europe, where governments are increasingly worried by threats to energy supplies and the need to meet energy-reduction goals agreed to under the Kyoto accords. Many are issuing grants and tax breaks for energy-efficient builders as well as tightening regulations. A European Union directive that takes effect at the end of next year will require house builders, landlords or sellers to show an energy-efficiency certificate setting out how well a building performs.

10

There's growing cooperation in this field between government, scientists and the environmental lobby. At the government-funded Lawrence Berkeley National Laboratory in California, Steve Selkowitz's windows-and-building-technology team has produced such innovations as dimmable windows that can minimise hot sunlight while preserving the view; the windows could save homeowners thousands of dollars a year in air-conditioning costs.

11

It's too early to know whether the public will embrace such measures fully. 'From the marketing point of view, energy efficiency is still a very hard sell,' says David Strong of Britain's Building Research Establishment. Who cares if warmth is leaking out through the roof when heating your home costs a relatively small amount?

12

'The technologies will be able to support each other,' says Thorne Amann. 'Solar panels, appliances, heat-pump water heaters – the synergy will improve the whole building.' And the outlook for world energy supplies.

A Much of the technology involved is not flashy, and could be used much more widely today. Things like triple-glazing windows to add extra insulation, tightening duct systems and using insulated panels in the construction of floors and walls are easy and cost-effective – and could cut the fuel consumption of the world's buildings by twenty percent before the end of the decade. 'You can accomplish a tremendous amount with the technologies that we have already,' says one official working on energy efficiency for the European Commission in Brussels.

B Still, as governments, scientists and builders continue to provide the 'market push' toward energy efficiency, the 'consumer pull' will be stimulated. Each new innovation will push us closer to what one might call the hybrid home, in which energy is conserved through a combination of increasingly efficient appliances and building techniques.

C The US government, too, has been doing its part. Through the Energy Star programme, it has set tough regulations on everything from home construction to major appliances and consumer electronics. 'Energy Star is transforming the market so that energy-efficient technologies become standard practice – and a money maker for companies, too,' says Jennifer Thorne Amann of the American Council for an Energy-Efficient Economy.

D Both of these regions still make every possible attempt to meet energy consumption guidelines as governments around the world attempt to come to grips with the threat of global warming. There seems every likelihood that this project could lead the way – one can only hope that others will follow.

E Even more exciting developments are creeping onto the market. Solar power is becoming more affordable, as are tankless water heaters, composting toilets and biomass heating systems like stoves that burn corn instead of declining resources like wood. In India, Development Alternatives, a New Delhi-based non-profit organisation devoted to sustainable development, has helped supply mini power stations fuelled by weeds and agricultural wastes to villages across the country. And beneath thousands of new houses in Sweden, a system of fluid-filled pipes taps the warmth of the surrounding earth to heat the home.

F This might sound like a high-tech oasis for the super-rich. But it's actually an 84-home development called BedZED on the site of a disused sewage treatment plant in an unfashionable patch of South London. Its residents aren't well-meaning ecology enthusiasts: many are tenants of a housing charity. But they are all at the forefront of a global trend toward reducing energy consumption in the home.

G The key is finding ways to maximise efficiency in the simplest ways possible: the 'ZED' in BedZED stands for 'zero energy'. Whatever little juice the London homes need after taking advantage of their built-in energy savers comes from an on-site power plant fuelled by waste timber. Simple also means cheap; build 5,000 ZEDHomes and the economies of scale mean the cost is no more than that of constructing a normal home: the price of components tumbles as production numbers rise.

PAPER 1 Reading ▶	Part 1
PAPER 2 Writing	Part 2
PAPER 3 Use of English	Part 3
PAPER 4 Listening	Part 4
PAPER 5 Speaking	

You are going to read a magazine article. For questions **13–19**, choose the answer (**A, B, C** or **D**) which you think fits best according to the text.

Mark your answers **on the separate answer sheet**.

Learning to Run

An article published recently in the prestigious scientific journal *Nature* is shedding new light on an important, but hitherto little appreciated, aspect of human evolution. In this article, Professors Dennis Bramble and Daniel Lieberman suggest that the ability to run was a crucial factor in the development of our species. According to the two scientists, humans possess a number of anatomical features that make them surprisingly good runners. 'We are very confident that strong selection for running – which came at the expense of the historical ability to live in trees – was instrumental in the origin of the modern human body form,' says Bramble, a biology professor at the University of Utah.

Traditional thinking up to now has been that the distinctive, upright body form of modern humans has come about as a result of the ability to walk, and that running is simply a by-product of walking. Furthermore, humans have usually been regarded as poor runners compared to such animals as dogs, horses or antelopes. However, this is only true if we consider fast running, or sprinting, over short distances. Even an Olympic athlete can hardly run as fast as a horse can gallop, and can only keep up a top speed for fifteen seconds or so. Horses, antelopes and greyhounds, on the other hand, can run at top speed for several minutes, clearly outperforming us in this respect. But when it comes to long-distance running, humans do astonishingly well. They can maintain a steady pace for miles, and their overall speed compares favourably with that of horses or dogs.

Bramble and Lieberman examined twenty-six anatomical features found in humans. One of the most interesting of these is the nuchal ligament, a band of tissue that extends from a ridge on the base of the skull to the spine. When we run, it is this ligament that prevents our head from pitching back and forth or from side to side. Therefore, we are able to run with steady heads, held high. The nuchal ligament is not found in any other surviving primates, although the fossil record shows that *Homo erectus*, an early human species that walked upright, much as we do, also had one. Then there are our Achilles tendons at the backs of our legs, which connect our calf muscles to our heel bones – and which have nothing to do with walking. When we run, these tendons behave like springs, helping to propel us forward. Furthermore, we have low, wide shoulders, virtually disconnected from our skulls, an anatomical adaptation which allows us to run more efficiently. Add to this our light forearms, which swing out of phase with the movement of our legs to assist balance, and one begins to appreciate the point that Bramble and Lieberman are trying to make.

But what evolutionary advantage is gained from being good long-distance runners? One hypothesis is that this ability may have permitted early humans to obtain food more effectively. 'What these features and fossil facts appear to be telling us is that running evolved in order for our direct ancestors to compete with other carnivores for access to the protein needed to grow the big brains that we enjoy today,' says Lieberman.

Some scientists speculate that early humans may have pursued animals for miles in order to exhaust them before killing them. Running would also have conferred an advantage before weapons were invented: early humans might have been scavengers, eating the meat and marrow left over from a kill by lions or other large predators. They may have been alerted to the existence of a freshly-killed carcass by vultures, and the faster they got to the scene of the kill, the better.

'Research on the history of human locomotion has traditionally been contentious,' says Lieberman. 'At the very least, I hope this theory will make many people have second thoughts about how humans learned to run and walk and why we are built the way we are.'

13 According to the text, the human ability to run

    A was only recently described in a scientific journal.

    B is now regarded as more important than the ability to climb trees.

    C played an important part in human evolution.

    D is surprising when we consider evolutionary trends.

14 According to the text, scientists used to believe

    A that the human body owes its form to the ability to walk.

    B the human ability to walk adversely affected the ability to run.

    C that only modern humans could walk upright.

    D that humans can run because they stand upright.

15 According to the text, humans

    A are better runners than most other animals.

    B are not good at running short distances.

    C cannot run at top speed for long distances.

    D compare unfavourably with horses and dogs.

16 It appears that the nuchal ligament

    A is found only in modern primates.

    B is associated with the ability to run.

    C prevents the head from moving.

    D is a unique anatomical feature.

17 The text implies that

    A we do not need calf muscles in order to walk.

    B without shoulders we could not run very fast.

    C the movement of our forearms is out of phase.

    D our Achilles tendons are an adaptation for running.

18 According to the text, early humans

    A killed animals by exhausting them.

    B may have evolved big brains for running.

    C competed with other animals for food.

    D could probably run before they could walk.

19 Professor Lieberman hopes to

    A dispel any remaining doubts about the nature of the human body.

    B prove conclusively that humans did not always walk in an upright position.

    C make people reconsider previously-held ideas about human anatomy.

    D inform people of the real reason why humans are able to run and walk.

PAPER 1 Reading ► Part 1
PAPER 2 Writing   Part 2
PAPER 3 Use of English   Part 3
PAPER 4 Listening   **Part 4**
PAPER 5 Speaking

You are going to read a newspaper article in which people talk about starting up their own business late in life. For questions **20–34**, choose from the people (**A–F**). When more than one answer is required, these may be given in any order.

Mark your answers **on the separate answer sheet**.

In which section of the article are the following mentioned?

the unexpected demands of the business	**20**	
a cautious approach to doing business	**21**	**22** ....
an established network of business contacts	**23**	
a prejudicial assessment of a person's value	**24**	
taking advantage of modern communications	**25**	
realising an ambition	**26**	
the cost of setting up a business	**27**	**28** ....
the confidence that comes with maturity	**29**	
plans to branch out	**30**	
a product that aims to help people fill in official forms	**31**	
the fact that few companies cater for a certain group of people	**32**	
the advantage of employing older people	**33**	
the competitive nature of a business	**34**	

STARTING OVER

*More and more people over fifty
are starting up in business for themselves.
What are their reasons — and why are so
many of them successful?*

A When I was fifty-three, I was made redundant almost literally overnight when the company I worked for was taken over by a multinational. The managing director called me into his office the following Monday and told me I was no longer on the payroll. It was a shock and I felt really depressed. I was also anxious about the future because we still had a mortgage to pay off on our house, and my husband's income couldn't cover our hefty monthly expenses. At the same time, I didn't feel I was ready for retirement, and to be honest, I was infuriated by the arrogance of the company, which appeared to believe I was too old to be useful any longer. So I gave some serious thought to starting up a business of my own. I'm an accountant, and for years I'd been advising friends about finances and helping them sort out their books, so I knew there were plenty of small businesses out there who would welcome the sort of services I could offer. The initial outlay for office equipment was pretty low, all things considered. So I set up as a consultant to people who want to branch out on their own, like me, and I find it extremely rewarding.

B About seven years ago, after being more or less forced to take early retirement, I looked around for an occupation to fill up my days and eventually decided I'd set up a company specialising in all-inclusive trips for retired people to domestic UK resorts. There seemed to be a dearth of companies catering for the over sixties, which is ironic because they're the ones who often have the leisure and the income to take advantage of opportunities for travel. I'd say someone like me has certain advantages when it comes to setting up in business. I spent years running a travel agency and I know a lot of people in the industry. They have been great, offering advice as well as concrete help. At first, there was a lot of work involved and

I had to travel around the country a great deal making new contacts, but now I don't have to be away from home very often at all. I enjoy what I do, especially because I've always worked with people, and without the daily contact I'd go mad!

C Three years ago I decided I'd had enough of being a teacher, so I retired and started a pottery business. Now we've got a fair-sized factory, and we're about to expand into glassware as well. Most of the people who work for me are more or less my generation. I find they tend to be more loyal; they don't rush off if they think they can see a better prospect elsewhere. It's also good for the economy when some of these older workers return to employment. It seems to me that people who start up businesses at my age are realistic: they don't aim to be millionaires, and they are less inclined to take unnecessary risks. So I'd guess that fewer businesses started by older people go bust in the first few years. As for me, I must admit I miss teaching at times, but we now have a few apprentices, and working with them is rather like being a teacher in some ways. Of course, running a business is a responsibility, especially since I know the people who work for me rely on the income from their jobs, but it's also a very stimulating, challenging experience.

D When I left the company I'd been with for twenty-five years, they gave me a rather good retirement package, which meant I had a reasonable amount of cash to invest in my own company. It was something I'd longed to do for years. I've always been a keen gardener, you see, so I started a landscape gardening company. All the physical work involved means I'm fitter than I have been for years! One thing that did surprise me at the start was how much official paperwork I have to deal with. It's exhausting filling in all those forms, but apart from that, I find the work itself rewarding. As for the future, who knows? Obviously, I wouldn't want to be travelling around the country and working outdoors as much when I'm over seventy, although on the other hand, I firmly believe that working has kept me active and alert, so why should I give it up until I really have to?

E My career was in accounting, and I knew that there was shortly going to be a change in the way self-employed people fill in tax returns. So when I was made redundant, I thought it would be a good idea to produce software showing people exactly how to go about it, and that was the first item my company put on the market. With my experience it was relatively easy to come up with the material – I wrote it all myself – and then I got together with a software producer to make the CD-ROMs. My wife's first reaction was that I should try something completely different from what I'd been doing all my working life, but I figured I'd be better off sticking to what I know. Things are going well, although I've deliberately not tried to expand the business – it can be stressful for a boss when a company expands fast, and I prefer to take things easy and enjoy what I do. Of course, there have been some tricky moments, but I can honestly say I've never regretted starting my own firm. I'm sure I wouldn't have had the nerve to do it when I was younger, but I'm very glad I did.

F I was in advertising for almost thirty years, but it's a very cut-throat business, and when we got a new boss he decided to make his mark by sacking quite a few people. It was particularly painful for me because I love advertising; it's a very creative line of work. So once I got my breath back, I decided to start working freelance. It occurred to me that a lot of companies need not only an advertising campaign but also a consultant, an independent expert to give them an honest view of their situation. I do almost all my work from home, using my PC for e-mails and video conferencing, and it's extremely satisfying as well as being financially rewarding. I believe older entrepreneurs like us play a vital though unsung role in the economy because we're not only generating money, we're also saving the country money by not claiming our pensions. Since I started my company, I've come into contact with a fair number of people in a similar position to me – older people who have set up by themselves – and if I have the choice, I prefer to do business with older people. We're so much more reliable!

PAPER 1 Reading

PAPER 2 Writing ▶   Part 1
                        Part 2
PAPER 3 Use of English

PAPER 4 Listening

PAPER 5 Speaking

You **must** answer this question. Write your answer in **180–220** words in an appropriate style.

1   A friend of yours wants to go to Britain to improve his/her English. He/She has sent you an advertisement for a study holiday in Britain, asking you for your opinion about it. Read the advertisement on which you have made some notes. Then write a letter to your friend, giving your views on the suitability of the study holiday he/she is considering and suggesting what further information he/she should request before making a final decision.

KINGLAND SCHOOL STUDY HOLIDAYS IN BRITAIN

Come and learn English in one of the most exciting cities in the world!

Kingland School has many years' experience in organising summer study holidays for students wishing to improve their English and enjoy life in Britain at the same time.

By train?
Exact location?

Located just half an hour from London, Kingland School provides simple but comfortable accommodation for students.

With families?
Or what?

What size?
What level?

Classes are small, with a friendly atmosphere, and students have plenty of time to themselves. And of course, there are numerous recreational facilities in the area!

How much? Class hours per week?

What sort?
Sports?
Cinema?
Music?

For full details, contact us at:
Kingland School

Now write your **letter.** You do not need to write postal addresses.

PAPER 1 Reading

PAPER 2 Writing ▶

PAPER 3 Use of English

PAPER 4 Listening

PAPER 5 Speaking

Part 1
Part 2

Write an answer to **one** of the questions **2–5** in this part. Write your answer in **220–260** words in an appropriate style.

2 You see the following announcement in a magazine called *Education World*:

> ### What sort of secondary education do young people really need?
>
> Is it better to specialise at an early age with a view to becoming an expert in one field, or should young people have as broad an education as possible? What do employers want from someone they hire?
>
> Send us an article expressing your views and the reasoning behind them.

Write your **article**.

3 You have seen the following advertisement in an in-flight magazine:

> ### *Competition*
>
> We are bombarded on all sides by information: from TV and radio, the Internet and mobile phones, newspapers and magazines. Are we in danger of suffering information overload? Is there a danger that people will switch off completely and not want to know anything about the world around them?
>
> Write and tell us your views. We will publish the best entry.

Write your **competition entry**.

4 The tourist board of your country is planning to publish a travel guide aimed at young visitors from abroad. You have been asked to write a short contribution describing the attractions and popular features of your region that young people aged 16–25 might find particularly interesting.

Write your **contribution** for the travel guide.

5 Answer **one** of the following two questions based on your reading of **one** of the set books.

Either

5(a) An online bookstore has announced a competition, and is inviting customers to write a review of a book they have read recently. Reviews must mention aspects of the book which they found attractive and also ones which they feel could have been improved. You have decided to enter the competition, and write about the book you have been reading.

Write your **review**.

Or

5(b) Your teacher has asked you to write an essay proposing an alternative ending to the book you have been reading. You should say if you think there is anything wrong with the ending as it is, and discuss whether you think your alternative ending is preferable. Refer to events in the novel to support your views.

Write your **essay**.

For questions **1–12**, read the text below and decide which answer (**A, B, C** or **D**) best fits each gap. There is an example at the beginning (**0**).

Mark your answers **on the separate answer sheet**.

Example:

0   **A** define   **B** adopt   **C** generate   **D** cause

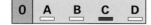

A new look at the Middle Ages

The Institute for Medieval Studies is holding a series of lectures to (**0**) ...... interest in a period of history which is all too often (**1**) .... It is hoped that these lectures will (**2**) ...... some of the misconceptions that (**3**) ...... to this day about the long and eventful span of time between the crowning of Charlemagne and the Renaissance.

It is true that Europe was (**4**) ...... by the plague in the latter part of the fourteenth century, while the terrors of the Inquisition cast a grim shadow over the continent. Living (**5**) ...... for the majority of people were appalling by modern standards, and life (**6**) ...... was low. The peasants suffered under a brutal feudal system and the (**7**) ...... of learning was open only to the clergy and the small minority who were literate.

However, these (**8**) ...... negative aspects of medieval life cannot be properly evaluated unless they are viewed in the broader (**9**) .... The Middle Ages saw the construction of the magnificent cathedrals that grace so many European cities and the (**10**) ...... of a middle class. Many institutions we think of as modern were a(n) (**11**) ...... part of medieval life. Progress was being made in science and technology, and artists were forging styles that had a powerful and (**12**) ...... influence on subsequent centuries.

1	**A** neglected	**B** abandoned	**C** subdued	**D** deserted
2	**A** respond	**B** refuse	**C** rectify	**D** revive
3	**A** insist	**B** persist	**C** consist	**D** desist
4	**A** injured	**B** eliminated	**C** wounded	**D** ravaged
5	**A** states	**B** circumstances	**C** conditions	**D** situations
6	**A** estimate	**B** forecast	**C** prediction	**D** expectancy
7	**A** pursuit	**B** chase	**C** desire	**D** quest
8	**A** comprehensively	**B** admittedly	**C** dubiously	**D** potentially
9	**A** background	**B** setting	**C** context	**D** environment
10	**A** debut	**B** invention	**C** introduction	**D** rise
11	**A** total	**B** entire	**C** seamless	**D** integral
12	**A** maintaining	**B** enduring	**C** remaining	**D** sustaining

For questions **13–27**, read the text below and think of the word which best fits each gap. Use only **one** word in each gap. There is an example at the beginning (**0**).

Write your answers **IN CAPITAL LETTERS on the separate answer sheet**.

Example:

0	CAN	0

Speed limit

A recent proposal to limit the speed cars (**0**) .... reach is proving controversial. The idea, put (**13**) .... by the Institute for Road Safety, involves fitting vehicles with a communications box containing a digital map of the road network. (**14**) .... a car is in motion, the communications box – which knows (**15**) .... fast the vehicle is legally permitted to travel on a particular section of road – automatically regulates the car's speed. (**16**) .... therefore becomes impossible for a vehicle fitted with (**17**) .... a device to exceed the speed limit.

There are plans (**18**) .... charge motorists to drive into the centre of major cities, and a communications box could be used to identify vehicles that enter this zone. At present, (**19**) .... time a vehicle does so, its number plate is photographed. (**20**) .... the number is compared against a list of authorised vehicles, but this system is costly and (**21**) .... from foolproof.

The system (**22**) .... be put in place quickly if the government wished as part (**23**) .... the technology has already been developed for another purpose. Electronic vehicle identification is unpopular with some people, who regard it (**24**) .... an infringement of their rights. (**25**) .... would certainly object to the plan to restrict the speed of their cars, (**26**) .... may make the government hesitate to go through with it. But by forcing drivers to slow (**27**) .... , the scheme would save lives, and this is likely to be popular with the general public.

For questions **28–37**, read the text below. Use the word given in capitals at the end of some of the lines to form a word that fits in the gap **in the same line.** There is an example at the beginning (**0**).

Write your answers **IN CAPITAL LETTERS on the separate answer sheet.**

Example:

0	*WESTERN*	0

The Origins of Halloween

Halloween is celebrated in many parts of the (**0**) .... **WEST**
world, and is a time when people dress up as witches or ghosts,
and go 'trick-or-treating'. It is (**28**) .... one of the most **DOUBT**
popular traditions in the United States and Britain.

The celebration (**29**) .... about two thousand years **ORIGIN**
ago with the Celts. These people were the (**30**) .... **INHABIT**
of an area that includes Britain, Ireland and Brittany. They
relied on the land for their (**31**) .... , and this meant **LIVE**
that they were at the mercy of (**32**) .... weather **PREDICT**
conditions, especially during the winter.

The Celtic new year began on 1st November, which also marked
the beginning of winter, a period (**33**) .... associated **TRADITION**
with death. On the eve of the new year, it was believed that the
barriers between the worlds of the living and the dead were
(**34**) .... withdrawn, and it was possible to **TEMPORARY**
communicate with spirits. The Celts believed that the spirits
offered them (**35**) .... and protection, and the Druids **GUIDE**
(Celtic priests) were (**36**) .... able to predict the **REPUTE**
future on this night.

When the Romans completed their (**37**) .... of Celtic **CONQUER**
lands, they added their own flavour to this festival. The advent
of Christianity brought about yet other changes. In the seventh
century, Pope Boniface IV declared November 1st All Saints' Day,
also known as 'All Hallows Day', and the night before it was
'All Hallows Eve', which was eventually abbreviated to 'Halloween'.

For questions **38–42**, think of **one** word only which can be used appropriately in all three sentences. Here is an example (**0**).

Example:

0
- We will do all the work, but they will .... all the credit, as usual!
- She will .... offence if you tell her that hairstyle doesn't suit her.
- They threatened to .... David to court unless he stopped playing his drums all night.

| 0 | *TAKE* | 0 ▭ ▭ |

Write **only** the missing word **IN CAPITAL LETTERS on the separate answer sheet.**

38
- They turned left and .... towards the port.
- Two students holding a banner .... the demonstration.
- Terry .... the team of researchers as he was the acknowledged expert.

39
- A meal at the restaurant will cost you an .... and a leg.
- I've got a list of people to phone as long as your .... !
- If you keep jumping on the .... of the chair like that, you'll break it.

40
- My new boss .... fault with everything I do.
- If my mother .... out I've crashed the car, I'll be in big trouble!
- Kirsten is shy, so she .... it hard to talk to strangers.

41
- Which .... are you interested in test-driving, madam?
- Nicky has made a beautiful .... of a Spitfire fighter plane.
- Ronaldinho is a role .... for many an aspiring young footballer.

42
- I've decided to paint the house in .... colours like cream and beige.
- Doris hid her anger by keeping her voice .... when she spoke.
- The two sides agreed to meet on .... ground to discuss a truce.

For questions **43–50**, complete the second sentence so that it has a similar meaning to the first sentence, using the word given. **Do not change the word given.** You must use between **three** and **six** words, including the word given. Here is an example (**0**).

Example:

0   Jane regretted speaking so rudely to the old lady.
     MORE
     Jane .... politely to the old lady.

0	*WISHED SHE HAD SPOKEN MORE*	0

Write the missing words **IN CAPITAL LETTERS on the separate answer sheet.**

---

43   They believe that Oliver failed his exam because he was nervous.
       DOWN
       Oliver's failure in his exam .... the fact that he was nervous.

44   'Why didn't I ask Linda for her phone number?' thought Vince.
       ASKED
       'If .... Linda for her phone number!' thought Vince.

45   Gillian was the only person who didn't enjoy the party.
       WITH
       Everyone enjoyed the party .... Gillian.

46   We didn't think he was going to recover, so it was a relief when he did.
       PULLED
       We were relieved when he .... we didn't think he would.

47   'I really don't like what you are saying about me!' said Tina.
       OBJECTED
       Tina .... about her.

48   I don't mind you staying out late, but your father does.
       NOT
       It's .... minds you staying out late.

49   'One thing you can do is give up smoking,' said the doctor.
       WERE
       'If .... give up smoking,' said the doctor.

50   They think that students vandalised the school last night.
       WAS
       It is .... by students last night.

You will hear three different extracts. For questions **1–6**, choose the answer (**A, B** or **C**) which fits best according to what you hear. There are two questions for each extract.

Extract One

You hear part of an interview with an aromatherapist.

1 Fiona thinks people
- **A** shouldn't feel embarrassed about what they look like.
- **B** shouldn't choose aromatherapy if they don't like being massaged.
- **C** shouldn't be massaged if they feel uncomfortable about it.

[| 1]

2 According to Fiona, the main advantage of the foot reflex treatment is that
- **A** it doesn't require you to undress.
- **B** the benefit you receive is two-fold.
- **C** it is more relaxing than a massage.

[| 2]

Extract Two

You hear part of a radio programme in which two people are discussing hybrid cars.

3 Both speakers agree that hybrid cars are
- **A** noticeably slower than they expected them to be.
- **B** expensive to buy but economical in the long term.
- **C** safer to drive and more economical than petrol-run cars.

[| 3]

4 The woman implies that
- **A** people who travel as part of their job prefer ordinary cars.
- **B** young male drivers are generally not safety-conscious.
- **C** most drivers want their cars to look impressive.

[| 4]

Extract Three

You hear part of an interview with a film maker, Tony Dupois.

5 Tony believes that the film school he went to
- **A** did not cater for people with backgrounds in video and television.
- **B** offered a broad curriculum that inspired him to be creative.
- **C** gave him the opportunity to make valuable contacts.

[| 5]

6 The interviewer mentions a character from one of Tony's films in order to
- **A** illustrate the importance of guilt as a theme in Tony's work.
- **B** exemplify the complexity of the characters Tony creates.
- **C** highlight the problem of stereotyping villains in films.

[| 6]

You will hear an archaeologist talking about an experience he had in South America. For questions **7–14**, complete the sentences.

An Unpleasant Adventure

The archaeologist's original task was to [_____ **7**] the ruined city and the area around it.

He was then asked to suggest ways to [_____ **8**]

It appears that the [_____ **9**] air exhaled by visitors is damaging the walls.

The archaeologist wanted to survey a tomb near the site of a proposed [_____ **10**]

Unfortunately, the tomb had been damaged by flood water from [_____ **11**]

The archaeologist lost his footing on some [_____ **12**]

As he fell, he broke his [_____ **13**]

He was found when a [_____ **14**] heard his shouts for help.

You will hear part of an interview with Professor Hector Williams, a linguist. For questions **15–20**, choose the answer (**A, B, C** or **D**) which fits best according to what you hear.

15 What was the assumption behind medieval interest in an artificial language?
   A   It would be easy to learn a logical language.
   B   The language would be more suited to classification.
   C   The universe was constructed on linguistic principles.
   D   The language would be a key to understanding the universe.

16 The artificial language based on the names of the notes in the scale
   A   had a vocabulary of single-syllable words.
   B   could be understood by people in the west.
   C   simplified the task of reading music.
   D   was intended to be easy to learn and understand.

17 How did Professor Williams feel when he first heard Esperanto spoken?
   A   He thought it was a dialect of Italian.
   B   He felt it had a pleasant sound.
   C   He considered it was successful in its aims.
   D   He wanted to know the logic behind it.

18 According to Professor Williams, what is the main objection to an artificial language?
   A   It is not very expressive.
   B   It cannot be used to talk about the past.
   C   It does not have any native speakers.
   D   It has a limited vocabulary.

19 What characteristic of Esperanto speakers does Professor Williams find most striking?
   A   their optimism
   B   their naivety
   C   their dedication
   D   their elitism

20 Professor Williams considers that no artificial language will ever become universal because
   A   the language instinct is fundamental in all human beings.
   B   identity and language are strongly linked for most people.
   C   it is impossible to invent a completely artificial language.
   D   too few people would ever consider learning one.

You will hear five short extracts in which people talk about the Internet.

While you listen you must complete both tasks.

Task One

For questions **21–25**, choose from the list **A–H** what each speaker says about starting to use the Internet.

A I first used it when I needed some historical information.

B I was obliged to start using it in my job.

C I first began using it for academic purposes.

D I wanted to buy books online.

E I first learnt to use it for recreation.

F I was put off by my initial experiences of using it.

G The commercial potential attracted me in the first place.

H I have always taken it for granted.

Speaker 1		21
Speaker 2		22
Speaker 3		23
Speaker 4		24
Speaker 5		25

Task Two

For questions **26–30**, choose from the list **A–H** the view each speaker expresses about the influence of the Internet.

A It is a source of information about current affairs.

B It threatens the security of our society.

C Lack of access to the Internet can perpetuate inequalities.

D Online games will come to dominate the leisure industry.

E Our reading habits will be transformed.

F Standards of literacy will decline still further.

G It may one day replace interpersonal communication.

H There are considerable temptations attached.

Speaker 1		26
Speaker 2		27
Speaker 3		28
Speaker 4		29
Speaker 5		30

Part 1 (3 minutes)

The examiner will ask you a few questions about yourself and then ask you to talk to your partner. For example, the examiner may ask you:

- What means of transport did you use to get here today?
- What sort of public transport is available in this area?
- Which forms of transport do you prefer, and which do you dislike?

Part 2 (4 minutes)

You will each be asked to talk on your own for a minute without interruption. You will each be given a set of three photographs in turn to talk about. After your partner has finished speaking, you will be asked a brief question connected with your partner's photographs. You will have thirty seconds to answer.

> **Anxiety** (compare, contrast and speculate)

Turn to pictures 1–3 on page **205**, which show people feeling anxious.

Candidate A, compare and contrast two of these pictures and imagine what might be making these people anxious. Which situation do you think is the most stressful?

Candidate B, which situation would you least like to be in?

> **Achievement** (compare, contrast and speculate)

Turn to pictures 1–3 on page **206**, which show people who have achieved something.

Candidate B, compare and contrast two of these pictures and say what you think these people have achieved. How might they be feeling?

Candidate A, in what situations do you find a sense of achievement most satisfying?

Part 3 (4 minutes)

> **Appearance** (discuss, evaluate and select)

Turn to the pictures on page **207**, which show examples of the outward appearance people present to the world.

Talk to each other about what each person is expressing by his or her appearance, and then decide which two pictures you would choose to demonstrate the wide variety of messages that appearance can give out.

Part 4 (4 minutes)

The examiner will encourage you to develop the topic of your discussion in Part 3 by asking questions such as:

- In what sort of situations do you think someone's appearance is most important?
- Do you think it is possible to ignore fashion? Why (not)?
- To what extent do you judge a person by his or her appearance?
- How important is appearance to someone who cares what other people think of them?

PAPER 1 Reading

PAPER 2 Writing

PAPER 3 Use of English

PAPER 4 Listening

PAPER 5 Speaking

Part 1
Part 2
Part 3
Part 4

You are going to read three extracts which are all concerned in some way with endurance sports. For questions **1–6**, choose the answer (**A, B, C** or **D**) which you think fits best according to the text.

Mark your answers **on the separate answer sheet**.

Running For Fun

About two years ago I was persuaded by my girlfriend to go to Paris with her so that she could run the marathon. At least, that was the idea initially. But then I started wondering if I could run the marathon with her, so I began a fairly intensive training programme. She was quite an experienced runner, so I didn't want to make a fool of myself! Luckily, I was already fairly fit, and I found a good trainer at my local gym who gave me some excellent advice, so it wasn't too hard for me to prepare for the race. It was an amazing experience. The planners who designed the course appear to have made sure it goes past every major sight in the city, including the Arc de Triomphe and the Louvre. The second half of the route also takes you past Notre Dame and the Eiffel Tower, along the banks of the Seine – it's hard to concentrate on running when you have such magnificent distractions!

Three-quarters of the way through the marathon, I started to get tired and I was rather dubious about completing it. But then I reminded myself that there wasn't much further to go, and the thought of finishing gave me an extra spurt of energy. I've decided that the most appealing thing about running a marathon is that it's basically an illogical thing to do, but you share it with literally thousands of other people, and you are cheered on by enthusiastic spectators. As far as the practicalities are concerned, we discovered how important it is to find a hotel near the start line. That eliminates race-day nerves about getting there on time.

My girlfriend and I now run in several marathons every year, and even arrange our holidays around them. One aspect I really enjoy is meeting up with some of the same people each time. You build up friendships, and it certainly beats meeting friends down at the pub!

1 How did the writer first become involved in marathon running?
   A His girlfriend persuaded him to take part in a race.
   B He decided to share the experience with his girlfriend.
   C His trainer recommended the sport to him.
   D He thought it would be a good way to see Paris.

2 What does the writer like most about marathon running?
   A the sights you can see along the route
   B meeting people before the race
   C the intensive training programme
   D sharing an interest with so many people

Nutrition and Competition

Olivia MacFarlane is a registered sports coach who specialises in training athletes for endurance sports competitions. Below, she provides some useful advice on nutrition for endurance athletes.

When you are training for any competition, a balanced daily diet is essential since it affects both your performance and how well you will progress towards competition level. Remember to eat regularly and drink sufficient amounts of water. The latter is particularly important. Don't wait until you are thirsty. Make drinking water at regular intervals a habit since it is something we often forget to do.

Studies have shown that certain nutritional 'tactics' in the days leading up to the competition can definitely enhance performance. These 'tactics' work in conjunction with 'taper training' during the last week, and may vary slightly from sport to sport. If you are competing in an endurance sport, it is vital that you fill up on glycogen before competing. Increase your intake of carbohydrates by eating such foods as potatoes, bread, cereals and pasta, and eat smaller amounts of meat, fish and eggs than normal to reduce your high-protein levels. Also, keep your fat intake to a minimum. During the last few days prior to the competition, sixty to seventy per cent of your energy intake should be coming from carbohydrates.

Athletes often ask whether they should eat on the day of a competition. The answer to this question is that food is the body's source of fuel. A car cannot run without petrol. It follows that our bodies need fuel if they are to perform. Again, carbohydrates are the key, so on the morning of the competition, stick to those foods. Then make sure you are well-hydrated, and have a supply of water and carbohydrate snacks to sustain you throughout the competition. Drink at regular intervals to prevent dehydration setting in.

3   According to Olivia, during the last week before a race you should
   A   combine taper training with a high-protein diet.
   B   increase your intake of meat and other proteins.
   C   make carbohydrates form the bulk of your diet.
   D   reduce your overall intake of food.

4   On the morning of a race, you should
   A   drink more water than usual.
   B   eat food that contains mainly carbohydrates.
   C   save energy by using a car to get to the event.
   D   eat carbohydrate snacks at regular intervals.

Endurance riding – The equestrian challenge of the future!

Attention all horse lovers! Endurance riding is a new equestrian sport which is really taking off! For those of you already familiar with the cross-country competition, endurance riding is the next step up. You are expected to cover longer distances within a restricted time limit. But don't be fooled into thinking it is simply a long pony trek. This sport presents a real challenge, and demands high levels of fitness in both horse and rider. For this reason, there are veterinary checks before and after each event, and, in the longer distance competitions, even during the ride, to ensure that the horse is in optimum health. Riding clubs all over the country are now organising endurance events under the guidance and supervision of our organisation. So there are now more opportunities to enjoy this sport.

Careful planning is essential before taking part. Event organisers provide riders with a map of the route well in advance so that they can scrutinise the route to work out what the terrain is like and which sections are likely to be more difficult. This allows them to anticipate how their horse will perform, and also decide where their backup crew will meet them along the way. Riders are largely autonomous, relying on their own map-reading skills to get them round the course, rather than chasing the horse in front. It is possible to get lost, so learn the route well before the start of the race!

One of the most enjoyable aspects of this sport is the sense of camaraderie among the riders. It is generally accepted that endurance riding is not so much about competing against other riders but rather against the elements and one's own stamina. Our organisation believes that completing the course is an achievement in itself, so riders tend to be supportive of one another, and particularly of inexperienced competitors.

So if you and your pony enjoy riding long distances and fancy a challenge, why not sign up today? There's an Endurance Centre near you, so visit our web site below for a complete list of centres nationwide.

5 According to the advertisement, endurance riding is
   A not as easy to do as it may at first appear.
   B a kind of long-distance pony trekking.
   C for riders who are not very competitive.
   D a sport which demands physical strength.

6 The advertisement emphasises the fact that riders should
   A compete against one another to win.
   B rely on their backup crew during the race.
   C aim to complete the course.
   D be able to follow a map.

PAPER 1 Reading ▶
PAPER 2 Writing
PAPER 3 Use of English
PAPER 4 Listening
PAPER 5 Speaking

Part 1
Part 2
Part 3
Part 4

You are going to read a magazine article. Six paragraphs have been removed from the article. Choose from the paragraphs **A–G** the one which fits each gap (**7–12**). There is one extra paragraph which you do not need to use.

Mark your answers **on the separate answer sheet**.

All This Jazz

What makes someone give up a stable career for the uncertainty of playing the saxophone in a jazz band? Walter Williams finds out.

Marjorie Anderson is terrified. We're sitting backstage in a small theatre that constitutes one of the few amenities the tiny French town of Villeneuf can boast of. In a few minutes she will walk on stage with the jazz band she plays with, Les Jazzistes. They have been together for two years now, slowly but steadily building up a loyal following, and there is little doubt that tonight's gig will be a success. An enviable position to be in, especially for someone who, like Marjorie, has managed to make a living in a notoriously precarious profession, and in a foreign country to boot.

7 [   ]

Marjorie lives in France and does little else other than play the sax professionally. She has a distinctive technique, honed to perfection by hours of practice and, some would claim, plays with added passion by virtue of the fact that she has made huge sacrifices in order to devote herself to jazz. In addition to being a fine musician, she's a vet by training: an extraordinary combination.

8 [   ]

She grew up in Sydney and was something of a child prodigy – as a flautist. She studied with a distinguished teacher and played with a youth orchestra, but then she abruptly decided that music was not for her. What happened? 'I auditioned for a prestigious orchestra, but nothing came of it.' Her sense of rejection at the time was overwhelming, but perhaps her failure was due to her attitude. 'I was abrasive

in the interview,' Marjorie admits. 'I was very thin-skinned in those days. I felt threatened every time someone commented on my playing or my technique.'

9 [   ]

However, it emerged a decade later that contentment of this sort was not what Marjorie really yearned for. Her brother treated her to a week in Paris for her thirty-fifth birthday, and on the final evening they went to a club whose lively jazz scene has been attracting a demanding clientele for over seventy years. The effect on Marjorie was immediate; it was as if she was hearing music for the first time.

10 [   ]

'I moved here because it hit me that for thirty-five years, I had never been in touch with my inner self, with my needs and desires,' she told me. 'Oddly enough, I didn't consider taking up the flute again. It was the saxophone that grabbed my attention. It was so much more expressive in terms of my own essential being.'

11 [   ]

I ask her if she has any regrets about dropping out to follow her dreams. She says no, but that she feels a bit guilty. 'I realise playing the sax in a band isn't saving the world. Sometimes I feel I ought to be doing something more useful.'

12 [   ]

There seems a good chance that her latest project will provide what's missing. Marjorie has decided to reinvent herself yet again – as a writer this time. She has just finished her autobiography, entitled *Why Not Try It?* It's a question many readers, envious of her courage, will find uncomfortable.

A Yet she is clutching her saxophone like a petrified child. 'I'm scared of the audience,' she says. 'You've got to be kidding,' I tell her. 'No,' she says with a snort. 'I freeze up when I look at them.' With a slightly shamefaced expression she reaches for her sunglasses. Wearing them throughout her appearance in front of this small crowd – maybe 250 people – is one of the methods she uses to control her nerves.

B Marjorie works hard, but being a musician, even a respected one, leaves her little opportunity to feed her brain in other ways. She's frustrated that her French isn't good enough to allow her to communicate at a depth she's accustomed to. And sitting around her tiny apartment reading books only goes a small way towards intellectual fulfilment.

C Marjorie refused to let such a minor problem daunt her. Soon she was playing music again, this time with renewed determination to be one of the best sax players in the world. Then, without any warning, she developed a fear of performing in public that nearly paralysed her the first time it struck. It was time to take action.

D 'I thought I'd gone to heaven,' she says. 'It was a turning point. The experience told me I had to play more music, hear more music and really live before it was too late.' This was the moment when she decided to make a radical change in her life.

E As if this weren't unusual enough, five years ago, seemingly on a whim, she suddenly decided to sell her thriving veterinary practice in Australia and moved to Villeneuf – without knowing a single word of French or how long she might stay. What would make someone abandon her entire life and take up playing music with a bunch of amateurs at the age of thirty-five?

F Her new-found stagefright was the other curious factor about this return to public performance. Marjorie believes her terror is related to the sense that she is baring her soul when she performs. 'The other thing I do to make myself less scared is stand completely still on stage,' she explains. 'Paradoxically enough, this seems to get me more attention!'

G So she went to college instead, and trained as a vet. She threw herself into her profession, channelling her energy into building up a practice. 'I became stronger psychologically because I was successful in my career,' she says. 'I see it as a positive thing. I was satisfied with my life.'

PAPER 1 Reading ▶

Part 1
Part 2
Part 3
Part 4

PAPER 2 Writing

PAPER 3 Use of English

PAPER 4 Listening

PAPER 5 Speaking

You are going to read a newspaper article. For questions **13–19**, choose the answer (**A, B, C** or **D**) which you think fits best according to the text.

Mark your answers **on the separate answer sheet**.

Saving the Big Birds

At first glance, why anyone would want to save California condors is not entirely clear. Unlike the closely related Andean condors with their white neck fluff or king vultures with their brilliant black-and-white colouring, California condors are not much to see. Their dull black colour – even when contrasted with white underwings – featherless head and neck, oversized feet and blunt talons are hardly signs of beauty or strength. Their appeal begins to become evident when they take flight. With nine-and-a-half-foot wingspans and weights up to twenty-eight pounds, California condors are North America's largest fully flighted birds. In the Americas, only Andean condors are bigger. California condors can soar almost effortlessly for hours, often covering hundreds of miles a day – far more than other creatures of the air. Only occasionally do they need to flap their wings – to take off, change direction or find a band of warm air known as a thermal to carry them higher.

When it was discovered that the condor population was becoming dangerously small, scientists and zookeepers sought to increase condor numbers quickly to preserve as much of the species' genetic diversity as possible. From studying wild condors, they already knew that if a pair lost an egg, the birds would often produce another. So the first and sometimes second eggs laid by each female in captivity were removed, artificially incubated, and the chicks raised using hand-held puppets made to look like adult condors. Such techniques quickly proved effective.

Despite these successes, the effort to save California condors continues to have problems, evoke criticisms and generate controversy. Captive-hatched condors released to the wild have died at what to some people are alarmingly high rates. Others have had to be recaptured after they acted foolishly or became ill. As a result, the scientists, zookeepers and conservationists who are concerned about condors have bickered among themselves over the best ways to rear and release the birds.

Some of the odd behaviour on the part of these re-released birds is hard to explain. At times they landed on people's houses and garages, walked across roads and airport runways, sauntered into park visitor centres and fast food restaurants, and took food offered by picnickers and fishermen. None are known to have died by doing so, though. More seriously, one condor died from drinking what was probably antifreeze. Others died in collisions with overhead electrical transmission wires, drowned in natural pools of water, or were killed by golden eagles and coyotes. Still others were shot by hunters and killed or made seriously ill from lead poisoning. Some just disappeared. Most recently, some of the first chicks hatched in the wild died after their parents fed them bottle caps, glass shards, pieces of plastic and other man-made objects that fatally perforated or blocked their intestines. These deaths may be due to the chicks' parents mistaking man-made objects for bone chips eaten for their calcium content.

Mike Wallace, a wildlife specialist at the San Diego Zoo, has suggested that some of the condors' problems represent natural behaviour that helps them survive as carrion eaters. The real key to successful condor reintroduction, he believes, lies in properly socialising young condors as members of a group that follow and learn from older, preferably adult birds. That, he argues, was missing from earlier condor releases to the wild. Typically, condors hatched in the spring were released to the wild that autumn or winter, when they were still less than a year old. Especially in the early releases, the young condors had no adults or even older juveniles to learn from and keep them in their place. Instead, the only other condors they saw in captivity and the wild were ones their own age. Now, condor chicks at several zoos are raised in cave-like nest boxes. The chicks can see older condors in a large flight pen outside their box but cannot interact with them until they are about five months old. Then the chicks are gradually released into the pen and the company of the social group. The group includes adult and older juvenile condors that act as mentors for younger ones. It is hoped that this socialisation programme will help the birds adapt to the wild when they are released.

13 According to the writer, the most impressive feature of the California condor is

    A its resemblance to the Andean condor.

    B its ability to glide.

    C its colourful plumage.

    D its blunt talons.

14 In the first stage of the conservation programme,

    A eggs were removed from the nests of wild condors.

    B female condors were captured and studied carefully.

    C scientists and zookeepers tried to create genetic diversity.

    D condors were induced to lay more than one egg.

15 What are we told about the attempts to save these birds from extinction?

    A There is disagreement about the methods employed.

    B The majority of condors released into the wild have died.

    C Attempts to breed condors in captivity have failed.

    D Condors reintroduced into the wild are unable to hunt.

16 Some of the condors released into the wild

    A died from ingesting too much fast food.

    B displayed a tendency to seek out human contact.

    C kept altering their eating habits.

    D adapted surprisingly quickly to their new surroundings.

17 Some chicks hatched by condors released into the wild died because

    A they were neglected by their parents.

    B they fell prey to other animals.

    C they suffered from lead poisoning.

    D they swallowed dangerous objects.

18 According to Mike Wallace, there will be fewer problems

    A if young condors are taught not to eat so much carrion.

    B if the chicks are kept in cave-like nest boxes for five months.

    C if young condors are taught appropriate behaviour by older birds.

    D if the chicks are in the company of older birds when they hatch.

19 The purpose of the article appears to be

    A to gain financial support for the California condor conservation project.

    B to evaluate the need to preserve the California condor.

    C to analyse factors surrounding the condors' failure to adapt to the wild.

    D to examine developments in the condor conservation programme.

PAPER 1 Reading	Part 1
PAPER 2 Writing	Part 2
PAPER 3 Use of English	Part 3
PAPER 4 Listening	**Part 4**
PAPER 5 Speaking	

You are going to read a newspaper article about different types of camera. For questions **20–29**, choose from the sections of the article (**A–D**). For questions **30–34**, choose from the sections of the article (**E–H**).

Mark your answers **on the separate answer sheet**.

Which sections of the article (A–D) mention the following?

hidden costs **20** ....

adding data to images **21** ....

taking pictures from a particular distance **22** ....

developing technical skills **23** ....

the compatibility of component parts **24** ....

the danger that you will not be able to access your photos **25** ....

protecting fragile items **26** ....

a joint venture **27** ....

the loss of quality that comes with enlargement **28** ....

similar quality for less money **29** ....

Which sections of the article (E–H) mention the following?

taking people unawares **30** ....

the tendency of some devices to develop faults **31** ....

the views of others **32** ....

evaluating one's work **33** ....

difficulties in obtaining supplies **34** ....

Buying Your First Camera

With so many different cameras on the market nowadays, how can you choose what to buy? We describe the four main types and ask a group of experts which one they would recommend to a beginner with £400 to spend.

The Cameras

A Compact/Point-and-shoot

These cameras are small and simple, making them ideal for use on holidays or taking snaps when you are out and about. There are no adjustments to be made, no settings to check: you simply aim the camera and press the button. And since they have a built-in flash as well as automatic focus, you get a good, clear image every time you press that button. On the other hand, the flash will probably be of poor quality, with an effective range of only about four metres. This means that even with 400 ASA film (the kind that needs least light), you will be unable to get a reasonable picture of anything further away. Another disadvantage is that the lens is not very good: the image will not be clear if you blow up the picture bigger than 15cm x 21cm. If you buy one of these cameras, it should have red-eye reduction for the flash so that people in your pictures do not have red dots in their eyes. Also, the larger and clearer the viewfinder, the better. Bear in mind that you will not be able to control the settings, so if you want pictures that look at all unusual (by being deliberately out of focus, for example), you won't be able to take them.

B APS

The Advanced Photo System (APS) was launched in 1996 by several manufacturers who established a common standard. Instead of the 35mm film used by compacts and Single Lens Reflex (SLR) cameras, APS cameras use little film cartridges. Consequently, APS cameras can be extremely small. And this isn't the only advantage: you can put your own information on each picture you take, such as the time, day and place where it was taken. The cartridges are easier to insert into the camera than normal film, and you can take one out before it's finished and use it again later. On the other hand, you don't have much choice about the texture of the picture – it has to be gloss, and it more or less has to be colour, since black and white cartridges are hard to find. While APS cameras are new, and some people feel it is best to stick to famous brand names for new technology, remember that – as with most types of camera – these famous names have their cameras made by the same factories that produce cameras for lesser-known brands. These often offer comparable features, build qualities and guarantees for a lower price.

C SLR

Single Lens Reflex (SLR) cameras are the oldest and simplest type of camera discussed here, with a comparatively large body and lenses that screw on to the front. The old-fashioned type had no electronic components at all, though now many SLR cameras have automatic features; one advantage here is that they can be turned off, in contrast to compact cameras. With SLRs you must make sure the lens and body will fit together since they come in different sizes. It is also worth thinking carefully about whether to buy a camera with an automatic focus lens. Naturally, this lets you take photographs quickly, without having to adjust anything yourself, but this is not always the advantage it may seem. Firstly, an automatic focus lens does not always produce the same quality of picture as a manual focus lens. Furthermore, the fact that an automatic focus lens is so easy to use will also encourage you to take far more photographs. So learning how to use a manual focus lens will not only save on film, your camera will work out to be less expensive altogether because manual focus lenses are cheaper – and you will learn how to make all the adjustments yourself, for different types of light etc. Get a camera with a metal body – some are made of plastic – because metal is far more sturdy, and delicate lenses are less likely to come to grief.

D Digital

Digital cameras don't need film: the picture you take is stored on a computer memory card, and then you can delete it, give it to a shop to print or print it on your own computer printer. You can even edit the picture yourself. These new and popular cameras are ideal if you just want to use them for basic holiday and home snaps that you intend to e-mail to others, post on a website or play around with on a computer. However, the lenses are not as good as SLR lenses, except on the most expensive cameras, and storing images can be a problem. You will have to store your photos on your computer, which can quickly get full, and what happens if it breaks down or you decide to get a new one? And though manufacturers stress the saving on film, they may fail to mention that you need expensive memory cards. What's more, some digital cameras use up batteries at an alarming rate. Depending on the printer you normally use, you may need to invest in special paper and ink, too.

The Experts

E I'd say a beginner should go for the best digital camera he or she can afford. You develop as a photographer by taking lots of shots, studying them and throwing away the vast majority; this is how you learn what makes a good picture. Digitals let you do this more easily than any other type, and some have software that enables you to do very sophisticated things on your computer in the way of editing. Plus you can always get normal prints if you want.

F A beginner who wants to become a good amateur, and maybe join an amateur photography club, needs an SLR. The basic technology is fairly old, but it's very reliable, and since they've been making these cameras for years, there are lots of second-hand models on the market. You learn better without the modern electronic gadgetry, which will probably break down in a couple of years anyway. Nobody will take you seriously as a photographer with anything other than an SLR.

G Spend around £400 on a good compact. You can take it everywhere with you and photograph interesting or amusing incidents that simply crop up in everyday life. That's what professionals do. You know you'll get a good picture every time, so you never waste film. Unlike APS and digital cameras, you can use any 35mm film with a compact – a definite advantage when you're in some tiny village where shops only have normal films.

H Get the best APS camera you can – that's my advice. It's tiny, so you can have it in your pocket or handbag and get those special shots without anyone realising they're being captured on film. You have a lot more control over the pictures than with compacts. You can choose the size of the print format, and you can change the print format at a later date.

You **must** answer this question. Write your answer in **180–220** words in an appropriate style.

1   You are a member of the student council at Whitewall College. You recently received a memo from the principal announcing changes to the college library. The student council is opposed to these changes.

You have offered to write an article for the college newsletter to inform students about the planned changes and to invite them to a council meeting in order to discuss the matter. Read the principal's memo to which you have added your comments. Then, using the information carefully, write the article in **180–220** words.

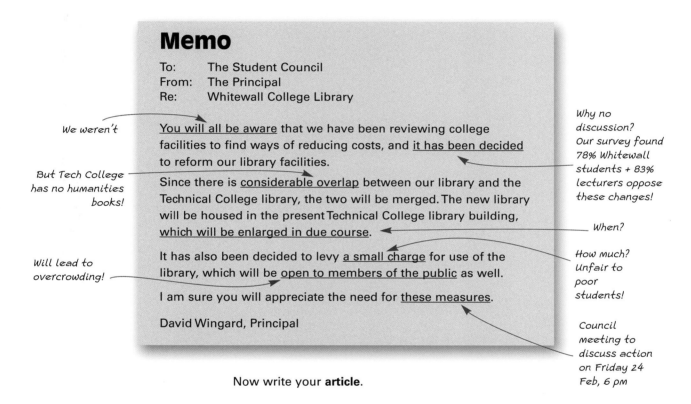

Memo

To: The Student Council
From: The Principal
Re: Whitewall College Library

We weren't

You will all be aware that we have been reviewing college facilities to find ways of reducing costs, and it has been decided to reform our library facilities.

Why no discussion? Our survey found 78% Whitewall students + 83% lecturers oppose these changes!

But Tech College has no humanities books!

Since there is considerable overlap between our library and the Technical College library, the two will be merged. The new library will be housed in the present Technical College library building, which will be enlarged in due course.

When?

It has also been decided to levy a small charge for use of the library, which will be open to members of the public as well.

How much? Unfair to poor students!

Will lead to overcrowding!

I am sure you will appreciate the need for these measures.

David Wingard, Principal

Council meeting to discuss action on Friday 24 Feb, 6 pm

Now write your **article**.

Write an answer to **one** of the questions **2–5** in this part. Write your answer in **220–260** words in an appropriate style.

2 You have seen the following advertisement in a magazine on books:

> ## Long Live Books!
>
> In the future most books will be available online for people to download and read on their computer screens. Will this mean the end of books as we know them?
>
> Write and tell us why the printed book will never die! The best entry will win a complete set of the novels of Charles Dickens!

Write your **competition entry**.

3 You see the following notice in a magazine called *International Restaurants*:

> **Do young people care about good food?**
> **Does it matter to youngsters today if food is tasty and made from fresh ingredients – or do they prefer fast food?**
> **What could school and college canteens do to encourage an interest in the art of cooking?**
> **Write an article for the magazine giving your views.**

Write your **article**.

4 This is an extract from a letter you received from a magazine called *Family Matters*:

> We are very interested in finding out how the family is perceived in different parts of the world. Please write a report for us describing the importance of both the nuclear and extended family in your country, and how family relationships might evolve in the foreseeable future.

Write your **report**.

5 Answer **one** of the following two questions based on your reading of **one** of the set books.
Either
5(a) A market research company are conducting a survey on books which have been made into films, and how the popularity of the film affects sales of the book. They have asked people to send in reports comparing a book of their choice to its film version, and saying whether they feel the latter affects book sales positively or negatively. You have decided to write a report on the book you have been reading.

Write your **report**.

Or
5(b) The literary supplement of your local newspaper has invited readers to send in articles in response to the following statement made in a review recently: *'I despair at the number of stereotyped characters in most modern novels. Where are the bad guys with a conscience, or the protagonists with weaknesses?'* You have decided to write an article in response to the statement, citing examples of characters in the novel you have been reading to illustrate your views.

Write your **article**.

PAPER 1 Reading

PAPER 2 Writing

PAPER 3 Use of English ▶ Part 1

PAPER 4 Listening   Part 2

PAPER 5 Speaking   Part 3

                            Part 4

                            Part 5

For questions **1–12**, read the text below and decide which answer (**A, B, C** or **D**) best fits each gap. There is an example at the beginning (**0**).

Mark your answers **on the separate answer sheet**.

Example:

0   **A** common   **B** expected   **C** usual   **D** normal

Vanilla Surprise

Vanilla is such a(n) (**0**) ...... flavour that it comes as a surprise to learn that it is also one of the world's most expensive crops. The vanilla plant is a(n) (**1**) ...... of the Americas. Its flowers grow in (**2**) ...... , and in nature they are pollinated by hummingbirds and bees. The (**3**) ...... seed pods resemble oversized French beans, and develop their (**4**) ...... flavour and fragrance during the curing process. After harvesting, the beans are treated with heat or hot water and are placed in the sun every day for many weeks. When they have (**5**) ...... to a fifth of their original size, they are (**6**) ...... according to size and quality.

Like other spices that we (**7**) ...... for granted today, vanilla has a fascinating history. In the sixteenth century, the Spanish imported the spice to Europe. However, attempts to grow vanilla in other locations (**8**) ...... with failure: the plants would not produce pods, and it was only when a way was found to pollinate the flowers artificially that the commercial exploitation of this valuable crop (**9**) ...... under way.

Today vanilla is used in the manufacture of perfumes and cosmetics, as well as in the culinary arts, where it is often a(n) (**10**) ...... of puddings. Recently, it has also been used in more (**11**) ...... ways. Lobster and vanilla is now a popular dish in certain restaurants – proving that chefs can (**12**) ...... up with amazing ideas to tickle the taste buds.

1	**A** resident	**B** aborigine	**C** native	**D** inhabitant
2	**A** groups	**B** bouquets	**C** teams	**D** bunches
3	**A** deriving	**B** resulting	**C** producing	**D** arising
4	**A** distinctive	**B** appetising	**C** tasteful	**D** potential
5	**A** reduced	**B** shrunk	**C** diminished	**D** lessened
6	**A** classed	**B** split	**C** divided	**D** sorted
7	**A** consider	**B** do	**C** make	**D** take
8	**A** resulted	**B** ended	**C** met	**D** finished
9	**A** got	**B** went	**C** came	**D** began
10	**A** substance	**B** element	**C** additive	**D** ingredient
11	**A** imaginative	**B** fabulous	**C** unimaginable	**D** different
12	**A** get	**B** come	**C** make	**D** run

For questions **13–27**, read the text below and think of the word which best fits each gap. Use only **one** word in each gap. There is an example at the beginning (**0**).

Write your answers **IN CAPITAL LETTERS on the separate answer sheet**.

Example:

0	*OF*	0

The First Cartoons

The technique of telling a story through a sequence (**0**) .... pictures, though associated with modern cartoons, was (**13**) .... fact in use about 500 years ago. Some wonderful examples of these early cartoons can now be seen at an exhibition in London, all of (**14**) .... were produced to order for wealthy clients. (**15**) .... makes this art form so interesting is that it flourished in one small part of Europe – Flanders, today a region of northern Belgium – (**16**) .... to die out as printing was developed.

Many of the tiny pictures were (**17**) .... larger than a postage stamp. They (**18**) .... painted by hand in books about (**19**) .... size of a modern paperback. The artists, whose skills were rewarded by high salaries, worked slowly, and the buyers sometimes (**20**) .... to wait years for the work to be completed. In the (**21**) .... of one four-volume example, the buyer waited for (**22**) .... than a decade.

(**23**) .... the majority of these cartoons depict religious stories, other subjects are illustrated, (**24**) .... Episodes from history were popular, (**25**) .... were fairy tales. And yet the artists had a visual style that seems oddly modern. (**26**) .... made full use of perspective and techniques familiar to us today from films, such as following a long shot (**27**) .... a dramatic close-up.

For questions **28–37**, read the text below. Use the word given in capitals at the end of some of the lines to form a word that fits in the gap **in the same line**. There is an example at the beginning (**0**).

Write your answers **IN CAPITAL LETTERS on the separate answer sheet.**

Example:

0	CREATOR	0

Sir Arthur Conan Doyle

Famous the world over as the (**0**) .... of Sherlock Holmes, Sir Arthur Conan Doyle was born in Edinburgh in 1859 into an Irish family who were (**28**) .... in the art world. Unfortunately, Arthur's father was an alcoholic, and his behaviour caused his family much (**29**) .... Arthur probably inherited the ability to tell stories from his mother, who was a source of (**30**) .... to him.

CREATE

INFLUENCE

HAPPY

INSPIRE

Thanks to the (**31**) .... of some relatives, Arthur was able to study medicine at Edinburgh University. He was a bright student, but (**32**) .... , and his zest for adventure led him to accept a contract as ship's surgeon aboard a whaler. Returning home, he completed his (**33**) .... studies in 1881. He eventually settled in the south of England.

GENEROUS

REST

MEDICINE

Telling stories had always been a part of his life, but the creation of a (**34**) .... detective called Sherlock Holmes turned Conan Doyle into a popular writer. It is believed that he based Holmes' character on one of his university tutors, Dr Joseph Bell, whom he regarded with respect and (**35**) .... for his logic and powers of (**36**) .... The first Sherlock Holmes story was so well received that Doyle was encouraged to write more. In 1893 he killed off his hero in order to concentrate on writing what he saw as more serious work, but this caused a public (**37**) .... , and he was forced to bring Holmes back to life.

FICTION

ADMIRE
DEDUCE

CRY

For questions **38–42**, think of **one** word only which can be used appropriately in all three sentences. Here is an example (**0**).

Example:

0
- We will do all the work, but they will .... all the credit, as usual!
- She will .... offence if you tell her that hairstyle doesn't suit her.
- They threatened to .... David to court unless he stopped playing his drums all night.

0	*TAKE*	0

Write **only** the missing word **IN CAPITAL LETTERS on the separate answer sheet**.

38
- The weather is exceptionally .... for November.
- I chose a .... curry from the menu as I don't like very hot food.
- The politician was lucky to come in for such .... criticism over the affair.

39
- I tried to make it clear I wasn't interested, but she wouldn't take the ....
- When we left this morning, there wasn't even a .... of a cloud in the sky!
- I can't remember the answer, so please give me a ....

40
- When she saw the balloons, Gina .... her hand over her mouth in amazement.
- Adam .... James on the shoulder and said, 'Well done!'
- As the comedian finished his performance, the audience .... politely.

41
- Zoos make a useful contribution to conservation, but animals are better off in their .... habitat.
- Nick's got a .... talent for music, and can play several instruments.
- I don't like eating anything heavy in the evening, but prefer some .... yoghurt with honey.

42
- Look at the situation from every .... before you make a decision.
- The picture was hanging at a peculiar .... , so I straightened it.
- The photographer took this shot from an unusual ....

PAPER 1 Reading

PAPER 2 Writing

PAPER 3 Use of English ▶

PAPER 4 Listening

PAPER 5 Speaking

Part 1
Part 2
Part 3
Part 4
Part 5

For questions **43–50**, complete the second sentence so that it has a similar meaning to the first sentence, using the word given. **Do not change the word given.** You must use between **three** and **six** words, including the word given. Here is an example (**0**).

Example:

0 Jane regretted speaking so rudely to the old lady.
MORE
Jane .... politely to the old lady.

| 0 | *WISHED SHE HAD SPOKEN MORE* | 0 |

Write the missing words **IN CAPITAL LETTERS on the separate answer sheet.**

---

43 Money is the only thing that matters, really.
COMES
It .... in the end.

44 Sally showed absolutely no fear when climbing the wall.
DISREGARD
Sally showed .... own safety when climbing the wall.

45 The identity of the murderer was never discovered.
WHO
The police .... was.

46 'It's not a good idea to call him just yet,' said Valerie.
AGAINST
Valery advised .... for a while.

47 If we leave now, it won't make any difference.
MIGHT
We .... now.

48 It was only after I left the office that I realised I had forgotten the file.
DID
Only after .... I had forgotten the file.

49 If I lose this match, people will never let me forget it!
LIVE
If I lose this match, I .... down!

50 Internal Affairs are investigating allegations of police fraud.
INTO
Allegations of police fraud .... Internal Affairs.

You will hear three different extracts. For questions **1–6**, choose the answer (**A, B** or **C**) which fits best according to what you hear. There are two questions for each extract.

Extract One

You hear part of a radio discussion between a nutritionist and a medical expert.

1 The woman's main argument is that

   A conventional doctors prescribe too many medicines for common ailments.

   B conventional medicine has been negligent in its attitude towards nutrition.

   C bad or inadequate nutrition is responsible for all allergies and illnesses.

   `1`

2 How does the man view the latest findings?

   A He thinks they exaggerate the influence of diet on a person's health.

   B He believes more research is needed before cancer can be linked to diet.

   C He feels optimistic about the direction conventional medicine is taking.

   `2`

Extract Two

You hear part of a radio programme in which an interior designer is giving advice on colour in the home.

3 According to Eugene, orange

   A calms and relaxes you.

   B stimulates and inspires you.

   C is a natural cure for insomnia.

   `3`

4 The interviewer believes the living room is difficult to decorate because of

   A the need to consider several other factors.

   B the paintings on the wall.

   C the need to be sociable.

   `4`

Extract Three

You hear a conversation between a man and a woman about something that has just happened.

5 What experience is the man describing?

   A He knocked down an old man with his car.

   B He was involved in a head-on collision with a lorry.

   C He hit another car while trying to avert an accident.

   `5`

6 The man thinks the police

   A may prosecute the lorry driver.

   B are unlikely to take action against the old man.

   C will hold the old man responsible for the accident.

   `6`

You will hear part of a talk by a writer who has written a book about bread. For questions **7–14**, complete the sentences.

Our Daily Bread

Supermarket [**7**   ]
believe that baking bread on the premises attracts customers.

About [**8**   ] of bread in Britain
is no longer baked in the old-fashioned way.

In the past, it took [**9**] for the yeast to ferment.

Nowadays, the fermentation process is faster,
and less [**10**   ] is used.

Unless salt is added,
bread baked in the modern way is [**11**]

Calcium propionate can be sprayed on the bread
to prevent it from going [**12**]

The speaker believes certain [**13**   ]
may be caused by modern bread-making methods.

Supermarkets [**14**   ] on the sale of bread.

You will hear part of a discussion between Velma Andrews, a lawyer, and Sergeant William Bailey, a police officer. For questions **15–20**, choose the answer (**A**, **B**, **C** or **D**) which fits best according to what you hear.

15 How did William feel the first time he gave evidence in court?
   A humiliated
   B nervous
   C furious
   D indifferent

16 Velma suggests that police officers giving evidence should
   A study the evidence more carefully.
   B ignore the lawyer for the defence.
   C not take comments personally.
   D demonstrate that they are honest and reliable.

17 Velma compares a police officer's evidence to a piece in a jigsaw puzzle because
   A it is unimportant unless it is part of a bigger picture.
   B it may not fit in with the rest of the evidence.
   C the defence lawyer will try to destroy it.
   D the police officer should only talk about his or her evidence.

18 William suggests that lawyers
   A adopt a special manner in the courtroom.
   B can be detached about a case.
   C might actually be close friends.
   D do not take their work seriously.

19 Velma's advice suggests that police officers should
   A never volunteer a personal opinion.
   B not answer a question unless they are sure of the answer.
   C remember they are not really addressing the lawyer.
   D not get into an argument with the judge.

20 William's main concern is that
   A a criminal could get away with his or her crime.
   B a court case could be confusing.
   C young police officers find courts terrifying.
   D police officers might argue with the lawyer.

You will hear five short extracts in which people talk about wind power.

While you listen you must complete both tasks.

Task One

For questions **21–25**, choose from the list **A–H** the attitude each speaker has towards wind power.

A Placing wind turbines out at sea is perfectly acceptable.

B Wind power is one of the sources of renewable energy we need to exploit.

C Wind turbines are a serious threat to birds in the area.

D Wind power has created attractive business opportunities for some people.

E Wind turbines in the countryside are an unpleasant sight.

F There are valid objections to situating wind turbines offshore.

G Wind power is grossly inadequate as a means of generating our electricity needs.

H Wind power is one of the most practical ways to generate a country's electricity.

Speaker 1	21
Speaker 2	22
Speaker 3	23
Speaker 4	24
Speaker 5	25

Task Two

For questions **26–30**, choose from the list **A–H** what each speaker says about the alternatives to wind power.

A Nuclear power should be considered if it can be made safe.

B The idea that enough energy can be generated from hydroelectric power is ludicrous.

C Other renewable energy-generating schemes would be expensive to set up.

D Only if various renewable sources are exploited collectively will they produce enough energy for our needs.

E Hydroelectric power is a feasible way of generating enough electricity for our needs.

F Fossil fuels cannot be completely replaced by wind power.

G Nuclear power is the safest and most reliable alternative to fossil fuels.

H The best way forward is to use fossil fuels more efficiently.

Speaker 1	26
Speaker 2	27
Speaker 3	28
Speaker 4	29
Speaker 5	30

Part 1 (3 minutes)

The examiner will ask you a few questions about yourself and then ask you to talk to your partner. For example, the examiner may ask you:

- What job do you do, or what job would you like to do?
- What kind of working environment would suit you best?
- What sort of job would you dislike, and what working conditions would not appeal to you?

Part 2 (4 minutes)

You will each be asked to talk on your own for a minute without interruption. You will each be given a set of three photographs in turn to talk about. After your partner has finished speaking, you will be asked a brief question connected with your partner's photographs. You will have thirty seconds to answer.

Respect (compare, contrast and speculate)

Turn to pictures 1–3 on page **208**, which show people expressing respect.

Candidate A, compare and contrast two of these pictures and imagine what could be prompting people to show respect in these situations. How might the people receiving the show of respect feel?

Candidate B, what sort of people do you respect?

Partnership (compare, contrast and speculate)

Turn to pictures 1–3 on page **209**, which show people in partnerships.

Candidate B, compare and contrast two of these pictures and say what kind of partnerships they illustrate. How do you think the partners feel about each other?

Candidate A, would you prefer to work with a partner or on your own?

Part 3 (4 minutes)

Recreation (discuss, evaluate and select)

Turn to the pictures on page **210**, which show different forms of recreation.

Talk to each other about the wide variety of activities people can do in order to relax, and then decide which two pictures best illustrate this diversity.

Part 4 (4 minutes)

The examiner will encourage you to develop the topic of your discussion in Part 3 by asking questions such as:

- Why do you think some people choose to do dangerous recreational activities like mountain climbing?
- Do you think everyone needs some sort of recreational activity? Why (not)?
- Would it be possible to encourage more children to take up recreational activities other than sports: hobbies such as collecting stamps or gardening?
- Which recreational activities are more beneficial: those that exercise the mind or those that exercise the body?

You are going to read three extracts which are all concerned in some way with travel. For questions **1–6**, choose the answer (**A, B, C or D**) which you think fits best according to the text.

Mark your answers **on the separate answer sheet**.

Winter Weekend Break

Hilary Blaine recommends a cosy retreat as a way to escape from those winter blues.

If you are looking to get away from it all for a few days this winter, but don't want to break the bank, then you could do a lot worse than book a weekend break at the Cog in the Wheel Inn, at Ashton Falls. Set in the beautiful Yorkshire Dales, this country retreat boasts a spacious yet cosy restaurant with a cuisine to be envied for miles around. Settle down in the comfortable, oak-panelled dining area and prepare to give your taste buds a real treat. Tuck into juicy local English lamb or Scottish venison accompanied by roasted root vegetables grown on the premises, and let the roaring log fire warm your toes and drive away all your worries.

Then retire to the lounge for homemade fudge and freshly ground coffee or perhaps a hot drink before wending your way up the four hundred year-old staircase to your room. Luxuriously furnished in William Morris prints, with a four-poster bed and en-suite bathroom, each of the inn's ten bedrooms affords magnificent views of the rolling countryside, creating the perfect atmosphere for a satisfyingly deep sleep.

The inn is a popular choice for ramblers as it is ideally positioned for well-known hiking routes, so make sure you don't forget your walking shoes. It is easy to reach by car, and anyone travelling by coach or train can contact the inn to arrange for the mini-bus to pick them up at Ripley Station.

1 According to the writer, the Cog in the Wheel Inn
  A is many miles from the nearest town.
  B serves unusual food to its guests.
  C has a fireplace in every room.
  D is pleasant and reasonably priced.

2 What does the writer think is the most favourable aspect of this inn?
  A its relaxing atmosphere
  B its proximity to the railway station
  C its popularity with walkers
  D its luxurious furnishings

Green Valley Travel –

for the conscientious traveller

Green Valley Travel is a growing, privately run travel company with a commitment to responsible sustainable tourism for singles. Every year our holiday packages undergo rigorous checks by a team of ecological experts before we offer them to our customers, and the owners of the eco-lodges in our network sign a pledge promising to maintain that commitment throughout the year. This, in turn, allows us to fulfil our mission: to provide the discerning traveller with an unforgettable experience which will change his or her outlook on life.

Eco-lodge is a term coined by the tourist industry to describe tourist accommodation which has been constructed using sustainable materials, and which operates with respect towards both the local community and the environment. Our network of eco-lodges covers a wide range of locations, from the rainforests of South America to the coastal regions of northwest Australia, so we are able to offer deals to suit the budget of every type of responsible tourist. Accommodation varies from the rustic to the luxurious, depending on your taste and means, but across the board, the emphasis is on providing a healthy, sustainable environment for the traveller.

Our commitment to making your experience a memorable one includes offering a variety of activities at each location, which will enable you to meet people. At one end of the spectrum, you could choose to simply relax and enjoy the scenery. At the other end, you could volunteer to get involved in local conservation projects; this has the added bonus of providing you with the opportunity to meet and work with members of the local community. The experience will be both enriching and rewarding.

Further details can be obtained from our website, or by contacting our office.

3   You are unlikely to choose one of Green Valley Travel's holidays if you
  A   don't like volunteer work.
  B   want to relax on a beach.
  C   have a restricted budget.
  D   want a family holiday.

4   The advertisement's main emphasis is on
  A   the affordable packages.
  B   the locations available.
  C   the ethics of the company.
  D   the activities on offer.

A charming hotel

The advert described 'a charming family hotel with swimming pool, a hundred metres from the beach'. I looked at the sight before me and wondered exactly what the writer of the brochure had been looking at when he wrote it.

'This *is* the Paradise Beach Hotel, isn't it?' I asked the taxi driver for the third time.

His English was not very good, and my Italian even worse, so I had hopes that perhaps he hadn't understood me. Or perhaps this was the *wrong* Paradise Beach Hotel? For paradise it most certainly was not!

'No, no, ees the *only* Paradise Beach 'otel,' he said, beaming at me.

I stared in dismay at what was in effect a building site, and waited for the inevitable eruption that was brewing beside me. From somewhere around the corner of the building came the dulcet tones of a pneumatic drill, and that triggered it.

'Looks like another one of your successful little projects, Ann,' came the razor-edged comment through gritted teeth. 'Well, this is going to be interesting. Kids! Let's go and see the pool, shall we?' And with a withering look in my direction, Geoff and the boys disappeared around the corner, leaving me standing alone surrounded by our bags. Not so much an eruption as a rumble, I thought, slightly relieved.

I looked towards the hotel entrance hopefully. No sign of anyone coming out to greet us, let alone relieve me of any luggage. The facade was finished, and I could see how the photograph in the brochure had duped us, the camera lens carefully focusing on this aspect, and concealing the pile of sand and tiles waiting to be laid out front. As I philosophically considered this ability of photographers to contrive and distort images, I caught sight of my brood returning from their reconnaissance trip. Things didn't look promising.

'Well, we found out what all the drilling is about,' said Geoff, bristling. 'They're digging out the swimming pool. Boy, are we in for a treat this holiday!'

5   What is the writer's initial reaction to the hotel?
   A   She fears it may be the wrong one.
   B   She worries about Geoff's reaction.
   C   She hopes there has been a mistake.
   D   She is concerned about the noise.

6   How does the writer feel about the holiday?
   A   optimistic
   B   concerned
   C   philosophical
   D   cynical

PAPER 1   Reading   ▶   Part 1
PAPER 2   Writing   Part 2
PAPER 3   Use of English   Part 3
PAPER 4   Listening   Part 4
PAPER 5   Speaking

You are going to read a magazine article. Six paragraphs have been removed from the article. Choose from the paragraphs **A–G** the one which fits each gap (**7–12**). There is one extra paragraph which you do not need to use.

Mark your answers **on the separate answer sheet**.

Close Encounters of the Wild Kind

The rise of the wildlife-watching experience

Wildlife observation has always proved inspirational for humans. It led Charles Darwin to provide us with a better understanding of how we evolved and inspired such everyday innovations as Velcro. US author Peter Matthiessen wrote: 'The variety of life in nature can be compared to a vast library of unread books, and the plundering of nature is comparable to the random discarding of whole volumes without having opened them and learned from them.' While there is indeed much to learn from many species not yet known to science, it's the already opened 'books' that attract the majority of us – in ever increasing numbers.

| 7 |

Awareness and understanding of the state of the planet and its wildlife has been spurred on by the efforts of conservation groups and natural history television. This, in turn, has led to an increased demand for wildlife tours or the addition of a wildlife-watching component to traditional holidays. It seems people want to discover nature for themselves.

| 8 |

Although the term is overused, 'ecotourism' allows tourists both to see and help wildlife. This encouraging development within the wildlife-tourism industry offers an added hope for the future of many endangered species, as money from clients is often given directly to conservation organisations. Tour operators who are listed with independent bodies such as Responsibletravel.com have ethical policies in place to ensure that proper procedures are followed. They use the services of local communities, train local guides and have close ties to conservation projects.

| 9 |

Conservation organisations have also realised that tourism can help educate people and provide a valuable source of revenue and even manpower. The World Wildlife Fund, for example, runs trips that give donors the chance to see for themselves how their financial aid is assisting conservation projects in the field. But not all wildlife watching trips are so hands-off. Some offer the opportunity to participate in research and conservation.

| 10 |

Similarly, Biosphere Expeditions takes about 200 people every year on what its field operations director, Dr Matthias Hammer, calls an 'adventure with a conscience'. Volunteers can visit six destinations around the world and take part in various activities including snow leopard, wolf and bear surveys and whale and dolphin research.

| 11 |

Of course, to go in search of wildlife doesn't always mean you will find it. That sightings of animals in large wild areas don't come on tap is simply a fact of life. Although potentially frustrating, it makes sightings all the more rewarding when they are made.

| 12 |

Indeed, some of the best wildlife-watching opportunities on offer are on our doorstep, according to author and ornithologist Malcolm Tait. 'People assume you have to go a long way to do it, which is simply not the case – your garden or even a railway cutting can bring constant surprises.'

A 'If done properly, wildlife-watching tourism can be a win-win situation,' says Hammer. 'People have a unique experience while contributing to conservation directly. Local people and habitats benefit through job creation, research and an alternative income. Local wildlife benefits from our conservation and research work.'

B 'What is interesting is how much people are willing to pay to be in a wilderness environment,' says Julian Matthews, director of Discovery Initiatives, which takes people on small group trips to more than thirty-five countries and works directly with conservation organisations such as the Orang-utan Foundation. 'It's still a small part of the tourism industry – maybe four or five percent of the whole – but it's undoubtedly expanding. There are definitely more and more people seeking wildlife experiences now.'

C A comparable problem is found in various parts of East Africa, though government intervention has, in these cases, done little to alleviate the hardships. Would it be possible for ethical tourism to play a role in the future of this region? Ken Logan, Director of the African Wildlife Association, is not optimistic about the chances.

D 'There's no way to compare seeing an animal in the wild with watching one on TV,' says Matthews. 'While a filmmaker may spend six months shooting an animal and will get closer to it than you will when watching it in the wild, there's no greater pleasure than seeing an animal in its own environment. On film, you're only getting the visuals and the sound. As impressive as they may be, it's not the real McCoy and misses other aspects that you can appreciate only by being there.'

E Earthwatch is a nonprofit international environmental group that does just that. 'Participation in an Earthwatch project is a positive alternative to wildlife-watching expeditions, as we offer members of the public the opportunity to be on the front line, not the sidelines, of conservation,' says Claudia Eckardt, Earthwatch volunteer programme manager.

F Wildlife covers all wild creatures, not just those that are big, dangerous or exotic. As people are able to travel to more extreme places in search of the ultimate wildlife experience, it's worth remembering that you don't have to go to the ends of the Earth to catch rewarding glimpses of animals.

G Thus tour operator Rekero has established its own school – the Koyiaki Guide School and Wilderness Camp – for young Maasai in Kenya. Maasai have largely been excluded from the benefits brought to the region by tourism; they make up just fifteen percent of employees in tourist camps. 'It is a concerted effort to put the running of the reserve into the hands of indigenous people,' says Ron Beaton, founder of the school.

You are going to read a magazine article. For questions **13–19**, choose the answer (**A, B, C or D**) which you think fits best according to the text.

Mark your answers **on the separate answer sheet**.

Are you a slumper?

Ashley Seager was, but cured bad posture – and her chronic back pain – with the Alexander technique

Many people will have heard of the Alexander technique but have only a vague idea what it is about. Until earlier this year, I didn't have the faintest idea about it. But, hunched over a computer screen one day, I noticed that the neck- and backache I regularly suffered were more painful than usual. I consulted an osteopath, who said: 'I can treat the symptoms by massaging your neck and upper back. But you actually have bad posture. That is what you need to get sorted out. Go off and learn the Alexander technique.'

I had regularly been told by friends and family that I tend to slouch in chairs but had thought bad posture was something one was born with and could do nothing about. That is not true. Dentists and car mechanics, among others, tend to develop bad posture from leaning over patients or engine bays. Mothers often stress and strain their necks and backs lifting and carrying children, and those of us who sit in front of computers all day are almost certainly not doing our bodies any favours.

A few clicks on the web and I found an Alexander technique teacher, Tanya Shoop, in my area of south London and booked a first appointment. Three months later I am walking straighter and sitting better, while my neck and back pain are things of the past. I feel taller, too, which I may be imagining, but the technique can increase your height by up to five centimetres if you were badly slumped beforehand.

The teaching centres on the neck, head and back. It trains you to use your body less harshly and to perform familiar movements and actions with less effort. There is very little effort in the lessons themselves, which sets apart the Alexander technique from pilates or yoga, which are exercise-based.

A typical lesson involves standing in front of a chair and learning to sit and stand with minimal effort. You spend some time lying on a bench with your knees bent to straighten the spine and relax your body while the teacher moves your arms and legs to train you to move them correctly.

The key is learning to break the bad habits accumulated over years. Try, for example, folding your arms the opposite way to normal. It feels odd, doesn't it? This is an example of a habit the body has formed which can be hard to break. Many of us carry our heads too far back and tilted skywards. The technique teaches you to let go of the muscles holding the head back, allowing it to resume its natural place on the summit of our spines. The head weighs four to six kilos, so any misalignment can cause problems for the neck and body.

The Alexander technique teaches you to think of the space above your head. This may sound daft, but it is an important element in the process of learning to hold yourself upright. You learn to observe how you use your body and how others use theirs – usually badly. Look how a colleague slumps back in a chair with his or her legs crossed. That puts all sorts of stresses and strains on the body. Even swimming can harm the neck. The Alexander technique can teach you to swim better, concentrating on technique rather than clocking up lengths. 'In too many of our activities we concentrate on how we get to a destination rather than the means or way of getting there,' says Shoop.

So who was Alexander and how did he come up with the technique? Frederick Matthias Alexander, an Australian theatrical orator born in 1869, found in his youth that his voice was failing during performances. He analysed himself and realised his posture was bad. He worked on improving it, with dramatic results. He brought his technique to London 100 years ago and quickly gathered a following that included some very famous people. He died in 1955, having established a teacher-training school in London, which is thriving today.

So if you are slouching along the road one day, feeling weighed down by your troubles, give a thought to the Alexander technique. It could help you walk tall again.

13 The writer learnt about the Alexander technique
  A after telling someone about her problems.
  B when she suddenly developed a bad back.
  C when massage failed to alleviate her back pain.
  D after a doctor told her she had bad posture.

14 The writer had been
  A concerned that her neck and back problems were caused by bad posture.
  B under the impression that poor posture was innate and could not be rectified.
  C aware that she had problems similar to those experienced by car mechanics.
  D uncertain about placing her trust in the Alexander technique.

15 The Alexander technique teaches that familiar movements
  A have been learnt by incorrect methods.
  B need more energy and effort than we think.
  C do not have to be performed so strenuously.
  D are the most common cause of backache.

16 It appears that the body forms habits that
  A inevitably cause physical pain.
  B can be difficult to change.
  C are a consequence of actions we perform.
  D develop in early childhood.

17 The Alexander technique
  A makes you aware of other people's faults.
  B has immediate and dramatic results.
  C helps athletes perform better.
  D brings about a change in body posture.

18 It is suggested that Frederick Alexander
  A believed in the benefits of exercise.
  B invented an alternative to yoga.
  C developed a form of exercise for actors.
  D recovered his vocal powers.

19 What is the writer's main purpose in the article?
  A to recommend regular physical exercise
  B to explain how debilitating backache can be
  C to suggest that back problems can be remedied
  D to explain the widespread occurrence of back pain

PAPER 1 Reading   ▶   Part 1
PAPER 2 Writing   Part 2
PAPER 3 Use of English   Part 3
PAPER 4 Listening   Part 4
PAPER 5 Speaking

You are going to read a newspaper article which discusses alternative power systems for vehicles. For questions **20–34**, choose from the sections of the article (**A–F**).

Mark your answers **on the separate answer sheet**.

In which section of the article are the following mentioned?

the advantages of conventional cars	**20** ....
a more compact version of existing technology	**21** ....
a willingness to invest in new technologies	**22** ....
limitations concerning where a vehicle can be used	**23** ....
a power source associated with a space programme	**24** ....
recycling waste products	**25** ....
a negative aesthetic impression	**26** ....
laws that encourage the development of new technologies	**27** ....
the inability to transport many people	**28** ....
devices that function best when conditions are constant	**29** ....
the rate of acceleration of a vehicle	**30** ....
the possibility of returning to a source of power used in the past	**31** ....
the existence of a market for a certain type of vehicle	**32** ....
the ability to switch from one power source to another	**33** ....
a car that is expensive to buy, and that has relatively low running costs	**34** ....

Vehicles of the Future

A The motor industry is finally showing some serious interest in developing cost-effective and environmentally-friendly technologies to power vehicles, as can be seen by the amount of money they are spending on research and development. There are some sound reasons for this: nowadays a significant number of people would prefer to buy a vehicle that did not emit greenhouse gases into the atmosphere or pollute the environment in other ways. But there are other forces at work in the industry as well. Governments throughout the world are demanding restrictions on gas emissions, and the goals they have set can only be met in the long run if conventional cars with internal combustion engines are phased out and replaced by vehicles that run on alternative power sources. Naturally, public opinion is ultimately behind legislation like this, which is aimed at protecting the environment. Governments, after all, need to respond to the wishes of their voters.

B For the last few decades innovators have been coming up with ideas for alternative power sources for automobiles, though so far none has had a significant appeal for consumers. The alternative technologies we have at present are lagging far behind the petrol-guzzling internal combustion engine in terms of speed and the distance that can be travelled before refuelling. But what does the future hold? At present a hybrid car propelled by a combination of an electric motor and petrol engine may be the best compromise for those who want to help save the planet and still have the convenience of a car. When you start the hybrid car and when you are driving normally, power is provided by the electric motor, which works with a battery. However, when the battery starts to go flat, the petrol engine starts automatically and drives a generator to recharge the battery. Similarly, when the car needs extra power – in order to accelerate, for instance – the petrol engine provides that power. This vehicle performs respectably, though not spectacularly: it can go from 0 to about 100 kph in around 10 seconds, has a top speed of 165 kph, and below average fuel consumption.

C And what of cars powered solely by electricity? Here the main stumbling block has always been storing the electricity: batteries may have come a long way, but they are still bulky and have to be charged for long periods. The latest completely electric car, for example, has a top speed of 60 kph and a range of 60 kilometres. It takes 6 hours to charge the battery fully. But the makers claim this is perfectly acceptable for city driving, when people are unable to go much faster or further in any case. Many cities provide benefits such as free parking for drivers of electric cars. But these vehicles are virtually confined to urban settings, which is off-putting, and most people find electric cars have a toy-like appearance which is definitely not appealing. Moreover, environmentalists point out that while the car itself may not emit poisonous fumes, as is the case with petrol-driven vehicles, this is of little real benefit to the environment if the electricity used to drive the car has been generated by coal or oil power stations, as is generally the case.

D First developed for use in missions to the moon, fuel cells appear to be the most serious challenger to the internal combustion engine as an alternative source of energy for both mobile and stationary applications. A fuel cell uses relatively straightforward technology that converts chemical energy into electrical energy with benign by-products. In fact, the only by-products are water, which is harmless, and heat. The other advantage is that fuel cells have no complex moving parts that need to be cooled or lubricated. But rather than replacing the internal combustion engine as the source of power for the vehicle itself, the fuel cell – in the view of some manufacturers – will only replace the battery and alternator, supplying electricity to vehicle systems, operating independently of the engine. The actual drive power for the vehicle itself would still be provided by the combustion engine. However, while fuel cells certainly hold a great deal of promise, there are some drawbacks. They need a steady supply of hydrogen, which needs to be extracted from some source, such as methanol gas, and this process can be cumbersome. In one model that uses fuel cells, the reformer required to extract the hydrogen from methanol takes up so much space that the vehicle can only seat the driver and one passenger.

E Another possibility is represented by turbines. Gas turbines have long been considered a possible mobile and smaller stationary power source, but their use has been limited for a variety of reasons, including cost, complexity and size. These large turbines shine when in steady-state applications but are not as efficient when speed and load are continually changing. However, a new generation of turbines – microturbines – has been developed in large measure for use in vehicles. They are small, high-speed engine systems that typically include the turbine, compressor and generator in a single unit with all the other vital components and control electronics. A different possibility in terms of energy supply for cars is household gas. A special device installed in a garage can compress the gas, which is then fed into the car. A gas car is cheaper to run, as well as being cleaner than a conventional car. On the other hand, the vehicle itself is expensive because the technology is new, and environmentalists argue that a gas car will produce only a little less carbon dioxide than petrol-driven vehicles.

F In the meantime, various compromises are being employed as temporary measures. For example, most diesel cars can now be converted to run on biodiesel fuel, which is made from used vegetable oils and animal fats. However, the environment lobby is not convinced that biodiesel helps cut local air pollution by any significant amount. Many experts believe that the ultimate solution to the problem of reducing dangerous emissions ultimately lies with electric vehicles once the battery technology has improved. Some experts even believe that the future may lie with steam cars, and since the first genuine 'automobile' – a vehicle capable of moving itself – was powered by steam more than two centuries ago, it could be that the wheel is coming full circle.

You **must** answer this question. Write your answer in **180–220** words in an appropriate style.

1 You are the secretary of the student council at the college where you are studying. Recently you came up with the idea of having a career day, when companies can send representatives to talk to students and help them plan their careers. You mentioned the idea to the principal of the college, and as a result, he sent you a memo supporting the idea and asking for a more detailed proposal.

Read the principal's memo and the notes you have made on it. Then, using the information carefully, write your proposal.

Memo

To: The Secretary, Student Council
From: The Principal
Re: Career Day

I feel you have a basically sound idea here. I'd like more details, and please bear in mind the following:

Friday, early June – end of semester?

* What day and time of year would be best?

Large lecture theatre? Set out desk for each company so students can approach them.

* What space will you need?

Overhead projector?

* Any equipment?

Not sure – about 10. Will write to 15 big local companies.

* How many companies will send reps?

Posters + note in college newspaper

Could you give me an idea what sort of publicity you need?

Thanks,

David Oliphant, Principal

Now write your **proposal**.

PAPER 1 Reading

PAPER 2 Writing ▶ Part 1

PAPER 3 Use of English | **Part 2**

PAPER 4 Listening

PAPER 5 Speaking

Write an answer to **one** of the questions **2–5** in this part. Write your answer in **220–260** words in an appropriate style.

---

2 You see the following announcement in a magazine called *Leisure Today* and decide to enter the competition.

> ### DO YOU HAVE AN INTERESTING OR UNUSUAL INDOOR LEISURE ACTIVITY?
>
> It could be anything from calligraphy to making models or embroidery! If so, write and tell us about the activity, explaining its attraction. The writer of the best entry will win £250.

Write your **competition entry**.

3 You see the following notice in a magazine called *Career Management International*:

> ### 'Soon nobody will spend all their working lives with the same employer – or even in one single type of work.'
>
> What do young people today feel about the necessity of having a range of skills and qualifications rather than knowledge of one specialised field? Are they stimulated or disconcerted by the prospect of performing a range of professional activities? Would they miss the security of a job for life – or see the alternative as a challenge?

Write your **article**.

4 You are a regular contributor to a magazine for young people called *Film Scene*. You have been asked to write a review of two films which you saw recently, and of which most people had great expectations. You enjoyed one of the films, but found the other one very disappointing.

Write your **review**.

5 Answer **one** of the following two questions based on your reading of **one** of the set books.

Either

5(a) Your teacher has asked you to write an essay on the following topic, based on your reading of the book: *'The protagonist in the novel grows as the plot unfolds, learning from his/her experiences.'* Discuss this statement in relation to the book you have been reading.

Write your **essay**.

Or

5(b) The teacher of the creative writing class you have been attending has asked you to write a review of a book you have read examining how the relationship between two of the main characters affects developments in the story. You must include examples from the book to illustrate your views.

Write your **review**.

For questions **1–12**, read the text below and decide which answer (**A, B, C** or **D**) best fits each gap. There is an example at the beginning (**0**).

Mark your answers **on the separate answer sheet.**

Example:

| 0 | **A** band | **B** scale | **C** range | **D** scope |

Raising Awareness

In cities around the world a wide (**0**) ...... of schemes is being instigated to promote environmental awareness. 'It's just as easy to (**1**) ...... of litter properly as it is to drop it on the streets,' says city councillor Mike Edwards, who has (**2**) ...... on the government to mount a concerted campaign to deal with the problem of litter. 'It's just a matter of encouraging people to do so as a (**3**) ...... of course. Once the habit is ingrained, they won't even (**4**) ...... they are doing it. After all, think what we have achieved with recyclable waste in the home. Sorting paper, glass, aluminium and plastic waste and then depositing it in the appropriate container outside is (**5**) ...... a great chore any more. People have become accustomed to doing this, so it doesn't (**6**) ...... to them that they are spending any additional time in the process. Only if they have to carry this waste for some appreciable distance to find a suitable container do they feel they are (**7**) ....'

Most people know they should behave in a responsible way and just need (**8**) ...... to do so. So a quirky, (**9**) ...... gimmick might be enough to change behaviour. With this in (**10**) ...... , the city of Berlin is introducing rubbish bins that say 'danke', 'thank you' and 'merci' – Berlin is a(n) (**11**) ...... city – when someone drops an item of rubbish into them. It might just (**12**) ...... the trick in this city, too.

1	**A** dispose	**B** discard	**C** jettison	**D** throw
2	**A** appealed	**B** called	**C** approached	**D** urged
3	**A** principle	**B** system	**C** matter	**D** duty
4	**A** notice	**B** remark	**C** comprehend	**D** appreciate
5	**A** almost	**B** barely	**C** virtually	**D** hardly
6	**A** concern	**B** occur	**C** impress	**D** strike
7	**A** inconvenienced	**B** sacrificed	**C** complicated	**D** imposed
8	**A** ordering	**B** prompting	**C** forcing	**D** obliging
9	**A** lighthearted	**B** mundane	**C** subjective	**D** intense
10	**A** context	**B** thought	**C** spirit	**D** mind
11	**A** worldly	**B** mixed	**C** cosmopolitan	**D** international
12	**A** serve	**B** do	**C** make	**D** play

For questions **13–27**, read the text below and think of the word which best fits each gap. Use only **one** word in each gap. There is an example at the beginning (**0**).

Write your answers **IN CAPITAL LETTERS on the separate answer sheet**.

Example:

0	THESE	0

Flying in Style

(0) .... days commercial airliners are becoming larger, (13) .... makes flying cheaper but in many ways more impersonal. Perhaps (14) .... a response to this, a more old-fashioned way of taking to the air is gaining popularity in Britain. (15) .... number of companies today offer charter flights in small aircraft. You hire the plane and pilot, just as you might hire a chauffeur-driven car, and (16) .... are yours for the day.

If you are flying on a short trip (17) .... Britain to the continent, a light plane can get you (18) .... almost as quickly as a jet airliner. In fact, the whole journey takes far (19) .... time, since you don't need to be at the airport hours (20) .... advance. And if you share the cost with friends, it can be cheaper than a scheduled flight.

The atmosphere (21) .... board is relaxed and friendly, with formalities (22) .... passport control and customs, if not entirely eliminated, at least kept (23) .... a minimum. Instead of walking for (24) .... seems like miles through a vast airport terminal, (25) .... it's time to take off, you simply stroll over and ease (26) .... into the plane. Even the flight itself is more fun, as (27) .... as the weather is fine. And if you want to descend and take a closer look at something on the ground, just ask the pilot; you're the boss!

For questions **28–37**, read the text below. Use the word given in capitals at the end of some of the lines to form a word that fits in the gap **in the same line**. There is an example at the beginning (**0**).

Write your answers **IN CAPITAL LETTERS on the separate answer sheet.**

Example:

0	*NOTORIETY*	0

Black Widow Spider

The black widow spider's (**0**) .... is not without foundation. However, an element of exaggeration has led to certain (**28**) .... regarding its evil nature.   **NOTORIOUS**

CONCEPT

Firstly, this spider is not as dangerous as is often thought. While it is indeed one of the most (**29**) .... species of spider, its venom being fifteen times stronger than that of the prairie rattlesnake, its bite injects such a small amount of venom by (**30**) .... that it is unlikely to kill humans. In fact, (**31**) .... are rare.   **VENOM**

COMPARE

FATAL

Black widows bite only if they are touched or their web is threatened. Furthermore, only the adult female is poisonous. Those most at risk from the female are the spider's natural prey – insects – and male black widow spiders. The latter are vulnerable as the female is (**32**) .... by nature, and has been known to kill and eat the male after mating. Such (**33**) .... are rare, but they explain how the spider got its name – and its reputation.   **SOLITUDE**

OCCUR

Nevertheless, the (**34**) .... effects of this spider's bite should not be (**35**) .... , and if you live in a temperate climate and have a fireplace in your home, it is advisable to take (**36**) .... Black widow spiders often inhabit wood piles, so you should wear gloves when handling firewood. Furthermore, since black widow spiders are (**37**) .... to many insecticides, you should regularly clean out likely hiding places.   **PLEASE**

ESTIMATE

CAUTION

RESIST

PAPER 1 Reading

PAPER 2 Writing

PAPER 3 Use of English ▶

PAPER 4 Listening

PAPER 5 Speaking

Part 1
Part 2
Part 3
Part 4
Part 5

For questions **38–42**, think of **one** word only which can be used appropriately in all three sentences. Here is an example (**0**).

Example:

0
- We will do all the work, but they will .... all the credit, as usual!
- She will .... offence if you tell her that hairstyle doesn't suit her.
- They threatened to .... David to court unless he stopped playing his drums all night.

| 0 | *TAKE* | **0** |

Write **only** the missing word **IN CAPITAL LETTERS on the separate answer sheet**.

38
- The college offers a wide .... of courses, from business studies to hair styling.
- We looked out of the plane window as we flew over the .... of mountains.
- The bird is just out of .... of my binoculars, so I can't make out what species it is.

39
- Sally .... on her soup to cool it down.
- A sudden gust of wind .... out the candle.
- They were making counterfeit money, but somebody .... the whistle on them, and they got arrested.

40
- There's a .... chance that she's still in her office, although she did say she was going out for lunch.
- Alicia has a small cottage on a .... island off the coast of Scotland.
- He was a cold, ... person, who was difficult to talk to, let alone get close to!

41
- The project was going really well until we .... a snag, and that delayed us.
- Sue and Raymond really .... it off, and I'm delighted they liked each other!
- The old lady .... her attacker on the head with her walking stick.

42
- George was so exhausted that he was in no .... to drive a car.
- Tanya has been training all winter, and she's in peak ....
- On no .... are children under ten allowed on this fairground ride.

For questions **43–50**, complete the second sentence so that it has a similar meaning to the first sentence, using the word given. **Do not change the word given.** You must use between **three** and **six** words, including the word given. Here is an example (**0**).

Example:

0   Jane regretted speaking so rudely to the old lady.
MORE

Jane .... politely to the old lady.

| 0 | WISHED SHE HAD SPOKEN MORE | 0 |

Write the missing words **IN CAPITAL LETTERS on the separate answer sheet.**

---

43   The police have issued a description of the man wanted in connection with the robbery.
BEEN

A description .... wanted in connection with last night's robbery.

44   I can't work because Joey won't leave me alone!
KEEPS

Joey .... I can't work!

45   'You really must stay and have dinner with us!' said Laura.
STAYING

Laura .... for dinner.

46   Alan split up with Julie because he couldn't stand her constant nagging.
WITH

Alan split up with Julie because he .... her constant nagging.

47   If you need me, call me any time, night or day.
MATTER

Call me if you need me, ... be.

48   I don't want to be disturbed at all this morning!
ACCOUNT

On .... disturbed this morning!

49   If Maurice hadn't told Beth about that letter, we wouldn't have argued.
FOR

Had .... telling Beth about that letter, we wouldn't have argued.

50   We're going to miss the start of the film if we don't hurry.
TIME

Unless we hurry, the film .... we get there.

You will hear three different extracts. For questions **1–6**, choose the answer (**A, B** or **C**) which fits best according to what you hear. There are two questions for each extract.

Extract One

You hear part of an interview with a woman who has changed her lifestyle.

1 The idea for buying an olive farm came from
 A a contact in Greece.
 B Kathy's husband.
 C a site on the Internet.

> 1

2 Kathy says she had expected to
 A miss her home and family in Britain.
 B find life in Greece more difficult.
 C feel nostalgic about her old job.

> 2

Extract Two

You hear part of a radio discussion in which two teachers are talking about teaching poetry.

3 The man feels that generally poetry
 A is not taken seriously by teachers.
 B is not a popular subject to teach.
 C makes for an uninspiring lesson.

> 3

4 The woman's main argument is that
 A teachers should encourage students to respond to poetry in their own way.

 B students need guidance if they are to understand and appreciate poetry.

 C only the poet can give us a valid interpretation of his or her work.

> 4

Extract Three

You hear two people talking about an unusual kind of competition.

5 According to Jake, he stopped at the pub
 A out of curiosity.
 B to eat something.
 C to meet someone.

> 5

6 The object of the competition is to
 A tell the most convincing lie.
 B tell the funniest anecdote.
 C tell the most obvious tall story.

> 6

You will hear part of a talk by the director of a sports academy. For questions **7–14**, complete the sentences.

The Waterman Sports Academy

The Waterman Sports Academy offers training in several sports, including swimming and [**7**]

Helen coached a girl who wanted to compete in the [**8**]

Her interest in sports medicine dates back to the time when her [**9**] suffered a back injury.

To be successful in a particular sport, an athlete must have the right [**10**]

Helen says that fitness is important, even in sports like [**11**]

She stresses that a [**12**] is vital in physical development.

Athletes who do not have the latest [**13**] are handicapped in competitions.

In Helen's opinion, the most important factor for success is having the right [**14**]

You will hear part of an interview with Harold Mackenzie, who has written a book about early adolescence. For questions **15–20**, choose the correct answer (**A**, **B**, **C** or **D**) which fits best according to what you hear.

15 According to Harold, what is the main reason pre-teens are receiving more publicity?
A Psychologists now understand the importance of the pre-teen years.
B A great deal of research is being done into the way children develop.
C Pre-teens are now demanding more attention from the media.
D People now realise pre-teens have economic power.

16 Harold suggests that pre-teens
A cannot keep up with their peers.
B start to choose their own clothes.
C develop unusual tastes.
D become more aware of their image.

17 Harold claims friendships are important to pre-teens because
A these relationships help them establish their identities.
B the children are beginning to rebel against their families.
C friends are starting to replace family members.
D the children are now capable of reacting to other people.

18 He suggests that an alternative method of academic evaluation would
A enable parents to be more supportive.
B be more effective than examinations.
C mean less stress for pre-teens.
D delay the onset of tension in adolescence.

19 How does he suggest parents can help pre-teens develop confidence?
A by allowing them to buy whatever they like
B by allowing them a certain degree of independence
C by allowing them to make decisions about their spare time
D by allowing them to control unimportant aspects of their lives

20 According to Harold, what is the greatest challenge facing parents of pre-teens?
A deciding what kinds of toys to buy for their children
B developing the correct approach to material possessions
C establishing a way of communicating effectively with their children
D discovering what kind of help their children really need

You will hear five short extracts in which people talk about their experiences at the theatre.

While you listen you must complete both tasks.

Task One

For questions **21–25**, choose from the list **A–H** what each speaker says about the show he or she enjoyed most.

A   The atmosphere was intimate.

B   I loved the period costumes.

C   The play was very moving.

D   I saw the play a couple of times.

E   The play had a large cast.

F   I went along reluctantly.

G   The star of the show was very talented.

H   The show was performed by a foreign company.

Speaker 1	21
Speaker 2	22
Speaker 3	23
Speaker 4	24
Speaker 5	25

Task Two

For questions **26–30**, choose from the list **A–H** the view each speaker has about why theatre is an interesting medium.

A   The thrill of watching big stars is unforgettable.

B   You can get carried away by the performance.

C   The theatre can be a communal experience.

D   It is interesting to learn from the cast.

E   Ideas can be conveyed with stunning force.

F   Each performance is a unique experience.

G   You sometimes feel transported to a different era.

H   The theatre can surprise and stimulate the audience.

Speaker 1	26
Speaker 2	27
Speaker 3	28
Speaker 4	29
Speaker 5	30

Part 1 (3 minutes)

The examiner will ask you a few questions about yourself and then ask you to talk to your partner. For example, the examiner may ask you:

- How popular are the cinema and theatre in your town or region?
- Which do you prefer, going to the cinema or watching films on television?
- What was the last film that you enjoyed?

Part 2 (4 minutes)

You will each be asked to talk on your own for a minute without interruption. You will each be given a set of three photographs in turn to talk about. After your partner has finished speaking, you will be asked a brief question connected with your partner's photographs. You will have thirty seconds to answer.

> **Stress** (compare, contrast and speculate)

Turn to pictures 1–3 on page **211**, which show people in stressful situations.

Candidate A, compare and contrast two of these pictures and say what is stressful about these situations. Which might be the most stressful and why?

Candidate B, what sort of situation causes you the greatest amount of stress?

> **Struggling against the elements** (compare, contrast and speculate)

Turn to pictures 1–3 on page **212**, which show people who have to struggle against the elements.

Candidate B, compare and contrast two of these pictures and say what kind of problems the people face. How might they be feeling in their current situation?

Candidate A, what sort of struggle against the elements would you find most difficult?

Part 3 (4 minutes)

> **Creativity** (discuss, evaluate and select)

Turn to the pictures on page **213**, which show different forms of creativity.

Talk to each other about the type of creativity in each of these situations and then decide which picture best shows the rewards of being creative.

Part 4 (4 minutes)

The examiner will encourage you to develop the topic of your discussion in Part 3 by asking questions such as:

- How important is it to people to feel they are creative in some way?
- Do you feel people get a similar sense of satisfaction from other activities?
- It is sometimes said that everyone has the potential to be creative in some way. Do you agree? Why (not)?
- Does modern society encourage people to be creative more or less than was the case in previous times?

UNIVERSITY *of* **CAMBRIDGE**
ESOL Examinations

Do not write in this box

Candidate Name
If not already printed, write name
in CAPITALS and complete the
Candidate No. grid (in pencil).

Candidate Signature

Examination Title

Centre

Supervisor:

If the candidate is ABSENT or has WITHDRAWN shade here ⬚

SAMPLE

Centre No.

Candidate No.

Examination
Details

0	0	0	0
1	1	1	1
2	2	2	2
3	3	3	3
4	4	4	4
5	5	5	5
6	6	6	6
7	7	7	7
8	8	8	8
9	9	9	9

Candidate Answer Sheet

Instructions

Use a PENCIL (B or HB).

Mark ONE letter for each question.

For example, if you think B is the right answer to the question, mark your answer sheet like this:

0   A B̲ C D E F G H

Rub out any answer you wish to change using an eraser.

1	A B C D E F G H
2	A B C D E F G H
3	A B C D E F G H
4	A B C D E F G H
5	A B C D E F G H
6	A B C D E F G H
7	A B C D E F G H
8	A B C D E F G H
9	A B C D E F G H
10	A B C D E F G H
11	A B C D E F G H
12	A B C D E F G H
13	A B C D E F G H
14	A B C D E F G H
15	A B C D E F G H
16	A B C D E F G H
17	A B C D E F G H
18	A B C D E F G H
19	A B C D E F G H
20	A B C D E F G H

21	A B C D E F G H
22	A B C D E F G H
23	A B C D E F G H
24	A B C D E F G H
25	A B C D E F G H
26	A B C D E F G H
27	A B C D E F G H
28	A B C D E F G H
29	A B C D E F G H
30	A B C D E F G H
31	A B C D E F G H
32	A B C D E F G H
33	A B C D E F G H
34	A B C D E F G H
35	A B C D E F G H
36	A B C D E F G H
37	A B C D E F G H
38	A B C D E F G H
39	A B C D E F G H
40	A B C D E F G H

A-H 40 CAS

denote
Print Limited 0121 520 5100

DP594/300

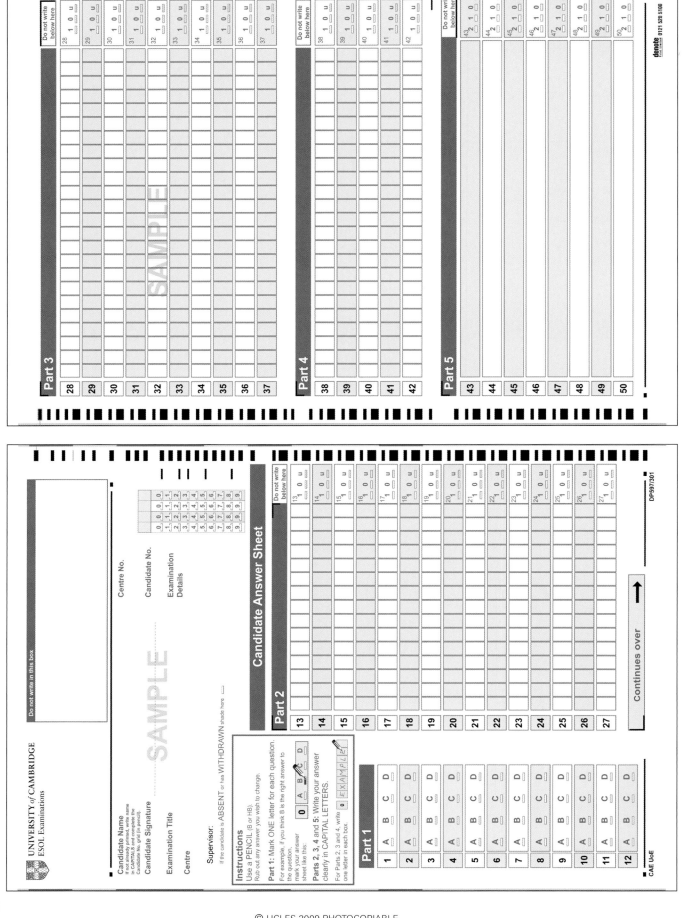

Paper 4 Listening

UNIVERSITY of CAMBRIDGE
ESOL Examinations

Do not write in this box

Candidate Name
If not already printed, write name in CAPITALS and complete the Candidate No. grid (in pencil).

Candidate Signature

Examination Title

Centre

Centre No.

Candidate No.

Examination Details

Supervisor:
If the candidate is ABSENT or has WITHDRAWN shade here ☐

Test version: A B C D E F J K L M N   Special arrangements: S H

SAMPLE

Candidate Answer Sheet

Instructions

Use a PENCIL (B or HB).
Rub out any answer you wish to change using an eraser.

Parts 1, 3 and 4:
Mark ONE letter for each question.

For example, if you think **B** is the right answer to the question, mark your answer sheet like this:

0   A ☐ B ▇ C ☐

Part 2:
Write your answer clearly in CAPITAL LETTERS.

Write one letter or number in each box.
If the answer has more than one word, leave one box empty between words.

For example:

0 N U M B E R   1 2

Turn this sheet over to start.

CAE L   DP600/304

Part 1

	A	B	C
1	A	B	C
2	A	B	C
3	A	B	C
4	A	B	C
5	A	B	C
6	A	B	C

Part 2 (Remember to write in CAPITAL LETTERS or numbers)

Do not write below here

SAMPLE

7	1 0 u
8	1 0 u
9	1 0 u
10	1 0 u
11	1 0 u
12	1 0 u
13	1 0 u
14	1 0 u

Part 3

	A	B	C	D
15	A	B	C	D
16	A	B	C	D
17	A	B	C	D
18	A	B	C	D
19	A	B	C	D
20	A	B	C	D

Part 4

	A	B	C	D	E	F	G	H
21	A	B	C	D	E	F	G	H
22	A	B	C	D	E	F	G	H
23	A	B	C	D	E	F	G	H
24	A	B	C	D	E	F	G	H
25	A	B	C	D	E	F	G	H
26	A	B	C	D	E	F	G	H
27	A	B	C	D	E	F	G	H
28	A	B	C	D	E	F	G	H
29	A	B	C	D	E	F	G	H
30	A	B	C	D	E	F	G	H

denote 0121 520 5100

TEST 1

▶▶ **PART 2**

Candidate A

Language bank

These people could be ...

They seem to be ...

I imagine ...

I suppose ...

I'm fairly sure ...

I'd say they're probably ...

Apparently, ...

Judging by the fact that ...

Similarly, ...

I can't tell who/where/what ...

actors
amateur
annual tradition
bow to the audience
brightly coloured costumes and
   masks
clown in a circus
curtain call
on the stage
professional
put on a performance
revellers
street party
take part in a festival/carnival/
   performance/play
well-equipped theatre

- • Why are the people dressed in this way?
- • How do you think they are feeling?

▶▶ **PART 2**

Candidate B

Language bank

The picture shows/depicts ...

They must be ...

It might/could be ...

He/She seems to be ...

In contrast to ...

As in the previous picture, ...

There are a number of advantages/
disadvantages to working ...

One advantage/disadvantage would
be ...

I imagine it's very satisfying to ...

agricultural workers
cheap labour
craft
create something with your hands
cut off from contact with the outside
  world
executive
exhausting
field on a hillside
highly paid/badly paid
indoors/outdoors
job satisfaction
make objects from clay
manual labour
mentally/physically exhausting
potter
sophisticated modern office
spectacular view of the city
stressful
suffer from the heat/stress
well-equipped office

• **What are the advantages and disadvantages of working in these environments?**

▶▶ **PART 3**

   Candidates A and B

- **What aspects of modern life do these pictures show?**
- **Which two would you choose to illustrate that modern life has both advantages and disadvantages?**

Language bank

The benefits/drawbacks of ... are obvious, I think.

What about the advantages/disadvantages, in your view?

Do the disadvantages outweigh the advantages in your opinion?

It's easy to see the benefits of laptop computers, don't you think?

Mobile phones certainly make it easier to keep in touch, wouldn't you say?

I'm not sure whether there are any health risks associated with heating food in a microwave oven. What do you think?

It's usually more convenient to drive somewhere than to take public transport, but surely the pollution caused by cars is too high a price to pay?

I'd find it difficult to think of any disadvantages connected with electricity.

Perhaps we have to distinguish between electricity itself and the means of generating it.

Is this a nuclear power station?

I'm not sure whether this photo is meant to illustrate modern western medicine in general or operations in particular.

microwave oven meal	laptop computer	sports coupé
operating theatre	power station	mobile phone

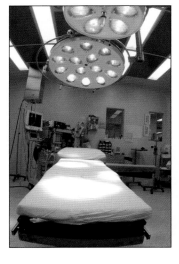

▶▶ **PART 2**

Candidate A

Language bank

I guess/I imagine ...

He/She appears to be ...

He/She may be ...

He/She looks as though ...

On the other hand, he/she might be ...

To judge from the clothes he/she's wearing, ...

To judge from his/her posture, ...

about to dive
apprehensive
bathing trunks
business suit
concentrate on what you are about to do
diving board
interview for a job
nervous
overcome your fears
have your arms outstretched
wait in the wings

- **What could the people be anticipating?**
- **How do you think they are feeling?**

• **Why are the people alone?**

• **How do you think they are feeling?**

Language bank

I can't tell whether the person is a man or a woman.

It looks as if/though …

I can't see the expression on his/her face, but I think he/she must be …

Perhaps he/she feels …

It's also possible that he/she …

If I were him/her, I'd probably feel …

The landscape/room might make me feel …

The sun appears to be setting because the scene is bathed in red light.

The person is dwarfed by the landscape.

Perhaps she's waiting …

She might simply be looking at something outside.

alone	long shadows
depressing atmosphere	peer through the curtains
dry grass	remote
elderly lady	rugged
formal clothes	spectacular
insignificant	suffer from loneliness
inspiring	tracksuit
lonely	uplifting

▶ 1

▶ 2

▶ 3

▶▶ **PART 3**

   Candidates A and B

> • **How important is motivation in these situations?**
> • **In which situation might motivation have a positive effect, and in which one might it have a negative effect?**

Language bank

I'd imagine that anyone who wishes to ... would have to be motivated.

He/She's probably motivated by ...

He/She must be motivated by ...

People can be motivated to excel/overcome difficulties.

Judging by ... , I imagine he/she works very hard.

A powerful sense of motivation could be negative if a person became obsessed with his/her goals.

Do you think such people might put others at risk?

Surely this sort of motivation is the most harmful type that we have seen?

depressed
discouraged/encouraged
inspired
jealous
miss out on other aspects of life
overcome physical hardships
personal ambition
push yourself to achieve a goal
ruthless and unfeeling
single-minded
the desire for knowledge
the desire to acquire material possessions
the desire to be admired by your colleagues
the desire to be the first
the desire to excel
the desire to gain the approval of others
the desire to impress others
the desire to overcome hardship/difficulties
the desire to pursue a career

▶▶ **PART 2**

   Candidate A

> • **Why might the people be leaving?**
> • **How might they be feeling?**

Language bank

It looks as if/though ...

They appear to be ...

They must be ...

I would say he/she's probably ...

Perhaps they're going somewhere on holiday.

They're about to leave on a holiday, not a business trip.

Like the man in the second picture, ...

Unlike the man in the second picture, these people are ...

The mode of transport in this case is very different.

about to board a spaceship
about to set off
boot of the car
briefcase
business trip
casual clothes
crew of a spaceship
embark on a journey/mission
family car
intercity train
load the luggage
members of a family
space mission
spacesuit
station platform
suit and tie
suitcase on wheels

▶▶ **PART 2**

Candidate B

Language bank

He/She looks very tired.

He/She must be feeling exhausted.

This makes me think he/she's been working ...

In all likelihood, ...

Of course, it's also possible that ...

I suppose they feel satisfied as well as exhausted.

In contrast to the previous two images, this picture shows ...

excited by the prospect of (doing something)
look after a young child
loosen your tie
mental/physical work
renovate a house
rest your head on your hand
stare at a computer screen
stiff muscles
wear a shirt and tie

- Why might the people be tired?
- What kind of exhaustion – mental or physical – is each person feeling, and why?

▶▶ PART 3

Candidates A and B

Language bank

They seem very proud of ...

Judging by their expression, ...

He/She's probably proud of his/her achievement.

Naturally, he/she must be proud of this accomplishment.

This kind of pride is very natural.

I'd say he/she's probably a ... .

Is his/her pride due solely to the fact that he/she ... ?

Obviously, he/she's just ...

cheer
dedicate yourself to achieving your
   goal
delighted
justifiably proud
lean against the car
own an impressive car
parental pride
politician
proud of your child/offspring
public acclaim
push a stroller
satisfied with yourself
trophy
victory
vote for someone
win an election
work and save in order to buy
   something

- **In what way are the people proud?**
- **Which two pictures would you choose to show that pride has different forms?**

▶▶ **PART 2**

Candidate A

Language bank

Presumably, this sport appeals to people who ...

It attracts people who are ...

People who are ... are inclined to do this sport.

People who want to excel in this sport must be ...

This sport does not demand the same level of fitness as ...

In contrast to ... , this sport ...

aim
archer
archery
bow and arrow
bull's eye
concentration
co-ordination
head a ball
hit the target
individual/team sport
powerful physique
take part in
score a goal
training and practice
weightlifting

- **What kind of training do these sports require?**
- **What are the advantages and disadvantages of taking part in a team sport, as opposed to an individual sport?**

▶1

▶2

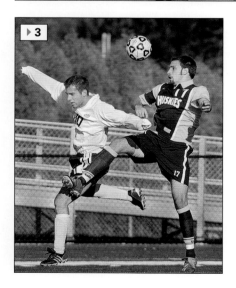

▶3

▶▶ **PART 2**

Candidate B

> • **What might be the advantages of living in these places?**
> • **What might be impractical about living in them?**

Language bank

I should think a home like this would be ...

In contrast to the other buildings, this home ...

The house seems to be made of ...

One advantage/disadvantage of a home like this would be ...

Its location would be a disadvantage in case of illness or other emergencies.

The building itself would be expensive to keep up because ...

It would require a large staff to look after a home like this.

Some people may dislike feeling that their home is just like all the rest.

Privacy might be a problem in a home like this.

(lack of) privacy
cut off from civilisation
flats in a high-rise block
high heating and maintenance costs
insulation
isolated
log cabin
mansion
rural/urban environment
stately home
unsuitable for domestic purposes

▶ **1**

▶ **2**

▶ **3**

▶▶ **PART 3**

Candidates A and B

Language bank

Why couldn't we use this picture to show an interesting aspect of the city?

I think ferries are an interesting means of transport, don't you?

I'd say it shows the city is concerned about the environment.

I hardly feel buses are interesting enough to feature on a brochure.

I completely agree with you about that.

I think you're absolutely right about that.

I take your point.

I agree with you up to a point, but I think there are other factors to be taken into consideration.

I'm afraid I have to disagree with you on that point.

cause less pollution than other forms of transport
cycle path
efficient
extensive transport system
ferry
highway
lane
tram
underground train

- Which three photographs should be used on the front cover of a tourist brochure in order to give the impression that this is an interesting city to visit?

▶▶ **PART 2**

Candidate A

- **What are the advantages of doing these activities in a group?**
- **What might be the negative aspects of these activities?**

Language bank

These people are wearing some sort of uniform ...

They're wearing white shirts and dark trousers.

They're all looking in the same direction and saluting.

They look as if they're in the army or some branch of the armed forces.

They look as if they're parading.

They're musicians in an orchestra.

Clearly, they feel part of a group because ...

As far as I can tell, the orchestra is made up of people of different ages.

Presumably, the sense of belonging to a group comes from their shared interest in music.

They may be amateur musicians, but they might also be professionals.

belt
blue and white helmet
brass instrument
bright red jacket
conductor
military uniform
music stand
officer
protest
sense of shared danger
wind instrument

▶ 1

▶ 2

▶ 3

▶▶ **PART 2**

Candidate B

- What sort of experience have the people gained?
- What might be the difficulties of gaining this experience?

Language bank

The farmer appears to be examining his crops.

Although the plants look healthy to me, it's possible that the harvest won't be as good as he had hoped.

His experience may allow him to predict how good the harvest will be.

It's not entirely clear from his expression how he feels about ...

The maize may be infected with some kind of disease.

He seems to be a teacher.

He may be demonstrating something to his pupils.

Perhaps his experience has led him to conclude that ...

I suppose he's learnt how to use discipline in a class/gain the respect of the children he's teaching.

He seems to be examining the horse's hoof.

Perhaps he is a cowboy or a farrier.

▶ 1

▶ 2

▶ 3

▶▶ PART 3

Candidates A and B

Language bank

Do we agree that better time management is necessary?

Would you say he/she's managed his/her time badly?

It's very obvious that ...

Maybe he/she should/shouldn't ...

If this situation occurs regularly, I think he/she needs to manage his/her time better.

This illustrates one of the problems connected with bad time management.

It must be frustrating to be in this situation.

I can imagine exactly how he/she feels.

Maybe he/she has no choice but to ...

badly organised
chat idly
deliver stationery supplies
ensure you get to the bus stop
   on time
have too much time on your hands
inefficient
miss the bus
point at your watch
queue at a post office counter
run to catch a bus
the baby in the high chair is
   screaming
the child is tugging at her dress
waste time

- How could these problems be helped by better time management?
- Which situation would benefit most, and which would benefit least from better time management?

▶▶ **PART 2**

Candidate A

Language bank

I imagine he/she's anxious about ...

My impression is that he/she ...

My guess would be that he/she ...

Maybe he/she's already ... and is now ...

Whereas the first picture shows someone worried about ... , this picture depicts someone in a state of anxiety about ...

The person's facial expression shows he/she's anxious or worried.

deal with a problem
exam results
notice board
patient
physician
possible treatment.
talk about the prognosis

• **What might be making these people anxious?**
• **Which situation is the most stressful?**

▶ 1

▶ 2

▶ 3

▶▶ **PART 2**
Candidate B

Language bank

It's obvious that he/she ...

I suppose he/she's pleased/relieved that ...

He/She's probably feeling pleased because ...

He/She's happy because he/she's finally managed (to do something).

I would guess that he/she ... for the first time, and he/she's delighted that he/she's achieved this.

He/She's expressing his/her pleasure at this achievement.

It's not entirely clear what/who ...

academic gown
bicycle fitted with outriders
congratulate someone on his/her promotion
degree/diploma
sense of elation
give the 'thumbs-up' sign
graduate from college/university
sign a mutually beneficial business deal
successful negotiation

- What have these people achieved?
- How might they be feeling?

▶▶ PART 3

Candidates A and B

- What is each person expressing by his or her appearance?
- Which two pictures would you choose to illustrate the wide variety of messages that appearance can give out?

Language bank

The clothes he/she's wearing give the impression that he/she's ...

Perhaps he/she intends his/her appearance as some sort of statement.

Surely his/her appearance is a symbol of what he/she's attained/what he/she believes?

Don't you think he/she's trying to show the world ... ?

He/She doesn't seem to care about convention/fashion.

Would you say his/her appearance shows ... ?

He/She's wearing what looks like ...

He/She comes across as ...

anti-establishment
arrogant
capable
catwalk
cloak trimmed with fur
coat/gown with a large fur collar
conservative
diamond necklace
efficient
extravagant clothes
fashion victim
formal event
haughty
loose-fitting
member of the armed forces
rank
scruffy
three-piece suit
unorthodox clothes
veil

▶▶ **PART 2**
Candidate A

• **What could be prompting people to show respect in these situations?**
• **How might the people receiving the show of respect feel?**

Language bank

She might be his grandmother.

He/She's looking at ... with a friendly but respectful expression.

He/She may respect ... for several reasons.

He/She may have been brought up to behave respectfully towards older people.

He/She appears to have made a speech.

I expect an audience is obliged to applaud a speaker out of politeness, but the facial expressions of these men suggest that their respect is genuine.

I know he's a famous politician, but I can't remember his name.

I think the man in the photo is Nelson Mandela, but I'm not sure.

applaud
bow to someone
express your respect and
    admiration
honour someone for his/her
    achievements
make a speech
politeness/courtesy is important in
    this culture
politician
(regrettable lack of) respect for old
    people
statesman
western society

▶ 1

▶ 2

▶ 3

DIRECTOR GENERAL

▶▶ **PART 2**

Candidate B

- •What kind of partnerships are these?
- • How do the partners feel about each other?

Language bank

There's no way of telling whether they're the architects or the owners.

In all likelihood, they're colleagues.

They're wearing ... , so they're probably ...

An undertaking like this must involve working closely with other people, all of whom have different skills to contribute.

If they're partners, they must have a great deal of confidence in one another.

Trust would be the basis of their working relationship, I imagine.

In this kind of partnership, I imagine respect for the other person's ability must be crucial.

architect
building site
busker
collaboration
colleague
contribution
co-operation
engineer
hard hat
have confidence in someone
intellectual ability
lab technician
laboratory
mutual trust
rely on your colleague
street musician
white lab coat

▶▶ **PART 3**

Candidates A and B

> • **How do the pictures show different ways of relaxing?**
> • **Which two pictures best illustrate the diversity in the ways people can relax?**

Language bank

This is a physically taxing activity, but I suppose it represents a way of relaxing for some people.

I imagine there's some danger involved as well.

Personally, I don't understand why people would choose to ...

This game usually requires a partner, but it's also possible to play against a computer program.

This is a solitary/creative/exciting pastime.

Gardening is a very popular hobby, especially with older people.

battle of wits
chess
competitive
croquet
croquet mallet
danger of dehydration
easel
lawn
recreation
rucksack
sand dune
weed the flower bed

TEST 8

▸▸ **PART 2**

Candidate A

- • What is stressful about these situations?
- • Which might be the most stressful and why?

▸ **1**

▸ **2**

▸ **3**

▶▶ **PART 2**

Candidate B

| • What kind of problems do the people face? |
| • How might they be feeling in their current situation? |

Language bank

The people in the boat are probably there from choice.

Probably they feel exhilarated, even though there are dangers involved.

They may not have realised how dangerous the situation would be.

They might regret ...

In contrast, the man probably has no alternative but to do battle against the elements.

He might be facing starvation.

They are trying to protect their homes or property against flooding.

(the river) burst its banks
coastline
drown
flood/flooding
in danger of capsizing
rough sea
sandbags
scorching heat
scratch a living from the land
skinny cow
sparse vegetation
starve
subsistence farmer
suffer from drought
survive
take part in a race/regatta
the soil is parched
water shortage

▶ **1**

▶ **2**

▶ **3**

▶▶ **PART 3**

Candidates A and B

Language bank

Do you feel this is a good illustration of the rewards that creativity can bring?

Talent is not enough; you have to work at your craft.

Many people believe they could write a novel, but I think creative writing requires talent.

Is composing music one of the most rewarding forms of creativity? After all, everyone can appreciate music.

Carpenters are not generally regarded as being creative.

It must be immensely rewarding to know that people live and work in a building you've designed.

Top designers are often in the public eye.

architect
carpenter
composer
craft
fine craftsmanship
functional as well as aesthetically
    pleasing
invent
landscape gardener
prune a bush/tree/shrub
social status
sturdily built
take pride in your work
topiary

> • **What kind of creativity does each picture depict?**
> • **Which picture best shows the rewards of being creative?**

1 Formal letter

▶▶ Exam task – Part 2

A colleague of yours, Alice Watson, has applied for a job in the public relations department of a large charity, Poverty Action. You have been asked to write a letter providing a character reference for her. Indicate how long and in what capacity you have worked with her, and how her personal characteristics would make her suited for the job. Here is part of the letter you received from Poverty Action:

> The job of Public Relations Co-ordinator consists mainly of supervising PR work, and entails travelling around the country and working with various people in our large organisation. The successful applicant will need good managerial skills and be committed to the philosophy of our charity.

Write your **letter**.

▶▶ Approach

▶ A character reference is almost always addressed to the organisation where someone has applied for a job or a place to study. Generally, you should use the heading line 'To whom it may concern', rather than writing to a specific person. If the exam question asks you to refer to certain characteristics of a person, make sure you do so. You should also imagine what other information may be required, bearing in mind the position the person has applied for.

▶ All character references are formal in style. Generally, you should write at least three paragraphs: introduction, main body and conclusion.

Useful phrases

Introduction

To whom it may concern

I have been asked to write this reference for (Ms Watson).

With reference to your letter of (3rd March), ...

I have known (Ms Watson) for the last (four) years ...

I was her supervisor/superior in (the publicity department of Children in Need) ...

Main body

(Ms Watson) has always shown great dedication/commitment to her work.

She has (excellent managerial skills) ...

Her duties/tasks here included ...

She proved to be ...

competent

dependable

efficient

popular with colleagues

trustworthy

Conclusion

I understand that (Ms Watson) has applied for ...

I am certain that (Ms Watson) would be extremely capable ...

I have no hesitation in recommending her for ...

I should be very happy to supply any further information.

Please do not hesitate to contact me ...

This is the standard heading for character references.

State the name of the person for whom you are writing the reference.

Explain what sort of jobs the person did, and describe the positive characteristics she showed.

End the letter formally.

Say how you know the person and explain in what way you worked together.

Refer to the person's suitability for the tasks involved in the new job.

To whom it may concern

Ms Alice Watson

I have been asked to write this reference for Ms Alice Watson, who worked with me for almost four years in the Head Office of the charity Children in Need. I was her immediate superior in the publicity department of that organisation, so I was able to observe her work at close quarters and feel qualified to evaluate her suitability for similar positions.

Ms Watson was extremely committed to her work and always performed to the highest standard. Her tasks included checking press releases and writing letters to a wide variety of recipients, and she displayed first-class communication skills. The executives of the organisation found her entirely trustworthy, and she always carried out her work cheerfully and efficiently. At various times of the year our department employed a number of temporary staff in order to send out appeals for donations, and in her dealings with these people Ms Watson exhibited very good managerial skills. She was also popular with the permanent staff, though she never allowed this to interfere with the work that had to be done.

I understand that Ms Watson has applied for the position of Public Relations Co-ordinator, which I imagine entails considerable responsibility. I have no hesitation in recommending her for this position, and I am certain she will prove an excellent and hard-working member of your organisation. Naturally, I would be very happy to supply any further information, so please do not hesitate to contact me if this should be required.

Yours faithfully,

Emma Lyons
Public Relations Officer
Children in Need

2 Informal letter

▶▶ **Exam task – Part 1**

Your penfriend Antonio has written to you for advice on a study holiday in Britain. Read his letter and the advertisement he has sent you, on which you have made some notes. Then, using the information carefully, write a letter to Antonio, expressing your views on the study holiday, and suggesting what further information he should request.

> You've lived in Britain, so could you give me your opinion of this study holiday? Would the programme give me a good insight into the sports, traditions and history of Britain?

How close?
Public transport
to Oxford itself?

QUEENSBRIDGE HERITAGE Study Holidays

Situated near Oxford, Queensbridge Heritage has been offering cultural study holidays to visitors from abroad since 1974. These holidays combine fascinating lectures by qualified experts on aspects of major British historical periods with field trips to sites of interest all around the country. with field trips to sites of interest all around the country.

Included in price? Or extra?

Qualified experts provide detailed summaries of the key aspects of British artistic and cultural life, including notes on the major historical periods such as Victorian Britain and the Swinging Sixties.

What kind and where?
Included in price?

Suitable accommodation is provided.

Fees from £500 per week.

Now write your **letter**. You do not need to include postal addresses.

▶▶ **Approach**

▶ Be careful you understand exactly who you are writing to, and what you must include in your letter. Here you are writing to a penfriend, giving him your views about a study holiday he is planning. You must answer all your friend's questions and mention all the notes you have made on the advertisement.

▶ You are writing to a penfriend, so the register should be informal or semi-formal.

Useful phrases

▶▶ **Model answer**

Begin with a brief reaction to your friend's letter. In a few words, express your opinion of his idea, and link to the main body of the letter by indicating what you are going to say next.

Use your own words to express the points mentioned in the input material. For example, you can talk about 'hidden extras' instead of 'Included in price?'

Dear Antonio,

Thanks for your letter last week. I was delighted to hear you're going to study British History – congratulations on getting a place at university! I think getting some background knowledge first would be a great help, but I feel you need more information about Queensbridge Heritage Study Holidays. The advertisement doesn't go into much detail, and there are some basic questions that need to be answered.

It seems to me that the advertisement isn't very clear about the price. You should find out if there are any hidden extras, such as charges for accommodation and field trips, which may not be included in the basic price. To be perfectly honest, I think £500 per week is rather inexpensive, so this might not include everything. In addition, if I were you, I would establish exactly what sort of accommodation they offer, and whether you might be expected to share a room. You should also find out exactly where the school is, what facilities it has, and what sort of public transport is available to the centre of the city.

On balance, I think this holiday might be very good, but it's impossible to say until you get more information. And you might find it doesn't give as broad a background in culture as you want; it seems to focus mainly on academic subjects, but sports aren't mentioned at all in the advertisement.

End by summarising the main ideas in your letter.

I hope I've been some use. Don't forget to write and tell me what you decide in the end.

Take care of yourself.

Alan

As this is a letter to a friend, you can end informally.

3 Article

▶▶ **Exam task – Part 1**

You are a student at Whitebridge College, which recently held a party for the elderly people who live in the area. An article in the local newspaper was critical of the party, and when you phoned the editor of the newspaper to express your disagreement, she suggested you write an article expressing your own views.

Read the extract from the newspaper article and the notes you have made on it. Then, using the information carefully, write an article for the newspaper.

Several letters praising Jones

Stand-up comedian Jimmy Jones failed to get many laughs, and was often inaudible. There was also swing music from the Walt Mitty Jazz Band, but jazz is too energetic and loud for an elderly audience!

Many elderly people love jazz

During lunch at least one of the guests, Mrs Nelly Allbridge (82), complained that the chicken dish was 'too spicy by half'.

Most people loved it!

Write your **article**.

▶▶ **Approach**

▶ When you write in response to an article, you should refer to all the points made in that article. You also need to include information from the other input material.

▶ You are asked to write an article for a local newspaper, so the register should be neutral or formal.

Useful phrases

Introduction

In last week's edition, you published an article that ...

I am writing on behalf of my fellow students ...

I would like to refer/respond to the article in last week's edition ...

Main body

The article suggested/stated that ...

The article was unfairly critical of ...

On the contrary, ...

Conclusion

In conclusion/To summarise, ...

There can be little doubt that ...

I hope I have succeeded in putting the record straight.

In your introduction, refer to the first article and say who you are and why you are writing.

Whitebridge College Party for the Elderly

In last week's edition, you published an article that was unfairly critical about the Whitebridge College Summer Party for the Elderly. As a student who was actively involved in planning the party, I should like to respond to the points made in the article: your readers may have got the impression that the party was a dismal failure. In fact, the party was a great success!

Your correspondent criticised the choice of entertainment, but in fact we had had discussions with residents at old people's homes in order to find out exactly what would be popular. We have been assured that the guests enjoyed it, and Mr Jones, the comedian, was very popular, though admittedly, he was not audible at all times. The music was neither too energetic nor too loud. Many elderly people love jazz, and several danced at the party. Furthermore, with regard to the lunch provided, most people commented favourably about the food, and we went to a great deal of trouble to cater for most tastes.

Respond to specific points in the previous article.

Nevertheless, I have to agree that the acoustics for the entertainer could have been better, and we shall certainly endeavour to improve this next year. In the meantime, I hope I have succeeded in setting the record straight.

It is a good idea to admit there were mistakes, as long as you stress that these mistakes will not be repeated.

4 Contribution to a longer piece

▶▶ **Exam task – Part 2**

A travel book is being produced which focuses on famous monuments around the world. You have been asked to write a contribution to the book describing a well-known monument in your country, saying why it is an important symbol of your country's culture, and why it is worth visiting today.

Write your **contribution to the travel book**.

▶▶ **Approach**

▶ Contributions are often required by people or organisations who are in the process of collecting information for a large book or a piece of research. The main purpose is to supply information and opinion. The register of your contribution will depend on the purpose of the longer document, but will usually be fairly formal.

▶ You should practise identifying the styles that are suitable for different documents. For example, a piece of research may require a neutral, factual style, and headings may be necessary, while a piece for a book may require a more descriptive, discursive style, similar to that of an essay.

Useful phrases

Introduction

Without doubt, ...

It is generally understood that ...

One of the most impressive places/buildings/monuments/cities ...

To date, the ... is one of the greatest examples of ...

Main body

Built in the (fifth century BC), ...

The city's heyday was in the (1960s), when ...

It is a symbol of excellence to local people, ...

It is generally believed that ....

One of the most significant developments ...

Thanks to the hard work of ...

It attracts people from all over the world, who ...

Conclusion

For the visitor, (Rome) offers ...

To local people, this monument symbolises ...

It is an enduring symbol of human achievement ...

For this reason, among others, a visit to (Paris) should not be missed.

Give your contribution a suitable title even if you do not use headings in the main body.

The Parthenon, the Acropolis, Athens, Greece

Without doubt, the Parthenon is Greece's most magnificent monument, but it is also one of the world's most impressive examples of human achievement. The geometrical precision of its structure amazes architects to this day.

Keep your introduction brief, with a general comment on the place or building.

Built in the fifth century BC, after a previous temple had been destroyed during a battle with the Persians, the Parthenon was constructed in honour of the goddess Athena, the city's protector. Pericles, the Athenian leader of the time, ordered its construction, and the temple was designed by the architects Ictinus and Kallicrates under the supervision of Phidias, the sculptor. Rectangular in shape, it was surrounded by forty-six columns, and housed a magnificent statue of the goddess, known as Athena Promachos, or Athena the Champion.

If you are writing about a historical place or building, some general facts or background information is useful.

Over the centuries, the Parthenon suffered a great deal of damage, and many of the beautiful sculptures carved by Phidias were stolen or removed. However, the outer structure of the building still stands, and it is possible to see the remaining sculptures and friezes which adorned the building in the Acropolis museum. Thanks to a lot of campaigning, a new museum is being constructed, and it is hoped that one day, most of the missing artifacts will be returned.

You may need to give a description of the place or building as it is today, or mention current developments.

The Parthenon is an important symbol of Greece, for Greek people regard Pericles as the father of democracy, and this building – his dream – is seen as an enduring symbol of Greek democracy. For the visitor, it provides an image of the artistic genius of the Ancient Greeks, and for this reason, should not be missed.

The conclusion should answer the last part of the question. You will usually be expected to make some kind of recommendation.

---

5 Report

▶▶ **Exam task – Part 1**

An international magazine is investigating tourism in various areas around the world. You have been asked to write a report for the magazine's editors, addressing the following questions:

- How has tourism in your region changed over the last decade?

- What are the reasons for these changes?

- What problems exist and can anything be done to solve them?

Write your **report**.

▶▶ **Approach**

▶ Read the question carefully to see whether you should include your own opinions in the report, and if this is the case, make it clear in the report when you are describing objective facts and when you are giving your interpretation. Depending on the task, you may need to describe something, give an account or narrate an event, express an opinion, and possibly compare and contrast.

▶ You can use headings and possibly bullet points or numbered lists to make it easier for the reader to find information quickly. The introduction and conclusion can be short. You are usually asked to write a report for some sort of organisation or publication, so the language you use should be semi-formal or formal. Even if you use bullet points or numbered lists, you should write complete sentences, not just notes. Remember that in formal writing we often use the passive voice.

Useful phrases

Introduction
The following report evaluates/ describes/presents/provides an account of ...
This report aims to provide an overall view of the situation.
I shall describe the situation below.

Main body
a popular destination
easy to reach by rail/road/air
holidays to (Prague) are widely advertised
overcharge

service in hotels
It is generally accepted that ...
The vast majority of visitors ...
This is probably due to the fact that ...
While data is hard to come by, it is thought that ...

Conclusion
One measure which may improve the situation would be to introduce ...
I am of the opinion that ...
It is my view/opinion that ...
On balance, it appears that ...

Give your report a suitable title.

Tourism in Prague

Introduction
The last decade has seen a dramatic increase in the number of tourists visiting the Czech Republic in general and Prague in particular. The following report presents a brief overview.

Write a brief introduction that provides a few important facts and summarises what your report is about.

Background
Until 1989, Prague was not a popular destination for tourists from western Europe due to a number of factors:
▶ The city was difficult to reach; visitors often had to wait for long periods at border crossings.
▶ There was little information about trips to Prague in foreign travel agencies.
▶ Some people felt nervous about trips to countries in central and eastern Europe.

Use bullet points to provide a list, but make sure each point is grammatically the same; here each point is a complete sentence.

Changes
All the above factors have changed dramatically: Prague is now easy to reach by road, rail and air; trips to Prague are widely advertised in western countries; few visitors feel nervous about visiting a country in eastern Europe any more.

You can use semi-colons to separate items in a list, but as with bullet points, make sure each item is the same grammatically.

Criticisms
The majority of visitors to Prague are extremely satisfied on the whole; however, there are a few complaints about two specific areas:
▶ taxi drivers acting in a rude manner and, in many cases, overcharging.
▶ hotels providing less than adequate service.

Future development
The city council is at present considering stricter laws relating to taxi drivers. Moreover, the local tourist authority is reclassifying the hotels in the city.

Conclusion
While Prague can offer visitors a generally positive experience, there are some issues which need to be addressed. I am of the opinion that better regulation of taxi drivers and hotels will solve these problems.

Make sure each section is clearly separated from the others.

6 Proposal

▶▶ **Exam task – Part 1**

You work at a language school that offers summer courses to students from abroad. This year the director of the school wants to hold an introductory weekend for the students, and has asked you to suggest what should be on the programme.

Read the memo she sent you and the notes you have made on it. Then, using the information carefully, write a proposal.

Memo

To: Ann Smith
From: The Director of Studies
Re: Introductory weekend for foreign students

Take them to town centre?

We have decided that it would be a good idea to give students a brief introduction to the college and local facilities – public transport, places of interest, etc. – during the weekend when they arrive.

Trial bus run?

I'd welcome your suggestions for a programme of introductory events, including informal, ice-breaker activities.

Disco, Saturday night?

Sandra Joyce, Director of Studies

Write your **article**.

▶▶ **Approach**

▶ Since a proposal is, by definition, a piece of writing that makes suggestions, you will often need to use conditional sentences and structures. Read the question carefully and make sure everything you suggest fits in with the information you are given about who and what the proposal refers to.

▶ Your ideas should be clearly presented, and the use of headings will assist in this. Generally, bullet points are not required, since you do not need to go into much detail, and you do not have much space to do so in any case. The introduction and conclusion can be short. As with a report, you are usually asked to write a proposal for some sort of organisation or publication, so the language should be semi-formal or formal.

Useful phrases

Introduction
In view of the fact that ...

Considering the fact that ...

At present, the situation is that ...

My experience suggests that ...

Main body
It would be helpful to students to be told ...

It would be of great benefit to students if ...

One possible solution would be to ...

Providing the event is properly organised, it could be of great assistance to students.

Students could also be ...

You might also like to consider ...

In all likelihood, ...

The chances are ...

Conclusion
Any teething troubles could quickly be overcome ...

In conclusion, I feel (quite) strongly that this is the best way to ...

In spite of/Despite the effort required, this would be a worthwhile step ...

▶▶ **Model answer**

Think of a suitable title for your proposal.

In the introduction, briefly outline the situation and indicate your position.

Refer to two or three examples or ideas under each heading.

Use a variety of structures to make suggestions. For example: 'would be' and 'might also be'.

In your conclusion, offer to help in other ways if required.

Introductory Weekend for Foreign Students

The vast majority of foreign students who come here for language courses have not visited this country before, so some introduction would be very beneficial.

Social life
The bus trip could be combined with a brief tour of the town centre, culminating in a drink at one of the cafés to show them how to order and pay in cafés, pubs and restaurants. This would be a fun way to introduce them to the town and each other. Also, they could be shown where the local cinema, theatre and sports facilities are, and be given information about local places of interest. Then we could hold a disco on Saturday night so that students could meet their teachers and fellow students in a relaxed atmosphere.

Public transport
Saturday morning could be devoted to explaining the system of tickets for buses and local trains, and providing students with a local street map would also be useful. Then perhaps they could be taken into the town centre by bus for a trial run.

In conclusion, the introductory weekend should be enjoyable for students since they are coming here to have a holiday as well as learn. I would be glad to explain my ideas in more detail if required.

7 Leaflet

▶▶ **Exam task – Part 2**

You are the secretary of the student council at the college where you are studying. The college is about to hold its first career day, when companies send representatives to talk to students and help them plan their future careers. You have been asked to write the text for a leaflet for students explaining what a career day is, why they should attend, and any other points you think necessary.

Write your **text for the leaflet**.

▶▶ **Approach**

▶ Your leaflet must deal with the points mentioned in the question, but it is also important to provide additional information from your own experience or imagination. Your writing needs to be organised clearly, and a layout that enables the reader to find information easily is also important. As with reports and proposals, you can use headings and bullet points or numbered points.

▶ In general, there are two types of leaflet for which you might be asked to write the text: those that give information (about a company, for example, or a place such as a museum), and those that try to motivate the reader (such as advertising leaflets). The use of headings and bullets or numbered points is particularly advised for leaflets that give information.

▶ The tone and register will depend on the target audience for your leaflet, so think carefully about who will be reading it. A clear and effective title and introduction are useful; you might want to use a rhetorical question if your leaflet is advertising something or trying to encourage the reader to do something. It is also important to have a good conclusion, perhaps summarising the main ideas in the leaflet.

Useful phrases

Introduction

Why should you ... ? Because ... !

Wouldn't you like to ... ?

Have you ever wanted to ... ? Now is your chance!

Come to ... for the time of your life!

Main body

If you want to ... , you will need ...

Please bear in mind that ...

You may be interested to know that ...

Take this opportunity/chance to ...

Conclusion

Don't forget to ...

We are sure you will find (the experience) a useful one.

▶▶ Model answer

Give your text a title that will attract the reader's attention.

The introduction should be short and clear.

Headings can ask questions which you then answer.

Career Day – A Chance You Shouldn't Miss!

On 12ᵗʰ June St Mary's College is organising its first Career Day. Why should you attend? Because you need to start thinking about a career now. It's never too soon to take your future seriously!

What is a Career Day?

At a Career Day you have the opportunity to speak to Human Resources Managers from big companies about your possible future with them, and about planning your career in general. We have invited over 30 companies, many of them major international companies, to send representatives. Each company will have a desk in the Main Hall, and students will have the chance to talk to representatives face to face.

Why should I be there?

Even if you have no clear idea what sort of career you would like in the future, talking to people from major companies will help you clarify what options are open to you. And if you do feel fairly sure about the type of career you want, this is a perfect opportunity to ask for advice on how to achieve your goals.

What should I bring?

You don't really need to bring anything, apart from a notebook and pencil to keep notes. If you are graduating soon and are interested in a job with one of these companies in the near future, then it's a good idea to bring several copies of your curriculum vitae with you, describing your education, past employment, interests etc.

Don't forget: June 12ᵗʰ is Career Day. Make sure you are there!

The conclusion can be short and should leave the reader with a clear idea of what has been described or discussed.

Preparing, planning and checking

▶▶ Preparing for the Writing Paper

Producing a piece of writing that fulfils a certain function is a difficult task for anybody, even in their native language. To prepare for the Writing Paper, it goes without saying that you need to have read widely. Then, you need to have studied all the basic text types you may be asked to produce, and understood the basic features that characterise them: layout, organisation, style and register. You should also practise completing writing tasks in the time allowed in the exam. Remember the criteria the examiners will use in awarding marks:

- Has the candidate achieved the purpose stated in the instructions?
- Does the text have a positive general effect on the target reader?
- Does the text cover all the content points?
- Is the text well organised and are ideas linked appropriately?
- Has language been used accurately?
- Does the text exhibit a good range of vocabulary and grammatical structures?
- Is the register appropriate for the task?
- Is the layout appropriate?

Ideally, the pieces of writing you produce should be checked by an experienced teacher who can provide useful feedback. Such feedback can help you compile a list of useful expressions, such as the useful phrases you find with the model answers in this section. You can also learn what sort of mistakes you make habitually so you can avoid them. For instance, if you find that you frequently make mistakes with a certain tense, you should consult a good grammar guide to clear up your confusion.

▶▶ Planning your answer

Perhaps the most useful lesson that experienced writers learn is the importance of planning what to write before they actually begin writing. Most good writers usually write several drafts of a text before they are satisfied with the result. Unfortunately, in the exam you do not have time to produce several drafts, and it would be a serious mistake to try: you only have time for a single draft. But you do have time to make a plan.

Always read the question carefully and make sure you understand the following:

- Who are you writing for?
- What are the points you must include in your answer?
- Does the text type have any particular layout requirements?
- Do you have the necessary vocabulary to answer the question?

Then prepare a plan or outline of what you are going to write. Its purpose is to help you, so it doesn't matter if you change it or cross things out – nobody else is going to read it. But it has to show clearly the different sections of your writing and what points you must include in which section. When you look at the plan closely, you might want to change it; for instance, something might be better in a different paragraph, or you might realise you will be repeating yourself. When you are satisfied with your outline, you will find it much easier to write your text. Planning takes time, so allow a minimum of fifteen minutes for it.

▶▶ Question 5, the set text task

If you choose to write about one of the set texts, remember that the question may ask for an article, an essay, a review or a report. You may be asked about the characters, relationships and themes in the book, and whether you would recommend it to others. Make sure you know the story well as you will need to support your views with examples from the book. When answering the question, think carefully about the target reader, and plan your answer accordingly.

▶▶ Checking

Most people make more mistakes than normal under exam conditions, so always allow at least ten minutes at the end to read through your work. Think of your task here as having two parts. First, check that you have answered the question correctly and that you have included all the information that was required. Secondly, check for mistakes in grammar, spelling, punctuation etc. You should by now have had enough experience to know where you often make mistakes – the spelling of certain words, for instance, or a particular type of punctuation.

If you need to correct something, make the correction neatly and legibly. If you need to cross out something you have written, just put one line through the word or words.

TEST 1

▶▶ **PART 1**

Text 1

flair (n) a natural talent for something

innovative (adj) clever, new or using new ideas

accessible (adj) easy to understand and enjoy

layman (n) someone who is not an expert

resumé (n) a short written account of your education and work experience

Text 2

ascertain (v) to determine; to find out (facts)

proximity (n) nearness; closeness

preclude (v) to prevent; to make impossible

rule out (phr v) to decide that something is not possible

pinpoint (v) to locate exactly

Text 3

retrospective (n) a show of all the kinds of work an artist, actor or film maker has done

buff (n) someone who is very interested in something

intercept (v) to stop something or someone as they are travelling from one place to another

compelling (adj) very interesting or exciting

interweave (v) to combine (with)

▶▶ **PART 2**

contemplate (v) to think about something that might happen in the future

verdict (n) someone's opinion about something

naive (adj) inexperienced and believing only good things will happen

take off (phr v) to increase or succeed quickly

figure out (phr v) to solve; to understand

budding (adj) (someone who is) starting to do an activity and (will) probably (be) successful at it in the future

overdraft (n) the amount of money owed to a bank when you have spent more money than you had in your account

unadulterated (adj) not containing unwanted substances; pure

dash (n) a small amount of a quality that is added to something else

quirky (adj) unusual, especially in an interesting way

soundbite (n) a short, quotable statement

asset (n) something or someone that is useful because they help you succeed

status quo (n) the way things are now

fiendishly (adv) extremely

preach (v) to give someone advice in a way that they think is boring or annoying

pint (n) a unit for measuring liquid: 0.568 litres

lager (n) a light-coloured beer

falling-out (n) a quarrel

munch (v) to chew strongly on something

preservative (n) a chemical that keeps food from going bad

communal (adj) shared by a group of people

complementary (adj) complementary things go well together, although they are usually different

bust-up (n) a serious quarrel, especially one that ends a friendship

down (v) to drink or eat something quickly and finish it off

premium (adj) of very high quality

▶▶ **PART 3**

etching (n) a picture formed by cutting lines on a metal plate, piece of glass, stone, etc.

depict (v) to paint; to draw

on a variety of counts (phr) in several ways

sheer (adj) used to emphasise that something is very large, good, etc.

staggering (adj) extremely great or surprising

hold your own (phr) to perform satisfactorily

epoch (n) a period of history

albeit (conjunction) even though; despite

inadvertently (adv) not on purpose; unintentionally

cordon off (phr v) to enclose an area

intimidating (adj) frightening

show up (phr v) to become visible

convey (v) to communicate or make known

preliminary (n) a preparation for an event

rigid (adj) very unwilling to change ideas or behaviour

tentatively (adv) provisionally

vulnerable (adj) exposed; unprotected

envisage (v) to imagine

PART 4

devise (v) to invent (something clever); to dream up

convention (n) a method or style often used in literature, the theatre, etc. to achieve a particular effect

prompt (v) to cause someone to do something

distressingly (adv) in a way that causes emotional pain

confined (adj) limited; restricted

ingenuity (n) skill at inventing things and thinking of new ideas

mount (v) to plan, organise and begin an event or a course of action

impose (v) to force someone to do something

upright (piano) (n) a piano with strings that are in a vertical position

pronounce (v) to officially state that something is true

medley (n) melodies from different tunes that are played one after the other

entrance (v) to hold someone's attention and give delight; to enchant

detract (v) to lower the value of someone or something

practitioner (n) a person who does skilled work

pier (n) a structure built over and into the water so that boats can stop next to it or people can walk along it

repertoire (n) the group of musical pieces, roles, etc. that an artist can play, sing or speak

venue (n) the location of an event

prop (n) a small object such as a book, weapon, etc., used by actors in a play or film

demise (n) death

rave (v) to praise greatly

ensemble (n) a small group of musicians, actors or dancers who perform together regularly

churlish (adj) rude; unpleasant

engage (v) to employ someone to do a particular job

scrupulously (adv) in a way that shows you are attentive to detail and correctness

percussionist (n) a musician who plays a percussion instrument like a drum or cymbals

acquit yourself well (phr) to perform or behave well

connoisseur (n) a person with knowledge of fine things

tribute (n) expression of praise, honour or admiration

initiate (v) to tell someone about something, or show them how to do something

piercing (adj) sharp and painful

ooze (v) if a thick liquid oozes from something, that liquid flows from it very slowly

sleuth (n) a person who tries to solve mysteries; a detective

condense (v) to shorten

PART 1

govern (v) to control the actions or behaviour of a person, a system, an organisation, etc.

stimulus (n) something that makes someone or something move or react

fluctuation (n) the process of varying irregularly

impose (v) to force someone or something to behave or react in the way that you want them to

at will (phr) whenever and in whatever way you want

adjust (v) to change so as to fit particular conditions or situations

PART 2

pursuit (n) an activity such as a sport or hobby

boom (v) to flourish; to thrive

sow the seeds of (phr) to do something that will cause a bad situation in the future

disperse (v) to break up and send or go away; to scatter

reinforce (v) to make part of a structure stronger

far-fetched (adj) not likely to happen; improbable

notion (n) an idea, belief or opinion

spell (v) if a situation or action spells trouble, etc., it makes one expect trouble

TEST 2

PAPER 1 Reading

PART 1

Text 1

hip (adj) doing things according to the latest fashion

jump on the bandwagon (phr) to start doing something that a lot of people are doing (used to show disapproval)

collaborate (v) to work with someone else on something

ostensibly (adv) supposedly; said to be true, but which isn't really true

alleviate (v) to make something less serious

fad (n) a trend; a fashion; a temporary enthusiasm

fickle (adj) likely to change very quickly and suddenly

Text 2

stomp (v) to walk with very heavy steps, making a lot of noise

supple (adj) soft and easily bent

bio-degradable (adj) which can be changed by bacteria into substances that are not harmful to the environment

Text 3

discarded (adj) thrown away; rejected

decompose (v) to decay

revamp (v) to change something in order to modernise it

customise (v) to make something look special or different from others

▶▶ PART 2

linguist (n) a person who knows several languages and their structure

forge ahead (phr) to proceed with strength and speed despite problems or difficulties

consummate (adj) perfect

wary (adj) concerned about danger; cautious

corpus (n) a body of written work

competent (adj) having the ability to do something well

mouthpiece (n) a spokesperson; a representative

blunt (adj) frank

trek (v) to travel with difficulty

expectant (adj) pregnant

score (n) twenty

tonic (n) a medicinal liquid that gives energy

rub (n) a medicinal lotion or cream that is rubbed on the skin

potion (n) a strong liquid medicine

▶▶ PART 3

bewitch (v) to charm; to captivate

smitten (adj) very attracted or in love

amid (preposition) in or into the middle of; surrounded by

stock (adj) commonly used

spirit (n) a mental disposition characterised by firmness or assertiveness

enduring (adj) lasting; surviving

shortcoming (n) a fault; a deficiency

sibling (n) a person with the same parents as someone else; a brother or sister

enlightened (adj) freed from ignorance and misinformation

villain (n) a bad person, especially a criminal

empathise (v) to understand another's feelings, attitudes, reasons, etc.

▶▶ PART 4

enhance (v) to improve; to add to

engage (v) to take part

venture (n) an undertaking involving chance, risk or danger; a speculative business enterprise

break (n) a piece of good luck

dabble (v) to work superficially or intermittently, especially in a secondary activity or interest

downside (n) a disadvantageous aspect

burnt out (phr) unable to work any more, usually from exhaustion

down the line (phr) at a point in the future

lucrative (adj) producing a lot of money; profitable

from scratch (phr) from the beginning

avid (adj) enthusiastic; eager

the ropes (phr) knowledge about a job or situation

dogsbody (n) a person who does hard, menial or monotonous work for someone else

---

PAPER 2 Writing

▶▶ PART 1

sloppy (adj) untidy; careless

surly (adj) rude and hostile in manner or attitude

PAPER 3 Use of English

▶▶ PART 1

feat (n) a notable act or deed

lock (n) an enclosure in a canal with gates at each end, used in raising or lowering boats as they pass from level to level

freight (n) goods to be shipped

cramped (adj) small and uncomfortable

weed (n) a wild plant that is not wanted in a yard or garden

▸▸ **PART 2**

all told (phr) in total

duplicate (v) to repeat an action or words

▸▸ **PART 3**

ubiquitous (adj) seeming to be everywhere

engraver (n) someone who carves, cuts or etches a text, design or picture into a block or surface used for printing

dissect (v) to cut apart or separate

mount (v) to place or fix something on or in a support or setting for display or study

controversy (n) an argument or disagreement, especially a public one, between sides holding opposing views

TEST 3

PAPER 1 Reading

▸▸ **PART 1**

Text 1

implication (n) a possible consequence

pesticide (n) a chemical used to kill insects and other small creatures that are harmful to crops

hindsight (n) an opinion about something after it has happened

naive (adj) inexperienced and not aware of how complicated life can be

tackle (v) to begin a job with a lot of energy

succumb (v) to show weakness; to give in to a desire or to someone or something stronger than you

concerted (adj) agreed on by all those involved

Text 2

thriving (adj) very successful

jurisdiction (n) the right to officially make legal decisions in a particular area

indiscriminately (adv) without thinking what harm an action might cause

aforementioned (adj) that has been mentioned before

implement (v) to take action that you have officially decided upon

Text 3

suffice it to say (phr) the statement that follows is enough to express my meaning

derisive (adj) showing that you think someone or something is stupid

yarn (n) a long cotton or woollen thread used in knitting or to make cloth

sweat-shop (n) a small factory where people work under bad conditions for little money

fume-belching (adj) which emits a lot of unhealthy smoke

▸▸ **PART 2**

surmise (v) to make a reasonable guess

perch (n) a resting place or vantage point

slog (v) to walk with difficulty, for example, in deep snow or mud

loot (v) to rob, especially on a large scale and usually by violence or corruption

aqueduct (n) a waterway made of stone blocks

carbon dating (n) chemical analysis used to determine the age of materials

fire (v) to fill with passion or enthusiasm

tantalise (v) to offer but not satisfy; to tempt

wry (adj) humorous, ironic or dry in manner

blue-collar (adj) blue-collar workers work with their hands in jobs that require some training

intricate (adj) having many complex interrelating parts or elements

toil (v) to work hard with little reward or relief

pore over (phr v) to study carefully; to examine carefully and for a long time

blunder (v) to move unsteadily or confusedly

annals (n pl) a written record or collection of historical events, discoveries, etc., on a certain subject

proponent (n) a person who argues in favour of something

vigorous (adj) energetic; strong

undeterred (adj) refusing to be prevented from acting

hail (v) to greet, especially with enthusiasm

swashbuckling (adj) flamboyantly adventurous

rugged (adj) hilly; (land that is) difficult to travel over

▸▸ **PART 3**

emblematic (adj) symbolic; representative

terrain (n) land; landscape

squat (adj) disproportionately short, low or thick

ungainly (adj) hard to handle; having an awkward appearance

hare (v) to go quickly

indulgence (n) something one enjoys, even though it may be bad or wrong

would-be (adj) desiring; professing; having the potential to be

goggles (n pl) plastic glasses that protect the eyes

usurp (v) to take the place of someone or something

▶▶ PART 4

transgression (n) a crime; a violation

fusion (n) a merging of diverse, distinct or separate elements into a unified whole

credible (adj) believable

evocation (n) imaginative re-creation

foster parent (n) an adult who is paid by the government to take care of a child that is not their own

inherent (adj) naturally belonging to or part of something

hard-hitting (adj) very effective; forceful

out of the blue (phr) suddenly; unexpectedly

enchant (v) to charm; to delight

floppy (adj) loose and usually oversized, like a soft toy

dilapidated (adj) falling apart; in disrepair

genre (n) a category of artistic, musical or literary composition characterised by a particular style, form or content

undertone (n) an implied meaning; an undercurrent

cuddle (n) a close embrace

premise (n) a basis for a line of reasoning; an assumption

chunky (adj) short and thick or broad

sparse (adj) with much space between; of few and scattered elements

interweave (v) to mix or blend together

overtly (adv) obviously

didactic (adj) intended to instruct

indulge (v) to allow someone to do something, even if it is not good or wise

drab (adj) dull in colour; uninteresting

hint (v) to make reference to something in an indirect way

mismatch (n) something unequal in ability, personality, strength, etc.

address (v) to deal with

unreserved (adj) given without reservation; unqualified

articulate (v) to put into words

portal (n) a door or entrance

plausible (adj) appearing worthy of belief

thorny (adj) difficult; complex

nullify (v) to make invalid; to cancel

quaint (adj) unusual or different in character or appearance

backdrop (n) the general events during which something else, such as a person's life, happens

dawn on (phr v) to begin to be perceived or understood

figurative (adj) related to a word or phrase that expresses meaning in a colourful way, usually through comparison; metaphorical

medieval (adj) of, relating to, or characteristic of the Middle Ages

depict (v) to describe

alike (adv) equally; to the same degree, form or manner

PAPER 3 Use of English

▶▶ PART 1

newsworthy (adj) of sufficient interest or importance to the public to warrant reporting in the media

fad (n) a fashion that lasts a short time

▶▶ PART 2

cater for (phr v) to provide a particular group of people with the things they need or want

outlet (n) a shop or company through which products are sold

reclamation material (n) useful materials or items that come from old buildings

▶▶ PART 3

urge (v) to encourage strongly

disembodied (adj) a disembodied sound or voice comes from someone who cannot be seen

▶▶ **PART 1**

Text 1

disconcerting (adj) confusing, embarrassing or worrying

gratifying (adj) pleasing; satisfying

overwhelm (v) to overpower in thought or feeling

Text 2

renovation (n) the act of repairing a building so that it is in good condition

restoration (n) the act of repairing an old building so that it looks as it did when it was first built

Text 3

mannerism (n) a way of moving or speaking that is special to a particular person or group of people

downtrodden (adj) a downtrodden person is shown little respect and is badly treated

▶▶ **PART 2**

policy (n) a rule or group of rules for doing business by industry and government

incorporate (v) to unite in or as one body

national grid (n) a network of conductors for distribution of electric power

consideration (n) a matter taken into account when formulating an opinion or plan

embrace (v) to accept an idea

electorate (n) a body of people entitled to vote

eyesore (n) an unpleasant sight

offshore (adj) away from the shoreline in the water

phase out (phr v) to remove something in gradual steps

decommission (v) to withdraw from active service

impact (n) an effect; an impression

migrate (v) to move from one place to another, as animals, birds and fish do

exploitation (n) productive use of something

▶▶ **PART 3**

uproar (n) clamour; people complaining or shouting

constitute (v) to make up; to compose

infringement (n) an act that is against a law or someone's legal rights

instructive (adj) with useful information; educational

turn a blind eye (phr) to avoid seeing something wrong; to overlook

prosecute (v) to bring legal action against someone because one considers that they have broken the law

a laughing stock (phr) an object of jokes or ridicule

sue (v) to seek justice or right from someone in a court of law

consensus (n) general agreement

wrath (n) anger

innocuous (adj) harmless; unobjectionable

distort (v) to cause to be perceived unnaturally

whine (v) to complain; to act irritably

resentment (n) a feeling of anger at something you regard as a wrong, insult or injury

steep (adj) expensive

evanescent (adj) of short duration; passing away quickly

▶▶ **PART 4**

paramount (adj) supreme; foremost

rural (adj) of or relating to the country, country people or life, or agriculture

commute (v) to travel back and forth regularly

enervate (v) to drain of energy; to weaken

write-off (n) something that is ruined

robust (adj) strongly formed or constructed; sturdy

on its last legs (phr) worn out; close to failure or death

woefully (adv) lamentably bad or serious; deplorably

unequivocal (adj) definite; clear; unambiguous

dismissive (adj) considering something unimportant or worthless

PAPER 3 Use of English

▶▶ **PART 1**

profound (adj) all-encompassing

heavenly body (n) an object in the sky

auspicious (adj) favourable; good

resort (v) to have recourse to something or someone

exempt (adj) free or released from some liability or requirement to which others are subject

▶▶ **PART 2**

constitution (n) the set of laws and principles that govern a country or organisation

revenue (n) the money that a business or organisation receives over a period of time

valid (adj) a valid document is legally or officially acceptable

combat (v) to fight

fleet (n) a group of vehicles that are controlled by one company

▶▶ **PART 3**

conduct (v) to carry out a particular activity or process

devise (v) to invent a way of doing something

merchant (n) someone who buys and sells goods for profit

intricate (adj) elaborate; having many complex elements

counterfeit (v) to make an exact copy of something in order to deceive people

issue (v) to circulate or publish; to make available

TEST 5

PAPER 1 Reading

▶▶ **PART 1**

Text 1

root (n) the basis of something; source; origin

avidity (n) keenness; enthusiasm

scan (v) to look at something to see as much information as possible in a short time

gullible (adj) too willing to believe what others tell you so that you are easily tricked

hard-headed (adj) tough-minded; sober; realistic

portfolio (n) a set of investments for a person

insight (n) the ability to see or know the truth; perception

riddle (n) a puzzle; a question that requires cleverness to answer

mechanistic (adj) capable of explanation by the laws of physics and chemistry

observance (n) behaviour according to laws, rules and customs

fervour (n) the state of being emotionally aroused and worked up

Text 2

abound (v) to exist in large numbers

acclaimed (adj) recognised and praised by a lot of people

scathing (adj) very severe (criticism)

empirically (adv) tested scientifically, not just based on ideas

probing (adj) searching through information carefully and intelligently

scrutinise (v) to examine in great detail

Text 3

efficacy (n) effectiveness

property (n) a quality or power that a substance has

apothecary (n) a person who mixed and sold medicines in the past

definitive (adj) the best in existence

credibility (n) the quality of deserving to be believed or trusted

▶▶ **PART 2**

plight (n) an unfortunate, difficult or dangerous situation

shed light (phr) to make clear; to explain

range (v) to live or occur in or be native to a region

come by (phr v) to get; to acquire

reclusive (adj) living alone and avoiding contact with others

inhospitable (adj) difficult to live in because of bad weather or geography

poacher (n) a hunter or trapper who takes game animals illegally

logger (n) someone involved in cutting down trees

bush (n) land far from towns and cities; wilderness

range (n) the region throughout which an animal naturally lives or occurs

canopy (n) the uppermost spreading branchy layer of a forest

replenish (v) to replace something that was used

fare (v) to get along; to succeed

convention (n) an assembly of people who meet for a common purpose

dwindle (v) to become steadily less or fewer

ominous (adj) being a sign of something evil, bad or threatening

slash (v) to cut with rough sweeping strokes

eden (n) a delightful place; a paradise

take a toll (phr) to cause damage

allocate (v) to plan to use an amount of money for a specific purpose; to allot

stark (adj) not cheerful; brutal

draw to a close (phr) to come to an end

roam (v) to go freely over a large area; to wander

glacier (n) a large mass of ice which moves slowly down a mountain valley

submerge (v) to cover something with water

deluge (n) a flood

lush (adj) having thick, healthy growth

verdant (adj) green with vegetation; covered with green growth

tusk (n) a long, thick front tooth, such as of elephants, warthogs, etc.

ledge (n) a narrow flat piece of rock that sticks out on the side of a mountain or cliff

pinpoint (v) to locate exactly

scathing (adj) very severe (criticism)

maritime (adj) related to the sea

aggregate (n) mineral materials, such as sand or stone, used in making concrete

quarry (v) to dig stone or sand from a quarry

dredge (v) to dig up sand, mud and debris from a harbour, river, etc.

artefact (n) an object produced or shaped by human craft, especially a tool, weapon or ornament

topography (n) the physical landscape

outraged (adj) feeling great anger

perception (n) the way a person sees something; a point of view

▶▶ PART 4

prospective (adj) likely to do something or achieve a position in the future

apprehensive (adj) worried or nervous about something that you are going to do

transaction (n) the act of doing business; a deal; a negotiation

interpersonal (adj) between people

babble (v) to talk without making sense

get carried away (phr) to do too much of something and lose control of yourself

go off at a tangent (phr) to leave the main point; to digress

evasive (adj) not direct, clear or frank

pedantic (adj) paying too much attention to rules and details

come across (phr v) to seem to have particular qualities

promotional (adj) related to advertising

penetrating (adj) showing an ability to understand things quickly and completely

size up (phr v) to form an opinion of someone

blurt out (phr v) to speak suddenly

component (n) one of several parts that make up a machine, system, etc.

swollen-headed (adj) arrogant

complacent (adj) pleased with a situation, especially something you have achieved, so that you stop trying to improve or change things

at fault (phr) responsible for something bad

diffident (adj) shy and not wanting to make people notice or talk about you

PAPER 3 Use of English

▶▶ PART 1

foolhardy (adj) reckless; rash

▶▶ PART 3

mainstream (adj) accepted or including most of the people in society

musing (n) the act of expressing something you have thought about carefully

full-blown (adj) having all the qualities of something that is at its most complete stage

call into question (phr) to cast doubt upon someone or something

bypass (v) to avoid

distort (v) to report an event, story, etc. in a way that is not completely true or correct

verify (v) to confirm; to say that something is true

TEST 6

PAPER 1 Reading

▶▶ PART 1

Text 1

barrister (n) a lawyer who speaks in the higher courts of law

ingénue (n) a naive, innocent girl or young woman

induce (v) to persuade; to influence

stage struck (adj) enthralled by the theatre; eager for a career in acting

sneak off (phr v) to go quietly; to try not to be seen

matinée (n) an afternoon film or theatre performance

Text 2

constitution (n) a set of basic laws and principles that a country is governed by

bill (n) a written proposal for a new law that is presented to parliament

cite (v) to mention something as an example in order to support an argument

wrest (v) to take power or influence away from someone by force

revere (v) to respect or admire someone or something very much

set the ball rolling (phr) to cause something to start

Text 3

litigation (n) the process of preparing and defending claims in a court of law in non-criminal matters

arbitration (n) the process of judging officially how a dispute or argument should be settled

liaise (v) to share information with someone who works in another department or organisation so that you can both work more effectively

confidentiality (n) trusting someone not to reveal secret information to anyone else

▶▶ **PART 2**

glaze (v) to cover or fit with glass

ventilation (n) a system of providing fresh air

conservatory (n) a greenhouse for growing or displaying plants

modish (adj) stylish

trim (v) to free of excess or extraneous matter by cutting

momentum (n) strength or force gained by motion or through the development of events

accord (n) agreement

break (n) a deduction that is granted in order to encourage a particular type of commercial activity

dim (v) to lower the force of, especially a light

synergy (n) the extra energy, power or capability produced by combining two or more agents, operations or processes

outlook (n) a prediction for the future

duct (n) a tube or passage in buildings, especially for air

come to grips with (phr) to confront squarely and attempt to deal decisively with something

compost (v) to convert (plant debris) to compost, usually for use as fertiliser

biomass (n) plant materials and animal waste used especially as a source of fuel

forefront (n) the most advanced part

juice (n) gas, electricity, etc.

tumble (v) to decline suddenly and sharply

▶▶ **PART 3**

hitherto (adv) up to this time

instrumental (adj) helpful; causing something to happen

by-product (n) something that happens as a result of something else

outperform (v) to do better than others

ligament (n) a strong, flexible band of tissue holding bones or other body parts in place

tendon (n) tough, fibrous tissue connecting muscles to bones or to other muscles

calf (n) the back part of the lower leg

confer (v) to give

scavenger (n) an animal that feeds on dead or decaying matter

carcass (n) a dead body

vulture (n) a type of bird that eats dead animals

locomotion (n) the ability to move from place to place

contentious (adj) controversial

▶▶ **PART 4**

prejudicial (adj) related to or causing harm by holding a biased opinion not based on fact

payroll (n) a list of employees to be paid and the amounts due to each

mortgage (n) a long-term loan from a bank for buying property, which is used as security

hefty (adj) of considerable size or amount

infuriate (v) to make very angry

outlay (n) money spent for something

dearth (n) little or none of something

concrete (adj) about real, specific things and situations, not general ideas

go bust (phr) to become bankrupt

landscape gardening (n) the art or profession of improving the ground around a building with trees, plants, etc.

cut-throat (adj) relentless or merciless in competition

unsung (adj) unpraised; not seen as important; overlooked

▸▸ PART 1

misconception (n) a mistaken idea about something

span (n) a period (of time)

plague (n) an epidemic disease causing a high rate of mortality

grim (adj) ghastly; repellent; sinister

appalling (adj) shocking; deeply offensive

feudal (adj) relating to a political and social system in which a king and the people of the upper classes owned the land and people of the lower classes worked it

clergy (n) the official leaders of religious activities in organised religions

▸▸ PART 2

exceed (v) to be greater than something; to go beyond the limits of something

infringement (n) an act that is against a law or someone's legal rights

▸▸ PART 3

withdraw (v) to remove

advent (n) the time when something first begins to happen or exist

TEST 7

PAPER 1 Reading

▸▸ PART 1

Text 1

distraction (n) something that draws someone's attention to a different object or in a different direction from the one they are concentrating on

dubious (adj) having doubts; suspicious

spurt (n) a sudden burst

Text 2

tactics (n pl) methods you use to achieve something

taper training (n) the practice of gradually reducing the amount of training in the days immediately before a competition

carbohydrate (n) a substance in foods that gives you heat and energy, found in potatoes, bread, cakes, etc.

prior to (adj) coming before

Text 3

terrain (n) a type of ground

anticipate (v) to expect a certain situation and be prepared for it

autonomous (adj) independent; able to make decisions and work alone

camaraderie (n) a feeling of friendship within a group of people, especially people who are working together

elements (n pl) the weather, particularly bad weather

▸▸ PART 2

amenity (n) something that adds to people's comfort, convenience and pleasure

boast (v) to be proud of something

following (n) a group of admirers or followers

gig (n) a performance by musicians or comedians

precarious (adj) dependent on chance, unknown conditions or uncertain developments

to boot (phr) in addition; also

hone (v) to improve

prodigy (n) a highly talented child

flautist (n) someone who plays the flute

abrasive (adj) rough; making people feel bad

thin-skinned (adj) touchy; sensitive to criticism

yearn (v) to have a strong desire for something; to long for something

demanding (adj) requiring high performance

clientele (n) a group of customers

kid (v) to make jokes

snort (n) the act of forcing air violently through the nose with a rough harsh sound

daunt (v) to make afraid; to discourage

whim (n) a sudden desire, especially an unreasonable one

bunch (n) a group

▸▸ PART 3

blunt (adj) not sharp

talon (n) a bird's claw, especially of predators

wingspan (n) the distance from the tip of one of a pair of wings to that of the other

soar (v) to fly high through the air with no difficulty

diversity (n) variety

incubate (v) to sit on an egg so as to hatch it by the warmth of the body

bicker (v) to argue about little things

rear (v) to help children or young animals to grow

saunter (v) to walk without hurrying

antifreeze (n) a liquid used in engine radiators to lower their freezing point

coyote (n) a kind of wolf similar to a medium-sized dog found mainly in western North and Central America

shard (n) a piece of a brittle substance such as glass or metal

perforate (v) to make a hole through something

carrion (n) the flesh and bones of a dead animal that is unfit for human food

juvenile (n) a youth or child; a young animal

pen (n) a small area of land surrounded by a fence and used to keep animals in

mentor (n) a teacher and friend

glide (v) to fly through the air without power

plumage (n) the covering of feathers on a bird

▶▶ **PART 4**

compatibility (n) the ability of machines to be used together

fragile (adj) easily broken; delicate

unawares (adv) without warning; by surprise

viewfinder (n) a device on a camera that indicates, either optically or electronically, what will appear in the field of view of the lens

texture (n) the way a surface or material feels when you touch it, especially how smooth or rough it is

gloss (n) a photograph that has been made shiny

come to grief (phr) to be harmed or destroyed in an accident

PAPER 3 Use of English

▶▶ **PART 1**

pollinate (v) to transfer pollen to the stigma of a plant so that it can reproduce

pod (n) a long narrow structure that grows on various plants like peas and beans, and contains seeds

fragrance (n) a pleasant smell; an aroma

cure (v) to preserve food, tobacco, etc. by drying it, hanging it in smoke or covering it with salt

harvest (v) to gather a crop from the field or plantation

treat (v) to put a substance on something or use a chemical process in order to protect, clean or preserve it

exploitation (n) the use of something for profit

culinary (adj) relating to cooking

tickle (v) to stimulate pleasantly

▶▶ **PART 3**

zest (n) intense interest and enjoyment

whaler (n) a boat used to hunt whales

 TEST **8**

PAPER 1 Reading

▶▶ **PART 1**

Text 1

break the bank (phr) to cost more money than you can afford

cog (n) a small wheel with bits sticking out that fit together with bits in another wheel as they turn in a machine

retreat (n) a place that you can go to for peace and quiet

oak-panelled (adj) (walls) lined with flat pieces of oak wood

wend your way (phr) to move slowly and in a leisurely way towards a destination

rambler (n) a person who goes for long walks for pleasure

Text 2

sustainable (adj) able to work without causing damage to the environment

rigorous (adj) very strict

pledge (n) a formal promise

discerning (adj) showing the ability to make good judgements

rustic (adj) simple and unaffected by modern developments; countrified

spectrum (n) a complete range of options to suit different tastes

Text 3

inevitable (adj) bound to happen

dulcet (adj) sweet and harmonious

withering look (phr) a disapproving look that makes the other person feel stupid and embarrassed

brood (n) a family of young creatures

reconnaissance (n) the act of searching an area to find out what is happening before deciding on action

Velcro (n) a material used to fasten clothes, consisting of two pieces of material which stick to each other when you press them together

plunder (v) to steal; to take others' property by force and in large quantity

random (adj) happening at any time; unplanned

spur (v) to encourage someone to do something

hands-off (adj) left alone; not to be touched

on tap (phr) available on demand

win-win (adj) a win-win situation is one that will end well for everyone involved in it

intervention (n) the act of becoming involved in a difficult situation in order to change what happens

alleviate (v) to make less difficult

the real McCoy (phr) something real or authentic

concerted (adj) strong; intense

indigenous (adj) born in a place; native to a place

▶▶ **PART 3**

slump (v) to lose an upright position by bending or falling

vague (adj) not clearly defined, grasped or understood

hunched (adj) formed into a hump

slouch (v) to walk, stand or sit with an ungainly stooping of the head and shoulders or excessive relaxation of body muscles

pilates (n) a system of exercise that increases flexibility

tilt (v) to move upwards or to the side

daft (adj) silly

orator (n) someone who is good at making speeches and persuading people

▶▶ **PART 4**

phase out (phr v) to gradually stop using or providing something

lag (v) to not keep up; to delay

stumbling block (n) an obstacle

bulky (adj) big and heavy; bigger than other things of the same type and difficult to carry or store

stationary (adj) standing still; not moving

benign (adj) harmless

lubricate (v) to put a substance like oil on something in order to make it move more smoothly

cumbersome (adj) slow and difficult

PAPER 3 Use of English

▶▶ **PART 1**

instigate (v) to make something happen

ingrained (adj) firmly established and therefore difficult to change

gimmick (n) a clever or unusual method or object used to attract attention

▶▶ **PART 3**

element of exaggeration (phr) an small amount of exaggeration

venom (n) a liquid poison produced by animals such as snakes, spiders or scorpions when they bite or sting

temperate climate (n) a type of weather that is never very hot or very cold

 TEST 1

▶▷ **PART 1**

1 A: Correct. 'to help develop a magazine that will be accessible to the layman'
   B: Incorrect. The magazine will publish articles about 'life in the universe', not on Earth.
   C: Incorrect. The magazine will report on research, not conduct it.
   D: Incorrect. The magazine specialises in 'astrobiology and astrophysics'.

2 A: Incorrect. 'The suitable candidate will have a Bachelor's degree in journalism or science'
   B: Incorrect. Knowledge of 'standard office computer software' is required, not 'specialist software'.
   C: Correct. 'The ability to handle stress and meet tight deadlines is of the utmost importance.'
   D: Incorrect. 'The suitable candidate will have a Bachelor's degree in journalism or science'

3 A: Incorrect. The technique could determine to some extent the amount of light a star was giving off.
   B: Incorrect. The technique could detect large objects, but it could not detect planets small enough to support life.
   C: Incorrect. The text does not discuss this.
   D: Correct. 'At first, the technique could only establish the existence of a very large planet with an elliptical orbit that brought it into close proximity to the star. This was one of the limitations of the technique: life could not exist on such large planets.'

4 A: Incorrect. They have discovered a large planet that resembles Jupiter in a way, but it is not this planet itself that is of importance.
   B: Correct. 'And this is the vital point about their discovery: there is at least a theoretical possibility that smaller planets could be orbiting inside the orbit of this planet.'
   C: Incorrect. This information is true, but it is not the vital point about the discovery.
   D: Incorrect. There is a possibility that life may exist on the smaller planets inside its orbit.

5 A: Incorrect. Jodie Foster is a very fine actress, but this is not why the film is so convincing.
   B: Correct. 'The film is based on the novel by the celebrated astronomer Carl Sagan. Its strength lies in the fact that it manages to retain much of the power and compelling nature of the book, while at the same time maintaining a relatively high level of technical accuracy. This is largely thanks to Sagan's involvement in the making of the film.'
   C: Incorrect. The film has a high level of technical accuracy, which is not the same thing, as 'accurate techniques'.
   D: Incorrect. The film was directed by Zemeckis, but this is not why the film is so convincing.

6 A: Incorrect. They are an important aspect of the film, but not the most important.
   B: Incorrect. The opposite is true.
   C: Correct. 'special effects are used both creatively and effectively, serving to enhance the plot rather than swamp it'
   D: Incorrect. They enhance the plot, not the actors' performances.

▶▷ **PART 2**

7 D: Link between 'asked their customers for a verdict' in the previous paragraph and 'We originally wrote this massive long questionnaire'.

8 F: Link between 'Britain's leading brand of smoothie, selling about 40% of the 50 million downed annually by British drinkers' and 'The appeal of Innocent's products' in the following paragraph.

9 C: Link between 'so-called "natural fruit drinks" ' and 'Most are made from concentrated juice with water – and perhaps sweeteners, colours and preservatives – added' in the following paragraph.

10 B: Link between 'extending their range of products into desserts' and 'Innocent plans to simply freeze some of its smoothies' in the following paragraph.

11 G: Link between 'is there a temptation to sell up and go and live on a desert island' and Richard's answer in the following paragraph.

12 F: Contrastive link between 'They also seem to have managed to stay friends' and 'We have got annoyed with each other' in the following paragraph. Also, link between 'each member of the team ... complementary set of skills' and 'the areas we have had fallings-out over are things where we each think we have reasons to be right' in the following paragraph.

▶▷ **PART 3**

13 A: Incorrect. They are 'extremely rare', not 'unique'.
   B: Incorrect. They are etchings, not paintings.
   C: Incorrect. The images are not compared to other cave art in Britain.
   D: Correct. 'But more importantly, the Church Hole etchings are an incredible artistic achievement.'

14 A: Incorrect. This is not stated or implied in the text.
   B: Incorrect. The point made is that ancient Britons *were part of a culture* that spread across the continent.
   C: Correct. 'Britons were part of a culture that had spread right across the continent'
   D: Incorrect. Britons were 'at least as sophisticated as' people in Europe.

15 A: Incorrect. The discovery of the images was made public, but the writer does not suggest this should have been avoided. She implies the images should have been protected.
   B: Correct. 'As a result, some etchings may already have been damaged, albeit inadvertently, by eager visitors.'
   C: Incorrect. The text states that many people *knew* about the etchings within hours of their discovery, but it does not say that they *visited* the cave within hours of the discovery.
   D: Incorrect. Measures were taken too late to prevent damage that had already been done, but the text does not say that the measures themselves are ineffective.

16 A: Correct. 'However, the Church Hole images are modifications of the rock itself, and show up best when seen from a certain angle in the natural light of early morning.'
   B: Incorrect. 'They had been looking for the usual type of cave drawing or painting'
   C: Incorrect. The images 'show up *best*' in natural light.
   D: Incorrect. The text does not suggest that the power of the light was a problem.

17 A: Incorrect. This statement does not express the conclusion Dr Samson draws about the function of the etchings.

B: Incorrect. They intended the images to be visible in the early morning.

C: Correct. 'I think the artists knew very well that the etchings would hardly be visible except early in the morning.'

D: Incorrect. The text mentions 'rituals involving animal worship', but this does not mean that ice-age hunters worshipped animals in the cave.

18 A: Incorrect. It is implied that we can make inferences, but we cannot 'insist on any rigid interpretation'.

B: Incorrect. Dr Caruthers does not think their function 'can be determined with any certainty', but she does not imply they serve no particular function.

C: Incorrect. Saying someone knows 'so little' is not the same as saying they know nothing.

D: Correct. 'We should, in my view, begin by tentatively assuming ... while of course being prepared to modify this verdict at a later date'

19 A: Incorrect. This is not stated or implied in the text.

B: Correct. 'To which I can only add that I felt deeply privileged to have been able to view Church Hole.'

C: Incorrect. This is not stated or implied in the text.

D: Incorrect. This is not stated or implied in the text.

▶▶ PART 4

20 B: 'Besides, who can afford to work only during the summer months?'

21 A: 'The other art form that I adore – ballet – could hardly be performed in the confined space of a normal house'

22 D: 'Death Calls ... had me fondly recalling a production of 2001, A Space Odyssey at the Edinburgh Fringe Festival'

23 A: 'We had made it clear that no particular requirements would be imposed upon the performers'

24 C: 'a colleague of my wife's started raving about a particular jazz ensemble. It seemed churlish to do otherwise than engage them'

25 C: 'The Hot Jazz Quintet ... appeared to make a point of being scrupulously polite and tidy. It was as though the stereotype image of the egocentric musician were being overturned in front of my very eyes'

26 D: 'In fact, one could claim that it doesn't really come under the category of theatre at all, and it is not normally presented on a stage, either.'

27 B: 'There was once a time when no seaside resort in the country was complete without a Punch and Judy show on the pier'

28 A: 'my daughter – who had previously been of the view that opera was unspeakably idiotic – was entranced'

29 B: 'They arrived with a surprising number of boxes and cases. Naively, I had expected a miniature theatre to require a minimal amount of equipment.'

30 D: 'There we stumbled – literally – over a body oozing fake blood that was so convincing it almost caused my wife to faint.'

31 B: 'William Daniels ... was suffering from a terrible cold ... . Like a true pro, though, he struggled through the performance bravely.'

32 A: 'so they gave us a medley of familiar pieces from popular operas'

33 C: 'As luck would have it, Mike is a percussionist with his school orchestra, and he was able to acquit himself creditably, to the delight of the professionals performing for us.'

34 D: 'my wife proved to be a brilliant sleuth, solving the mystery in record time'

PAPER 2   Writing

▶▶ PART 1

Question 1
Style: Semi-formal or formal
Content: 1 Describe the planning department's intentions.
2 Say that there is a lot of opposition to the plan.
3 Present the arguments against the plan.
4 Say what residents hope to achieve.

▶▶ PART 2

Question 2
Style: Neutral or semi-formal
Content: 1 Suggest that travel is good for young people.
2 Give a number of reasons, e.g. learning to be independent, learning to make decisions, seeing interesting places.
3 Say how you would benefit from a trip, what you would like to see etc.

Question 3
Style: Semi-formal or formal
Content: 1 Introduction: explain what you will write about.
2 Give an example of a useful machine.
3 Give a second example of a useful machine.
4 Give an example of an unnecessary machine.
5 Give a second example of an unnecessary machine.
6 Conclusion: express your opinion whether on balance technology makes our lives easier.

Question 4
Style: Semi-formal or formal
Content: 1 Introduction: give some relevant information about your region.
2 Describe young people's attitude to your region's culture, giving examples.
3 Describe young people's attitude to your region's history, giving examples.
4 Conclusion: express your view on how the situation may change in the future.

Question 5(a)
Style: Semi-formal or formal
Content: 1 Introduction: state the title of the book you are going to write about.
2 Describe the plot, commenting on what you find interesting/exciting/disappointing, etc.
3 Say whether you would recommend it or not, giving reasons.

Question 5(b)
Style: Formal
Content: 1 Introduction: state the title of the book and then say which characters you are going to write about.
2 Describe their personality.
3 Choose two or three examples from the book to illustrate whether their actions are justified or not.
4 Say what you think of the characters overall.

PAPER 3   Use of English

▶▶ PART 1

1 C   **2** D   **3** B   **4** A   **5** C   **6** D   **7** B   **8** A   **9** C   **10** A   **11** D   **12** C

▶▶ PART 2

13 Some **14** while/whereas/but **15** in **16** However **17** be
18 the **19** how **20** Another **21** not
22 will/may/might/can/could **23** take **24** with **25** by
26 time **27** off

▶▶ PART 3

28 incredibly (adjective to negative adverb) **29** majestic (noun to adjective) **30** keeping (verb to noun) **31** lifelong (noun to compound adjective) **32** abilities (adjective to plural noun)
33 beneficial (noun to adjective) **34** stimulation (verb to noun)
35 captivity (verb to noun) **36** extensive (verb to adjective)
37 daily (noun to adjective)

▶▶ PART 4

38 side **39** cold **40** deep **41** faced **42** key

▶▶ PART 5

43 denied (1) having cheated/that he had cheated (1)
44 you (ever) happen (1) to be (1)
45 had Paula reached (1) the gate than (1)
46 it was Mark (1) who wrote (1)
47 though (1) it may be (1)
48 to tell the truth (1) will mean (1)
49 may/might have got lost (1) as/since/because (1)
50 rather (1) spend money (1)

PAPER 4 Listening

▶▶ PART 1

1 C **2** B **3** B **4** A **5** A **6** C

▶▶ PART 2

7 ancient Egypt **8** willow tree extract **9** 1829
10 stomach **11** German company **12** research **13** fifty/50
14 vegetables

▶▶ PART 3

15 B **16** A **17** D **18** D **19** C **20** A

▶▶ PART 4

Task One
21 B **22** H **23** A **24** D **25** F

Task Two
26 G **27** F **28** H **29** D **30** B

TEST 2

PAPER 1 Reading

▶▶ PART 1

1 A: Incorrect. It is a 'network of designers and businesses connected with the industry'.
   B: Incorrect. Its aim is to promote 'sustainable practices in the manufacture of clothing'.
   C: Incorrect. It is not made up only of fashion designers.
   D: Correct. 'Its aims are, ostensibly … to promote sustainable practices in the manufacture of clothing … . The Ethical Fashion Forum encourages manufacturers to improve working conditions by reducing the use of dangerous chemicals and dyes in the treatment of fabrics.'

2 A: Incorrect. This, according to the writer, is what *appears* to be one of their motives.
   B: Incorrect. The writer mentions 'all the components in the global garment supply chain', but she doesn't imply that the Forum's *real* motives are to coordinate them.
   C: Correct. 'Or is it simply capitalising on the eco-friendly fad of the moment … by marketing the idea that the fashion industry is also now socially and environmentally aware? The industry appears to be saying that it is still acceptable, in fact *necessary*, to buy lots of clothes and accessories.'
   D: Incorrect. The writer mentions 'the use of dangerous chemicals and dyes', but she suggests that alleviating 'the negative impact it has on the environment' only *appears* to be one of their motives.

3 A: Incorrect. The advertisement states they use bio-degradable materials 'where possible'.
   B: Incorrect. They are made in European factories.
   C: Correct. 'the full range of the colours and styles we offer'
   D: Incorrect. The materials used are animal-friendly and the footwear is aimed at people who are environmentally aware, not specifically at vegetarians.

4 A: Correct. 'worker-friendly environments'
   B: Incorrect. The advertisement merely says that customers can see the full range of colours and styles on the web site.
   C: Incorrect. The advertisement does not imply that the styles are unique.
   D: Incorrect. Stomping Green have a shop in Portsmouth, but the advertisement does not imply anything about the quantities that the shop sells.

5 A: Incorrect. It does not mention being adventurous when buying clothes.
   B: Correct. 'Did you know that in Britain alone, people throw away an estimated one million tonnes of clothing material every year?'
   C: Incorrect. It does not mention individual styles.
   D: Incorrect. It does not mention fashion.

6 A: Incorrect. The article suggests that people can save money by recycling old clothes.
   B: Incorrect. The article does not suggest that people should stop buying clothes altogether, but recycle old ones.
   C: Correct. 'There is a wealth of sites on the Internet devoted to recycling old clothes, and several offer useful practical advice on how to revamp items like old suits, aprons, curtains, etc.'
   D: Incorrect. Buying clothes from charity shops is just one of the ways in which people can recycle clothes.

▶▶ PART 2

7 F: Link between 'As many as 1,000 languages have died in the past 400 years. Conversely, the handful of major international languages are forging ahead' in the previous paragraph, the description of the status of the world's major languages today, and the description of what is happening to many languages in the following paragraph.

8 A: Frederik Kortlandt is mentioned for the first time in paragraph A. Also, link between 'Frederik Kortlandt … has a mission to document as many of the remaining endangered languages as he can' and 'Documenting a threatened language can be difficult' in the following paragraph.

9 C: This paragraph continues the theme of languages threatened with extinction developed in preceding paragraphs.

10 E: Link between 'Kortlandt knows a language is disappearing' and the main theme of preceding paragraphs. Also, link between 'turned up at a conference in Tallinn' and 'like-minds met in Kathmandu for a conference' in paragraph C. Link between 'Every now and then language researchers get lucky. Kamassian ... was supposed to have died out, until two old women ... turned up at a conference in Tallinn' and 'To non-linguists it must seem an odd issue to get worked up about' in the following paragraph.

11 D: Link between 'Language is the defining characteristic of the human species. These people say things to each other which are very different from the things we say, and think very different thoughts, which are often incomprehensible to us' in the previous paragraph and 'If you want to understand the human species, you have to take the full range of human thought into consideration'.

12 B: Link between 'For centuries forest tribes have known about the healing properties of certain plants ... . All this knowledge could be lost if the tribes and their languages die out' in the previous paragraph and 'There are hundreds of known remedies in Fiji's forests. ... If the languages die, so too will the medicinal knowledge of naturally occurring tonics, rubs and potions'.

▶▶ PART 3

13 A: Incorrect. It is implied that this is Ellen MacIntosh's view, but it is not the writer's view.
   B: Incorrect. 'simplicity' refers to the 'stock, two-dimensional characters', not the stories themselves.
   C: Correct. 'Indeed, although her comment does make one wonder why simplicity of this sort should be out of place in a story for children.'
   D: Incorrect. This is not stated or implied in the text.

14 A: Incorrect. This is a true statement in itself but it is not what Ellen objects to.
   B: Correct. 'Instead of standing up to her cruel stepmother ... Cinderella just waits for a fairy godmother to appear and solve her problems. But wouldn't you want a daughter of yours to show more spirit?'
   C: Incorrect. The two sisters are 'absurd', which is not the same as saying they are figures of ridicule. Also, this is not what Ellen objects to.
   D: Incorrect. This is implied in the text, but it is not what Ellen objects to.

15 A: Incorrect. 'The character of the rich and handsome stranger, however, is retained, *and in some cases really is a prince*.'
   B: Correct. 'the Cinderella character no longer has to clean the house and *has no siblings to make her life a misery*'
   C: Incorrect. 'The role of the fairy godmother is often replaced by coincidence or sheer luck.' This does not say that she no longer exists.
   D: Incorrect. 'the Cinderella character no longer has to *clean the house*' and 'In the majority of film versions, the heroine has a profession'

16 A: Correct. 'In these versions for the silver screen, the Cinderella character ... persists in not showing much backbone.'
   B: Incorrect. This is not stated or implied in the text.
   C: Incorrect. This is not stated or implied in the text.
   D: Incorrect. This is not stated or implied in the text.

17 A: Incorrect. 'In the majority of film versions, the heroine has a profession', but the text does not indicate whether she is successful in her profession.
   B: Incorrect. 'marrying her prince' is used metaphorically, to imply that Cinderella will 'live happily ever after', not that she will become a real princess.

   C: Incorrect. This is not stated or implied in the text.
   D: Correct. 'In the majority of film versions, the heroine has a profession and is even permitted to continue working after marrying her prince – *this is the twenty-first century, after all*.'

18 A: Correct. 'Most children ... empathise with the protagonist ... challenge.'
   B: Incorrect. The text does not state or imply that little girls like to be challenged themselves.
   C: Incorrect. This is not stated or implied in the text.
   D: Incorrect. This is not stated or implied in the text.

19 A: Incorrect. This is not stated or implied in the text.
   B: Correct. 'This can be seen in the original story of Cinderella ... . She has to grow spiritually, and by maturing, she becomes attractive to the prince ... In the later versions, this element is missing'
   C: Incorrect. This is not stated or implied in the text.
   D: Incorrect. This is not stated or implied in the text.

▶▶ PART 4

20 B: 'I enjoyed putting on plays at the local youth centre, especially coaching budding actors'
21 D: 'I also offered to help my uncle out in his studio. ... I'd go along at the weekends and act as general unpaid dogsbody.'
22 A: 'now I can really understand why someone's using a certain technique or piece of equipment'
23 E: 'I was hardly a model employee. I loathed my job, and instead of selling insurance, I used to wander around the city's numerous art galleries'
24 C: 'I'm thinking either of expanding – more shops, managers and so on – or diversifying, perhaps producing my own surf boards'
25 B: 'The classes themselves aren't terribly lucrative, but I supplement my income ... organising trips to see shows in London.'
26 F: 'and the next thing I knew, my wife was urging me to set up my own company'
27 B: 'Then someone at an organisation called Business Link ... suggested advertising on the Internet!'
28 D: 'I've had to find another way to switch off. In fact, I've taken up fishing.'
29 A: 'If I hadn't realised early on that I'd never make it as a performer, I probably would have carried on dreaming that my big break would come.'
30 B: 'I couldn't work out how to find customers who would pay for their children to attend the kind of courses I wanted to run'
31 C: 'He said he wanted to sell up and I jumped at the chance to buy the business from him!'
32 E: 'To my surprise, I've turned out to be quite a good saleswoman.'
33 F: 'I had to take a very deep breath before I finally took the plunge.'
34 B: 'I studied medicine, but when I finished medical school I had a sort of crisis. I suddenly knew I couldn't go on with it!'

PAPER 2 Writing

▶▶ PART 1
Question 1
   Style: Formal
   Content: 1 Suggest that the writer of the article is mistaken in some ways.

2 Explain that the new sports centre has replaced the old sports pavilion.

3 Mention increased student numbers, more students from abroad and the need for accommodation.

4 Indicate that academic standards are actually better now, not worse. Also, mention the greater range of courses now offered.

5 Add that the college contributes to the cultural life of the community.

▶▶ PART 2

Question 2

Style: Formal

Content: 1 Introduction: explain the basic idea.

2 Describe the benefits of the radio station, e.g. a service for students, its usefulness for communicating information etc.

3 Describe possible programme types.

4 Describe the support you would need, e.g. rooms, funding, equipment.

5 Conclusion: end with a summary of your arguments.

Question 3

Style: Semi-formal or formal

Content: 1 Introduction: describe the situation you are going to discuss (people moving to cities).

2 Describe the attractions of city life.

3 Describe the problems of country life.

4 Describe the disadvantages of city life.

5 Discuss what cities may be like in the future.

6 Conclusion: end with a summary of your views.

Question 4

Style: Semi-formal or formal

Content: 1 Introduction: give some basic information about the geography of your region.

2 Describe the most popular public transport facilities, and say why they are popular.

3 Describe what is being done to improve and promote the use of public transport.

4 Discuss what more could be done.

5 Conclusion: end with a summary of your views.

Question 5(a)

Style: Semi-formal or formal

Content: 1 Say which book you have chosen to write about and who the protagonist is.

2 Explain why you think this character is a hero/heroine.

3 Use examples from the book to show why this character is exceptional, and perhaps compare him/her with the hero/heroine from another popular book.

4 Say why you think this character deserves to be considered the most popular fictional hero/heroine.

Question 5(b)

Style: Formal

Content: 1 Introduction: state the purpose of the report and the title of the novel you are going to write about.

2 Describe the most dramatic events in the story.

3 Describe how these events affect the characters.

4 Say who you would recommend this book to, and why.

PAPER 3 Use of English

▶▶ PART 1

1 A **2** D **3** B **4** B **5** C **6** A **7** C **8** A **9** B **10** D **11** A **12** D

▶▶ PART 2

13 may **14** but **15** apart **16** their/the **17** far **18** any
19 they **20** into **21** better **22** When **23** to **24** every
25 as **26** do **27** so

▶▶ PART 3

28 originated (noun to verb)
29 inventor (verb to noun)
30 undisputed/indisputable (verb to negative adjective)
31 initially (adjective to adverb)
32 educational (noun to adjective)
33 invariably (verb to negative adverb)
34 discoveries (verb to plural noun)
35 updated (noun to verb)
36 inconclusive (verb to negative adjective)
37 conceivable (verb to adjective)

▶▶ PART 4

38 feet **39** heavy **40** rate **41** view **42** bent

▶▶ PART 5

43 as/so long as (1) he did (1)
44 was Ned who (1) told him (1)
45 came up with (1) the idea (1)
46 having our living room (1) done up (1)
47 to being (1) spoken to (1)
48 on the point of (1) calling him (1)
49 no circumstances (1) am I (1)
50 it hadn't been (1) for Kevin (1)

PAPER 4 Listening

▶▶ PART 1

1 C **2** B **3** A **4** C **5** B **6** A

▶▶ PART 2

7 an amateur historian **8** farmer **9** a doctor **10** articles and essays **11** personal correspondence **12** wife's brother
13 Roman history **14** Italy

▶▶ PART 3

15 A **16** B **17** C **18** D **19** A **20** A

▶▶ PART 4

Task One
21 G **22** E **23** B **24** C **25** F

Task Two
26 D **27** H **28** C **29** E **30** G

PAPER 1 Reading

▶▶ PART 1

1 A: Correct. 'With hindsight, I think we were naive.'

2 D: Correct. 'This is because problems like global warming are so huge that ordinary individuals don't feel they could possibly make any difference. I think that's the real danger facing us today – that we'll succumb to a feeling of helplessness instead ... future generations.'

3 C: Correct. 'The main problem is that the high seas do not fall under the jurisdiction of any one country, making restrictions difficult to impose. Advances in fishing technology mean that large factory ships can stay out for weeks on end, using huge nets which indiscriminately scoop up everything in their path'

4 B: Correct. 'The overfishing of krill in the Antarctic threatens wildlife further up the food chain such as whales, seals and penguins, which rely on the krill for food. In some Canadian coastal areas, cod fish populations have been fished to commercial extinction, thereby destroying the livelihood of whole communities.'

5 C: Correct. 'Suffice it to say, they do *not* care. In fact, they don't approve of those who do, and do little to disguise their feelings. ... I ... was met with a brick wall from the husband and derisive sarcasm from the wife.'

6 B: Correct. 'Bruce (the husband) scoffs at our neat row of separate recycling bins for plastic, paper and metal'

▶▶ PART 2

7 G: Link between 'remnants of the Inca civilisation' in the previous paragraph and 'the greatest Inca discovery of them all'. Also, link between 'But this region of southern Peru is still full of ruins' and 'an advanced civilisation existed here' in the following paragraph.

8 D: Link between 'firing the ambitions of those hoping to make similar spectacular finds' in the previous paragraph, 'That amounts to an awful lot of culture buried under the ground' and 'It is the mountains of the Vilcabamba range that perhaps hold the most tantalising, spectacular ruins' in the following paragraph.

9 A: Link between 'foundations of buildings, foundations of roads, water channels' and 'The finds' in the following paragraph.

10 E: Contrastive link between 'About ninety percent has not been investigated' in the previous paragraph and 'vigorous exploration combined with serious scientific research'. Also, Johan Reinhard's name is mentioned for the first time in paragraph E.

11 C: Contrastive link between 'It's the Indiana Jones fantasy' in the previous paragraph and 'But exploring is not all about adventure'.

12 B: Link between 'In two lengthy expeditions to Qoriwayrachina in 2001 and 2002' and 'future expeditions to Qoriwayrachina' in the following paragraph.

▶▶ PART 3

13 A: Correct. 'Later came the beach buggy, a briefly fashionable, wildly impractical, single-terrain vehicle' and 'there is no doubt which pointless recreational vehicle ... it's the quad bike'

14 C: Correct. 'There's nothing cool about a quad' and 'Spoilt children get them for Christmas.'

15 B: Correct. 'Originally, the ATV ... was developed in Japan as a three-wheeled farm vehicle, an inexpensive mini-tractor that could go just about anywhere.'

16 D: Correct. 'the quad's recreational appeal lies in its potential to deliver a safe thrill' and 'The quad bike, in short, provides middle-aged excitement for men who think a Harley might be a bit dangerous.'

17 C: Correct. 'Employers are required to provide training to workers who use quad bikes'

18 B: Correct. 'they have all but replaced the tractor as the all-purpose agricultural workhorse'

19 D: Correct. 'this squat, ungainly, easy-to-flip machine' and 'Outside of racing, quad bikes are growing in popularity and injuries have trebled in the last five years'.

▶▶ PART 4

20 E: 'Books and films for older children (and adults) that deal with time travel indicate just how, well, timeless, that interest is.'

21 B: 'The haunting pictures of the dilapidated farm buildings and scruffy animals are just one of the outstanding features in this first novel'

22 H: 'nobody must look at the old oak. Everyone in the village knows this ... except Arthur ... We learn what happens to Arthur when he looks at the tree'

23 C: 'The sparse text is cleverly interwoven with the line drawings in such a way as to encourage reading without being too overtly didactic.'

24 F: 'But a new teacher at nursery school brings out the artist in Viji'

25 E: 'As Heather ventures backwards and forwards in time, she learns fascinating details about life in different epochs, each of which is entirely plausible and very real.'

26 H: 'as in her first novel, Carson depicts brilliantly the isolation of childhood'

27 D: 'Problems begin to emerge when he discovers he is slipping in and out of his imaginary world without realising it – and then he finds he can't control which world he is living in.'

28 C: 'Even toddlers who show no interest in the usual baby bathtime books will be entranced by the delightful narrative.'

29 F: 'A useful message for every child who is unwilling to try something new because of doubts about his or her ability.'

30 D: 'the younger members of the target market for this work may find the material too unsettling' and 'If this marketing mismatch could be addressed'

31 G: 'Wilmot captures brilliantly the ... uniformity, but also the quaint quality of life in that decade' and 'their house, number 54 Mafeking Place'

32 A: 'the breathtaking finale comes right out of the blue'

33 B: 'This enables young readers to understand fully the awkward issues facing the grown-ups in this world'

34 G: 'Wilmot's ability to demonstrate what is going on in the minds of the adults in the story without talking down to his young readers, as so many writers do'

PAPER 2 Writing

▶▶ PART 1

Question 1

Style: Formal

Content: 1 Introduction: briefly describe the trip (dates, number of people, places visited).

2 Say what criticisms have been expressed:

- the coach was slow
- a train with sleeping cars would save time
- practice with Scottish accents needed
- the language classes were hard for some people
- the lectures were boring for some people

3 Describe the positive feedback:
- people enjoyed the guided tour of the city
- country dancing was popular
- people enjoyed the museums and art galleries, though this was too much for one day

4 Conclusion: end with your suggestions for future trips.

▶▶ PART 2

Question 2

Style: Semi-formal or formal

Content: 1 Introduction: give some basic information about the region.
2 Describe the sports played in the region and the facilities.
3 Describe what other recreation possibilities there are.
4 Give some basic information about cinemas and theatres (how to get there, the kinds of films, plays one can see etc.).
5 Give some basic information about cafés and restaurants (how to get there, prices, type of food etc.).
6 Conclusion: perhaps suggest where students can get more detailed or additional information.

Question 3

Style: Semi-formal or formal

Content: 1 Introduction: describe a situation when you did manual work.
2 Describe exactly what you had to do.
3 Say how the work proved to be satisfying.
4 Conclusion: perhaps end with a reflection on the value of doing manual work.

Question 4

Style: Informal

Content: 1 Introduction: explain what you are going to write about.
2 Describe the events leading up to the accident.
3 Describe the accident itself in some detail.
4 Describe the reactions of the drivers and other people.
5 Describe your experience with the police.
6 Explain what was interesting about the whole experience for you.

Question 5(a)

Style: Formal

Content: 1 Introduction: state which two characters you are going to write about with regard to the question of guilt and responsibility in the book.
2 Examine one character and the extent to which he or she is guilty/responsible.
3 Compare him or her with the second character, using examples from the book.
4 Conclusion: sum up your comparison.

Question 5(b)

Style: Semi-formal

Content: 1 Introduction: comment briefly on the film version of the book.

2 Compare the portrayal of the characters in the film with those in the book, using examples.
3 Compare the development of themes in the film with that of the book.
4 Conclusion: say whether you think the film is as good as the book.

PAPER 3 Use of English

▶▶ PART 1
1 C **2** B **3** D **4** D **5** C **6** D **7** A **8** C **9** B **10** B **11** C **12** A

▶▶ PART 2
13 than **14** number **15** them **16** in **17** as **18** what
19 why **20** worth **21** less **22** though/if **23** the **24** such
25 will/can/could/may/might **26** mind **27** in

▶▶ PART 3
28 popularity (adjective to noun)
29 increasingly (verb to adverb)
30 censorship (verb to noun)
31 powerless (noun to negative adjective)
32 growth (verb to noun)
33 tendency (verb to noun)
34 critical (noun to adjective)
35 sophistication (adjective to noun)
36 applicable (verb to adjective)
37 equally (adjective to adverb)

▶▶ PART 4
38 charged **39** dead **40** tied **41** idea **42** alien

▶▶ PART 5
43 no matter (1) how hard (1)
44 have made (1) their getaway (1)
45 seem to be (1) taken into consideration (1)
46 placed the blame (1) on herself/her/Carrie (1)
47 not only our computer (1) but (also) (1)
48 take back (1) what I said (1)
49 despite the fact that (1) it was (1)
50 accused Joe of (1) leaving his (1)

PAPER 4 Listening

▶▶ PART 1
1 C **2** B **3** C **4** A **5** A **6** C

▶▶ PART 2
7 a (new) motorway **8** skeleton **9** ceremonial **10** cattle
11 leader **12** France **13** west **14** the British Museum

▶▶ PART 3
15 C **16** C **17** D **18** B **19** A **20** A

▶▶ PART 4
Task One
21 A **22** H **23** G **24** E **25** B

Task Two
26 F **27** D **28** B **29** H **30** C

PAPER 1 Reading

▶▶ **PART 1**

1 C: Correct. 'I enjoy being invited to parties'

2 D: Correct. 'some aspects of performing came as a surprise. I never would have imagined I'd get back pain from standing on stage for so long'

3 D: Correct. 'more boarding facilities'

4 A: Correct. 'Opportunities are available for donors to receive naming rights.'

5 C: Correct. 'his body movements speaking volumes to people the world over in a universal language which knew no racial or cultural boundaries. This made him accessible to a wider audience than almost any other theatrical artist'

6 D: Correct. 'Marceau was inspired by both the great novelist and Charlie Chaplin … for both were champions of the downtrodden, the have-nots, the little people.'

▶▶ **PART 2**

7 D: Link between 'almost eight percent of the electricity that the country needs will be generated in this way' in the previous paragraph and 'This is in line with the target … of producing ten percent of Britain's electricity from renewables'.

8 A: Link between 'the principle … has only very recently been used successfully' and 'the delay' in the following paragraph.

9 G: Contrastive link between the risks described in the previous paragraph and 'In fact, there is very little risk involved'. Also, contrastive link between 'Britain may well become a world leader in offshore wind exploitation' and 'The way ahead is not without problems, however' in the following paragraph.

10 F: Link between the problems and complaints described in the previous paragraph and 'Another cause for concern'.

11 C: Link between 'solar energy is hardly going to be a great success here' in the previous paragraph and 'Some form of water power would seem a far more likely candidate for development'.

12 E: Link between 'Existing nuclear power stations are to be phased out' in the previous paragraph and 'this is only a small step in the right direction'. Also, link between 'when the existing power stations are shut down' and 'In the meantime' in the following paragraph.

▶▶ **PART 3**

13 C: Correct. 'the industry actively pursues and prosecutes pirates. Now the Music Recording Association has announced that it regards individuals downloading music from the Internet as pirates'

14 B: ' "The industry is completely overreacting; it'll be a laughing stock," says Mayes.'

15 A: Correct. 'There is a general consensus that CD pirates should be subjected to the full wrath of the law'

16 D: 'The scratchy, distorted cassette copy is a poor version of the original recording, whereas an MP3 file is of high quality and can be stored'

17 C: 'The companies are simply hoping that one of these new bands or singers will be a hit'

18 B: 'the recording industry can't be held responsible for the evanescent nature of fame, given the teenage appetite for anything novel'

19 C: 'The problem isn't going to vanish if the industry carries on trying to make a quick profit.'

▶▶ **PART 4**

20 A: 'Consequently, she uses a car mainly to commute to her office'

21/22 B: 'when the weather is bad she has to drive the children to their school nearby'

21/22 C: 'she mostly uses the car to stock up with groceries from the local supermarket on Friday evenings'

23 D: 'she only passed her driving test three and a half years ago'

24 C: 'She is rather dismissive of SUVs … they are a danger to cyclists because SUV drivers tend not to notice them.'

25 B: 'When asked about what influenced her choice of vehicle, she is unequivocal: safety was the crucial point'

26 A: 'They wanted a car that would be fuel-efficient and that would produce as few harmful emissions as possible.'

27 D: 'Heather herself then reluctantly took charge of the car'

28 A: 'Megan left the choice of car to her husband; she claims she is ignorant of the technical issues involved'

29 C: 'The new charges for drivers … she would far rather take the train to the city'

30 B: 'Vera is one of the growing number of people who have purchased an SUV.'

31 B: 'her SUV seats eight people … she needs this room'

32 D: 'She says she never expected to get such enormous pleasure from sitting behind the wheel … a sense of independence and confidence that she lacked when she was younger.'

33 A: 'She stresses she would rather be able to manage without a car at all. However, … a viable option'

34 C: 'Some good neighbours … were thinking of buying a new one … use hers whenever they wanted to.'

PAPER 2 Writing

▶▶ **PART 1**

Question 1

Style: Formal or semi-formal

Content: 1 Suggest that the writer of the article is mistaken in some ways.
    2 Answer the writer's criticisms:
- most people were satisfied
- refreshments were served from twelve to two
- other entertainment was available, apart from rides
- students paid for the party, not the college

    3 Admit that the layout was bad and apologise.
    4 Conclusion: perhaps end with a summary.

▶▶ **PART 2**

Question 2

Style: Neutral or semi-formal

Content: 1 Introduction: Describe how the situation came about.
    2 Say who was involved.
    3 Describe what you felt.
    4 Say whether you succeeded in concealing your feelings.
    5 Conclusion: perhaps discuss any lessons you learnt from this experience.

Question 3

Style: Semi-formal or formal
Content: 1 Introduction: give some basic information about the area.
2 Describe one or two places of historical interest.
3 Describe one or two areas of natural beauty.
4 Describe one or two theme parks/amusement parks.
5 Conclusion: perhaps tell readers where to find additional or more detailed information.

Question 4

Style: Semi-formal or formal
Content: 1 Introduction: describe where and when you had this teacher.
2 Describe the teacher's appearance and personality and how he/she taught.
3 Describe the response of the pupils.
4 Discuss what made him/her a good teacher.
5 Discuss what you learnt from this teacher.
6 Conclusion: summarise what makes a good teacher.

Question 5(a)

Style: Semi-formal or formal
Content: 1 Introduction: briefly describe the novel you are going to write about, and outline the role the central character plays in it.
2 Discuss the character as victim, giving examples from the book.
3 Say if the character stops being a victim, and explain how and why. If the character persists in being a victim, explain why.
4 Conclusion: summarise your views on this character.

Question 5(b)

Style: Formal
Content: 1 Introduction: Say which novel you have chosen to write about, and briefly summarise its plot.
2 Outline its most successful aspects.
3 Outline its shortcomings.
4 Conclude why it remains popular.

PAPER 3   Use of English

▶▶ **PART 1**

1 B **2** A **3** A **4** D **5** B **6** D **7** C **8** D **9** B **10** A **11** C **12** D

▶▶ **PART 2**

13 due **14** how/where **15** keep **16** which/that **17** despite
18 its **19** can/could **20** everyone/everybody/anyone/anybody
21 or **22** back **23** on/to **24** against **25** In **26** whether/if
27 no

▶▶ **PART 3**

28 inconvenience (adjective to negative noun)
29 transactions (noun to plural noun)
30 tendency (verb to noun)
31 nickname (noun to compound noun)
32 transferable (verb to adjective)
33 Initially (adjective to adverb)
34 accompanied (noun to verb)
35 identification (verb to noun)
36 withdraw (verb to verb)
37 widespread (verb to compound adjective)

▶▶ **PART 4**

38 gift **39** mixing **40** left **41** regular **42** under

▶▶ **PART 5**

43 was taken (1) aback by (1)
44 is not worth (1) trying to persuade (1)
45 would involve (1) (her) travelling (1)
46 it not been (1) for (1)
47 may/might/could accidentally (1) have taken (1)
48 to (1) our expectations (1)
49 was only (1) when she took off/after she took off/had taken off (1)
50 suggested (that) (1) I/we (should) go (1)

PAPER 4   Listening

▶▶ **PART 1**

1 C **2** A **3** C **4** A **5** B **6** B

▶▶ **PART 2**

7 winter **8** two/2 **9** direct **10** not descended
11 became extinct **12** tools **13** groups **14** a mystery

▶▶ **PART 3**

15 B **16** A **17** C **18** A **19** D **20** C

▶▶ **PART 4**

Task One
21 B **22** E **23** A **24** G **25** H

Task Two
26 D **27** G **28** F **29** A **30** C

TEST 5

PAPER 1   Reading

▶▶ **PART 1**

1 A: Correct. 'In fact, most cultures throughout history have believed that the stars influence our lives, and ... astrology is as popular today as ever it was.'

2 C: Correct. 'After all, ... science seems to have provided answers to many of the riddles and mysteries of nature. Paradoxically, however, the resultant mechanistic view of life has caused many to feel that their life has no purpose ... . Is this, perhaps, why growing numbers of people are turning to astrology with such fervour?'

3 B: Correct. 'Few people are willing to examine the subject empirically or objectively. Tom Maine is one of the few who has attempted to do so. His approach is impartial'

4 C: Correct. 'As to my own conclusion regarding the validity of astrology, I am keeping that to myself!'

5 B: Correct. 'People saw astrology as directly affecting the efficacy of plants' healing properties.'

6 D: Correct. 'Believing that medical knowledge should be made available to whoever was interested, Culpeper made himself unpopular ... by writing and publishing guides in English, rather than Latin'

▶▶ **PART 2**

7 C: Link between 'Gorillas, chimpanzees, bonobos and orangutans ... could vanish from the wild within fifty years' in the previous paragraph and 'The clock is standing at one minute to midnight for the great apes'. Also, link between 'They have appealed for £15 million to save the world's great apes' in the previous paragraph and 'the sum required'.

8 B: Link between 'the decline in ape numbers has not only continued but accelerated' in the previous paragraph and 'the rapidly dwindling numbers'.

9 G: Link between 'In one population studied, researchers knew of 140 gorillas. After an outbreak of the Ebola virus, they could only find seven alive' and 'The future looks equally bleak for the other African apes' in the following paragraph.

10 D: Link between 'To survive and breed, the great apes need undisturbed forest. But such earthly edens are becoming increasingly scarce' and the destruction of natural habitats discussed in the following paragraph.

11 E: Link between 'Unesco officials are working to improve law enforcement in African national parks' and 'We cannot just put up fences to try and separate the apes from people' in the following paragraph.

12 A: Link between 'one official' in the previous paragraph and 'Another official'.

▶▶ **PART 3**

13 C: 'all that remains to tell us that it was once lush and verdant – and inhabited – is the occasional tool stone, harpoon or mammoth tusk brought up from the sea bed by fishing boats'

14 C: Correct. 'bathymetry makes use of computers, satellite positioning devices and special software to create accurate and remarkably detailed maps'

15 D: 'While previous devices have only been able to produce two-dimensional images, bathymetry ... accurate and remarkably detailed maps. ... an ancient river bed leaps out of the three-dimensional image ... . The sites of pre-historic settlements can now be pinpointed, ... to see in stunning detail the sunken shipwrecks'

16 A: 'She is however, scathing about the scale of government funding' and 'it's an absolute scandal that we know so little about the area just off our shores'

17 B: 'The idea of Britain as a natural island kingdom will be challenged ... . It remains to be seen how far this new awareness is taken on board among our "island" people.'

18 D: 'In addition, commercial applications are a real possibility.'

19 A: Correct. 'mapping the sea bed will also identify places where rare plants and shellfish have their homes. Government legislation may prevent digging at such sites'

▶▶ **PART 4**

20 E: 'Preparation is of extreme importance; things like finding out what form the interview will have ... will you be talking to one person or a panel?'

21 A: 'But I got carried away and went off at a tangent, which made a bad impression.'

22/23 B: 'I wondered if perhaps I had been too direct, but I later discovered ... they were impressed by my enthusiasm and ambition.'

22/23 F: 'Show that your ambition is the force that drives you'

24 E: 'Actually, it's not so much what people say ... as the way they sit, how they hold their heads, whether they meet the interviewer's eye'

25 C: 'find out as much as you can about the company you have applied to from its website and promotional material'

26 D: 'I turned up in a smart business suit and tie, only to find that my prospective employers were in jeans!'

27 E: 'Another question interviewers sometimes ask ... is about mistakes you have made. ... admit that you were at fault'

28 B: 'Firstly, a candidate should not learn a speech off by heart; you will come across as insincere, as if you have practised everything in front of a mirror.'

29 D: 'A candidate should decide in advance on at least ten things to ask the interviewer'

30 F: 'Being nervous can make you forget things ... this will help you feel less nervous.'

31 D: 'I was so relieved that the interview was over that I just smiled and blurted out: "No thanks!"'

32 C: 'Make it clear that the interview is a two-way process'

33 D: 'They believed in being casual ... people all used first names with each other etc.'

34 A: 'The other lesson I learnt was that if you are asked what your weaknesses are, you shouldn't be evasive. You could mention a weakness that can also be a strength.'

PAPER 2 Writing

▶▶ **PART 1**
Question 1
Style: Formal
Content: 1 Introduction: briefly describe what you are going to propose.
   2 Describe the schedule you propose.
   ● Saturday morning: a talk on regulations
   ● Early Saturday afternoon: use of the library
   ● Late Saturday afternoon: visit the Sports Hall
   ● Saturday evening: disco
   ● Sunday morning: use of the computer room
   ● Sunday afternoon: an introduction to student societies
   3 Conclusion: make any other relevant comments and suggestions.

▶▶ **PART 2**
Question 2
Style: Semi-formal or formal
Content: 1 Introduction: perhaps explain how history can be boring.
   2 Summarise the relevant part of history.
   3 Describe the situation you were in.
   4 Explain why it made history come alive.
   5 Conclusion: write an appropriate ending to round off.

Question 3
Style: Formal
Content: 1 Describe briefly how you met the applicant.
   2 Describe his/her skills and abilities.
   3 Describe the personal characteristics that make him/her a good candidate for the position.
   4 Offer to supply more information if necessary.

Question 4
Style: Semi-formal or formal
Content: 1 Introduction: describe the situation (i.e. many young people leave school early).
   2 Discuss the benefits of further education.
   3 Discuss why many young people do not appreciate these benefits.
   4 Discuss what could be done to encourage young people to go to college.
   5 Conclusion: perhaps end with a brief summary of your points.

Question 5(a)

Style: Formal

Content:
1 Introduction: briefly outline the plot. Say how important truth is in the story, and which two characters you have chosen to illustrate this.
2 Examine the importance of truth through the first character.
3 Compare this character with a second character, who is perhaps entangled in lies.
4 Conclusion: describe the effect that events have on these two characters, and which illustrates the importance of truth.

Question 5(b)

Style: Formal

Content:
1 Introduction: state the purpose of the report.
2 Describe briefly a scene from the beginning of the book and discuss the possibilities and potential problems of creating the opening scene of the film from it.
3 Describe briefly a scene from the middle of the book and discuss the possibilities and potential problems of creating the opening scene of the film from it.
4 Conclusion: state which you think would be best and why.

PAPER 3 Use of English

▶▶ **PART 1**

1 C 2 D 3 A 4 B 5 C 6 A 7 C 8 B 9 D 10 C 11 B 12 A

▶▶ **PART 2**

13 any 14 on 15 which 16 for 17 do 18 have/need
19 like 20 why 21 In 22 not 23 If/When 24 without
25 account/consideration 26 As 27 their

▶▶ **PART 3**

28 daily/everyday (noun to adjective)
29 eloquently (noun to adverb)
30 conceivable (verb to adjective)
31 disrespect (noun to negative noun)
32 influential (noun to adjective)
33 discredited (verb to negative verb)
34 inevitably (adjective to adverb)
35 unmodified (verb to negative adjective)
36 disprove (noun to negative verb)
37 complacency (adjective to noun)

▶▶ **PART 4**

38 broad 39 mind 40 code 41 walk 42 approach

▶▶ **PART 5**

43 would benefit (1) from (taking/having) (1)
44 is out of (1) the question (1)
45 no time (1) were they (ever) aware (1)
46 pointed out (1) to Claire that (1)
47 had not been (1) for that accident (1)
48 are on very good terms (1) with (1)
49 can't have (1) burned the dinner (1)
50 had her bag (1) snatched (1)

PAPER 4 Listening

▶▶ **PART 1**

1 C 2 B 3 C 4 A 5 B 6 A

▶▶ **PART 2**

7 subject 8 on Earth/earth 9 extraterrestrial life 10 organisms
11 (geological) period 12 five million/5,000,000
13 (very) different from 14 (the) dinosaurs

▶▶ **PART 3**

15 A 16 D 17 C 18 B 19 A 20 C

▶▶ **PART 4**

Task One
21 B 22 C 23 G 24 A 25 D

Task Two
26 E 27 A 28 F 29 G 30 H

 TEST 6

PAPER 1 Reading

▶▶ **PART 1**

1 B: Correct. 'She went on to enjoy a considerable measure of success, yet, rather unusually, she also felt she was not being stretched intellectually.'

2 A: Correct. 'It wasn't an easy decision to make, but at that point of my life, it was the right thing to do.'

3 C: Correct. 'Magna Carta ... represented little more than a bargaining tool in King John's struggle with his rebellious barons'

4 D: Correct. 'Their intentions were in reality no nobler than the king's, ... so it is amazing that this paper has subsequently had such far-reaching effects on the judicial systems of the civilised world.' and 'Yet, however unwittingly, those rebellious barons of the thirteenth century set the ball rolling in the battle for human rights, a battle which is being fought to this day.'

5 C: Correct. 'The job is challenging and varied, so we are looking for someone who is versatile and confident.'

6 B: Correct. 'The successful candidate will occasionally be required to handle sensitive documents, so he/she must be trustworthy, as confidentiality is vital.'

▶▶ **PART 2**

7 F: Link between the description of the 'community for the deeply green' in the previous paragraph and 'This might sound like a high-tech oasis'.

8 G: Link between 'a matter of intelligent design' in the previous paragraph and 'The key is finding ways to maximise efficiency in the simplest ways possible'.

9 A: Link between 'more zero-energy communities are under construction' in the previous paragraph and 'Much of the technology involved'.

10 C: Link between the 'European Union directive' described in the previous paragraph and 'The US government, too, has been doing its part'.

11 E: Link between the innovations described in the previous paragraph and 'Even more exciting developments are creeping onto the market'.

12 B: Contrastive link between 'Who cares ... costs a relatively small amount?' in the previous paragraph and 'Still, as governments, scientists and builders continue to provide the "market push" towards energy efficiency, the "consumer pull" will be stimulated'. Also, link between 'a combination of increasingly efficient appliances and building techniques' and 'The technologies will be able to support each other' in the following paragraph.

▶▶ PART 3

13 C: 'the ability to run was a crucial factor in the development of our species'

14 A: Correct. 'Traditional thinking up to now has been that the distinctive, upright body form of modern humans has come about as a result of the ability to walk'

15 C: 'However, this is only true if we consider fast running, or sprinting, over short distances. Even an Olympic athlete can ... only keep up a top speed for fifteen seconds or so.'

16 B: 'When we run, it is this ligament that prevents our head from pitching back and forth or from side to side. Therefore, we are able to run with steady heads, held high.'

17 D: 'Then there are our Achilles tendons ... which have nothing to do with walking. When we run, these tendons behave like springs, helping to propel us forward.'

18 C: 'running evolved in order for our direct ancestors to compete with other carnivores for access to the protein needed to grow the big brains that we enjoy today'

19 C: Correct. 'At the very least, I hope this theory will make many people have second thoughts about how humans learned to run and walk and why we are built the way we are.'

▶▶ PART 4

20 D: 'One thing that did surprise me at the start was how much official paperwork I have to deal with.'

21/22 C: 'It seems to me that people who start up businesses at my age ... are less inclined to take unnecessary risks.'

21/22 E: 'I figured I'd be better off sticking to what I know'

23 B: 'I know a lot of people in the industry. They have been great, offering advice as well as concrete help.'

24 A: 'I was infuriated by the arrogance of the company, which appeared to believe I was too old to be useful any longer'

25 F: 'I do almost all my work from home, using my PC for e-mails and video conferencing'

26 D: 'It was something I'd longed to do for years.'

27/28 A: 'The initial outlay for office equipment was pretty low, all things considered.'

27/28 D: 'When I left the company ... I had a reasonable amount of cash to invest in my own company.'

29 E: 'I'm sure I wouldn't have had the nerve to do it when I was younger, but I'm very glad I did.'

30 C: 'we're about to expand into glassware as well'

31 E: 'software showing people exactly how to go about it'

32 B: 'There seemed to be a dearth of companies catering for the over sixties'

33 C: 'Most of the people who work for me are more or less my generation. I find they tend to be more loyal'

34 F: 'I was in advertising for almost thirty years, but it's a very cut-throat business'

PAPER 2 Writing

▶▶ PART 1
Question 1
Style: Informal
Content: 1 Introduction: advise your friend to ask for further information.
2 Your friend should ask about:
- the exact location and how he/she can get to London
- the kind of accommodation available; can he/she stay with a family to improve his/her conversational English?
- the number of students in each class
- classes for students who already have a good level of English
- the number of class hours per week
- facilities for sports and other activities

3 Conclusion: perhaps end by wishing your friend a pleasant stay if he/she eventually decides to attend the school and offer to help further if necessary.

▶▶ PART 2
Question 2
Style: Semi-formal or formal
Content: 1 Introduction: describe the situation (some young people have to specialise at an early age).
2 Discuss the benefits of specialisation.
3 Discuss the benefits of getting a more general education.
4 Discuss what employers might want.
5 Conclusion: perhaps end with some general conclusions and/or suggestions.

Question 3
Style: Semi-formal or formal
Content: 1 Introduction: describe the situation (there are many sources of information).
2 Discuss the benefits of access to so much information.
3 Discuss the possible problems, e.g. getting bored or becoming unable to absorb it all.
4 Conclusion: perhaps end with your views of what will happen in the future.

Question 4
Style: Semi-formal or formal
Content: 1 Introduction: give some basic information about the region.
2 Describe some sights that might be of interest to young people.
3 Describe some places of cultural interest.
4 Describe some places of historical interest.
5 Describe some places of entertainment.
6 Describe some places where young people can socialise.
7 Conclusion: perhaps end by telling readers where to find additional or more detailed information.

Question 5(a)
Style: Style: Semi-formal or formal
Content: 1 Introduction: state which book you are going to write about and briefly describe the story.
2 Describe the features of the book that you find appealing, using examples.

3 Say which aspects of the book you feel could have been improved, and suggest how.

4 Conclusion: express your opinion of the book overall.

Question 5(b)

Style: Formal

Content: 1 Introduction: briefly outline the ending of the book, and say what you think of it.

2 Present an alternative ending, and show how the events of the story would lead up to it.

3 Compare your alternative ending with the original.

4 Conclusion: say which ending you think is preferable and why.

PAPER 3 Use of English

▶▶ **PART 1**

1 A **2** C **3** B **4** D **5** C **6** D **7** A **8** B **9** C **10** D **11** D **12** B

▶▶ **PART 2**

13 forward **14** While/When/If **15** how **16** It **17** such
18 to **19** each/every **20** Then **21** far **22** could/would
23 of **24** as **25** They **26** which **27** down

▶▶ **PART 3**

28 undoubtedly (noun to negative adverb)
29 originated (noun to verb)
30 inhabitants (verb to plural noun)
31 livelihood (verb to noun)
32 unpredictable (verb to negative adjective)
33 traditionally (noun to adverb)
34 temporarily (adjective to adverb)
35 guidance (verb to noun)
36 reputedly (noun to adverb)
37 conquest (verb to noun)

▶▶ **PART 4**

38 headed **39** arm **40** finds **41** model **42** neutral

▶▶ **PART 5**

43 was (1) put down to (1)
44 only (1) I had asked (1)
45 with the exception (1) of (1)
46 pulled through (1) because/as/since (1)
47 objected to (1) what I was/we were/they were saying (1)
48 your father, (1) not me/I who (1) OR
not I/me (1) but your father who (1)
49 I were you, (1) I would (1)
50 thought (that) the school (1) was vandalised (1)

PAPER 4 Listening

▶▶ **PART 1**

1 C **2** B **3** B **4** A **5** C **6** B

▶▶ **PART 2**

7 map (out) **8** conserve the site **9** humid **10** coach park
11 an underground stream **12** (loose) stones **13** leg
14 tour guide

▶▶ **PART 3**

15 D **16** D **17** B **18** A **19** C **20** B

▶▶ **PART 4**

Task One
21 F **22** E **23** C **24** H **25** A

Task Two
26 A **27** G **28** H **29** C **30** E

 TEST 7

PAPER 1 Reading

▶▶ **PART 1**

1 B: Correct. 'But then I started wondering if I could run the marathon with her, so I began a fairly intensive training programme.'

2 D: Correct. 'I've decided that the most appealing thing about running a marathon is that it's basically an illogical thing to do, but you share it with literally thousands of other people, and you are cheered on by enthusiastic spectators.'

3 C: Correct. 'During the last few days prior to the competition, sixty to seventy per cent of your energy intake should be coming from carbohydrates.'

4 B: Correct. 'Again, carbohydrates are the key, so on the morning of the competition, stick to those foods.'

5 A: Correct. 'But don't be fooled into thinking it is simply a long pony trek. This sport presents a real challenge, and demands high levels of fitness in both horse and rider.'

6 C: Correct. 'It is generally accepted that endurance riding is not so much about competing against other riders but rather against the elements and one's own stamina. Our organisation believes that completing the course is an achievement in itself'

▶▶ **PART 2**

7 A: Contrastive link between 'An enviable position to be in' in the previous paragraph and 'Yet she is clutching her saxophone like a petrified child'.

8 E: Link between 'an extraordinary combination' in the previous paragraph and 'As if this weren't unusual enough'. Also, link between 'she's a vet by training' in the previous paragraph and 'she suddenly decided to sell her thriving veterinary practice'.

9 G: Link between 'I was satisfied with my life' and 'contentment of this sort' in the following paragraph.

10 D: Link between 'it was as if she was hearing music for the first time' in the previous paragraph and 'I thought I'd gone to heaven'.

11 F: Link between 'Oddly enough' in the previous paragraph and 'the other curious factor'.

12 B: Link between 'little opportunity to feed her brain', 'reading books only goes a small way towards intellectual fulfilment' and 'her latest project will provide what's missing' in the following paragraph.

▶▶ **PART 3**

13 B: 'Their appeal begins to become evident when they take flight' and 'can soar effortlessly for hours'

14 D: 'From studying wild condors, they already knew that if a pair lost an egg, the birds would often produce another. So the first and sometimes second eggs laid by each female in captivity were removed'

15 A: 'As a result, the scientists, zookeepers and conservationists who are concerned about condors have bickered among themselves over the best ways to rear and release the birds.'

16 B: Correct. 'At times they landed on people's houses and garages, walked across roads and airport runways, sauntered into park visitor centres and fast food restaurants, and took food offered by picnickers and fishermen.'

17 D: 'Most recently, some of the first chicks hatched in the wild died after their parents fed them bottle caps ... and other man-made objects that fatally perforated or blocked their intestines.'

18 C: 'The real key to successful condor reintroduction, he believes, lies in properly socialising young condors as members of a group that follow and learn from older, preferably adult birds.'

19 D: Correct. The article as a whole.

▶▶ **PART 4**

20 D: 'And though manufacturers stress the saving on film, they may fail to mention that you need expensive memory cards. What's more, some digital cameras use up batteries at an alarming rate.'

21 B: 'you can put your own information on each picture you take, such as the time, day and place where it was taken'

22 A: 'On the other hand, the flash will probably be of poor quality, with an effective range of only about four metres.'

23 C: 'you will learn how to make all the adjustments yourself, for different types of light etc.'

24 C: 'With SLRs you must make sure the lens and body will fit together since they come in different sizes.'

25 D: 'You will have to store your photos on your computer ... what happens if it breaks down'

26 C: 'Get a camera with a metal body ... delicate lenses are less likely to come to grief.'

27 B: 'The Advanced Photo System (APS) was launched in 1996 by several manufacturers who established a common standard.'

28 A: 'the image will not be clear if you blow up the picture bigger than 15cm x 21cm'

29 B: 'these famous names ... These often offer comparable features, build qualities and guarantees for a lower price.'

30 H: 'It's tiny, so you can ... get those special shots without anyone realising they're being captured on film.'

31 F: 'You learn better without the modern electronic gadgetry, which will probably break down in a couple of years anyway.'

32 F: 'Nobody will take you seriously as a photographer with anything other than an SLR.'

33 E: 'You develop as a photographer by taking lots of shots, studying them ... this is how you learn what makes a good picture.'

34 G: 'you can use any 35mm film with a compact – a definite advantage when you're in some tiny village where shops only have normal films'

PAPER 2 Writing

▶▶ **PART 1**

Question 1

Style: Semi-formal or formal

Content: 1 Explain what is being proposed:
- to merge the Whitewall College library with the Technical College library
- to house the libraries in the Technical College library building
- to introduce charges for borrowing
- to open the library to members of the public

2 Encourage opposition to this plan by explaining the disadvantages:
- the Technical College has no humanities books in its library
- the charge for borrowing will affect poor students unfairly
- the library will be overcrowded

3 Describe opposition to the plan from students and staff and say that there will be a meeting to discuss the situation. Give the place and time.

▶▶ **PART 2**

Question 2

Style: Semi-formal or formal

Content: 1 Introduction: describe the situation (it is getting easier all the time to download books).
2 Discuss the benefits of downloading.
3 Discuss the benefits of conventional books.
4 Discuss why conventional books have the ultimate advantage.
5 Conclusion: perhaps end with a brief summary of your points.

Question 3

Style: Neutral or formal

Content: 1 Introduction: describe the situation (the increasing number of fast food outlets).
2 Discuss the convenience of fast food, especially for young people.
3 Describe the attitude of young people to healthy foods.
4 Describe how an appreciation of good food and the art of cooking could be promoted in schools and colleges.
5 Conclusion: perhaps end with a brief summary of your points.

Question 4

Style: Semi-formal or formal

Content: 1 Introduction: state briefly what you are going to describe.
2 Discuss the role played by the family in the past, mentioning both the nuclear and the extended family.
3 Describe a typical family in your country today and the relationship between family members.
4 Say whether the situation today is different from what it used to be.
5 Discuss how the family might change in the future and the factors that may contribute to this change.

Question 5(a)

Style: Formal

Content: 1 Introduction: state the purpose of the report.
2 Compare the book with its film version, saying which seems to be more popular and why.
3 Discuss whether book sales have been affected positively or negatively by the film.
4 Conclusion: sum up the points raised.

Question 5(b)

Style: Semi-formal or formal

Content: 1 Introduction: reiterate the statement in your own words, and briefly express your view of it, making reference to the novel you have read.

2 Discuss a 'bad' character in your novel in relation to the point raised in the statement.

3 Discuss the protagonist in relation to the point raised in the statement.

4 Conclusion: consolidate your view of the statement.

PAPER 3 Use of English

▶▶ PART 1

1 C **2** D **3** B **4** A **5** B **6** D **7** D **8** C **9** A **10** D **11** A **12** B

▶▶ PART 2

13 in **14** which **15** What **16** only **17** no/little
18 were **19** the **20** had **21** case **22** more
23 While/Whereas/Although/Though **24** too **25** as
26 They **27** with

▶▶ PART 3

28 influential (noun to adjective)
29 unhappiness (adjective to negative noun)
30 inspiration (verb to noun)
31 generosity (adjective to noun)
32 restless (noun to negative adjective)
33 medical (noun to adjective)
34 fictional (noun to adjective)
35 admiration (verb to noun)
36 deduction (verb to noun)
37 outcry (verb to compound noun)

▶▶ PART 4

38 mild **39** hint **40** clapped **41** natural **42** angle

▶▶ PART 5

43 all comes down (1) to money (1)
44 complete/total disregard (1) for her (1)
45 never discovered (1) who the murderer (1)
46 against (1) calling him (1)
47 might as well (1) leave (1)
48 leaving the office (1) did I realise (1)
49 will never (1) live it (1)
50 are being (1) looked into by (1)

PAPER 4 Listening

▶▶ PART 1

1 B **2** C **3** B **4** A **5** C **6** A

▶▶ PART 2

7 chains **8** ninety-eight percent/98% **9** a few/several hours
10 flour **11** (rather) tasteless **12** stale **13** allergies
14 lose money

▶▶ PART 3

15 A **16** C **17** D **18** B **19** C **20** A

▶▶ PART 4

Task One
21 D **22** E **23** A **24** G **25** B

Task Two
26 C **27** F **28** A **29** H **30** D

PAPER 1 Reading

▶▶ PART 1

1 D: Correct. 'If you are looking to get away from it all … but don't want to break the bank, then … book a weekend break at the Cog in the Wheel Inn, at Ashton Falls. Set in the beautiful Yorkshire Dales, this country retreat boasts a spacious yet cosy restaurant with a cuisine to be envied for miles around.'

2 A: Correct. 'let the roaring log fire warm your toes and drive away all your worries' and 'Luxuriously furnished … each of the inn's ten bedrooms affords magnificent views of the rolling countryside, creating the perfect atmosphere for a satisfyingly deep sleep.'

3 D: Correct. 'Green Valley Travel is a growing, privately run travel company … for singles.'

4 C: Correct. 'with a commitment to responsible sustainable tourism', 'Every year our holiday packages undergo rigorous checks by a team of ecological experts', 'Eco-lodge is a term coined by the tourist industry to describe tourist accommodation which has been constructed using sustainable materials, and which operates with respect towards both the local community and the environment.'

5 C: Correct. ' "This is the Paradise Beach Hotel, isn't it?" I asked the taxi driver for the third time. His English was not very good, and my Italian even worse, so I had hopes that perhaps he hadn't understood me. Or perhaps this was the *wrong* Paradise Beach Hotel? For paradise it most certainly was not!'

6 B: Correct. 'I stared in dismay at what was in effect a building site' and 'I caught sight of my brood returning from their reconnaissance trip. Things didn't look promising.'

▶▶ PART 2

7 B: Link between 'There are definitely more and more people seeking wildlife experiences now' and 'an increased demand for wildlife tours or the addition of a wildlife-watching component to traditional holidays' in the following paragraph.

8 D: Link between 'It seems people want to discover nature for themselves' in the previous paragraph and 'There's no way to compare seeing an animal in the wild with watching one on TV'.

9 G: Link between 'They use the services of local communities, train local guides and have close ties to conservation projects' in the previous paragraph and 'Thus tour operator Rekero has established its own school – the Koyiaki Guide School and Wilderness Camp'.

10 E: Link between 'Some offer the opportunity to participate in research and conservation' in the previous paragraph, 'Earthwatch … does just that' and 'offer members of the public the opportunity to be on the front line, not the sidelines, of conservation'.

11 A: Link between 'Volunteers … take part in various activities including snow leopard, wolf and bear surveys and whale and dolphin research' in the previous paragraph and 'People have a unique experience while contributing to conservation directly'.

12 F: Link between 'it's worth remembering that you don't have to go to the ends of the Earth to catch rewarding glimpses of animals' and 'some of the best wildlife-watching opportunities on offer are on our doorstep' in the following paragraph.

▶▶ PART 3

13 A: 'I consulted an osteopath ... Go off and learn the Alexander technique.'

14 B: Correct. 'I had regularly been told ... that I tend to slouch in chairs but had thought bad posture was something one was born with and could do nothing about.'

15 C: 'It trains you to use your body less harshly and to perform familiar movements and actions with less effort.'

16 B: 'The key is learning to break the bad habits ... a habit the body has formed which can be hard to break.'

17 D: 'This may sound daft, but it is an important element in the process of learning how to hold yourself upright.'

18 D: 'Frederick Matthias Alexander, an Australian theatrical orator ... with dramatic results.'

19 C: The text as a whole.

▶▶ PART 4

20 B: 'The alternative technologies we have at present are lagging far behind the petrol-guzzling internal combustion engine in terms of speed and the distance that can be travelled before refuelling.'

21 E: 'However, a new generation of turbines – microturbines – has been developed ... . They are small, high-speed engine systems ... all the other vital components and control electronics.'

22 A: 'The motor industry is finally showing some serious interest ... as can be seen by the amount of money they are spending on research and development.'

23 C: 'But these vehicles are virtually confined to urban settings'

24 D: 'First developed for use in missions to the moon, fuel cells appear to be the most serious challenger to the internal combustion engine'

25 F: 'For example, most diesel cars can now be converted to run on biodiesel fuel, which is made from used vegetable oils and animal fats.'

26 C: 'electric cars have a toy-like appearance which is definitely not appealing'

27 A: 'Governments throughout the world are demanding restrictions ... replaced by vehicles that run on alternative power sources.'

28 D: 'the reformer ... takes up so much space that the vehicle can only seat the driver and one passenger'

29 E: 'These large turbines shine when in steady-state applications but are not as efficient when speed and load are continually changing.'

30 B: 'This vehicle ... can go from 0 to about 100 kph in around 10 seconds'

31 F: 'Some experts even believe that the future may lie with steam cars ... it could be that the wheel is coming full circle.'

32 A: 'nowadays a significant number of people would prefer to buy a vehicle that did not emit greenhouse gases into the atmosphere or pollute the environment in other ways'

33 B: 'When you start the hybrid car and when you are driving normally ... the petrol engine provides that power.'

34 E: Correct. 'A gas car is cheaper to run, as well as being cleaner than a conventional car. On the other hand, the vehicle itself is expensive because the technology is new'

PAPER 2 Writing

▶▶ PART 1

Question 1

Style: Formal

Content: 1 Describe the purpose of a career day.
2 Suggest a day and date for it.
3 Describe what space and facilities might be needed and describe the layout of the lecture hall.
4 Discuss how many companies should be invited.
5 Discuss what kind of publicity is needed.
6 Conclusion: end by stating what the next steps should be.

▶▶ PART 2

Question 2

Style: Neutral, semi-formal or formal

Content: 1 Introduction: say a few introductory words about the activity.
2 Describe how you became interested in this activity.
3 Describe what equipment is needed.
4 Describe the attractions this activity has for you.
5 Conclusion: perhaps end by describing what you plan to do in the future in connection with the activity.

Question 3

Style: Neutral or formal

Content: 1 Introduction: perhaps begin by stating that more and more people change employers or even careers these days.
2 Describe the attitude of young people to the traditional idea of working at one job for life.
3 Describe the attitude of young people to developing a range of skills.
4 Describe the attitude of young people to job security.
5 Conclusion: perhaps end by describing how you think most young people think about employment these days.

Question 4

Style: Neutral or formal

Content: 1 Introduction: explain that you are going to talk about two films that are supposed to be good: one that you liked and one that you didn't.
2 Discuss the first film:
  ● give a brief summary of the plot
  ● describe the characters briefly
  ● describe some interesting or appealing aspects of the film, e.g. the acting, the soundtrack, the dialogue etc.
  ● summarise why you liked the film
3 Discuss the second film:
  ● give a brief summary of the plot
  ● describe the characters briefly
  ● describe any aspects of the film that you think are worth mentioning, e.g. the acting, the soundtrack, the cinematography etc.
  ● summarise why you didn't like the film

Question 5(a)

Style: Semi-formal or formal

Content: 1 Introduction: briefly reiterate the statement in your own words and say whether you think it is true of the protagonist.

2 Discuss your view of the development of the protagonist's character, supporting what you say with examples from the book.

3 Conclusion: sum up how the character has changed by the end of the novel.

Question 5(b)

Style: Semi-formal or formal

Content:
1 Introduction: state which two characters you are going to discuss.

2 Examine the relationship between them in the novel.

3 Show how this relationship affects events using examples.

4 Conclusion: sum up with comments.

PAPER 3 Use of English

▶▶ PART 1

1 A **2** B **3** C **4** A **5** D **6** B **7** A **8** B **9** A **10** D **11** C **12** B

▶▶ PART 2

13 which **14** as **15** A **16** they **17** from **18** there
19 less **20** in **21** on **22** at **23** to **24** what **25** when
26 yourself **27** long

▶▶ PART 3

28 misconceptions (noun to negative plural noun)
29 venomous (noun to adjective)
30 comparison (verb to noun)
31 fatalities (adjective to plural noun)
32 solitary (noun to adjective)
33 occurrences (verb to plural noun)
34 unpleasant (verb to negative adjective)
35 underestimated (verb to verb)
36 precautions (noun to plural noun)
37 resistant (verb to adjective)

▶▶ PART 4

38 range **39** blew **40** remote **41** hit **42** condition

▶▶ PART 5

43 has been issued (1) of the man (1)
44 keeps bothering me, (1) so/and (1)
45 insisted (1) on my/our staying (1)
46 was (1) fed up with (1) OR
   couldn't (1) put up with (1)
47 no matter (1) what time it may (1)
48 no account (1) am I to be (1)
49 it not been (1) for Maurice (1)
50 will have started (1) by the time (1)

PAPER 4 Listening

▶▶ PART 1

1 C **2** C **3** B **4** A **5** B **6** A

▶▶ PART 2

7 (long-distance) running **8** long jump **9** nephew **10** build
11 shooting **12** proper diet **13** equipment **14** attitude

▶▶ PART 3

15 D **16** D **17** A **18** C **19** B **20** C

▶▶ PART 4

Task One
21 F **22** D **23** G **24** C **25** A

Task Two
26 C **27** H **28** D **29** B **30** F

TEST 1

▶▶ **PART 1**

You will hear three different extracts. For questions 1–6, choose the answer, A, B or C which fits best according to what you hear. There are two questions for each extract.

Extract One

You hear two friends talking about an experience one of them had as a volunteer.

Jenny: Nigel! I haven't seen you for a while! Where have you been?

Nigel: Madagascar.

Jenny: Never! Tell me about it!

Nigel: Well, you know I want to study marine biology? Anyway, I decided to get some hands-on experience while doing volunteer work, and this mate of mine put me in touch with a conservation operation called Blue Ventures in Madagascar. And off I went! We did a lot of diving to record the marine life around the reefs and monitor the effects of bleaching on the reefs themselves. Some of them were incredible – a myriad of fish of different shapes and sizes, with all these vibrant colours. Unfortunately, bleaching is wreaking havoc and threatening to destroy the coral. Now the Blue Ventures project is trying to both protect the marine life in the area and also help the local people find a way to survive. They're terribly poor, but so optimistic and friendly. It was an unforgettable experience!

Jenny: Really? Fascinating ... Did anything exciting happen while you were there?

Nigel: On one dive we saw a huge pufferfish! And then five minutes later, we actually saw a white tip reef shark! It was pretty mind-blowing. Then we ....

Extract Two

You hear two people talking on a radio programme about how to deal with a compulsive disorder.

Interviewer: So, Alice, how long were you a compulsive shopper?

Alice: Well, I wouldn't say I'm fully cured now! Still get urges, you know – and they can be quite strong. But I'd say it was really bad for about four years before I admitted to myself it was a problem and realised I had to put a stop to it.

Interviewer: What forced you to face up to the problem?

Alice: Well, the debts I'd run up on my credit cards might have had something to do with it!

Interviewer: What did you do?

Alice: I got professional help to start with, and then joined a self-help group. I was amazed how many of us there were! Talking about things really helped, and then I got rid of the credit cards. I only pay by cash now, and I'm strict with myself about how much I carry on me when I go out.

Interviewer: What do you do now when you get the urge?

Alice: Don't laugh, but I joined a gym with a friend of mine from the group. As soon as she or I feel a craving coming on, we call each other and we rush down there and work out for an hour – until the craving subsides.

Extract Three

You hear two friends talking about a football match that they have just watched.

Man: I can't believe it! We were this close! The referee was out of order! There was no way Rooney was offside!

Woman: Oh, come on, Dave! The replay showed that he was!

Actually, I thought England were complacent. They gave away too many chances. Look at Gerrard missing that open goal. That I couldn't believe!

Man: Don't remind me! But come on, Tracy. You can't say England played badly. Robinson made a couple of brilliant saves, and Owen had a good game. But it was the same old story: they just couldn't drive the ball home. Russia, though, were sloppy. They had no structure in their play, and Pavlyuchenko's goal was sheer luck.

Woman: It was well executed, and you know it. Our defence just didn't see him coming. No, Russia saw their chance and took it. England were too convinced they were going to win. That's what lost them the game.

Man: You can say that after the way Owen and Cole played?

Woman: They were only two players, Dave. The others looked like they were strolling throughout the match. Russia might not have played well, but England were no better.

▶▶ **PART 2**

You will hear a writer talking about a book she has written on the subject of aspirin. For questions 7–14, complete the sentences.

Writer: We are all familiar with aspirin, that common household remedy which provides relief from pain. But few people are aware of just how fascinating the subject of aspirin actually is.

The key ingredient of this wonderful drug is found in several plants, and five thousand years ago physicians in ancient Egypt were using an extract from the bark of the willow as a cure for a variety of complaints. But it was to be many centuries before the scientific basis of this medication was understood.

Then, in the eighteenth century, an Englishman, Edward Stone, accidentally rediscovered the medicinal properties of willow tree extract, although he mistakenly attributed its efficacy to its bitter taste and its supposed resemblance to another drug, quinine. Later on, in 1829, a pharmacist isolated the active ingredient, salicylic acid. Unfortunately, the chemical has several undesirable side effects, the most serious of which is that it can upset the stomach.

However, at the end of the nineteenth century, a chemist working for Friedrich Bayer, a German company, found a way of combining salicylic acid with an acetyl group. A few years later, Bayer marketed the first aspirins, and for the next seventy years it was regarded as a miraculous painkiller. Curiously, during all that time, hardly any research was done into the way aspirin works.

Then, in 1971, groundbreaking findings were published that showed how aspirin slows down swelling and the coagulation of the blood. This means it also dramatically reduces the risk of heart disease. As you can imagine, this was exciting news. Further research showed that a third of all people at risk from a heart attack will not have one if they take aspirin regularly. Although that sounds too good to be true, most doctors now accept that aspirin really does possess these miraculous qualities. More controversially, some scientists believe that nearly everyone over the age of fifty would benefit from taking aspirin regularly as a preventative measure.

Now it seems that the active ingredients of aspirin can also be found in many organically grown vegetables – and regular consumption of such foods might be an alternative to an aspirin a day ...

▶▶ PART 3

You will hear part of an interview with Stan Levin, a dance critic, about a modern ballet production involving animals. For questions 15–20, choose the answer, A, B, C or D which fits best according to what you hear.

Interviewer: Stan, you are known as being something of a conservative as far as dance is concerned, so I was intrigued when you told me you wanted to discuss Alain Platel's ballet *Wolf* on tonight's programme. *Wolf* generated a furore in certain circles when it was first performed, didn't it?

Stan: Yes, it's attracted its fair share of criticism, but it's also been welcomed as one of the most fascinating modern dance productions in recent years.

Interviewer: Some of our viewers may not have seen the ballet and they may be wondering why all the fuss, so could I ask you to describe briefly what *Wolf* is about.

Stan: Well, basically, it's about homeless people living in a disused shopping mall and returning to some sort of pre-civilised life. And it features some startling innovations, including the use of dogs as characters.

Interviewer: How do the dogs come into it?

Stan: Well, as I understand it, the pack of dogs represents this return to a primitive state. At least, that's the idea Platel is trying to convey.

Interviewer: What do you think of the idea of using animals on stage in this way? Can it be justified?

Stan: Well, more and more choreographers these days are moving beyond the traditional limits of dance, and I don't disapprove of this in principle. Many are turning to technology, for instance, using computers to plan the actual choreography.

Interviewer: Sometimes even using projections of dancers alongside the real ones ...

Stan: Exactly. I find all this very interesting – take the work of Annette Sanderson in New York, for instance – but I think it's now going beyond the genre of dance and turning into something else. Whereas I think Platel is coming from the other direction, if you like, working more with improvisation and basic ensemble techniques.

Interviewer: How do audiences respond to *Wolf*?

Stan: By and large, quite enthusiastically. I think some people are surprised at how well it all works. The dogs generally keep very close to one of the characters. Apparently, the dancer works intensively with them during rehearsal, and the dogs have learned to imitate his movements. That fascinates audiences. Of course, sometimes the dogs distract attention from an important piece of dancing, but I don't feel this is a real problem.

Interviewer: Do the dogs do anything special during the performance?

Stan: No. Their main function is to add atmosphere. It's not like a circus, with the dogs performing tricks! At the same time, you realise they have been trained and are, in a sense, putting on a show simply by remaining on stage with the human performers. During the performance I saw, a member of the audience in the front row tried to call the dogs over to him, which made them look away from the dancers towards the audience. It spoiled the mood – though of course, this wasn't the dogs' fault.

Interviewer: So the dogs fulfil a kind of symbolic function in the story?

Stan: Yes and no. They are attached to one of the characters, a tramp, and we are meant to understand that they have become a pack. I must say this works rather well: you really *do* get the impression that the dogs and the tramp have bonded to form a sort of community. But for me, the most striking aspect of the production was the lurking possibility of aggression, largely as a consequence of the presence of the animals.

Interviewer: Well, Stan, I must say it all sounds fascinating. Thank you for coming along tonight and sharing your insights with us.

Stan: My pleasure.

▶▶ PART 4

This part consists of two tasks. You will hear five short extracts in which people talk about fitness and health. Look at Task 1. For questions 21–25, choose from the list A–H what each speaker says about his or her reasons for attending a gym regularly. Now look at Task 2. For questions 26–30, choose from the list A–H what opinion each speaker expresses about fitness and health generally.

Speaker 1: I think getting fit is like many things in life: it's much easier if you arrange a regular routine for yourself. Then after a while it becomes a source of pride to continue the way you've started – as if you'd be breaking a promise to yourself if you stopped. And of course, having a definite goal helps, too. That's why I've entered for the London Marathon next year, despite being over forty! I want to be ready for it, and every time I go to the gym that's what I focus on while I work out.

Speaker 2: I'm not what you'd call a fitness fanatic but about three years ago I was knocked off my bike by a car, and I had to stay in hospital for a month. It took me a long time to regain the full use of my legs. And the physiotherapist made me promise to exercise in a gym at least three times a week. She also said I needed to stop smoking and lose weight, which makes sense. I mean, you can't expect to be fit if you have such unhealthy habits, can you?

Speaker 3: I suppose if I'm honest, one of the reasons I work out in the gym is that I've got to know a lot of people here, and I enjoy seeing them. Now and then we meet up outside the gym for a drink, or to go to the cinema. Of course, I do think keeping fit is important as well. Although I think it's harder for some people to keep slim and healthy. It's as though it's in the blood. I have a friend who doesn't eat much and takes regular exercise, but he's still overweight. It's as if his body doesn't *want* to be thin.

Speaker 4: It's getting harder and harder to stay fit. I used to go for a walk every morning to the local shops; plenty of healthy exercise. But now they've all closed, there's one of those massive supermarkets on the edge of town, and I have to take a bus there. I've decided I have to be serious about exercising, which is why I joined a gym, and I generally manage to get there three times a week. I have high blood pressure, you see, and I don't want to end up having a heart attack like my father and grandmother.

Speaker 5: As a professional golfer I don't really have any choice: I simply must do my three hours in the gym every morning to make sure I can play the game properly. Fortunately, I love golf and I like the lifestyle, so all the exercise doesn't bother me too much. In fact, it's become so much part of my life that I think it would be hard to stop. The people I admire are those who start doing serious exercise late in life; it must be so hard to do that when you aren't accustomed to it.

TEST 2

▶▶ PART 1

You will hear three different extracts. For questions 1–6, choose the answer, A, B or C which fits best according to what you hear. There are two questions for each extract.

Extract One

You hear part of an interview with a Tai Chi instructor.

Interviewer: So, Ruth, what exactly is Tai Chi?

Ruth: Well, Peter, it's not just a form of physical exercise. The term Tai Chi refers to harmony in all life forces. The double-fish symbol we in the West refer to as the yin and yang symbol is in fact the Tai Chi T'u symbol, representing perfect balance. The dividing line between the yin and yang sections is not straight, signifying the constant flow and interaction between the two opposites. This is reflected in everyday events and activities: night becoming day, hot becoming cold or winter changing to summer, are all examples of the Tai Chi in action.

Interviewer: Fascinating! So how is this connected to the form of exercise?

Ruth: The philosophy transfers directly to the sequence of exercises that make up the Tai Chi 'forms'. Each sequence of movements is designed to bring about harmony in your body, and should flow into one another in a continuous manner. And again, balance is everything. People laugh when they see us in the park because we look as though we're dancing in slow motion! In fact, it takes years of practice and concentration to get the flow between movements close to what it needs to be.

Extract Two

You hear two people discussing taking a year off before going to university.

Woman: For me, taking a year off between finishing school and going to university was the best thing I could have done.

Man: Yeah, too right! I had a great time. I taught English in this tiny school in China. It was unforgettable! I went off thinking that the job would be a doddle, you know, an easy way to earn some travelling money. Couldn't have been more wrong! I had to work really hard. But the thing was, I ended up loving it. The kids were great, and it was a real laugh. Of course, it had nothing to do with my studies – mechanical engineering – but it taught me a lot about how to get along with people, you know? So how about you? Why was your gap year so special?

Woman: Basically because it brought me to my senses! I'd been planning to study hotel management, and decided to use my gap year to get some practical experience by doing internship training abroad. I got placed in this hotel in Rio de Janeiro and, well, it was a real eye-opener, I can tell you! Within two weeks, I realised I wasn't cut out for that kind of thing, and when I got home, I re-applied to study Marketing!

Extract Three

You hear part of an interview with an illusionist.

Interviewer: So why become an illusionist, Daniel?

Daniel: Well, I started doing card tricks in high school ... the usual story ... there was this girl I had a crush on, and not knowing how to talk to her, I tried to get her attention that way.

Interviewer: Did it work?

Daniel: For a while, but the novelty soon wore off, and this made me realise I'd have to develop my skills if I wanted to hold people's attention! Then it became an obsession. I experimented and practised every day, and I got a buzz out of the effect my tricks had on people. And it went on from there.

Interviewer: You often draw parallels between magic and film making. Why is that?

Daniel: Ah! Sure now, they're both forms of entertainment, and their success depends on creating a convincing illusion. They also demand a suspension of disbelief from the audience, and technology has helped here, through the development of special effects. The master of illusion on the stage, just like the master of the cinema, is someone who is able to use such things most effectively. You only have to watch a famous illusionist like David Copperfield to see that. In my case, I ...

You will hear part of a talk by a writer who has written a biography. For questions 7–14, complete the sentences.

Writer: I've just finished writing the biography of Robert Tewbridge, an amateur historian who achieved a certain notoriety in his day. It probably comes as no surprise that I find him a fascinating character, and I hope I've managed to convey this in my book.

One of Tewbridge's most endearing personal qualities was his fierce independence of spirit. Throughout his life, he stubbornly followed his own instincts rather than sticking to the accepted norms. He was born in Scotland, the son of a farmer. Robert's parents had ambitions for their only son, a quick-witted lad, and hoped he would study medicine at Edinburgh University, the idea being that he would return to the highlands as a doctor and set up his own practice. But Robert was determined to see the world and so, at the age of nineteen, he left home for London with only a few shillings in his pocket.

In the great metropolis, Robert had to find some way to keep body and soul together, and being of a literary turn of mind, he started writing for newspapers and journals. Indeed, during his lifetime Tewbridge was known primarily for his articles and essays on some of the more controversial social and political issues of the day. I was able to study most of his published work while I was doing research for the biography, but I would hardly have had an insight into the private man without access to his personal correspondence. Tewbridge wrote literally thousands of letters during his lifetime, including an astonishing number to his wife's brother, a learned chap by all accounts. The two men became very intimate, and in these letters Tewbridge felt able to be frank and honest. It was while I was reading one of these letters that I discovered how Tewbridge first became interested in history. Apparently, it was after seeing a performance of Shakespeare's *Julius Caesar*. This prompted him to begin a lifelong study of Roman history, and the fascination never left him. In fact, when Tewbridge was in his fifties, he and his wife moved to Italy, where they lived for the next thirty years, until his death, in fact. Tewbridge did not live to publish his monumental work on Rome and died without seeing his native Scotland again, but it was ...

You will hear part of an interview with Betsy Boom, owner of a chain of fashion shops. For questions 15–20, choose the correct answer, A, B, C or D which fits best according to what you hear.

Interviewer: Betsy, it's only five years since you opened your first shop, but today your chain is one of the success stories of the retail market in the UK. Perhaps one way to gain an understanding of how you managed such a phenomenal feat would be to find out a little about your personal tastes. Shopping is your business, but is it one of your pleasures? Are you an avid shopper?

Betsy: Not really, which I think helps explain the philosophy behind my stores. I mean, I like finding a bargain as much as the next person, but what I adore is trying things on – seeing how I look in outfits I wouldn't normally buy. Then there's the other aspect of shopping: going from one shop to another, being ignored in the cheaper shops or treated with disdain by aloof staff in the expensive ones – and feeling you are obliged to buy something if you've been in a shop longer than ten minutes. I can't stand that.

Interviewer: Did your personal attitudes shape the concept of your first store?

Betsy: Absolutely. I thought: wouldn't it be wonderful to go into a shop that was fun! And for me, that means friendly staff who come up to you and suggest all sorts of ideas, some of them wild, about how you might like to look. So you're persuaded to try on loads of things – but nobody minds if you don't buy them! It's more like romping around a huge fancy-dress emporium than going shopping!

Interviewer: Did the idea for your shop take off right away?

Betsy: More or less. I mean, when we opened the first place, most people who came in felt a little stunned, not sure how to respond, I suppose. But once they got used to the idea they loved it! And it was the same with the staff. I asked the assistants to be far more outgoing and upfront than usual. They were a bit shy at first, partly because they weren't sure whether customers would take it the right way or get offended and storm out. But they get quite a kick out of it now.

Interviewer: Now that success is assured, can you pick out the most satisfying aspect of the work for you personally?

Betsy: Well, it's lovely being able to turn round to all the people who said it would never work and say: 'Look! I did it!' But what never fails to thrill me is the sight of someone who isn't at all sure at first about wearing something new, and then she thinks she might as well because the atmosphere's so friendly, and in the end she's delighted by a completely different, daring outfit she'd never have tried on otherwise. It's like seeing a person discover a new self.

Interviewer: So what comes next? Where do you go from here?

Betsy: Good question. To be honest, I haven't a clue! Or at least, I do have a few ideas, but I'm being careful. The shops have worked for me, but that doesn't make me a top business brain by any means! Having said that, I'm deeply aware that I tend to be lazy. I'm quite capable of just sitting back and letting the cash roll in.

Interviewer: That doesn't sound too bad!

Betsy: No, but after a while I'd become frustrated. I know I have to take a risk and try something else, even if it fails. Otherwise my self-respect will be in tatters within a couple of years.

Interviewer: Whatever you do try next, good luck. And thanks for being with us today, Betsy Boom.

Betsy: I've enjoyed talking to you.

▶▶ **PART 4**

This part consists of two tasks. You will hear five short extracts in which people talk about environmental initiatives in the workplace. Look at Task 1. For questions 21–25, choose from the list A–H the person who is speaking. Now look at Task 2. For questions 26–30, choose from the list A–H what view each speaker is expressing.

Speaker 1: I don't think offices are environmentally friendly places at all. All that stuff that gets thrown away! People just can't be bothered to recycle paper, and they leave equipment on, wasting electricity. Our organisation sends leaflets out all the time to try and raise awareness among employees in various companies, but, well, the average worker thinks it's up to the bosses to do something. They just don't realise they could make a significant difference just by turning off computer monitors and electrical equipment at the end of the day.

Speaker 2: Fortunately, these days more people are conscious of a company's environmental image when buying products and services, which is a big change when you remember the situation ten or fifteen years ago. I think it's the hard economics of the marketplace that's making companies do something for the environment. And I've got a new generation of university students looking to me to find them an employer whose environmental concerns are similar to their own. So recruitment is harder for companies without a good attitude towards the environment.

Speaker 3: I think we should feel more encouraged about the

environment these days. After all, there are some positive signs. For instance, the insurance company I work for no longer uses energy derived from the burning of fossil fuels. It uses clean, 'green' sources instead: solar energy and wind energy. We now drive company cars that run on gas fuel, so they don't burden the atmosphere with so many dangerous emissions. And considering how many of us travel all over the country every day to sell insurance, this does make a difference.

Speaker 4: One thing about environmental awareness: everyone agrees it's a good idea to encourage it. So companies benefit from a kind of association of ideas. But a business has to put real effort into making environmental initiatives work. It's no good simply introducing new regulations in the workplace. Here at Head Office, we show our employees exactly how much energy can be saved by adopting particular practices.

Speaker 5: Communication is definitely the key, because both staff and customers can easily think that environmental schemes are there simply to save money or as an advertising gimmick. Obviously, the fact that we publicise the initiatives taken by the company to support the environment enhances sales, so I'd be lying if I said it wasn't. After all, advertising is what my job's all about! But we also show our staff that we are sincere by giving them incentives to follow our environmental initiatives at work. I think that's also important.

 TEST **3**

▶▶ **PART 1**

You will hear three different extracts. For questions 1–6, choose the answer, A, B or C which fits best according to what you hear. There are two questions for each extract.

Extract One

You hear two people talking about the benefits of garlic.

Brenda: Cor! Gary! Have you been eating garlic again? It reeks in here!

Gary: Mm, well, you know, I've, mm, been reading up on it. Did you know that, aside from the obvious tried and tested cold remedy, garlic also helps combat high cholesterol levels, cures acne and even keeps mosquitoes at bay! They're averse to the smell, too, apparently.

Brenda: Hmph! I'm not so sure it's good for the skin. Helen was told to put it on her spots, and instead of making them disappear, her skin became red and felt like it was burning!

Gary: It's probably more effective when eaten – it tends to clean out the system from within, if you know what I mean. It's really good for getting rid of toxins in the body.

Brenda: You have to be careful even then, though. I've known people who are allergic to it.

Gary: You're joking!

Brenda: No, seriously. It can bring you out in a rash. Don't forget, it's a pretty powerful substance, and you know the saying: 'Too much of a good thing.'

Gary: Mm. I'd better cut down then!

Extract Two

You hear part of an interview with Rusty Upshaw, a bossaball referee.

Interviewer: So, Rusty, how do you play bossaball?

Rusty: Ah! It's the best, you know? This sport is a combination of all the good things in life: an element of football, volleyball, trampolining, mixed together with a lot of rhythm and soul. It's also played to music, so there's an element of capoeira in there, too. Now, it's played on a court of bouncy inflatables with a net in the middle. On either side of the net there's a circular trampoline. Two teams of between three and five players aim to ground the ball on the opponents' field. Players can use any part of the body to hit the ball, but can only touch it once with their hands, or make a double touch with their feet or head. The music is optional, but it creates atmosphere and gives a rhythm to the game. And you need a good samba referee.

Interviewer: And that's where you come in, Rusty! What does a 'samba referee' do?

Rusty: He creates the atmosphere of the game. A good one is a DJ with a nice selection of music to set the pace and get the crowd in the mood. Charisma is also useful 'cause then the game becomes a show, and people love it.

Extract Three

You hear two people talking about research into depression.

Man: What are you reading, Jan?

Woman: Uh? Oh, this article about the brain. It's quite interesting, actually. Scientists have managed to link positive thought with two specific regions in the brain. They believe the discovery could help them determine the causes of depression.

Man: *Fantastic!* Let's encourage society's preoccupation with depression! Perhaps if they didn't go on about it so much, people might stop fooling themselves that they're *suffering* from it!

Woman: According to the findings, having positive thoughts activates two areas in the brain which have traditionally been associated with depression. When people feel optimistic, these regions become highly active, while activity is noticeably reduced in depressed individuals.

Man: Well, that seems logical. I can't see what's so amazing about that!

Woman: Just listen a minute! Autopsies reveal that severely depressed people have fewer cells than normal in these regions. Positive thought causes increased activity, but if you have fewer cells than normal in these regions, then you might be prevented from thinking positively. What researchers don't know yet is whether reduced activity and a lower number of cells is a *cause* of depression or is caused *by* it. If they can clarify this, they'll be on the way to finding a more effective way to treat depression.

▶▶ **PART 2**

You will hear an archaeologist talking about a recent find. For questions 7–14, complete the sentences.

Archaeologist: This find was really the most astonishing stroke of luck! You see, while we know quite a lot about Roman Britain, comparatively little is known about the era before that, when various tribes inhabited different parts of the country. And then, quite by chance, builders excavating the foundations for a new motorway in Yorkshire unearthed a limestone chamber with the remains of a chariot from that period! The chariot is 2,500 years old and from it we can deduce quite a lot about the history of this region.

First of all, we know the chariot was rather special. It contained the skeleton of a man aged between thirty and forty years old, and this suggests that the chariot served a ceremonial, not a utilitarian purpose. The hypothesis was borne out when it was discovered that it did not have matching wheels, so it could not have been used for transport. The chamber also contained the bones of over 250 cattle, and slaughter on this scale can only be explained if the person interred in the chariot was very important – a tribal leader, in fact.

Secondly, burials like this indicate a belief that in the afterlife a person would have need of his worldly possessions. Such

beliefs were by no means confined to ancient Britain, of course – one immediately thinks of the ancient Egyptians. So in view of the similarities, we wonder if there had been any contact between Egypt and pre-Roman Britain.

Thirdly, we know from other sites that chariot burial was practised by a tribe known as the Parisii. These people had arrived on these shores from France, and it is not inconceivable that they were in communication with lands further south.

Finally, the finding is significant because it shows us that the Parisii inhabited regions of the country farther west than has previously been thought.

Unfortunately, the authorities have decided that work on the motorway has to continue, which means we are working non-stop in an effort to excavate as much of the surrounding area as we can in the time available. We're hoping that a place for the chariot will be found at the British Museum, if we can succeed in the very tricky task of lifting the remains out of the ground ...

▶▶ **PART 3**

You will hear part of a radio discussion with Ellen Harrington of the Meadow Lane Residents Group, and Tim Barlow from the Carton Town Planning Department. For questions 15–20, choose the answer, A, B, C or D which fits best according to what you hear.

Interviewer: Good morning, and welcome to *City Life*, our weekly look at some aspect of life in towns and cities. Today my guests are Ellen Harrington of the Meadow Lane Residents Group in the town of Carton, and Tim Barlow from the Carton Town Planning Department. Ellen, perhaps I can start by asking why you formed a residents' group?

Ellen: Because our lives have been a misery recently, that's why! You see, three months ago the town council decided to turn the centre of Carton into a pedestrian precinct – no cars at all. Which seemed like a terrific idea at first. I was over the moon. Until I realised that all the traffic diverted from the centre of town was going to come through Meadow Lane. And I suspect the planners knew all along this would happen.

Interviewer: And Meadow Lane is – or was – a quiet suburban street.

Ellen: Exactly! With two schools and lots of children playing in the street. Now it must be one of the most dangerous roads in the county! And we're not going to stand for it! We're livid, we really are, and we're going to do whatever it takes to get satisfaction, starting with our protest at the town hall tomorrow!

Interviewer: If I could turn to you now, Tim. What's your reaction to what Ellen has been saying?

Tim: Well, naturally, I have every sympathy with her situation. But I really don't think the Carton Town Planning Department is entirely to blame for this. Closing the town centre to traffic was the right thing to do, and I think it's to the credit of the town council that a measure like this was put into practice, despite considerable opposition. Changing the status quo is never an easy course of action – somebody's always going to be unhappy with the new situation. But in this case, if cars drive too fast along quiet streets, that's a matter for the police. Irresponsible drivers are to blame for the problem, which is why the protesters have chosen the wrong target. I'm not even sure exactly what Mrs Harrington's Meadow Lane Residents Group is trying to accomplish.

Interviewer: Do you accept that point, Ellen?

Ellen: I certainly do not! Drivers will take the shortest possible route to get where they're going – that's just human nature – and it's the Town Planning Department who decide what that route is. I think Mr Barlow is trying to dodge the responsibility for the problem – probably because the planners hadn't realised quite how bad the situation in our street would be. And I don't believe they can wash their hands of the whole matter. And even if they weren't entirely to blame for it, they could still do something now to solve it.

Interviewer: What would you like to see happen now?

Ellen: First of all, a new traffic system should be installed in the area of Meadow Lane to stop motorists using the street the way they do. Then we'd like a review of the whole road system in and around the town. Obviously, that will take some time to set up – in fact, we don't want any rush jobs here – but we want a firm commitment from the town council that they'll listen to our demands.

Interviewer: And this protest you're planning: do you feel it will be a success?

Ellen: I certainly do! You see, we plan to have a big demonstration outside the Town Hall, which will attract a lot of media interest – and that's what really makes people sit up and take notice these days. I'm sure we'll get some reaction. After all, the people in charge here are our representatives, councillors who should listen to the views of the people who elected them …

▶▶ **PART 4**

This part consists of two tasks. You will hear five short extracts in which people talk about children's free time activities. Look at Task 1. For questions 21–25, choose from the list A–H the explanation each speaker gives about how his or her child became interested in an activity. Now look at Task 2. For questions 26–30, choose from the list A–H what each speaker expresses about these activities.

Speaker 1: Michael's been a member of a rugby club for two years now. He'd never played until he went to the local comprehensive, but he was hooked immediately! We were nervous at first about him getting hurt, but he's never been injured, not really. I'm glad he's got a hobby, although it *is* quite expensive. We take him to away games, which could be anywhere in the country, so petrol costs mount up. But he's learning to be one of a team, which is a good skill to have in general.

Speaker 2: Our daughter Jane's wild about skiing! Obviously, she can only actually go skiing when we're on holiday or during skiing excursions. She got the idea from a novel about some girls at finishing school in Switzerland, and kept pleading with us to let her try it. Now she's got all the equipment, which cost quite a lot – but she enjoys it so much it's worth the money. She gets anxious about the exams they have at the ski club, which is not altogether a good thing. I mean, the whole point of a hobby is that it should be fun.

Speaker 3: Dan was spending the summer with some horsy friends in Cornwall, and so of course it was inevitable that they should take him riding one day. Their enthusiasm must have rubbed off, because when Dan came home, he asked us to arrange riding lessons for him. Luckily, there's a good stables nearby, and he goes twice a week – more in the summer holidays. I'm glad he has an outdoor hobby; before he started riding, he used to get colds all the time and was rather pale, but now he's full of beans and he's got a healthy glow.

Speaker 4: I enrolled Wendy in a ballet class when she was five because our doctor told me it would help strengthen her spine, and she took to it straight away. My mother had been a professional dancer, but I don't think that influenced Wendy in any way. She goes to classes three times a week, and although she'll never be good enough to be a professional, she still enjoys it. She's become friends with some of the girls in her class, and we have a fair bit of contact outside ballet, which is nice, especially since Wendy is an only child.

Speaker 5: One Sunday night, Jim suddenly announced he was going to be a painter! My brother had been taking him to various art galleries all summer, but it seems that an exhibition of Impressionists was what really began it all. At first, my wife and I thought it was just a passing craze, and we tried to dissuade him. We thought he should have a healthy outdoor hobby. But Jim's been attending art classes for a number of years now, and I must say, some of the things he's done are very nice. He's quite dedicated to his art!

TEST 4

▶▶ **PART 1**

You will hear three different extracts. For questions 1–6, choose the answer, A, B or C which fits best according to what you hear. There are two questions for each extract.

Extract One

You hear a mother talking to her teenage son about school.

Mother: Sam, this is just not good enough! You must concentrate! Look at all these spelling mistakes! And you haven't even bothered to answer question four. And what are all these drawings down the left-hand margin? Does your teacher allow this? I mean they're quite good, but you've obviously spent more time *doodling* than doing your exercises. You're not taking your school work at all seriously!

Sam: Oh, come off it, Mum! I do my homework!

Mother: In about *five* minutes! And forty per cent in your History test is *hardly* a mark to be proud of! At your age, you should be studying hard, not wasting your time sending emails, or listening to your MP3 player! How are you going to pass your exams?

Sam: Well, none of the other kids in my class did well in that test, and after all, I'm *fifteen*, Mum! Teenagers have got a natural aversion to studying! This is the age when we're discovering ourselves; asserting our personality.

Mother: Teenagers have got a natural aversion to *everything* that's not connected to fashion or music!

Sam: So aren't you pleased? I'm *normal*!

Extract Two

You hear part of a radio programme in which two people are discussing growing herbs.

Interviewer: So, Jerry, what useful tips have you got for us on growing herbs?

Jerry: Well, now, listeners will be delighted to know that herbs are not at all hard to grow. The ideal situation is to have a herb garden, of course. Or you could dedicate a corner of your garden to herbs – perhaps plant them in a knot pattern. They can be a very attractive feature. But if you don't have much space, you needn't feel deterred. Herbs grow just as nicely among other plants. In fact, they can help keep unwanted bugs at bay in vegetable patches. Growing basil among tomato plants, for instance, has a two-fold purpose: it acts as an insect repellent, and it adds flavour to the tomatoes. Some herbs can also be grown on kitchen windowsills or in window boxes. They're very versatile.

Interviewer: How many different kinds of herbs are there?

Jerry: Well, they fall into two main categories. There are your annuals – these grow and die in one season. Basil, parsley and dill are good examples, and all of these are widely used in cooking. Perennials, on the other hand, such as rosemary and thyme, grow year in, year out, and can make attractive borders for your flower beds.

Extract Three

You hear two friends talking about travelling alone.

Tim: Joy, you've been on singles holidays, haven't you? What are they like?

Joy: Why do you ask?

Tim: Well, I was wondering what to do about a holiday this summer. It's just, well, all my friends are married or have steady girlfriends and I'm at a loose end, if you know what I mean!

Joy: Yep, I certainly do! When I first started going it alone, I must admit, I found it a bit daunting. I didn't mind being on my own during the day – sightseeing and shopping and things. What bothered me was eating out alone in the evenings. The Internet saved me. I just typed in 'travelling solo' and hit the search button.

Tim: But I feel awkward about going off on my own. I've never done it before!

Joy: But that's my point; you don't have to! I joined Travelling Companions UK, and after emailing a few members and meeting up a couple of times, a group of us went away for a weekend. It really worked because we had company in the evenings, but during the day we did our own thing. I've now been on several holidays like that. Just take a look on the Net – there are things to suit all ages and tastes.

Tim: OK, I will. Thanks!

▶▶ **PART 2**

You will hear an anthropologist talking about a recent find. For questions 7–14, complete the sentences.

Anthropologist: A most exciting discovery has been made in a remote region of Ethiopia, and I don't think it's too much of an exaggeration to say this may change the way we think of evolutionary history! Last winter an international team of anthropologists unearthed some fossil hominid skulls that have been reliably dated as being 160,000 years old. Three of the skulls – two belonging to adults and one to a child – were in quite good condition, but fragments of other skulls were also found. Now, this in itself isn't the exciting part because skulls of hominids – we use the word to mean species similar to our own – have been found that are considerably older than this. But it seems that these people were our direct ancestors, whereas the older hominid skulls are from species which died out. To put it simply, the fossils were the skulls of *Homo sapiens*, the species to which modern humans belong.

Another reason why this discovery is causing great excitement in the world of anthropology is because it ties in with other research indicating that we are not descended from Neanderthals at all. You see, the Neanderthals only vanished from the fossil record about 30,000 years ago. So if the hypothesis is correct, it paints a fascinating picture. For an incredibly long time, tens of thousands of years in fact, at least two different species of humans co-existed on the planet, and then – for reasons we don't understand – the Neanderthals became extinct.

It is also interesting that a number of tools were found near the fossil skulls in Ethiopia, and it may well be that these people's superior technological skills allowed them to drive the Neanderthals away. Moreover, there are suggestions that they lived in groups, and there is a close correlation between advances in human development and social interaction. This may explain why *Homo sapiens* prevailed as the dominant human species! On the other hand, I must remind my listeners that the distant origins of mankind, those early days lost in the mists of prehistoric time, continue to be a mystery. Nobody really knows what happened – which naturally makes my work even more fascinating.

▶▶ **PART 3**

You will hear part of a radio discussion about iris recognition systems. For questions 15–20, choose the answer, A, B, C or D which fits best according to what you hear.

Interviewer: My guest on *Technology Matters* this week is Jim Davies, a leading expert in the field of IRS or iris recognition systems. Jim, perhaps I could start by asking you to explain exactly what IRS is?

Jim: In fact, it's a simple system in theory, one that was first suggested back in the 1930s. Basically, it's a way of recognising a person by analysing the pattern of his or her iris. This pattern is different for every individual on the planet; even identical twins have different iris patterns. The way it works is, you have a camera linked to computer software that can compare the iris pattern it sees with iris patterns on a database; the computer makes a match and then reports on the identification.

Interviewer: It just provides a report?

Jim: No. That's simply the first step. An iris recognition machine can be connected to any number of devices. For instance, at airports it will be possible for barriers to be opened by a machine, and this will, in turn, speed the flow of passengers through checkpoints. I must say, though, I don't think it's speed that is the biggest appeal of iris recognition machines – the fact that they are reliable will guarantee their popularity in the future.

Interviewer: Are iris recognition machines actually being used at the moment?

Jim: Oh, yes. As a matter of fact, we've just completed a pilot scheme in northern England. We installed machines at a school there to identify pupils as they came into the canteen. That way they could be given their correct meals automatically, which meant they didn't have to wait around to be served. It was a great success! And the kids loved it. I think they regarded it as something out of a science fiction film.

Interviewer: What about adults? Do you think they will be as impressed?

Jim: That's a good question. I admit there are many people who feel that the use of iris recognition machines is a civil liberties issue and infringes on their privacy, but I think people said the same thing about the use of X-ray machines at airports, and now everyone accepts them. So I'm confident that the vast majority of people will come to see the sense behind using these machines, especially when they realise how efficient they are. When they're properly set up, they take a mere twelve seconds to scan someone's iris, and of course the customs people themselves are very attracted to the idea because of the time it saves.

Interviewer: So is it simply a matter of time before we find iris recognition machines everywhere?

Jim: Nobody knows as yet just how widespread they'll be. A lot depends on how quickly the public comes to accept them, and I think the government wants to monitor public reaction before committing itself to the technology.

Interviewer: What about the costs involved?

Jim: The computerised cameras themselves don't cost a great deal, but the really huge cost will be when we have to register the whole population. I can quite understand that the government might be nervous about this sort of expense, although of course you wouldn't ever have to repeat it on such a huge scale once you'd done it.

Interviewer: So you believe the future lies with IRS?

Jim: I do, yes, primarily because every government wants to be able to confirm identity at places like airports, and iris recognition machines are simply the most effective way of doing this as yet available to us ...

This part consists of two tasks. You will hear five short extracts in which people talk about holidays that went wrong. Look at Task 1. For questions 21–25, choose from the list A–H the person who is speaking. Now look at Task 2. For questions 26–30, choose from the list A–H what each speaker is expressing.

Speaker 1: We went to Tunisia last year to celebrate my retirement. We were so looking forward to it, but the whole thing was a fiasco from start to finish. The flight was delayed for three hours, so we were in a foul mood even before we left! Then we were diverted to a different airport in Tunisia, and we spent an extra hour on the bus to get to our hotel – which turned out to be well below standard, and there were steep stairs everywhere! Poor George with his bad leg. Then when we got back and complained to the tour company that the advertisement for 'holidays tailored to the mature traveller's needs' was misleading, we were told a refund was out of the question…

Speaker 2: It was a walking tour 'for more mature walkers'. Well, some of them should have stayed at home, if you ask me! There were constant complaints about the difficulty of the terrain. But we were walking in the Lake District, so what did they expect? And I took them on the gentle route; very little walking uphill. It was hardly my fault that we got caught in such a bad storm that we had to cut short the trip. I did take them to a lovely little pub to dry off and warm up, but it didn't make much difference. They just moaned all the way home.

Speaker 3: I'd had a difficult term, and wanted to stay away from beaches full of kids! So I booked myself an all-inclusive trip to Russia, and everything was very interesting until the last day, when I woke up with awful abdominal pain. I couldn't keep anything down, not even water. It was clear I was running a fever. At the hospital they told me I had a ruptured appendix and an operation was unavoidable! Well, in a way, it was an interesting experience. Once I realised the doctor was first-rate, I was so relieved! I even felt fortunate to have been in Russia when my appendix burst!

Speaker 4: It was my fault, really. Driving all over the country to visit clients as I do, I thought I'd hire a car while we were in France. Anyway, I was involved in a minor accident with another car. The other driver was terribly decent and spoke excellent English, but when the police came, they said I'd have to go to the police station because I wasn't a resident! I lost my head and started yelling at them, which was a mistake. I ended up spending the night in jail, and that's no fun, I can tell you. In the end, I got away with just a small fine. But the whole experience shook me a bit.

Speaker 5: We had a group in Alicante last year and it was a disaster. Our rep had been assured the new hotel would be ready well before the dates we'd booked it for, but of course, it wasn't. Some of the bathrooms had no tiles on the floor, and the air conditioning hadn't been installed! There was no way we could convince the customers that it wasn't our fault, and even though we relocated them, several demanded a refund. But that comes with the business, and you just make sure you recuperate your losses with other, more successful holidays.

TEST 5

▶▶ PART 1

You will hear three different extracts. For questions 1–6, choose the answer, A, B or C which fits best according to what you hear. There are two questions for each extract.

Extract One

You hear part of a radio programme in which a man is being interviewed about an unusual sport.

Interviewer: Chris, I must admit, I was a bit bemused when I heard about cheese rolling. Tell us about it.

Chris: Well, it's an event that takes place on May Bank Holiday Monday every year in Gloucestershire. Basically, a large Double Gloucester cheese is rolled down the hill, and a bunch of idiots like me try to catch it. Whoever gets to the bottom of the hill first wins.

Interviewer: It sounds easy! But isn't it dangerous?

Chris: Well, the hill is really steep and the surface is rough and uneven. It's not so bad if it's dry, but if it's been raining and the ground's muddy, it can be tough. You get tangled up in the grass, and it's difficult not to fall. People have had to be carted off to hospital with broken limbs or concussion. But it's great fun, and people come from all over. The last three years, an Australian woman has won the women's race, and they've set up a similar competition down under.

Interviewer: So what advice would you give to someone wanting to take part for the first time?

Chris: Wear sturdy football boots or walking boots, pad yourself out in hardwearing clothes, and have fun!

Interviewer: I think a suit of armour would be more suitable for me! Now …

Extract Two

You hear a father and daughter discussing something that the daughter wants.

Sophie: It's not fair, Dad! I'm thirteen, and all my friends have got one!

Dad: Look, Sophie, I know it's hard, but I just think you're too young. Research has linked them with various health problems, and I don't like the idea.

Sophie: I wouldn't use it often! And I'd be able to call you if I needed you to come and get me. You and Mum would be able to contact me, too.

Dad: Yes, I know all the arguments, but you'd be talking to your friends all the time instead of doing your homework. I've seen Fiona and Anna when they're here, on the phone all the time.

Sophie: No, they're not! They send text messages and play jokes on our friends. It's fun! Oh, come on, Dad! I promise I won't use it much.

Dad: Mm. You say that now, but once you've got it …

Sophie: Please, Dad. I'll pay for calls myself out of my pocket money.

Dad: Well, I'll have to talk to your Mum. And if we let you have one, you're not to carry it about with you all the time, and you'll keep it switched off while you're at school, and ….

Sophie: Ooh! Thanks, Dad! You're the best!

Dad: Now, wait a minute, young lady. I haven't said yes yet!

Extract Three

You hear two people talking about yawning.

Man: So what you're saying is yawning actually wakes us up?

Woman: In a sense, yes. It's been known for a while that when we yawn, both our heart rate and blood pressure increase, but for a long time scientists believed its purpose was purely to increase our intake of oxygen. Research has proved that this is not true, and psychologists have put forward a theory that yawning helps make us more alert. That's why we yawn when we're tired or bored. It's our body giving us a warning, or 'wake-up' call, if you like.

Man: Interesting. So why is it if one person starts yawning, pretty soon all the people around are also at it?

Woman: Well, the same psychologists have a theory for that, too. They suggest that some kind of empathic mechanism in our brain is triggered when one member of the group yawns. It may be a way of keeping everyone in the group awake and on the alert. Monkeys do it as well. It seems that, instead of encouraging us to sleep, yawning is trying to do the opposite!

Man: OK, I'll buy that. But what about yawning during exercise? I sometimes yawn while I'm running, ...

▸▸ **PART 2**

You will hear an astrobiologist talking about her work. For questions 7–14, complete the sentences.

Astrobiologist: When I tell people what my particular branch of science is, I often get funny looks. In a way, I understand because astrobiology is the study of life on other planets. Well, obviously, life has *not* been discovered on other planets, which would appear to make astrobiology a science without a subject! However, everything we know about life on our *own* planet suggests we have to try to understand if there are any universal requirements for life to evolve, as well as the processes involved in evolution. Consequently, astrobiologists are deeply interested in the beginnings of life on Earth. Once we know more about what happened on home ground, as it were, we will be in a better position to understand any life forms we may one day find on other planets.

When most people think of extraterrestrial life, they conjure up images of so-called 'higher' life forms: they imagine humanoid creatures or bizarre and probably dangerous animals of some kind. But if we consider the whole history of life on Earth, a very different picture emerges. For billions of years the only forms of life on the planet were organisms consisting of single cells. It was only about 550 million years ago, during the geological period we call the Cambrian, that the seas suddenly became filled with a whole array of multi-cellular life.

So how do humans fit into this time frame? Well, human-like creatures first appear in the fossil record about five or so million years ago: in geological terms, this is just a blink of an eye compared to the long history of life on Earth. And *Homo sapiens*, our own species, has only been around for about 130,000 years. The point is if we *do* find life on other planets, it will almost certainly be relatively simple – of the sort that populated the Earth for most of its existence so far.

And of course, we must be prepared for these life forms to look very different from life on Earth. We must not forget that many modern life forms came about as a result of chance, their fate shaped by floods, continental drift and comet or meteor strikes. It is interesting to reflect that if a giant asteroid had not hit the Earth and wiped out the dinosaurs, they might still be ruling the planet and we might never have evolved ...

▸▸ **PART 3**

You will hear part of a radio interview with Pete Birtwhistle, a playwright. For questions 15–20, choose the answer, A, B, C or D which fits best according to what you hear.

Interviewer: This evening on *Arts Alive* I'm talking to Pete Birtwhistle, whose new play, *Time Talking*, has just opened at the Court Theatre in London. Pete, thank you for joining us.

Pete: Glad to be here.

Interviewer: Before we talk about your new play, I'd like to ask you how you started writing for the theatre in the first place. I think I'm right in saying that your background isn't exactly typical for a playwright?

Pete: I suppose you could put it like that! You see, I was a miner until my mid-thirties, but then my health got bad and I had to leave the pit. But the theatre was the last thing on my mind! I don't think I'd ever been to a play – apart from taking the kids to pantomimes at Christmas – and I wasn't even curious about it: I didn't feel it had any bearing on me and my life at all.

Interviewer: So what prompted you to write your first play?

Pete: Doctor's orders. Being out of work was terrible – it really got me down when I realised I had to stop working down the mine, and in the end I was in such a bad way that my local GP sent me to a psychiatrist. She suggested I write a story about what had happened to me, how I felt about working in the mine and then having to leave. All therapy, really. Well, of course, it was pretty hard at first, writing a play from scratch.

Interviewer: Getting the dialogue and story right, I imagine?

Pete: Funny you should say that. I started off thinking I could invent a group of characters and have them put forward different views. But when I sat down to write, I couldn't get them to do what I wanted, no matter how hard I tried. In the end, I discovered I had to let them do and say what *they* wanted.

Interviewer: What do you mean, exactly?

Pete: They took on a life of their own. So I had to sit back and let them go whichever way they wanted. And once I let myself give them that freedom, the play wrote itself. The odd thing is I feel all the characters I create are part of me, so I'm revealing different aspects of myself.

Interviewer: Is that the most profound effect writing has had on you?

Pete: I think so, yes. Practical things have changed as well, of course – we've just bought a new house – but material benefits are fairly peripheral in the end.

Interviewer: Turning to your new play about time travel – isn't that an unusual theme for the theatre?

Pete: Definitely! But it's not deliberate. I mean, I don't go round looking for novel subjects just to be different. It's more a case of finding an issue that doesn't have easy answers, a topic that stretches you when you start thinking about it.

Interviewer: I hear you're going to start work on a screenplay for a film in the next few months. Is that an exciting prospect?

Pete: Yes, but there are so many stories of films that never get made, writers and directors who throw themselves into the task of making a film and then get terribly disappointed when it all falls apart. So I have to watch out that I don't take the whole thing too seriously ...

▸▸ **PART 4**

This part consists of two tasks. You will hear five short extracts in which people talk about tracing their ancestors. Look at Task 1. For questions 21–25, choose from the list A–H what each speaker says about the discoveries he or she made. Now look at Task 2. For questions 26–30, choose from the list A–H the emotion aroused in each speaker by these discoveries.

Speaker 1: The first bit of new information was quite exciting. It turned out my grandfather's only brother had slipped out of the house one day when he was about sixteen and disappeared! At first, the family thought he'd gone off to Australia, but it turned out that he'd joined a circus and become a clown. Romantic, isn't it? I managed to track down his descendants, and I found out they were all circus performers, too. It's fantastic to know that the two branches of our family are in touch again.

Speaker 2: I wanted to know something about my roots, and with a name like O'Dwyer, I knew I probably had some Irish ancestors. Eventually, I did find out a bit about them, though this is going back to the end of the nineteenth century. It was my great-grandparents who came over to the States because life was so hard back home. People were starving in Ireland – literally. And apparently, my great-grandmother's family were worse off than most. I get furious at the idea of ancestors of mine having to leave their homes because they were so hungry.

Speaker 3: After a lot of work I established that one branch of the family exists to this day in Australia, though regrettably, the background to the story is a family row. Apparently, my great-grandmother's brother wanted to marry a girl his family didn't approve of, so he just walked out and never came back. He ended up in Australia with his wife, and his parents never saw their grandchildren. A family tradition has it that his mother died of a broken heart. Imagine a family being torn apart by something like that!

Speaker 4: My great-grandfather was a doctor, which has been a sort of family tradition ever since. He seems to have been a man of strong religious feeling, and he worked for years in a hospital in Africa. Apparently, he paid his own way over and volunteered his services to a missionary hospital. By all accounts, he never boasted about what he'd done; he seems to have thought everyone should help their fellow human beings if they can. It makes me glad to think there was someone so genuinely *good* in my family.

Speaker 5: There was a story passed down in the family that we're distantly related to an aristocratic family from Scotland, complete with an estate, manor house and so on. Well, it turns out that my great-great-grandmother really *did* live in a posh house, but only because she was a servant to the family who owned it! It wasn't exactly what I had been expecting, and it took me a while to get over it, but now I can see the funny side of the whole business.

TEST 6

▶▶ **PART 1**

You will hear three different extracts. For questions 1–6, choose the answer, A, B or C which fits best according to what you hear. There are two questions for each extract.

Extract One

You hear part of an interview with an aromatherapist.

Interviewer: ... and as I was saying, I'd feel *embarrassed* about having a massage. There's a lot of flab around at my age – too many rich meals.

Fiona: But an aromatherapist isn't interested in your figure! However, it's true that many people feel inhibited about their bodies, and a body massage might seem intrusive to them. My advice to anyone feeling that way would be not to bother with massage.

Interviewer: Surely you aren't advising them *against* aromatherapy?

Fiona: I didn't say that. But there are alternative ways to benefit from essential oils. One of them is to have a foot reflex treatment. All you have to take off is your shoes and socks – and it's as relaxing as a massage. In fact, it's *more* effective.

Interviewer: In what way?

Fiona: The foot reflex treatment offers you the benefits of reflexology combined with a specially prepared aromatherapy cream. So you have both the essential oils *and* the reflex massage addressing your particular health problems.

Interviewer: Sounds more up my street. But come on, Fiona, for an old sceptic like me, does it really do anything, apart from relax you?

Fiona: It certainly does! I regularly help clients with digestive and respiratory problems, and they're all amazed at the results.

Interviewer: Right! When can I book an appointment?

Extract Two

You hear part of a radio programme in which two people are discussing hybrid cars.

Man: ... I think people are coming round to the idea of hybrid cars, but it's taking time.

Woman: Mm. I think one problem is the price. Hybrid cars may be more economical in the long run, but the initial outlay is rather off-putting.

Man: True, but within a couple of years, you'll have made a *huge* saving on petrol. So what's the problem?

Woman: Well, another drawback is speed. Hybrid cars just can't keep up with conventional cars, and telling a twenty-five-year-old male that it's safer to drive slowly just doesn't appeal. He's also likely to tell you that the hybrid isn't as flashy to look at, either.

Man: Yes, but manufacturers are producing more sporty-looking models, and the Honda Insight is selling well.

Woman: What about the middle-aged market of supposedly environmentally-aware citizens, then? I don't see them going wild over hybrid cars. More importantly, you get lower mileage on hybrids. One company bought a fleet for their sales reps, and even advertised the fact in their marketing campaign. However, they said it wasn't cost effective because of the low mileage and lack of speed. A sales team has to travel all over the country, so this is important.

Man: Don't they see, though, that they're contributing to the future of the environment? I wish people would wake up to what's happening around them!

Extract Three

You hear part of an interview with a film maker, Tony Dupois.

Interviewer: Tony, you went to film school, yet many directors I've spoken to recently suggest that it's a waste of time. What's your view?

Tony: Well, my family had no background in film, so film school put me in touch with the right people. Yes, the curriculum was sometimes too rigid, hindering true creativity, but the important thing is that I met like-minded people, and was inspired by what was happening around me. But I can see that for someone whose father's an actor or director himself, film school could seem limited in scope. Dad's already their inspiration, while mine was one of my professors. He mapped out the whole film-making process for me, making everything seem possible.

Interviewer: Regarding your films, Tony. I find your characters fascinating. Even the bad guys in your films have a subtlety to them. A fine example is Carl Fraullet in *Games of the Gods*, who commits a heinous crime, then spends the rest of the film battling with his conscience.

Tony: It's vital that my characters are convincing human beings, not just stereotypes. There are many facets to the human psyche. Not one of us is completely good or completely bad. I wish my characters – all of them – to convey this ...

▶▶ **PART 2**

You will hear an archaeologist talking about an experience he had in South America. For questions 7–14, complete the sentences.

Archaeologist: A couple of years ago I was working in an ancient Aztec city in South America. This city is becoming more and more popular with visitors, and I was part of a team employed to map out the city and its environs. We were half-way through our contract when we were approached and asked if we could come up with some ideas about how best to conserve the site, because it was feared that the increasing numbers of visitors could be damaging it. The worst damage is caused by the mere presence of people. Their breathing makes the air very humid, which causes the plaster on the walls to crumble. At the time I'm talking about, this was one of my special interests, so I was only too pleased to undertake the job.

Anyway, one day I had to go into one of the minor tombs – we were making a survey of it because the authorities were going to build a coach park nearby, and we had to ensure the tomb wouldn't be damaged any further by the construction work. To my horror, the tomb was in a worse state than we thought it would be. There were signs of recent erosion, apparently caused when an underground stream flooded. But it was when I was climbing into the tomb itself that disaster struck. The stones underfoot were loose, you see, and I twisted my ankle. I fell awkwardly and rolled down a slope. I heard a terrible cracking noise, rather like a pistol shot, and I knew I had fractured my leg. The pain was excruciating, but once I got over the initial shock I became far more worried about the fact that it was now dark outside, which would lessen my chance of being discovered. As the hours went by, I began to feel very cold and pretty scared, but in the end I was incredibly lucky. A tour guide was out for an evening stroll and just happened to come close enough to hear me shouting from the hole in the ground, so he alerted the rest of the team. The break wasn't too bad, fortunately, but the whole thing was quite a frightening experience ...

▶▶ **PART 3**

You will hear part of an interview with Professor Hector Williams. For questions 15–20, choose the answer, A, B, C or D which fits best according to what you hear.

Interviewer: Professor Williams, I know you've made a special study of artificial languages. I suppose most people think of Esperanto when this subject comes up, but is Esperanto the most widespread of the various artificial languages in existence?

Williams: I think that's the case today, yes, but you must remember that the idea of an artificial language isn't new. Esperanto dates back to the 1880s, but even in medieval times people were fascinated by the idea of a language created by man. Of course, their aims would have been quite different back then.

Interviewer: What do you mean?

Williams: Well, in the Middle Ages there was a theory that the universe was constructed on logical principles and that everything in it could be classified and named according to a regular and logical system. Ultimately, the nature of the universe itself could be understood through a language created in this way.

Interviewer: That all sounds rather complicated. Would such a language be easy to learn?

Williams: That one wouldn't have been, no, but there were other artificial languages that did have this goal. One man, for instance, struck by the fact that the notes of the musical scale were known by the same syllabic value all over the western world, felt this could be of use in the creation of a universal language, so he invented words based on the syllables *do, re, mi, fa* etc.

Interviewer: Was there the same kind of logic behind Esperanto?

Williams: In a way, and if I may digress for a moment, I must confess that the first time I heard it, Esperanto did seem musical to my ears. I think it was because the syllables of Latin origin aroused in me vague memories of the operas my father used to play on the gramophone when I was a child. Anyway, the man who came up with Esperanto, Dr Zamenhof, wanted his artificial language to be easy to learn, so he chose word stems and roots from major European languages, hoping they would sound familiar to most Europeans. And most experts believe he did a remarkably good job in that sense. A person with average linguistic skills can gain a working knowledge of Esperanto in a matter of months.

Interviewer: So do you feel it could have a future as a universal language?

Williams: To be perfectly honest, I don't. And there are a number of reasons for this. I have some sympathy with those who claim that the words of an artificial language seem one-dimensional, as it were, because they don't have any flavour derived from past usage; no word could have connotations in such a language. And this is not just a theoretical problem; it really does make the language seem rather mechanical.

Interviewer: You'd describe advocates of Esperanto as idealists then, would you?

Williams: Possibly – though that isn't such a bad quality! In my experience, people who have taken the trouble to learn Esperanto are marked by a refreshing enthusiasm for the task; I imagine many language teachers would be delighted to have students with such single-minded determination to master the details of a language. The difficulties with imagining Esperanto as the language of the United Nations, say, or the European Union, are not based on any deficiencies among the speakers.

Interviewer: Well, you've mentioned one problem with artificial languages; what others are there?

Williams: The fundamental difficulty is psychological. For the vast majority of the world's population, the sense of self is inextricably bound up not just with location but also with what is aptly referred to as their mother tongue. So any attempt to replace that native language meets with very strong resistance – and that is why I am convinced that the applications of an artificial language are very limited.

Interviewer: Professor Williams, thank you for being with us.

Williams: My pleasure.

▶▶ **PART 4**

This part consists of two tasks. You will hear five short extracts in which people talk about the Internet. Look at Task 1. For questions 21–25, choose from the list A–H what each speaker says about starting to use the Internet. Now look at Task 2. For questions 26–30, choose from the list A–H the view each speaker expresses about the influence of the Internet.

Speaker 1: The problem was that my neighbour, who showed me how to use the Internet in the first place, didn't really know what he was doing – and of course, I didn't know that at the time! So it was pretty discouraging. Back then, everything was so slow, and you were always losing your connection. But now I wouldn't want to be without it. I even read my daily paper online, and I expect that's the way it is for lots of people, especially those of us who live in remote areas.

Speaker 2: A work colleague of mine was really into virtual reality games, you know, the sort you play with other users in real time online. Well, I watched him playing one day, and I got hooked! I still play games like that today, despite the fact that I'm now a grandmother. But I must admit, I wouldn't like my two-year-old granddaughter to grow up doing everything online and never interacting with real people! And that's the way I can see things going.

Speaker 3: While I was writing my thesis for my master's degree, I realised the best way to compile a list of the reading I had to do was to use the Internet, so I took a deep breath and started to learn. These days I use it at work, like most people, but the best aspect of the Internet for me personally is online shopping. I love ordering books and having them delivered to my door a couple of days later. The only problem is that it's so easy you sometimes forget how much money you're spending!

Speaker 4: Growing up with the Internet the way I did – we've had it at home since I was eleven – it never seemed a big thing. I mean, I'm used to having it around, the way I'm used to television. But I realise that there are parts of the world where people don't have Internet access, so if you're growing up there, you're missing out on a terrific resource. That should be changed so every kid has the same opportunities to learn.

Speaker 5: A couple of years ago I decided I wanted to know more about my family tree, and a friend told me there was a website listing the births, marriages and deaths during the last 150 years in many parts of the UK. I thought I'd give it a try, and it was fascinating! As for the future, I think the Internet's going to have a huge impact in lots of ways. For instance, libraries as we know them won't exist in a decade or so because we will all be able to access the book we want online and even print it out if we choose.

TEST 7

▶▶ **PART 1**

You will hear three different extracts. For questions 1–6, choose the answer, A, B or C which fits best according to what you hear. There are two questions for each extract.

Extract One

You hear part of a radio discussion between a nutritionist and a medical expert.

Woman: As I was saying, it simply confirms what we nutritionists have been saying for years. It's taken the medical profession far too long to recognise that poor diet is responsible for all kinds of diseases and allergies. A visit to any conventional doctor will result in a prescription for all kinds of medicines, but never a list of foods to be avoided!

Man: Now, Judith! It's not the doctor's job to look into a patient's diet.

Woman: But if that's where the root of the problem lies, then surely it's the doctor's responsibility to address it!

Man: Well, this report now officially empowers doctors to address diet as part of their treatment of patients by confirming fears that poor nutrition is linked to cancer.

Woman: OK, I accept that this report is a major milestone in the development of conventional medicine, but it's rather late in coming!

Man: Don't dismiss conventional medicine so scathingly! In the case of cancer in particular, it has often saved lives! This report, however, now enables general practitioners to go a step further. Don't be too hard on us, Judith! After all, …

Extract Two

You hear part of a radio programme in which an interior designer is giving advice on colour in the home.

Interviewer: So, tell me, Eugene, why shouldn't I paint my bedroom orange? It's my favourite colour, after all!

Eugene: Well, *you* might look lovely in orange, but on the walls of your bedroom? Orange is a wake-you-up, vibrant colour that stimulates and inspires. It's hardly going to *relax* you! No, what you want in your bedroom is a subtle shade of blue or green to promote tranquility. Or why not try a creamy yellow, which is optimistic and happy, without being too intense and dramatic?

Interviewer: OK. So what about the kitchen? I spend a lot of time there.

Eugene: Well, here you *could* use orange to create a lively atmosphere that will inspire you to create wonderful meals!

Interviewer: Mm. My cooking needs all the inspiration it can get! Now what about the living room? I find this room difficult to decorate because it's not just a communal room. It's also got a wild combination of colours in upholstery and paintings.

Eugene: Of course, if you've got lots of pictures on the wall, you need to tone down the colour behind them. Beige and brown can create a warm, welcoming atmosphere, and offset the colours in your paintings nicely. But you're so right. This is usually the most difficult room to get right.

Extract Three

You hear a conversation between a man and a woman about something that has happened.

Patrick: … so I'm driving along the road when out of nowhere, this old man starts to cross the road in front of me! It was pitch black, and he just walked out from behind the parked lorry! I had no time to stop, so I swerved out across the road and hit the Ford coming in the opposite direction!

Helen: Goodness, Pat!

Patrick: I couldn't believe it! The driver of the Ford started ranting and raving at me, but then the old man – who was pretty shaken himself – came up and apologised and offered to pay for damages, so the other driver calmed down a bit.

Helen: What did the police say about it?

Patrick: Well, they arrived fairly quickly, and a couple of other people stopped and asked if we needed help. I was feeling dizzy – shock, probably. The other guy was OK, except for a couple of bruises. But the police, well, they were more concerned about the lorry having been parked in such an awkward place. I think the driver's going to be in for it. They were OK with me, though. The old man's statement really helped. It's a good thing he admitted it was his fault.

Helen: You were lucky none of you got badly hurt!

Patrick: I know.

▶▶ **PART 2**

You will hear part of a talk by a writer who has written a book about bread. For questions 7–14, complete the sentences.

Announcer: Here in the studio with me today on *Food Matters* is Algernon Lacey, who's just written a book called *Half a Loaf* about that most basic of foods: bread. Algernon, what first aroused your interest in the subject?

Algernon: My grandmother, actually. One day she was describing to us how she used to make bread in the old days, and I was interested enough to start doing some research. I found out that all the big manufacturers use the same process to make bread these days. Even the supermarket chains, who think it makes them look good if customers see bread baking in their stores, use the same ingredients as everyone else. 98% of bread is made in this way – that's all the bread on sale in this country except for the products of small independent bakeries. And this process is a basic departure from the traditional techniques. You see, bread used to be made by allowing the yeast to ferment in water, which takes a few hours. But the modern method uses rapid mixing to shorten the time necessary for fermentation. This method is preferred because it saves money: less flour is needed to make bread. Unfortunately, there is a downside: you need a lot more water and fat, which makes the bread less wholesome. And since it's the fermentation process that gives bread its natural flavour, the modern method would produce rather tasteless bread if a great deal of salt weren't added. Some modern bread is also given a coating of calcium propionate to make sure it doesn't go stale. The loaf will last for a couple of weeks that way. But of course, there's a problem here, too – an increasing number of people are developing allergies to bread and wheat products, and I think there's a connection. The modern method doesn't ferment the ingredients properly, and it's hard for consumers to do anything about this because bread-making methods are dictated by the large supermarkets, who don't make a profit on bread. They don't even sell it at cost price.

They're prepared to lose money to bring customers into their stores. So they dictate the methods used in the big bakeries.

▶▶ **PART 3**

You will hear part of a discussion between Velma Andrews, a lawyer, and Sergeant William Bailey, a police officer. For questions 15–20, choose the answer, A, B, C or D which fits best according to what you hear.

Interviewer: Today on *Legal Issues* we have Velma Andrews, a lawyer, and Sergeant William Bailey, a police officer who helps to run a scheme which trains police officers in the art of giving evidence in court. William, perhaps I can start by asking you why this training scheme is necessary?

William: Well, you must remember that in a criminal case the police have gathered evidence to show that someone – the defendant – is guilty of a crime. And the defendant's lawyer is trying to show that this evidence is wrong or unreliable. Now, the way the defence lawyer goes about doing this can be very tricky. For instance, the first time I gave evidence in court twenty-five years ago, the lawyer for the defence made me look like a right fool. He annoyed me by interrupting me all the time, and when I tried to argue with him I got confused, and the people in court laughed at me. That made my evidence look bad. I simply had no idea what I was up against.

Interviewer: Velma, you are a defence lawyer; do you agree with William?

Velma: Absolutely. A police officer has to learn how the system works. You must get used to the idea that the lawyers are just doing a job, and even if it seems they are attacking your honesty in a rude or brutal manner, they have nothing against you as an individual.

Interviewer: It must be hard to think like that when you're giving evidence and some lawyer is trying to trip you up.

Velma: It is, but a police officer has to develop the right attitude. You need to think of your evidence as one piece in a jigsaw puzzle, the picture being the whole case against the defendant. If you start giving opinions about other pieces, other parts of the case that aren't your responsibility, it weakens the case as a whole. Your piece of the puzzle is the only thing you should think about!

Interviewer: Do you find Velma's advice helpful for police officers on your training scheme, William?

William: Definitely. For a young officer, appearing in court is an intimidating experience. It's hard to get used to the system. I mean, there are two lawyers, one acting for the defendant and one for the crown, and in the courtroom they are adversaries but they probably know each other professionally. They may even go off together after the trial and have dinner. As if it were all a game!

Interviewer: Would you advise William's trainees to treat a court case as a game, Velma?

Velma: I would tell them to remember that the defence lawyer is trying to discredit them and their evidence. One tip to help you develop the right attitude so you don't get drawn into an argument with the lawyer is to stand so you're facing the judge, and direct all your answers to the bench. That should make it easier to avoid any sort of personal exchange with the lawyer.

Interviewer: William, is your training scheme having results?

William: Yes. I think police officers are more confident in court. And this is not just about making people less nervous! I've seen some pretty terrible things happen in court. You get an inexperienced officer who starts arguing with the lawyer and ends up making the judge and jury think there's something wrong with the police case – there's a risk that dangerous criminals might be found not guilty and set free. That's the main reason why officers need this training.

Interviewer: Velma Andrews and William Bailey, thank you.

▶▶ **PART 4**

This part consists of two tasks. You will hear five short extracts in which people talk about wind power. Look at Task 1. For questions 21–25, choose from the list A–H the attitude each speaker has towards wind power. Now look at Task 2. For questions 26–30, choose from the list A–H what each speaker says about the alternatives to wind power.

Speaker 1: I've just been reading about some sheep farmers in Wales who were losing money and looked into a different way of earning a living. So they took the plunge and decided to set up a wind farm. But apparently, some neighbours resented the fact that they'd had a brilliant idea and capitalised on it. As a result, there was a good deal of opposition to the farm in the area. However, I did think it was an encouraging story, especially since wind farms aren't as expensive to set up as, say, it is to build a hydroelectric station. That's why so many people are interested in going into them.

Speaker 2: The whole issue is an emotional one, but it's the *look* of these wind farms that's causing the greatest outcry, it seems to me. I know quite a few people in rural areas are getting together and starting wind farms to serve their local community, and though I think they have the best of intentions, it does seem that they're going about it the wrong way. Wind turbines are not a reliable source of energy and still need a substantial backup, which can only be satisfactorily provided by fossil fuels at present.

Speaker 3: I find it odd that people object to having wind turbines miles offshore, where nobody except a passing ship would ever see them. What's wrong with that? After all, it's a question of using fossil fuels, other renewable energy sources or nuclear power. Obviously, there's no real future in fossil fuels, but I can't see any feasible way of generating enough electricity from wave power or hydroelectric stations either, at least not in this country. Which leaves the third option, though we have to make sure sufficient safeguards are in place.

Speaker 4: I get quite angry about the whole question, actually, because everyone goes on about how wonderful wind power is, but there's only enough wind to generate electricity about thirty per cent of the time. I think the whole method is fundamentally impractical. And the irony is that we could save more energy than wind can ever generate if we could make better use of existing coal and oil supplies. If only the government would formulate sound energy conservation policies and implement them!

Speaker 5: There's been a lot of talk about birds flying into turbines, and that has turned a lot of people against wind energy. But if you look at the figures, you'll see that the number of birds killed in this way is insignificant. On the other hand, I think we have to see wind power in perspective as just part of a move towards energy from renewables. We can't rely on any *one* source; a combination of wind, hydroelectric and solar power will be needed before we can realistically talk about replacing fossil fuels completely.

 TEST 8

▶▶ **PART 1**

You will hear three different extracts. For questions 1–6, choose the answer, A, B or C which fits best according to what you hear. There are two questions for each extract.

Extract One

You hear part of an interview with a woman who has changed her lifestyle.

Interviewer: Kathy, you gave up a job with a prestigious London law firm to become an olive farmer in Greece. Why?

Kathy: Does sound rather crazy, doesn't it? But working in the City isn't all it's cracked up to be, you know. There's so much pressure on you to perform, you're frowned upon for taking a day off sick, there's the traffic, the pollution ... the list is endless! It all got on top of me, and I suddenly realised how unhappy I was. My husband Kostas suggested moving to Greece for a while. I liked the idea, but I realised that I wouldn't be happy doing nothing but playing housewife. Then, while I was surfing the Net, I came across a site on olive growing, and it clicked. We made a few contacts, and found this lovely plot on the slopes of a mountain. Within six months, we'd left our jobs, put our furniture in storage, and moved. And I've never looked back!

Interviewer: And you're surprised by that?

Kathy: Yes. I thought I'd get bored, and miss the buzz of being in court. But it hasn't happened. I'm too busy! There's a lot more to olive farming than meets the eye, and if you want to be organic, there are rigorous procedures to follow. Great fun, though ...

Extract Two

You hear part of a radio discussion in which two teachers are talking about teaching poetry.

Mark: I think the main problem with teaching poetry is not so much the attitude of the students, but that of the teacher.

Marjory: How do you mean?

Mark : Well, teachers know that a lot of students are going to ridicule the lesson, so they are reluctant to teach it from the outset, which in turn is unlikely to inspire students!

Marjory: Oh, come on, Mark! I know some very good teachers who love their poetry lessons! I think the problem lies elsewhere. We need to break away from the 'I teach, you learn' dynamic in order to make the poetry class work. Kids need to be given the freedom to respond to a poem without too much 'guidance' from the teacher.

Mark: But the teacher has to point them in the right direction, surely! Otherwise some of them will understand next to nothing!

Marjory: What 'right' direction? You see, one of the limitations of saying we're going to teach poetry is just that – we 'teach' it. When perhaps we should just present it, and allow students to respond to it in their own way. Then they will learn to enjoy poetry ...

Extract Three

You hear two people talking about an unusual kind of competition.

Jake: It was incredible, really. I was driving through Wasdale, on my way back from the meeting, and I saw all these cars parked outside this pub in the middle of nowhere! So I thought, this one must be good, and stopped for a bite.

Sarah: Hm! But three hours later ... !

Jake: Well, I wasn't to know it was the World's Biggest Liar Competition in there! I mean, I'd never heard of such a thing! But it was excellent! Some of the stories! Half of them deserved a prize just for being so clever!

Sarah: So, how does the competition work?

Jake: Well, contestants make up a tall story – based on true events so that it sounds convincing – and try and deceive the people who are judging them. The story that won had us rolling about with laughter. It started out as a tale about a fishing trip, and ended up in a German submarine off the coast of Scotland! Brilliant! Oh, yeah! And do you know who was sitting next to me? Rowan Atkinson! Mr Bean himself!

Sarah: Really? Did you talk to him? What's he like?

Jake: Hah! Got you! Sarah, you're so gullible sometimes! I just might go in for that competition myself next year.

▶▶ **PART 2**

You will hear part of a talk by the director of a sports academy. For questions 7–14, complete the sentences.

Helen: I'm Helen Waterman, director of the Waterman Sports Academy, a school that helps promising young athletes fulfil their dreams. We coach youngsters who want to swim faster than anyone else in the world and children who dream of running the marathon at the Olympic Games one day.

I've coached many athletes in my life, going back to the day when the daughter of a friend announced she had entered for the long jump in an amateur athletics event. I enjoyed coaching her, and that was the start of my career. I also became interested in sports medicine at about that time, when my nephew fell off his bike and hurt his back. He'd been a keen athlete before his accident, but unfortunately, he never really got over his injury sufficiently to get back into serious training. That's when I realised the importance of sports medicine, and the staff of the academy includes two doctors.

Perhaps at this point I should answer a question often asked by young people when they enrol at the academy: how important is an athlete's build? Well, nobody can deny that build *does* matter, and one cannot hope to be a world-class long-distance runner, say, if one is built like a weightlifter. But other factors also play a vital role. For a start, good general health and fitness. These are important, even in sports where you might not think they are a priority. In shooting, for instance, athletes have to be fit to lower their heart rate. This enables them to fire between heart beats and so achieve maximum accuracy. At the academy, we encourage healthy eating habits. Without a proper diet, young athletes cannot achieve their optimum physique. Nor will they have the energy for training. Then there's the role of technology in sports. These days, athletes cannot compete successfully at the highest level without access to state-of-the-art equipment. I've already mentioned sports medicine, and it goes without saying that young athletes need to be able to consult specialists in case of an injury. But above all, at the academy we stress the importance of *attitude*. Without the will to succeed, you may as well not bother to take up any sport seriously. In my opinion, it is this that ...

▶▶ **PART 3**

You will hear part of an interview with Harold Mackenzie, who has written a book about early adolescence. For questions 15–20, choose the answer, A, B, C or D which fits best according to what you hear.

Interviewer: Harold Mackenzie, your book *Talking to Pre-Teens* is coming out later this month, and I'm sure that parents who read your best-selling *Talking to Teens* will be queuing up to buy it. But let's begin by asking you exactly what a pre-teen is.

Harold: A pre-teen – or 'tweenie' as some people prefer – is a child aged between eight and twelve, in other words, a child hovering on the brink of adolescence. Oddly enough, this age group didn't attract much attention in the past, but in recent years there has been quite a dramatic growth of interest. There are several reasons for this. Psychologists are beginning to understand how important this period is in an individual's development, and much more research is being done. However, that's not the main reason pre-teens are featuring in the news more and more. It seems that businesses have woken up to the fact that these youngsters are a force to be reckoned with. They have considerable spending power, so marketing managers who previously focused on teenagers are now also targeting these younger consumers. The trouble is that pre-teens are so impressionable.

Interviewer: Mm. In your book you suggest that marketing campaigns aimed at pre-teens should be carefully vetted. Can you expand on this?

Harold: We are all susceptible to advertising, but pre-teens are especially vulnerable. Advertisements can suggest that everything the child does – the food he eats, the clothes he wears, the toys he chooses to play with – are regarded as a statement by his or her contemporaries. He feels he has to 'keep up', so it's bewildering for a child when he tries to follow a fashion that is succeeded after a brief time by a different, equally arbitrary one.

Interviewer: Can you tell us something about the kinds of changes a child experiences during the pre-teen years?

Harold: Well, this is the age when children start to measure themselves against people outside their families for the first time, and one way in which they develop their sense of self is by forming friendships with other children. The way your peers react to you plays an enormous role in how you see yourself in later life.

Interviewer: It sounds as though the pre-teen years are quite eventful emotionally.

Harold: Yes, and they can be a trying time as well. It's unfortunate that for many children this period is full of stressful situations. For example, at this age children have to face real examinations at school for the first time – examinations that may determine what sort of education they will have in future. If a child's ability could be evaluated in different, less stressful ways, we might reduce the tensions that pre-teens are subjected to. I outline several possibilities in my book.

Interviewer: Harold, what can concerned parents do in concrete terms to help their pre-teen children?

Harold: Helping them gain self-confidence is crucial. Parents should respect their children's views about how their lives are conducted, but they should not make the mistake of indulging all their offspring's wishes and allowing them complete control of their lives. Children still need guidance! Buying them everything they want is not the best response; it can even be dangerous because it suggests that the things you have matter more than the kind of person you are. Find a way to discuss important issues with your children and listen – really listen – to what they tell you about their fears and desires.

Interviewer: Harold Mackenzie, thanks for being with us.

Harold: My pleasure.

▶▶ **PART 4**

This part consists of two tasks. You will hear five short extracts in which people talk about their experiences at the theatre. Look at Task 1. For questions 21–25, choose from the list A–H what each speaker says about the show he or she enjoyed most. Now look at Task 2. For questions 26–30, choose from the list A–H the view each speaker has about why theatre is an interesting medium.

Speaker 1: The first time I went to the theatre, I was twelve, and my mother had to drag me along. But it was a fantastic play – a murder mystery – and I was entranced. Ever since then I've enjoyed the theatre, and I go whenever I can. I love the atmosphere you get at a good play, as if you are all in an enchanted circle for those two hours the play is on. I don't think you get that feeling in the cinema.

Speaker 2: When I was at university, I saw a production of a comedy by Tom Stoppard called *After Magritte*. It was absolutely hilarious! I liked it so much that I went back the next night with two friends! There were some very simple jokes, there was slapstick humour, and there were some very witty lines. I don't think you'd get that in a film these days – the cinema has become so formulaic. For me, it's the theatre's ability to jolt you out of your complacency that makes it so special.

Speaker 3: As a child I saw a performance of the musical *My Fair Lady* with my Aunt Emily. My family weren't sure I'd enjoy it, but the actor playing the lead was marvellous! He could sing, his acting was great – he dominated the whole performance. I do some acting myself – I'm in an amateur dramatics society – and I love watching the way different actors go about interpreting a role. It definitely helps me when I have to take on a big part.

Speaker 4: My most memorable theatrical experience was a performance of Shakespeare's *Romeo and Juliet*. I went because we were studying it at school. I didn't expect to be affected, but to my intense surprise I was in tears at the end! That's when I finally understood how magical the theatre is. Seeing a play on stage is special; all the emotions come across to the audience if it's a good production. While you are watching there's a suspension of disbelief, and what's happening on the stage becomes real, at least for a while.

Speaker 5: I'd read a review of a production of *Antigone* by Sophocles in a very small theatre, so I went along. The acting was excellent, and because you were so close to the actors you felt very involved in the play – it became a sort of personal experience, as if you were in the play yourself! I suppose what I've come to love about the theatre is that no two performances are ever exactly the same: the actors do not always deliver their lines in the same way and there are subtle differences of timing and interpretation.